THE MOUNTBATTENS

ANDREW LOWNIE

THE MOUNTBATTENS

ANDREW LOWNIE

BLINK
bringing you closer

Published by Blink Publishing
2.25, The Plaza,
535 Kings Road,
Chelsea Harbour,
London, SW10 0SZ

www.blinkpublishing.co.uk

facebook.com/blinkpublishing
twitter.com/blinkpublishing

Hardback – 978-1-788-702-56-0
Trade paperback – 978-1-788-702-60-7
Ebook – 978-1-788-702-57-7

A CIP catalogue of this book is available from the British Library.

Typeset by Envydesign Ltd
Printed and bound in Great Britain by Clays Ltd, Elcograf S.p.A.

1 3 5 7 9 10 8 6 4 2

The publisher has made every effort to contact rights holders for permission to use their material, but in the event of any omission, will happily make amends and update the publication at the earliest possible opportunity.

Blink Publishing is an imprint of Bonnier Books UK
www.bonnierbooks.co.uk

Contents

Preface

No biography has any value unless it is written with warts and all.
LORD MOUNTBATTEN

Writing to Richard Hough about how he would like to be acknow-ledged in Hough's book, *Louis and Victoria,* Dickie Mountbatten suggested: 'Naval officer who became First Sea Lord after being Supreme Allied Commander and Viceroy of India and thus the best-known figure the Navy has produced since Nelson, as well as being the President of the Society of Genealogists.'[1]

The entry reveals much – Mountbatten's achievements, what he valued and his pomposity. No figure has a longer entry in *Who's Who,* apart from Winston Churchill, partly because every minor organisation is mentioned, but also because Dickie Mountbatten had a remarkable life.

As one obituary noted, 'It seemed almost unbelievable that one human being could have touched the history of our century at so many points.'[2] Head of Combined Operations, a Member of the Chiefs of Staff and then Supreme Commander of Allied Forces in South East Asia during the Second World War, the last Viceroy and first Governor-General of India, First Sea Lord and

Chief of the Defence Staff, member of the Royal Family and mentor of Prince Philip and Prince Charles: his life, which covered the first 80 years of the 20th century, also provides an opportunity to look at some of the most important and controversial issues of the period, from the 1942 Dieppe Raid to Indian independence. His biography cannot be told without also considering the life of his wife, Edwina, the richest heiress in the world when they married, whose reputation for her global humanitarian work endures.

Philip Ziegler's magisterial official life of Dickie was published in 1985 and Janet Morgan's deft authorised life of Edwina came out six years later. What is missing is a shorter, joint biography of these two remarkable figures, a book which is also a portrait of an unusual marriage – one that was loving and mutually supportive, but also beset with infidelities. As Dickie would later claim, 'Edwina and I spent all our married lives getting into other people's beds.'[3]

With the Mountbattens, the private life did intrude into the public life, not least in the question over the nature of the relationship between Edwina and the Indian Prime Minister, Jawaharlal Nehru, and how far it affected the perception of the impartiality of the Mountbattens during Independence.

Even after countless books on the couple, the questions remain. Was Mountbatten one of the outstanding leaders of his generation, or a man over-promoted because of his royal birth, high-level connections, film-star looks and ruthless self-promotion? What is the true story behind controversies such as the Dieppe Raid and Indian Partition and the love affair between Edwina and Nehru? The authorised biographies had certain subjects they had to cover and to avoid. Now 30 years later, with many of those involved in the story dead, with new papers released and different sensitivities, there is a case for a new book.

Preface

'The interesting biography will be the one that is published in 30 or 40 years' time when the dust has settled,' wrote Mountbatten's military assistant Pat MacLellan to Brian Kimmins, a wartime member of Dickie's staff, in 1980.[4]

This book is that attempt.

Prologue

TUESDAY, 18 JULY 1922

In spite of the rain, by breakfast, 600 people had gathered outside St Margaret's, the 12th-century church in the shadow of Westminster Abbey and a favourite for society weddings. By lunchtime the crowd would swell to 8,000. For the *Daily Telegraph,* this was to be the Wedding of the Year – the *Star* thought it the Wedding of the Century – between the beautiful Edwina Ashley, 'the richest girl in the world', and Lord Louis Mountbatten, the handsome naval officer and member of the extended Royal Family. King George V and Queen Mary and most members of the Royal Family were attending, with the Prince of Wales as best man.

At exactly 2.15 p.m., Edwina entered the church to Wagner's *Lohengrin.* The service was conducted by Dickie's former school tutor, Frederic Lawrence Long. 'The Lord is my Shepherd' was followed by the hymns 'Thine for Ever' and 'May the Grace of God our Saviour', whilst Beethoven's 'Hallelujah' was sung during the signing of the register.

The couple – Dickie at six foot two dwarfing his wife – emerged from the church to Mendelssohn's *Wedding March* just as the sun broke through the rain and they walked under the traditional arch of swords of a naval guard of honour. Mountbatten, his sharp-chiselled face set in a solemn expression, was dressed in a long, blue frock coat and golden epaulettes in the dress uniform of a naval lieutenant and carrying his father's gold-hilted sword.[5] Edwina, blue-eyed and fair-haired, was in a simple, ankle-length frosted silver dress, with a wreath of orange blossom on her head, and a four-foot train of silver cloth covered with 15th-century lace.

They climbed into the bridal car, a Rolls-Royce – a wedding gift from Edwina bought from the Prince of Wales – which was then drawn by a naval gun crew around Parliament Square. Around the corner, a flag-draped lorry took over, towing the car past Buckingham Palace to the reception at the bride's home, Brook House in Park Lane. There, at the entrance to the two ground-floor reception rooms, where a narrow dividing room had been made into an avenue of ten-foot orange trees, the couple received their 800 guests.[6] So large was the wedding cake, with its top tier shaped like a crown, plus miniature anchors, sails and hawsers, and tiny lifeboats hanging from silver davits, that it took four men to lift it.

The wedding had attracted attention around the world with entire issues of magazines devoted to it, postcards and souvenirs produced to commemorate the occasion, and a 14-minute film for Pathé News.[7] The list of presents took up a whole page of *The Times* and included, for Edwina, a pendant with the royal cipher in diamonds from Queen Alexandra, a brooch from the Aga Khan, a horse from the Maharajah of Jaipur, and the bracelet she had only recently returned to a previous suitor, Geordie, Duke of Sutherland. Mountbatten's gifts were of a more practical bent, reflecting his interests – a ship's telescope, a copper hot-water jug and an aneroid barometer – and from the King, the award Knight Commander Victorian Order to add to his cherished Japanese Order of the Rising Sun and Grand Cross Order of the Nile.

Finally, at 5 p.m., they set off in the Rolls-Royce for the bride's family home, Broadlands, to begin their married life together.

CHAPTER I

Beginnings

The marriage had brought together two of the most glamorous figures of the period.

Dickie Mountbatten, born on 25 June 1900 at Frogmore House, was a great grandson and godson of Queen Victoria – his mother, Victoria, born in 1863, was the daughter of the Queen's second daughter, Alice. Dickie's mother was to be an important influence, encouraging in her youngest child supreme self-confidence and acting as his tutor between the ages of five and nine. 'She taught me English, German, French and Latin. She taught me world history in a horizontal manner,' he later recalled. 'In the Elizabethan era, I knew what was going on in Europe and India as well as in England.'[8]

He was christened Louis Francis Albert Victor Nicholas – the Victor and Albert in tribute to his great-grandparents – though from an early age he was always known as Dicky or Dickie.

His father, Prince Louis, born in 1854 in Austria, was the son of Prince Alexander and Princess Julie of Hesse, the oldest ruling Protestant dynasty in the world, but, as it was a morganatic marriage, the children were excluded from the succession to the sovereignty of Hesse.[9] Instead, Prince Alexander was given the name and title of Battenberg, which came from a town in the upper part of the Grand Duchy. This genealogical flaw in Mountbatten's ascendance was to be an embarrassment, which he would seek to brush over in later life.

Dickie's father had joined the Royal Navy, aged 14, and enjoyed a successful naval career, becoming Director of Naval Intelligence shortly after his younger son's birth. Part of the slightly louche set around Edward VII – his torso boasted a tattoo of a dragon – in 1881 he had fathered a child, Jeanne Marie, with the King's mistress, Lillie Langtry.[10]

In 1884, Prince Louis had married his cousin, Victoria, eldest daughter of Grand Duke Louis of Hesse and a favourite granddaughter of Queen Victoria, and their children, Alice, Louise and George, were born respectively in 1885, 1889 and 1892. Fluent in French and German, a skilled pianist and artist, who had been elected to the Royal Institute of Painters in Water Colours, he was worshipped by his youngest child.[11]

As the youngest and with a gap of between 15 and eight years with his siblings, Dickie was used to amusing himself and getting his own way. He later recollected, 'I was spoilt and no one minded.'[12] His was an essentially female household, as his brother and father were seldom at home, where he was doted on by his mother, two elder sisters and various female members of staff. This was to have a powerful effect on him in later life. He was always to get on with women better than men, who were either to be admired, like his father and brother, or seen as antagonists to be defeated.

It was also, with his regular visits to German relations at the family homes at Heiligenberg Castle and Wolfsgarten, a much more cosmopolitan upbringing than that enjoyed by most British children of the time. Just after his first birthday, he had stayed with the Grand Duke Sergei Alexandrovich, the Governor of Moscow, before going on to the Peterhof Palace.[13] For Christmas 1905 he received from the Tsar, who was married to Dickie's aunt, a replica uniform of the crack *Chevalier Garde*, complete with helmet, breast-plate, boots, spurs and sword. It was to be the start of a lifelong love of uniforms.

The summer of 1908 was spent staying with various Russian relations where, at the Nicholas Palace in St Petersburg, he became friendly with his cousin the Grand Duke Dmitri, one of the two conspirators behind the death of Rasputin. This was followed by a week with Tsar Nicholas and his family at the Peterhof Palace.[14]

In 1910, Prince Louis, who had had a series of postings around the Mediterranean, was made Commander-in-Chief of the Atlantic Fleet, and decided to send Dickie to boarding school.[15] His parents picked Lockers Park, a fashionable prep school just north of London with strong naval connections, which Dickie's uncle Maurice and brother George had attended a few years previously.[16] Shortly after arriving, he wrote to his mother, 'Some of my nicknames are Baterpudding, 2 things beginning with P – prince and pig, also London Fire Brigade like LFB. One boy spelt my name Batumberg.'[17]

A diligent but unpredictable student, his term positions fluctuated widely. At the end of his first term he was eighth in a class of ten, but by the end of 1910, he was first. 'His behaviour has been excellent and I am pleased to see he is less inclined to worry over trivial matters' ran his report.[18] Throughout 1911, he remained in the bottom half of the class, with his best subjects history and geography, but by the following year, he was top and had received the form prize.

He was a kind and popular child. One contemporary, Sir Hamilton Kerr, later remembered how, when he was lonely and miserable at the school, he discovered that Mountbatten could speak German. 'We talked German on Sunday afternoons, walking up and down the school lawn. One never forgets these kindnesses of early youth.'[19]

Not naturally athletic, nevertheless, Dickie managed to reach the finals of the boxing competition and captain the second football team. Above all, his qualities of leadership were beginning to be recognised and he became a prefect. His headmaster wrote in his final report: 'He has always acted on the principle that if a thing is worth doing, it is worth doing well. We all regret that his stay at the school has come to an end and I am confident of his future success.'[20]

In May 1913, Mountbatten followed in his brother George's footsteps to Osborne, the Navy's training school on the Isle of Wight, passing in 15th out of the 83 candidates – his score was 440/600 with the top mark 498 – and English and German his best subjects. Osborne was very different from Lockers Park. The 430 boys, many from naval families, were subject to naval discipline and instead of school uniform, they wore naval dress, ranging from monkey jackets to dress uniforms for special occasions.

The curriculum was focused on subjects such as engineering, navigation and seamanship, and it was a tough environment aimed at developing self-discipline, initiative and confidence. There was lots of bullying and Dickie, cocky and feminine-looking, was frequently bullied. In May, he got into a fight with a boy who had been at Lockers Park, John Scott, who teased him about his name – the brass plate on his bedside sea chest described him as Serene Highness – earning the respect of his peers when he fought back.[21]

At the end of Dickie's first term, he was 33rd out of 81. His tutor, A.P. Boissier, who taught maths, wrote, 'He has made an excellent start. He invariably shows great keenness in everything and is always out to learn.'[22] By the next term he was second in English and history, with Boissier noting, 'He possesses the gift of thoroughly mastering a subject before he allows himself to pass on.'[23] This was to prove a characteristic throughout his life.

He was playing drums in the college band, taking fencing lessons, boxing, playing in the second eleven hockey, and in October he stroked the winning boat in the First Year Skiffs. Already he was showing an interest in wireless telegraphy and with a friend he spent hours trying to pick up broadcasts from the Eiffel Tower on a primitive crystal receiver.

The summer of 1913 was spent in Hesse with his older siblings – Alice, now married to Prince Andrew of Greece, Louise and George, now a lieutenant serving in the battle cruiser HMS *New Zealand*. They were joined in Hesse by the Tsar and Tsarina and their five children, with one of whom, 14-year-old Marie, Dickie fell in love. 'I was crackers about Marie, and was determined to marry her,' he remembered. 'She was absolutely lovely. I keep her photograph on the mantelpiece in my bedroom – always have.'[24] Within five years, all the family would be dead at the hands of the Bolsheviks.

On 28 June, the Archduke Franz Ferdinand was assassinated in Sarajevo and the countdown to war began. Prince Louis had become First Sea Lord in 1912 and Dickie was invited to watch a full test mobilisation of the Fleet on 18 July. Dickie was thrilled to watch the Royal Review at Spithead in front of King George V, with the full might of the Royal Navy laid out in front – some 59 battleships, 55 cruisers, 78 destroyers, 16 submarines and a host of lesser craft – and to meet Admiral Jellicoe and Winston Churchill, the First Lord of the Admiralty.

Dickie had met Churchill several times before, not least when he had paid an official visit to Osborne. When Churchill had asked the cadets if they had any requests, Dickie had been the first to respond. 'Please, sir, may we please have three sardines for Saturday supper instead of only two?' 'I'll see to that,' Churchill assured him. The sardines were never forthcoming. It was a lesson that Dickie was to remember.[25]

It was Prince Louis, alone on duty, on the fateful weekend before the outbreak of war, who had to make the decision not to stand down the Fleet, but keep them mobilised. It proved to be a wise decision. The following day, Germany and Russia declared war on each other and on 4 August, the United Kingdom declared war on Germany.

There was an almost instant wave of anti-German feeling, with assaults on suspected Germans – even dachshunds were targeted – and the looting of stores owned by people with German-sounding names. Mountbatten initially joked to his mother on 14 August, 'that Papa has turned out to be a genuine spy and has been discreetly marched off to the Tower, where he is guarded by beef eaters [*sic*] . . . I got rather a rotten time of it for about 3 days as little fools (like Stopsford) insisted on calling me German spy and kept on heckling me and trying to make things unpleasant for me.'[26]

In October, the German-accented Prince Louis, feeling that the criticisms of him as head of the Navy were a distraction from the war effort, resigned as First Sea Lord. He had faithfully served his adopted country for 46 years and yet Winston Churchill made no attempt to dissuade him. His son was devastated. Another cadet saw a contemporary standing in front of the Osborne mast with tears running down his cheeks. It was Dickie. From that day he was to have one consuming ambition, to avenge his father's dismissal and become First Sea Lord himself.[27]

* * *

A descendant of the Native American princess Pocahontas, the Prime Minister Lord Palmerston and the reformer and philanthropist the seventh Earl of Shaftsbury, Edwina was born on 28 November 1901. Her father, Wilfrid Ashley, was a former colonel in the Grenadier Guards, who would later become a Conservative Member of Parliament. Her maternal grandfather was the banker Sir Ernest

Cassell, financial adviser to Edward VII – the King was Edwina's godfather and she was named after him – and one of the richest men in the world.

Cassell, whose wife had died within three years of marriage, was very close to his only child and her first-born daughter and provided one of the few anchors in Edwina's rather rootless youth. Edwina's father was a remote figure, busy pursuing his parliamentary business or sporting interests, and her mother, Maud, frequently ill, had no idea how to be a parent to Edwina.

Maud died of tuberculosis in February 1911, when Edwina was nine and her sister Mary was five. Neither child was allowed to attend the funeral at Romsey Abbey. Edwina wrote to her father, 'I am so very sorry darling Mama left us all so suddenly and for ever, I wanted to kiss her once and now I didn't, but it is very nice to think her spirit will always be with me.'[28] She never spoke of her mother again in public.

Both daughters found it hard to come to terms with their mother's death, but displayed it in different ways. Edwina was forced to grow up quickly, became ever neater and more dutiful, while Mary responded by becoming more wilful and uncooperative. Motherless and starved of affection at home, Edwina poured her love into caring for her animals – puppies, ponies, rabbits, kittens, a goat and, a present from her grandfather, an Arab horse. Educated at home, she was a conscientious and organised student, who by the age of ten could read German, write in French and play the piano. She had a particular love for geography, noted one biographer. 'Maps fascinated her, talk of distant lands gripped her attention, and she would read travel books voraciously.'[29]

The situation improved with the arrival of a new governess, Laura Deveria, in September 1912. Young, warm-hearted and fun, she made lessons interesting and the two girls adored her, but their happiness did not last for long. In August 1914, Wilfrid, lonely and feeling he needed a wife for his political career, remarried. He had met Molly Forbes-Sempill on the political circuit and they married weeks after she had secured a divorce from her naval officer husband.

Molly quickly made herself unpopular with everyone through her bossiness, insensitivity and attempts to make changes, from replacing the brocade wall coverings at the family home in Hampshire, Broadlands, to strict new rules that the children should be sent to bed at half past six. A guest who came back early from fishing, because of the rain, was made to eat his lunch in the hall, rather than bring his wet boots into the dining-room.

She insisted the girls call her 'Madre' and when travelling by train she would go first class, but put them in third. Laura Deveria, regarded as a threat, was dismissed, which only increased the girls' unhappiness and sense of rejection. Wilfrid, fearful of confrontation and busy raising and training a battalion to take to France, turned a blind eye rather than stand up for his daughters.

The anti-German hysteria that had affected the Battenbergs was now directed at the German-born Ernest Cassell. In spite of being one of the largest subscribers to the War Loan and entrusted with an official mission to the United States to secure a loan of half a million dollars, he was accused of being friendly with the German Emperor and having a specially designed wireless set on the roof of Brook House to maintain contact with the country of his birth. Sir George Makgill, Secretary to the Anti-German Union, brought a lawsuit to strip Cassell of his membership of the Privy Council. It failed, but for Edwina – like her future husband remembering his father's experiences – it was something she would never forget.

CHAPTER 2

Students

Dickie had ended his Osborne career on a high note, graduating first in physics, second in engineering and third in seamanship. In January 1915, he moved on to Britannia Royal Naval College, more commonly known as Dartmouth, for the next stage of his naval training. He again threw himself into student life, editing a magazine with close friend Kit Bradford, beagling, running, fencing, playing cricket, rugger, tennis, fives and squash – generally with more enthusiasm than success – and attending the Saturday night dances with wives and daughters of officers on the station.

It is inevitable that boys going through puberty, thrown together and with very few girls, should indulge in adolescent homosexual experimentations, though Dickie's reaction to his colleagues' antics, to a later generation, may appear priggish and naïve. He wrote to his mother – her reaction is unknown – in June, 'Dr Moon is going to have the talk with me soon. People here are becoming too swinish for words. It is awfully difficult not to get contaminated by them, when you have them talking filth, or almost worse still, hinting at nasty things during meals and when we are in bed & in the gun room . . . some people in the other dormitory have even begun to do filthy things, I have heard.'[30]

His first holidays from Dartmouth were spent with George on

17

HMS *New Zealand*, steaming off Heligoland, guarding the edge of a large minefield and covering some 2,000 sea miles. He wrote in his diary, 'I am having the time of my life.'[31] George had been given a portable projector for 35mm films and he would borrow films from a local cinema and show them to the ship's company. It was to kindle a passion that his younger brother was to enjoy for the rest of his life.

Dickie had been in an isolation hospital with German measles for most of May. Then in July, he was ill again. Often prone to injury from his fearlessness, in February 1916 he sprained his ankle in a tobogganing accident and then broke his leg, requiring him to sit his final exams in hospital. Bored, he placed an advertisement in the personal column of *The Times*: 'A Young Naval Officer, injured and in hospital desires correspondence'. The reaction was immediate, as he told his mother: 'On the Saturday I got 100 letters and today I got 75 letters with a possible prospect of more to come . . . They vary from a society girl in Curzon Street & a merry widow in Stanhope Gardens to a typist in Whitechapel & a chauffeur, who looks after a Ford car.'[32] In the end, over 200 women, most of them in their twenties, wrote to him until he placed another ad regretting he could not respond individually.

Leaving Dartmouth in April 1916, he was disappointed not to go to sea, thereby missing the Battle of Jutland the following month, unlike his brother George. Instead, his cohort spent three months at Keyham, the engineering college, but it was to be a turning point in his career. Two days after his sixteenth birthday, he wrote to his mother, 'I was surprised myself to find that I had passed out first from Keyham.'[33]

His first posting in July 1916 was as a junior midshipman to Admiral Beatty's flagship HMS *Lion*, employed as a general dogsbody to the captain, John Chatfield. 'My action station is on the Fore Bridge, which I believe is about the best station going, only one suffers rather from the blast of one's own guns,' he wrote excitedly to his mother:

> I am awfully pleased to be up there, as one can see something
> of what's going on. My chief job is tending voice pipes & that
> is where the admiral & his staff are, as a rule. At sea I am in
> the white watch and keep watch at the 4 gns by night, with
> 2 other fellows. At day I keep submarine watch . . . I have
> been having a ripping time.[34]

The sub-lieutenant in charge of the gunroom was a bully and took every opportunity to curb the natural exuberance of the young midshipman, but Dickie thrived on the discipline and hard work and the demands of war.[35]

In August, *Lion* escaped a mine and a torpedo attack in the North Sea defending Sunderland from a German bombardment. Dickie was thrilled. He had achieved his ambition and been bloodied in war.

* * *

In order to divide and rule, Molly had sent Mary to boarding school to keep the sisters apart. Edwina continued her lonely childhood at Broadlands, her main enjoyment baiting her stepmother – a favourite ploy was to write in French or German, languages Molly could not speak. Most of the day was spent in lessons with her governess, Miss Atwood, but there was time to ride and hunt with the Hursley Hounds and she read voraciously – *A Study in Scarlet*, *Dombey and Son* being particular favourites. It was then her short-sightedness was discovered and she was prescribed spectacles, but discarded them whenever she could. From this point her eyesight worsened, as did the headaches that were to plague her throughout her life.

From an early age, Edwina was organised and tidy. The schoolroom books were catalogued, and her diary scrupulously listed everyone's birthday, as well as the names of all the visitors to Broadlands with the times of their arrival and, more importantly, departure. It was a means of her exerting control on a world in which she had little say. Evidence of that came in the summer of 1916, when she learnt that she, too, was being sent away to school. The excuse was that it was felt she had too few companions but, as she noted in her diary, it was clear the reason was 'that Madre wanted to get rid of me and Miss A. – the pig!'[36]

In September 1916, aged 14, she joined Mary at The Links in Eastbourne, which was run by Miss Jane Potts, a former governess to Queen Victoria's granddaughter Princess Alice, and known to the girls as Potty. Edwina quickly shone, coming top in French and German, excelling in music, drawing and English literature, and playing in the cricket and tennis teams. Now with schoolgirl companions, her strong competitive streak came out, but she champed at the petty rules and restrictions. She was used to being a free spirit, found the routine and discipline of school life irksome and, by the autumn of 1919, she had outgrown the school.

In autumn 1918, she followed several of her friends to Alde House, a mixture of finishing school and Domestic Science Training College, on the Suffolk coast at Aldeburgh.[37] Its aim, over the year's course, was to teach 20 girls at a time how to run a household. The training ranged from cleaning, cooking, dressmaking and doing their own laundry to comportment, etiquette, ordering stores and paying wages. As always, Edwina flourished and she was one of two students to represent the school at a Domestic Science display in London in July 1919. It should have been invaluable training, but from the day she left, Edwina never again picked up a broom or a kitchen utensil. Now free from the constraints of formal education, her adventurous nature determined she would see the world.

* * *

Naval policy was not to let two brothers serve together, so when George joined *Lion* in February 1917, Dickie was transferred to *Queen Elizabeth*. Again he threw himself into the ship's activities, appearing as a flower girl and in the chorus in *Three Peeps: A Musical Muddle in Three Acts* and editing a quarterly magazine, *Chronicles of Queen Elizabeth*, with a print run of 1,100 copies.[38]

Dickie had written short stories at school – one was about 'a midshipman called Richard Norman and a new type of motor-propelled destroyer called the "Okapi" which can act as a submarine.'[39] Now with time on his hands, under the *nom de plume*, N.O., he had been invited to write another for the naval magazine *Sea Pie*. 'Soapy – The Tale of a Dog', about a cocker spaniel on board a battleship, was based on his own experience with a spaniel called Bubbles.[40]

Both HMS *Lion* and HMS *Queen Elizabeth* were based at Rosyth, just outside Edinburgh, and the two brothers saw much of each other. In November 1916, George had married the vivacious and exotic Nada de Torby, a daughter of the Grand Duke Michael of Russia and great granddaughter of the poet Alexander Pushkin, and Dickie often visited them at their home on the Firth of Forth, riding there on his Douglas motorbike.

George was regarded as the more brilliant of the two brothers. The second master at Osborne thought him the cleverest and laziest cadet he had ever known. He had always been mechanically minded, reputedly aged five putting a family clock back together after dismantling it. By the age of ten, he had his own workshop, and by 15 was designing and constructing working models of steam engines.

He was constantly inventing gadgets to make life more comfortable, including an early form of air-conditioning, which worked by having a thermometer with electric contacts that switched on a fan if the cabin was too hot and a radiator if too cold. He produced hot and cold running water in his cabin, using small electric lathe-motors to pump the water, and created a device controlled by an alarm clock to produce an early morning cup of tea.

Shortly after leaving Dartmouth, he had ridden in the procession for George V's 1911 Durbar in Delhi, before specialising as a gunnery officer and taking part in the naval actions at Heligoland, Dogger Bank and Jutland. His younger brother revered him and vowed that if he could not compete on the same intellectual level, he would achieve success by hard work. Dickie, in contrast, according to his first biographer was 'found to be rather young for his age, full of enthusiasm, ready to try anything, but not very good at games. His youthfulness showed itself in lightning changes of mood, and this made some of those who served with him at that time question his stability of temperament.'[41]

The brothers' nomenclature was about to change. In June 1917, King George V was persuaded to change his German name of Saxe-Coburg and Gotha to Windsor and relinquish all German titles and styles on behalf of his relatives who were British subjects. Mountbatten's father, Prince Louis of Battenberg, was forced to change his name to Mountbatten – an earlier option had been Battenhill – and became the Marquess of Milford Haven, with George becoming the Earl of Medina and the younger brother Lord Louis Mountbatten. He would henceforth be known by many as simply Lord Louis.

In November, Dickie signed up for the steam submarine K6 for the first of two fortnight stints, as part of a scheme to broaden a midshipman's training and help them choose their specialism.[42] The wardroom, he wrote to his mother, was:

A grand and sumptuous compartment, in the centre of which you really can stand up without bumping your head. It looks for all the world like a tuppenny tube, except that in place of umpteen advertisements . . . they are bedecked with gaily coloured pictures of semi-nude females out of *La Vie (Parisienne)* . . . That department has been turned over to me, as has also our 'garden'. This is a wonderful piece of 'terra' of sorts, dug and sown in March with all manner of vegetables . . . cabins have no bulkheads but curtains. Bath is a LONG one at least 3 ft long!!! The WC is the most wonderful contraption of valves you have ever seen.[43]

After his second fortnight in January, he was able to tell his mother, 'I have spent the happiest month I've ever spent in the Service (6 years this May) in this ship and am more sorry than words could ever say my time in her is up . . .'[44] Part of the reason might also be that he had 'made the acquaintance of a very nice girl, who went to one of the "gun room dances" in Edinburgh where I met her, and her name is Hilda Blackburne. She is the daughter of Lady Constance Blackburne.'[45]

The submarine service was now to be his career, its attractions including better pay, longer periods of leave and more rapid promotion, though the new Marquess of Milford Haven counselled his son to keep his options open for the moment.

Whether through his father's contacts or as part of a scheme for naval officers – it's not clear – Dickie achieved his ambition to visit the Western Front, though of the ten days he spent in France in July 1918, because of a high fever, only two were actually spent with front-line troops.

In the autumn he left the *Queen Elizabeth* to broaden his experience, joining P31 (an escort and anti-submarine vessel) on the Dover Patrol. Now a sub-lieutenant, he was the second in command of 50 officers and men with a particular responsibility for organisation, paying the sailors and acting, in effect, as the ship's doctor, which during the flu epidemic claimed the lives of a quarter of the crew; and for several weeks in early 1919, he was the acting captain. It was his first real position of responsibility and he relished it.

When it appeared that P31 might not take part in the peace celebrations in August 1919 and be either mothballed or sent for scrap, Dickie contrived for Princess Mary, daughter of George V, to tell her father that she wanted to visit a P-boat and persuaded him to come as well. It was great publicity for the young naval officer and it saved the ship. Dickie was already showing that he was very happy to use his royal connections for the benefit of himself and the Navy.

The names of various women now begin to appear in his letters, but his first love remained the Navy – summed up by this ditty 'Soliloquy' (1st Lieutenant P31):

> Peggy was my only joy
> Poppy's now without alloy
> (Margery still gets a turn)
> Phyllis's letters I can burn
> Of all the P's there isn't one
> Can beat my best love '31'[46]

In the autumn, P31 was called to help with the intervention in Russia, but the Navy had other plans for Dickie. He was to go to Cambridge.

* * *

The same month that Dickie started at Cambridge, Edwina and her cousin Marjorie (accompanied by Sir Ernest and Marjorie's father) set out for their cultural tour of Europe. Cassell was anxious that his elder daughter should be prepared for her coming out. In Paris, where the party stayed at the Ritz, he bought her a fur coat, 'mole, with a very smart lining', gloves, new jewels and hats. After a week he had to leave and was replaced by Miss Cranston, secretary to their family friend, Lady Zia Wernher.[47] From Paris, they took the *Train de Luxe* to Rome.

Ostensibly, during their sojourn the girls were taking piano and Italian lessons, visiting historic sites, art galleries and museums, and taking tea with the formidable Mrs Strong of the British School in Rome, but there were other distractions:

> Captain Mott, with his cleft chin and neat moustache, or Mr Scott, so sleek that his hair looked like boot polish thinly applied to his perfectly shaped head. Still more attractive were the Italians: Galeazzo Manzi-Fe, olive-skinned, with brooding dark eyes; Folco Malaspira, in his uniform of high-buttoned jacket, well-cut breeches and tight, high boots; and Ricardo, a magnificent duke, by whom Edwina was utterly dazzled.[48]

The trip had been more educative than Sir Ernest could ever have realised. Edwina, by nature high-spirited and strong-minded, had blossomed in this new environment where she could reinvent herself. Her adolescent podginess had disappeared and she had turned into a confident, beautiful young woman, who knew how to flirt, dissemble, and that she was highly attractive to men. It was knowledge she never lost.

* * *

In October 1919, Dickie started at Christ's College, Cambridge, part of a scheme for naval high-flying junior officers whose education had been curtailed by the First World War. He was one of 400 officers sent to Cambridge – five to Christ's – for two terms on a special course covering mathematics, physics, engineering, navigation, naval history, literature, languages and ethnology. This post-war class differed from previous generations as many were war veterans, used to being in command, and considerably older than the usual undergraduate. The experience was to be a formative one for the young naval officer, widening his view of the world and training him to think for himself.

He quickly threw himself into college and university life. He represented the college against King's College in 100 yards, 220 and long jump and was elected to the university's sports club, the Hawks, and its most socially fashionable club, the Pitt, which, as he told his father, 'consists of all the snobs and little Eaton [*sic*] boys, but my word it is comfortable and the food is not bad. Also one does meet a lot of really nice fellows there of one's own class, besides the dreadful snobs.'[49]

One of the nice fellows he met was Peter Murphy, who was to become not only a lifelong friend, but a crucial confidant and influence. The biographical details for Murphy – full name James Jeremiah Victor Fitzwilliam Peter Murphy – are hazy. Three years older than Dickie and a talented linguist, he had been a scholar at Harrow, leaving shortly before his sixteenth birthday to spend a year at Frankfurt University.

At the outbreak of the First World War, he had joined the territorial battalion of the Bedfordshire Regiment before being commissioned as a second lieutenant in the Special Reserve in March 1915, serving later with the Irish Guards and the Royal Irish Fusiliers. He had been injured on the Somme at the end of 1916 with shell shock and ICT (Inflamed Connective Tissue), after losing his boots in the mud.

After a period of recuperation in London, he was given 'temporary employment in the Foreign Office . . . he is believed to possess capabilities which suit him for work of a confidential character'.[50] He had arrived at a neighbouring college, Magdalene, to read economics that term and Dickie had met him in the rooms of Christopher Tennant, later the 2nd Baron Glenconner. Murphy subsequently remembered Dickie:

> I immediately felt he was different, not only from the other young naval officers, but from the other undergraduates at Cambridge. Physically he was strikingly good-looking, with knock down charm, second only to that popular idol, the Prince of Wales himself . . . I was really astonished to find a member of the Royal Family so free of prejudice and reaction, with such a genuinely receptive, progressive outlook. I helped him to start reading intelligent books and papers. I tried to get him to take an interest in music, which he enjoyed, though his tastes were simple. In art his outlook was hopelessly conventional, but in politics he was certainly no reactionary.[51]

Under the influence of the left-wing Murphy, Dickie increasingly began to question his world view, not least the flaws in capitalism. By nature undogmatic and pragmatic, Dickie learnt to challenge the values and codes of his class. One manifestation of this was a growing interest in politics and debating, joining both the college debating society, the Junior Acton, and the university's Union Society.

Within weeks of arriving in Cambridge, he was a paper speaker at the Union – i.e., on the programme and not merely contributing from the floor – opposing the motion, 'That in the opinion of this house, the Ulster Party is principally to blame for the present chaotic conditions of Ireland'. Four days later, he unsuccessfully argued against reducing armaments and, at the end of term, he stood for the committee, coming fourth out of the 15 candidates and being elected. An assessment of his debating noted he has 'a ready wit and a genius for turning opponents' arguments. Is always an attractive speaker, especially in the unprepared parts of his speech. When he has nothing to say, he still says it very nicely.'[52]

His greatest triumph was perhaps the Inter-Varsity debate against Oxford in February 1920, successfully speaking with Winston Churchill (he later claimed he had persuaded him to appear) against the motion, 'That this House considers that the Time is ripe for a Labour Government', though the Union report noted that, 'He had a difficult task in attacking Labour, because (rumour has it) his sympathies ran strong that way.'[53]

At the end of term, Dickie learnt to fly at an aerodrome at King's Lynn. 'I've looped the loop three times and loved it,' he wrote to his mother.[54] He had been taken under the wing of Lady Cunard and was being invited to lots of dances.[55] He explained the reason for his success to his mother:

I've found that very few people seem to take the trouble to dance or even talk with any of the older people. Most extraordinary. They are usually far more interesting than all except a few of the young girls. Not only is it polite to do so but it pays. Because I danced with Lady Ribblesdale the first night I was asked again.[56]

Dickie, always attractive to women, and always besotted with someone, had now fallen seriously in love. The object of his affections was Audrey James:

The most beautiful girl of the season. This everyone admits, but I think she's the most beautiful thing I've ever seen. She's nearly 18, I think. The trouble, or perhaps the safeness of it all is that I am no. 9 of her young men, though being the latest, at present apparently the most favoured.[57]

Audrey James was the illegitimate granddaughter of Edward VII and the illegitimate daughter of Sir Edward Grey, 1st Viscount Grey of Fallodon. Dickie had first seen her in an October edition of *Tatler* and, through Peter Murphy, inveigled himself to escort Audrey to a dance. The next day he had 'got off' with her at tea with Peter Murphy. He had then been invited with her to an opera ball at Covent Garden – he went as a gondolier – and the romance continued.

In December he saw her again at a dinner party given by Peter Murphy and Christopher Tennant. He wrote enthusiastically to his mother:

How any girl can be so pretty and alive at the same time beats me. Mama you simply couldn't conceive how lovely she is. Beats everything I've ever seen to a Frazzle. Keeps 2 houses, a maid, a footman etc of her own and yet she is 'unspoilt'.

Deceitful yes but not spoilt . . . She's got the wee-est & most perfect eyebrows under marvellous grey eyes and the most kissable mouth that God ever made.[58]

But his friends were warning him about her, and the fact that she couldn't commit to any of her numerous admirers.

George V's sons Bertie, the future King George VI, and Henry, the future Duke of Gloucester, were also at Cambridge as part of their education, but living outside the city and being taught by tutors. 'Bertie & Harry are very nice & asked me to come to their house whenever I like as they know nobody & feel lonely,' wrote Dickie to his mother. 'I am getting up a dinner party for them here.'[59]

The three young royals became friendly, seeing each other in Cambridge but also at country house weekends, such as Philip Sassoon's home, Trent Park, north of London. Never one to miss an opportunity and hearing that the Prince of Wales was due to go on a world tour the following year, Dickie had asked Bertie to request his brother if Dickie could join him. At a dance at Lady Ribblesdale's in December, to which Mountbatten had engineered an invitation, the Prince of Wales approached him, asking if he would accompany him. In March, Dickie was about to set out on a new adventure in his life.

CHAPTER 3

First Loves

David, Prince of Wales, was six years older than Dickie and had also been educated at Osborne and Dartmouth. He had briefly served in the Navy before some educational travel in Europe and a brief stint at Oxford. During the First World War, he had held a staff job at Army HQ, but he had never got close to the fighting. After the war it was decided that, as part of his training to be king, he should conduct a series of world tours to demonstrate Britain's gratitude for the contribution of the Empire to victory. In 1919 he had visited Canada and the United States and the trip had been a great success. This new tour would take in Australia, New Zealand, the Pacific and West Indies.

Dickie's role on the trip was officially as flag-lieutenant to the Prince's chief of staff, Rear-Admiral Sir Lionel Halsey, but more practically, it was to act as a sort of minder, to provide the future king with company of his own age, to keep him amused, occupied and in a happy state of mind. David was deep in his affair with Freda Dudley Ward, the wife of a Liberal MP – it would last until he met Wallis Simpson in 1934 – and he had no wish to be parted from her.

In mid-March 1920, the party set off. The Prince of Wales immediately wrote to Freda:

Dickie is keen & cheery about everything although of course he is such a baby!! But he's a vewy [*sic*] clever boy & goes out of his way to be nice & kind & sympathetic & attentive to me as I think he guesses a little how I'm feeling. I'm so glad I've got him with me & I think we are going to be great friends, or as much so as our different ages will allow as of course he is terribly young. But he's been such a help to me today angel & I'm grateful to him.[60]

'David I like more and more, the more I see of him,' Dickie wrote to his mother:

We have long talks before he finally goes to bed at night in his sleeping cabin and exchange various confidences, mainly *affairs de coeurs*. Poor chap, with all these hundreds of people round him, he's as lonely & homesick as he can be and is (at present) HATING this trip! He says he'll cheer up later. But then he is very, very badly smitten I think.[61]

Mountbatten, meanwhile, kept his mother abreast of his own love life:

But please, please keep this secret. Nada has come to the amazing conclusion that Catherine now loves me. This I still don't really believe her but I am terribly afraid I'm falling in love with her. If I see Audrey at Panama it may change things though on the whole (as far as guts are concerned) I am heart free and shall keep a list of girls I meet on the trip.[62]

There were many, in his parlance, with whom he 'got off' as, apart from girls met at official functions, others were brought out to them on ship or at remote beaches.[63] They included: the daughter of the Mayor of San Diego, Lucia Wilde; a general's daughter who later married a prominent Australian politician, Gwenda Grimwade; and Mollee Little, a friend of Bertie's mistress Sheila Loughborough. In June, Peter Murphy wrote to Dickie to keep him abreast of the news, mentioning that 'there is a new debutante whom all the young men are mad about. Huge blue eyes, attractive hair, a gorgeous figure and lovely legs; just your cup of tea. Her name is Edwina Ashley and everybody tells me she is very sweet.'[64]

The men passed their time playing deck hockey, clay pigeon shooting, jumping on pongo sticks, posing for nude photographs and playing juvenile pranks in-between the official programme of teas, garden parties, dances, banquets, parades, meeting ex-servicemen, naval and troop reviews. The Prince of Wales was depressed, bored and petulant, and only briefly cheered up when the train from Sydney to Perth was derailed, leaving the local Minister of Works trapped in the lavatory. The Prince himself was found 'reclining amid the wreck of the costly compartment, smiling and smoking a cigar', later remarking that 'at last we have done something which was not on the official programme'.[65]

Dickie's natural enthusiasm and self-confidence had a calming effect on the highly temperamental Prince, but his close friendship – he was the only one allowed to call him David – also created some envy; Joey Legh, another courtier, in his letters home referred to Dickie as 'Dirty Dick' and 'the Hun' or 'The Boy'. Dickie wrote to his father in June after they had arrived in Australia:

This is very private but he <u>hates</u> his father & mother – both of them – and misses a father & mother so much . . . David felt rather sick so he has joined me in my cabin & never leaves it, save to go on Deck. I sleep in his cabin. He loves mine.[66]

'As I've told you Dickie & I have become very close friends & after all we are relations & he knows YOU & so means a great deal to me away from you,' wrote the Prince to Freda:

> The result is that we are more or less inseparable & are in & out of each other's cabins all day (he's generally in mine) & when we sleep on deck our beds are always next to each other! Well, would you believe it sweetie, the rest of the staff have for this reason become jealous of him & object to him & have gone to the Admiral with a long list of what they consider his misdeeds!! Of course they don't mention a word about me & our being so *intime* but I've just had a long yarn with the Admiral who has just had a long talk to Dickie.[67]

But it was also realised that Dickie's closeness could be a useful way of persuading the Prince to carry out tasks he didn't want to do.

Halsey had asked Dickie to keep an unofficial record of the trip designed for an inner circle of courtiers. Dickie tried to keep it light-hearted and felt able to share it with his mother, brother and the Prince's brother Bertie, but there was a brief furore when the official photographer, Ernest Brooks, disappeared with a copy and was tracked down to a London restaurant, Kettners, where he was caught trying to sell it to an American journalist for £5,000.[68]

Dickie had usurped the Prince of Wales's younger brother Bertie as confidant. In a letter to his mother, Mountbatten wrote:

> He told me that before he came out his best friend was Bertie but what a useless fellow as a true friend. He's a dear good stupid pompous & faithful old soul – as David himself describes him, but as for his having a good effect on David. It's all the good that's going out of David into him. I don't

know if I've ever told you before exactly what friends David
& I are. I've told him more about myself & he has told me
more about himself than either of us ever have told anyone in
our life before.[69]

On the final stretch of the trip, Dickie produced a film of
manoeuvres at sea, which could be used 'to facilitate the teaching
of fleet manoeuvres by means of a kinematograph film', and which
Halsey forwarded to the Admiralty, who adopted it. It became
known as the Mountbatten System Manoeuvre Tuition and became
a mainstay of naval training.[70]

HMS *Renown* returned on 11 October. The seven-month trip had
been a formative experience for the young naval officer. Not only
had he forged a close friendship with his future king, but he had
met a whole range of people and made connections that he would
usefully later exploit.[71] He had seen the world and had matured,
learnt how to meet and engage with crowds. Now all set for a sub-
lieutenant's course at Portsmouth, he felt ready to settle down.

* * *

Back from her travels, no one knew what to do with Edwina.
Cassell, aware of the difficult relationship with Molly and lonely
himself, suggested Edwina come and live at Brook House and act
as his hostess. With the end of the war, he had begun to entertain
more and Edwina took on the role not only of companion but,
working with his secretary, Stella Underhill, social secretary
responsible for table plans, invitations and supervising the staff;
not just at Brook House, but at Six Mile Bottom and Moulton
Paddocks, his shooting and racing estates outside Newmarket.

She was a natural, but it was an unexciting life for a teenager
living alone with a man almost 50 years older. Much as he loved

her, seeing in her all the lost promise of his dead wife and daughter, he could be very controlling – checking her post and forbidding any meetings outside the house without a chaperone. Charles (later Sir) Baring, three years her senior, often saw her when both were staying in the South of France during the winter of 1920. 'She talked very openly to me about life, and what she wanted from it,' he later remembered. 'She knew nothing at that time, but she did know that she was going to play some significant part in the world. She really had a great sense of destiny, but didn't know what it was.'[72]

Charming, curious about the world, intelligent but still quite childlike, without a mother to guide her, Edwina came out in May 1920. A huge party, shared with Marjorie, was held at Brook House, a black jazz band played in the drawing room and a more traditional orchestra in the ballroom. She was now recognised as one of the most beautiful debutantes of her year – intelligent, elegant, a good dancer and conversationalist.

Through her grandfather she had met Cornelius and Grace Vanderbilt, whose $100 million fortune derived from his grandfather's shipping and railroad interests. That summer she stayed with Grace, 30 years older and a sort of substitute mother figure, at Nuneham Courtenay in a house that they had taken for the summer. In August she was with the Barings at their house in Cowes – their daughter Poppy was a contemporary and friend – from whence she watched the racing during the regatta from the Vanderbilts' yacht *Sheela,* before going on to stay with the Earl of Crawford in Fife.

She was not short of admirers. In the autumn, Charlie Rhys, an Old Etonian, who had won an MC with the Guards during the First World War, proposed whilst she was staying with his parents in Wales.[73] 'She intended to say yes, but at breakfast she decided he looked like a frog, and changed her mind.'[74] Her life was, however, now about to take a new course.

* * *

Dickie spent the first three months of 1921 doing a sub-lieutenant's course at Portsmouth, coming top in navigation. He still had hopes for his relationship with Audrey and in January they were reunited: 'I had a marvellous 3 days in town with her and I never could have believed that I was ever going to love one small woman so much,' he wrote to his mother. 'Every time I see her she has grown more wonderful.'[75] He saw her whenever he could, staying the weekend with her and her sister near Guildford, seeing each other in London or in Portsmouth.

'Every time I see her I feel more and more sure of myself and she does too,' he wrote to his mother at the end of January.[76] There were plans for him to join her in Biarritz, where she was staying with a French family, after his course finished, especially as there were doubts about whether the Prince of Wales's next tour, on which Dickie had been invited again, was going ahead.

'The Admiral does not seem at all sure about the Indian trip. If it does <u>not</u> come off when shall we get married?' he told his mother. 'Early next year or this winter is what Audrey & I would like because it is so much harder to have to wait so long when one is living in the same country.'[77]

In April he was sent to Liverpool in command of a platoon of naval stokers to deal with a threatened strike in the coal mines. It was at the end of June, shortly after joining HMS *Repulse* for a three-month secondment as senior watch keeper and assistant torpedo lieutenant, that Audrey finally told him where he stood. 'She says how miserable she is to have made me unhappy & how she can't understand herself & how she has lost all faith in herself.

'She even said she wasn't good enough for me,' he explained to his mother:

> I have written back as nice a letter as I possibly could. It is hard to realise what we were to each other at one time (as she herself says in her letter) and to realise that all that is over. I try to be philosophical about it and to realise that it is probably all for the best & that I was anyhow too young – but it is rather hard.[78]

* * *

Edwina continued to act as her grandfather's hostess and visit friends around the country – in July she had been part of a house party with Bertie, Duke of York and Elizabeth Bowes-Lyon, before joining Sir Ernest at Cap Ferrat, where he was supervising the rebuilding of the Villa des Cèdres, which he had recently bought from King Leopold of the Belgians.[79] It was from the South of France that Edwina set off to stay, as customary for the Cowes Regatta, with Sir Godfrey and Lady Baring at their home, Nubia House in Cowes.[80]

Also in Cowes that August week was Dickie, still pining for Audrey ('I really am beginning to forget Audrey occasionally'), who had been invited by the Vanderbilts on their yacht *Venetia* in the hope he might take an interest in their daughter Grace.[81] It was not Grace who caught his eye, but Edwina, whom he continually ran into at social events throughout the week. She too was entranced.

Dickie and Edwina had already met at a ball at Claridge's hotel in October 1920. Mountbatten later remembered, 'We got on extremely well, had several dances, but nothing more followed.'[82] 'Dickie Mountbatten was not only virtually unknown to Edwina but also quite unlike the young men she did know,' wrote Edwina's biographer:

> She had spent the past year with admirers who wore plus-fours, tweed caps and stout shoes; Dickie, keen and trim, always looked as if he were in uniform, as he often was. Other men played tennis, Mountbatten did acrobatics on the court. He was always on the move, turning somersaults on the deck of *Venetia*, shinning up on the rigging with his friend Dick Curzon. On a cloudy day with high waves he would put on a rubber cap and a bathing suit and aquaplane on a flat board towed behind a launch.[83]

At the end of the week, Dickie was due to stay with the Prince of Wales at his house on Dartmoor and Edwina was meant to be joining her grandfather for a motor tour of France, but a better invitation presented itself. The Vanderbilts had organised a ten-day cruise along the coast of Belgium and Northern France. Both Dickie, still regarded as a possible suitor for Grace, and Edwina were invited. Both seized their opportunity and gave their respective excuses to the heir to the throne and the millionaire. 'There is no doubt that it was on this cruise that we really fell in love,' Dickie later remembered. 'It was lovely weather and we used to sit up in deck chairs by moonlight holding hands and we went ashore at each place and went to the local night club and had a very gay and amusing time.'[84]

Dickie's first action on his return was to take Edwina to meet his parents, then living near Southampton, though he was shocked to discover: 'When we went to catch the train to Southampton West, I found she had a third class ticket whereas I had got a first class ticket.'[85] He duly paid for an upgrade. His parents were charmed by her. 'Edwina is the most remarkable and charming girl of this generation that I have met,' Mountbatten later claimed his father told him. 'She's got intelligence, character, everything. Now, you're very young, but if you do decide to marry her, you have my whole-hearted approval. She'll make a wonderful wife for you.'[86]

The two lovers arranged to meet again as soon as they could. The *Repulse*, with Dickie's father on board as a guest of its captain, Dudley Pound, was due in Inverness in mid-September. The Prince of Wales and Bertie were shooting at the Duke of Sutherland's Dunrobin Castle, 60 miles north, and Dickie arranged not only for him to join them, but also Edwina. It was probably their last chance to meet before he left with the Prince of Wales on his tour of India in October.

At Inverness, Dickie headed for Dunrobin to be reunited with Edwina, whilst his father, who had caught a chill, took the night train from Inverness to London. It was a large house party, which included Randall Davidson, Archbishop of Canterbury, but the young couple had been partnered at tennis and it promised to be a fun few days. 'I spent most of the weekend in Edwina's company and we were getting on like a house on fire,' he later remembered, 'and I had made up my mind to pop the question the last night of the weekend.'[87]

But events were to further delay a proposal. On the second day of his stay, 11 September, Dickie received a telegram to be told that his father, the man he hero-worshipped, had had a heart attack following influenza. At the age of 67, he was dead. Dickie immediately returned to London to deal with the funeral arrangements, followed ten days later by Edwina. When she arrived at Brook House, she discovered that a second tragedy had also taken place. Sir Ernest had suffered a heart attack whilst at his desk in the library, as she travelled back by train. He had never met the man his beloved granddaughter wished to marry. Edwina's first thought was that she must see Dickie.

Early the next morning, she sent a note to him at York House, where he was staying. He arrived at noon and took her, unchaperoned, out of the house across the road into Hyde Park, where they walked and talked about the past and the future. They had been thrown together in their mutual grief and were now further brought together by others. Mrs Ronnie Greville, a great matchmaker, invited them to stay at the same time at Polesden Lacey; whilst George and Nada Milford Haven had them for the first weekend in October at their home, St George, in Southsea, along with Dickie's mother and two sisters.

Dickie was due to sail in three weeks, but he felt it unfair to declare himself when he was about to disappear for eight months. However, late one afternoon, the two young people found themselves alone in the billiard room. Deeply in love and emotionally drained by the events of the last few weeks, Dickie declared his love and the two came to an understanding.[88]

Cassell's death had changed Edwina's life in many ways, not least her financial position. He had left almost seven and a half million pounds – over 300 million pounds in current values – with a 25/64 share to Edwina, which she would fully inherit when she married, or on her twenty-eighth birthday, whichever was sooner. This left simply on bank deposit would give her a weekly income of £2,000, when the average was £2.

Concerns remained. Both of them were young and emotionally immature – Dickie on the rebound from Audrey and his father's death, and Edwina even keener, with her grandfather's death, to create the family unit she had missed in her youth. There was also the huge disparity in their wealth and backgrounds. Dickie had his £310 a year naval pay, which was doubled with his private income, but it was nothing beside that of Edwina. In the circumstances, given Dickie was about to leave for eight months, the couple decided to keep quiet.

CHAPTER 4

Duty

On 26 October, the *Renown* set sail. The Duke of York and Prince Henry saw their brother off, whilst Dickie's brother, mother and sister Louise came on board to say their farewells. Tactfully, Edwina was left for half an hour with Dickie in his cabin. He gave her a little watch to mark time whilst parted. As the ship pulled out, Dickie trained his telescope on the shore. That night he wrote:

> My own beloved Darling, when you get this we will have been parted for the last time for a long while, and so I want to tell you that you will be truly *ever* in my thoughts, and you will be my 'guiding spirit' throughout . . . I shall try very hard to be worthy of your great love, though darling – it is difficult for a poor sinner like me to look up to such a wonderful, wonderful girl.[89]

Whilst Dickie wrote every day, bought her a birthday present and continued to tell her how much he missed her, Edwina was determined that separation would not change her life. She continued to go to the theatre and out dancing, and thought nothing of mentioning her admirers, such as the Harvard-educated banker and international sailor, Paul Hammond, who had been with them at Cowes.

'I had great fun at Edwina's. Her cousin Marjorie Brecknock was also there – most amusing. I have found out (which will please Harold!) that Edwina is a real flirt and anything but as innocent as Dickie thought her to be!' wrote Michael 'Boy' Torby, brother of Nada Milford Haven, to their sister, Zia Werner. 'They were awfully funny, as they both had a go at me to find out what sort of chap I was and were delighted when they found out I had a dirty mind like their own!'[90] Dickie was left hurt and jealous. It did not augur well for a future marriage.

Edwina, in spite of her flirtations, was bored and lonely. Suggestions that she see Grace Vanderbilt in America or accompany Wilfrid and Molly to Italy came to nothing. What about India and seeing Dickie? She could always stay with family friends, the Viceroy Lord Reading and his wife. All she needed was the fare and a chaperone to accompany her. Her great aunt Mrs Cassell obliged with the first and a search through the passenger shipping lists provided a suitable, casual acquaintance – Mrs Carey Evans, a daughter of Lloyd George and the wife of the Viceroy's personal physician, who was taking her two small children to India.[91]

The two women played poker with some of the officers each evening and Carey Evans 'used to get cross with her because she always wanted to win. She was a spoilt little rich girl, and luck was usually with her'.[92] She thought Edwina mixed with people who were 'undesirable', but only exercised her role as chaperone once when Edwina wished to go out late in Aden:

As a person, Edwina was quite fearless. Nothing seemed to frighten her, and I suppose the idea of going ashore late at night, when there could be dangers lurking round every corner, simply exhilarated her. But I'm afraid I never really liked her, and she always seemed to me to be a woman completely without warmth.[93]

* * *

One purpose of the royal tour had been to improve Anglo-Indian relations, especially after the 1919 Amritsar massacre, but the reception was not always favourable. The Indian National Congress had organised a boycott of the tour, there were demonstrations, and at Patiala shots were fired at the ADC's car. In Allahabad, the young Jawaharlal Nehru and his father were locked up as the royal party passed through. The Prince pined for Freda and punished himself with violent exercise and a near-starvation diet.

Alongside the official functions, however, there was plenty of time for other pursuits. Apart from discovering polo, a sport that was to remain a passion all his life, there was pig sticking, hunting black buck from a Rolls-Royce with the Maharaja of Bharatpur, and shooting tigers and panthers – the latter taken from a zoo and doped.

At each port, Dickie's letters awaited Edwina with everything from pen portraits of the royal party she was about to meet – Fruity Metcalfe, 'the nicest fellow we have. Poor, honest, a typical Indian cavalryman'[94] – to lists of precedence. 'As a naval lieutenant mine is 78, as an ADC to the POW 74, and if I was out here as a member of the family you could take off 70.' Knowing his real ranking, he could 'laugh secretly at all these poor misguided people struggling to go even one place higher . . .'[95] It was clear Dickie cared very much about such things.

Edwina arrived in Bombay in early February and that night caught the fast mail train for the 25-hour, 700-mile trip to Delhi. She was staying in the Viceregal Lodge with another guest, Mrs Ronnie Greville. That night, 'We played happy families after dinner and then Edwina instructed me in all the new steps that have crept into London dancing since we left in Mrs Greville's sitting room,' Dickie scribbled in his diary.[96]

Writing to his mother a few days later, he confessed:

> I have been here since Saturday and seen Edwina all day long for three whole days – quite enough for me to realise that she is the most wonderful person in the world and that life without her would seem a very bleak prospect indeed. This isn't just purely physical attraction – it's her whole nature and character I love. In fact everything & though you mayn't believe it, it's quite, quite different from what I ever felt for Audrey. Would you mind if I tried my luck while she's out here – Mama? It's a devil of a long time to wait till we get home and I've already waited four months to ask her. If I wait much longer, the opportunity might pass.[97]

That night, suitably on Valentine's Day and four months after they had first met at the dance at Claridge's, Dickie proposed in the Prince of Wales's sitting-room, which he had put at their disposal. She immediately accepted. Only the Prince of Wales, who accepted the invitation to be best man, was told.[98] 'Miss Edwina Ashley is engaged to Lord Louis Mountbatten. What a waste,' Anthony Eden noted in his diary.[99]

The next day Dickie confided to his diary that he was 'happy beyond my wildest dreams' and how, after a state banquet, they had 'motored out to King Humayun's enormous tomb, which we saw at 3.00 am by moonlight. Very wonderful and romantic.'[100] Enthusiastic letters were written pledging his undying love and praising those bits of her body he had been allowed to see – a special pleasure was the discreet glimpse of her breasts, which he had named after two First World War campaign medals, Mutt and Jeff.

Now that Edwina had accepted, permissions had to be requested and arrangements made. Six days after proposing, the couple told their ostensible matchmaker Mrs Ronnie Greville, the Viceroy and his wife. Mrs Greville, in particular, had her reservations:

> My dear Viceroy, I am absolutely wretched about that child – I couldn't sleep a wink, I have grave misgivings. They were both at me last night – & she will not be reasonable, all I begged for was that no engagement should take place now, in a year she will be sick of him . . . this is absolutely confidential only I feel she is being thrown to the wolves . . . I don't dislike him but he is wily . . . she looked so white-faced and motherless last night. Dear Viceroy, please insist on no engagement.[101]

Lady Reading, writing to Wilfrid Ashley, put it more simply, 'I hoped she would care for someone older, with more of a career before him.'[102]

On 21 February, their last day together, the young couple rode at dawn to the site of the 1911 Durbar, then spent the afternoon together at the Pavilion. 'I took Edwina in to dinner tonight and danced with her and sat out with her till it was time to go (10.50),' Dickie wrote in his diary. 'She came to the station and saw us off. I hated leaving. I hated it very much.'[103]

That day he wrote as a courtesy to George V, asking his formal permission under the Royal Marriages Act to marry, and told his mother:

> I've done it and she has said 'Yes' – are you angry? I do hope not. I really do know what I am about this time and it isn't

just a physical infatuation – indeed the supremely physical attraction has only grown since I have got to love all the rest of her. Mama – I am just quietly convinced that there is no other girl living who is half so wonderful, sweet or sympathetic. I feel absolutely totally unworthy of her – indeed I know I am and I shall spend the rest of my life striving to be even a little worthy of her.'[104]

He added that he felt ready for marriage. 'I have never really sown any wild oats & as I never intend to, I haven't got to get over that stage, which some never have to.'[105]

He was to be the proud instigator of a new line, now that the name Battenberg had been abandoned and his brother's children were Milford Haven, and his thoughts were already turning to becoming a parent, buying children's toys in Malaya. For all his bravado about 'getting off' with women, Dickie remained an inexperienced lover. His only previous experience had been a visit to a brothel in Paris in January 1919. 'Please darling, don't get fussed or frightened,' he reassured Edwina. 'I'm a very patient chap, just out to please you . . .'[106]

From India, the royal party moved on to Ceylon, where they stayed at the King's Pavilion in Kandy before going on to Singapore and Hong Kong. On 12 April they arrived at Yokohama, Japan. Traditionally, Japan had been an ally of the British, but the long-standing treaty of friendship had not been renewed, nationalism was on the rise, and Japan had engaged in rapid rearmament. Attempts by the British naval attaché to visit their newest battleship, the *Mutsu*, had been rebuffed, so Dickie, regarded as simply a royal visitor, was recruited to do a little bit of espionage, producing a detailed report for the Admiralty.[107]

In mid-June the *Renown* reached Plymouth, escorted for the last stretch by four seaplanes and a flotilla of destroyers, and the party caught a special train to Paddington where huge crowds awaited, including the King and Queen and most of the Cabinet. From there, a convoy of State carriages took the party to Buckingham Palace and a celebration lunch. Edwina preferred to wait and be reunited that evening at Marjorie Brecknock's house, where she was staying.[108]

During the eight-month trip, Dickie had travelled over 40,000 miles and the trip had cemented his close friendship with the heir to the throne, enhanced his naval career and consolidated three great loves – India, Polo and Edwina.

Dickie, who loved organising things, threw himself into the preparations for his forthcoming wedding in deadly earnest. Wedding venue, presents and guests all had to be planned and furniture for their new home together bought, all neatly labelled with its country of origin.[109] It was nothing compared to Edwina's preparations, especially in terms of her wardrobe. To Queen Mary's shock, even her lingerie was described in the press – each marked with a tiny cypher E and M intertwined in a diamond-shaped frame.

There was also the business of catching up with friends and being entertained. That was how Edwina liked it, but there was little opportunity for them to spend time together alone. It was a pattern to repeat itself throughout their life.

CHAPTER 5

Honeymoon

Most couples return to their private lives after the public spectacle of a wedding, but the Mountbattens' marriage marked simply the start of a life where private life and public appearances would often be merged. Their first four days of honeymoon at Broadlands was hardly spent alone, with a church fair in the grounds of Broadlands, and a visit to the cinema in Romsey to see the Pathé News film of the wedding. Dickie himself, who liked to be the centre of attention, talked of the wedding being like a movie. The honeymoon was to be no different.

After hosting a dinner party for the Prince of Wales and Fruity Metcalfe, the couple left in the new Rolls-Royce – the chauffeur Rasdill and Edwina's maid Weller squashed in the back with the luggage – for the first part of their four-month honeymoon.[110] Their first stop was Paris, which represented for Edwina freedom and sophistication, and the main suite at the Ritz hotel. 'It's marvellous, Mama dear, being married,' Dickie wrote to his mother, 'quite the best thing I've ever done or am likely to do.'[111]

But the differences between the newlyweds were already apparent. For Dickie, everything had to be planned down to the last detail, for Edwina, the joy, after years of close supervision, was to run free without plans. Their next stop was Spain, where Dickie had carefully mapped out routes and overnight stops, much to the dismay of Edwina, who would have preferred more spontaneity and consultation. To please her, Dickie cancelled his bookings to find at their first stop, Tours, the only accommodation was a tiny attic room at a small hotel. After a sleepless night, Edwina agreed to let him pre-book in future.

Their next stop was Spain and a stay with King Alfonso and Queen Ena – Dickie's cousin – in Santander, followed by Wolfsgarten, near Darmstadt. After that a visit to Dickie's uncle Ernie, where they saw Heiligenberg Castle, the Battenbergs' country house, which Dickie's father had sold two years before. A surprise visitor was Peter Murphy, Dickie's Cambridge friend who, after entertaining his hosts at Wolfsgarten, disappeared as mysteriously as he had appeared. Back in Paris, the young couple were joined at the Ritz by Georgie and Nada for a much more exciting three days of cocktails and nightclubs, before returning to London at the end of August.

Dickie, who had taken leave on half pay until November, was now able to take up the second part of his honeymoon – a trip across America. At the end of September, the Mountbattens left on the *Majestic*, then the biggest passenger ship in the world, in a huge suite obtained for the price of a single cabin because of their publicity value. Press attention was something they were to generate throughout their American stay. In New York they gave a press conference, dined with the composer Jerome Kern, went to the cinema with Douglas Fairbanks and Mary Pickford, saw the Ziegfeld Follies, danced to Paul Whiteman's Big Show Band, watched a baseball game with Babe Ruth, and rode the roller coaster at Coney Island nine times.

Dickie had only briefly been to the United States – a short stop at San Diego with the Prince of Wales – and Edwina never. Their trip had been organised by a wealthy family friend, Robert Thompson, who had put his private railway carriage at the disposal of the honeymoon couple and also joined them with various members of his family. From New York they visited Niagara Falls, a meat factory in Chicago and the Grand Canyon, pulling in at sidings to visit power stations, museums and Colonel Thompson's friends. Douglas Fairbanks had invited them to use his home, Pickfair, and through Geordie, the Duke of Sutherland, they had an introduction to Charlie Chaplin. 'He is the most loveable, shy & pathetic little man & yet so full of humour that he can keep one amused by the hour,' wrote Dickie to his mother.[112]

Cecil B. de Mille showed them the sets for his new film at Paramount Studios and they even made their own film, *Nice and Friendly*, centring around Edwina's abduction by Colonel Thompson and rescue by Chaplin, with bit parts for Dickie as her lover, child star Jackie Coogan and even their own valet Thorogood in the role of a disdainful butler.[113]

And then it was back to the East Coast with Dickie giving an address at the Navy League dinner in Washington on Navy Day – Thompson was Honorary President of the League – to Florida, the Naval Academy at Annapolis, a brief visit to President Warren G. Harding, and finally ten days with the Vanderbilts at their house at 640 Fifth Avenue, where Edwina celebrated her twenty-first birthday.

It was not only Edwina, but Dickie who had come of age. Both blossomed, learning to work a crowd and politely answer the most inane questions, notably about their wealth and future. 'Career for Lady Louis? Why, she's going to be my wife, career enough!' Dickie told one paper.[114] Edwina was happy to go along with the conceit, claiming, without a blush, that 'Scrubbing floors, dishwashing and cooking . . . are her long suits.'[115] They had enjoyed the attention

– the Press called them Prince and Princess – the openness and the hospitality, and made many new friends and developed new passions, such as spirituals and jazz. America was, in future, to be another escape from the more curtailed lives in Britain to which they were about to return.

Dickie's naval future looked uncertain. The First World War had imposed huge financial burdens on Britain and the National Debt had risen from £677 million in 1910 to £7.8 billion in 1922 – larger than the country's GDP. Something had to be done. Sir Eric Geddes was appointed to look into cutting public expenditure. He recommended reductions in public spending of £87 million with much of it falling on defence – the budget was cut by 42 per cent in one year, and especially the Navy. It meant that 350 lieutenants would have to be retired. The view was taken that those with private incomes should be the first to be culled. It looked like Dickie's career might be over before it had even begun.

Amongst those on the committee deciding who should be retained was Admiral Ernle Chatfield. Dickie had been his 'doggie' – ADC and errand boy – and he knew the young officer was serious and ambitious. Other influential supporters included the Prince of Wales, who spoke to his father, and his brother Georgie, who argued that Dickie had the makings of a fine naval officer but, from recent evidence as a director of a gramophone company, was an indifferent businessman.[116]

On the other hand, many of Dickie's contemporaries saw him as a rich playboy, a lightweight more interested in accompanying the Prince of Wales on tour and making films in Hollywood than his naval career. By the end of 1923, more than half the officers from Dickie's year had left the service. Saved by his influential contacts, he was not one of them, but he knew that if he was to survive and prosper in the Navy, he would have to excel.

In January 1923, Dickie was posted to the battleship *Revenge* – part of the International Fleet in the Dardanelles – to deal with any problems in the Balkans. Edwina, Peter Murphy, John and Marjorie Brecknock accompanied him by train to Paris, where they spent a few days visiting the night spots of the capital. Presenting his wife with a toy rabbit called Bun, Dickie then caught another train to Constantinople. It was the first time they had been apart since marrying six months earlier.

The captain of the *Revenge*, Gilbert Stephenson, had initially asked the Admiralty not to post Mountbatten, concerned he was not serious about his career:

> Directly I saw the man at work I realised how tremendously intelligent he was, how full of life and vivacity. He had the gift of getting on with people; people, in other words, wanted to do what *he* wanted them to do. And, after all, that's a very valuable gift in anybody, especially an officer. He was, in fact, the most successful of all my officers when handling difficult men, though you would hardly have expected him to afford them the time they needed.[117]

Dickie made a point of knowing all 160 men in his division, preparing details of each with their career and background. He gave prizes for good shooting (until it was pointed out that other officers could not afford to do the same), introduced mah-jong and wrote a script for a black-and-white Pierrot show. The Communist Len Wincott, later ringleader in the Invergordon Mutiny, remembered that when Dickie 'left the *Revenge* . . . he received such a send-off from the men that I doubt any captain ever was so spontaneously or sincerely bid *bon voyage*.'[118]

The newlyweds missed each other enormously. On the first

anniversary of their engagement, he wrote her a 24-page letter recapping their life together since they had first met and confessing to dreams about her slim legs encased in soft leather riding boots. Edwina also faced uncertainty and a need to prove herself. She had rushed into marriage not knowing what else to do and now faced long periods apart from Dickie, as he single-mindedly pursued his naval career. She had no obvious purpose and around £50,000 a year after tax (when £1,000 before tax was a generous income) to pursue it.

Stella Underhill largely ran the Cassell bequests, trust and charities, and Brook House, so Edwina simply occupied herself by sleeping late, shopping, playing bridge, seeing friends, attending parties and country house weekends and, where possible, following Dickie on his naval postings. A particular pleasure was revue and cabaret shows, especially 'jerky syncopated dance music, sentimental love songs and the sound of a wailing saxophone'.[119] She was painted by the society painter Philip de László, but she felt bored and restless, her sharp brain and competitive nature not fully exercised.

She had already redecorated Brook House, papering and carpeting her bedroom in pale grey and installing a vast bath of Italian marble flanked by an enormous double washstand. Amongst her jars of cream and perfumed oils was a small bottle containing the blackened nerve of Dickie's left front tooth, damaged in a hunting accident in 1920, and a parting present before he left for Constantinople.

Dickie's bedroom had also been redone to resemble an officer's cabin, complete with regulation bunk, brass rail, folding washstand, the simulated noise of the throb of a ship's engine, and a porthole *trompe-l'œil*, which, at the flick of a switch, presented a diorama of Valetta harbour by either day or moonlight. Against a painted background was a collection of cut-out ships at 50 feet to an inch that, when darkness fell, twinkled real Morse signals to each other.

In one corner in a glass case was the comforting presence of his father's hat, uniform and decorations as First Sea Lord.

In April, the *Revenge* docked at Plymouth and the Mountbattens, reunited at the Grand Hotel, began their next joint operation – a child. Shortly afterwards, Edwina announced she was pregnant.

Another task that summer was to find a country house near Portsmouth where *Revenge* was now based. In May, Edwina took a six-week lease on Maiden Castle House, near Dorchester, a square, substantial brick villa with eight bedrooms and plenty of room for Dickie's polo ponies. At the same time, they cut back on their expenditure by renting out Brook House to Mrs Vanderbilt. The *Revenge* was now at Devonport and Edwina returned to London, where she danced every night with an old flame, Hugh Molyneux, heir to the Earl of Sefton, at a succession of nightclubs – the Riviera Club, the Grafton Galleries or the Blue Lagoon.

On 14 February, Dickie, cruising with the Atlantic Fleet at Madeira, received a signal informing him of the birth of a daughter born exactly two years after his engagement.[120] She was named Patricia (after her cousin and godmother, Lady Patricia Ramsay) Edwina Victoria (after Dickie's mother). He immediately wrote to Edwina:

> I could hardly hold myself in when I got the wireless message this morning saying that our daughter had been born. For a few days past I felt convinced it would be a girl and was praying it would be as I think it's so much nicer to have a daughter as one's first child. That I am a father I simply cannot believe, and oh! My dear, I am so excited I can hardly wait until I come home to see her. It is thrilling, isn't it, my dear? Bless you sweet – if anything could make me love you more dearly than I already do, it will be our baby.[121]

Edwina, having done her duty, quickly resolved to go back to her life of pleasure and the baby was handed over to Nannie Woodard. Shortly afterwards, she left for dress fittings and fun with Nada in Paris and then to stay at the Château de la Garoupe at Antibes. Amongst her new friends were Paula Gellibrand, a *Vogue* model, and her husband, the Marquis de Casa Maury. Bobby Casa Maury, known as 'The Cuban Heel', had been born in Cuba but brought up in Britain. A racing driver by profession, a playboy by inclination, he and his wife dazzled Edwina.

Dickie was granted leave for the christening in April at the Chapel Royal, attended by her godparents, who included the Prince of Wales. Immediately, Dickie was besotted, but Edwina was slower to appreciate her first child. Whilst her photograph albums of 1924 have scores of pictures of her friends, there are only nine of Patricia for the first months of her life. It sometimes appeared as if the infant was simply an ornament with whom her mother was occasionally photographed for society magazines.

Edwina continued her frantic social life – Wimbledon for the Ladies' semi-finals, Ascot for tea with the King and Queen, Cowes with the Vanderbilts and Barings. There were tennis parties when the weather was fine, mah-jong when wet, visits to the movies with friends such as Jean Norton and Hugh Molyneux, the occasional charity function and, every few months, shopping trips to Paris for shoes at Tetreau, hats at Reboux and dresses at Chanel.

She ate little and exercised frantically – golf or tennis daily, for which she had professional coaching, and then several hours dancing each night – with the result she remained fit and slim. She was desperate for new experiences and felt trapped by domesticity. Above all, she craved her own independence – having been denied it in her youth.

In August 1924, Dickie left the *Revenge* and after a week playing polo at Deauville and Le Touquet on the French coast, he and Edwina joined the Prince of Wales on the Cunard liner *Berengaria* to New York. Ostensibly, the purpose was to watch an international polo match between Britain and the United States on Long Island. Others on board included: Georgie and Nada; her sister Zia and husband Harold Wernher; the Duchess of Westminster; Jean Norton and her husband Richard, the heir to Lord Grantley; Diana (returning to appear on Broadway) and Duff Cooper, and Ivor Novello's mother. Indeed, so popular was the crossing that it had a waiting list of 500 – mainly marriageable daughters.

Dickie and Edwina spent much of their time with the Prince, who was travelling incognito as Lord Renfrew, playing mah-jong or swimming in the liner's swimming pool, a vast cave lined with marble columns and mock-Pompeian mosaics. Dickie organised a tug-of-war team from amongst the Prince's staff, who naturally were allowed to win. Edwina and Jean danced the night away in the ship's nightclub.

The royal party was staying on Long Island with James Burden, president of Burden Iron Works, the largest horseshoe and nail-producing concern in the world, and spent their time at polo meetings, dances, dinners and trips into New York, either by road or boat. The Prince of Wales conducted an affair with Pinna Cruger, the actress wife of a New York haberdashery millionaire, whilst Fruity Metcalfe took up with an 18-year-old dancer, Virginia de Lanty.[122]

The relationship between Nada, who had lesbian tendencies, and Georgie was under strain and Edwina saw much of her sister-in-law, especially as Dickie was taken ill with tonsillitis and spent much of the trip in bed. Edwina wasn't going to have her fun spoilt and continued to aquaplane behind fast boats, dance at parties, and stay until dawn at nightclubs in New York accompanied by other guests.

Once he recovered, Dickie gamely accompanied her, but he did not warm to Edwina's new social set, nor their nightclubbing antics. He much preferred a solitary round of golf or playing with a movie projector. Tensions built until Edwina, liberated by her newfound freedom and friends, announced she would not be returning with Dickie, but wanted to stay on. It was clear there were problems in the marriage. Edwina needed constant reassurance and Dickie, emotionally immature himself, did not always know how to give it. Confused by her own burgeoning emotions and newly assertive, she respected him all the less when he accepted her criticism of his various faults. Dickie returned home alone on the *Homeric* full of self-reproach.

Edwina remained a few more weeks, enjoying her new independence, but unsure what to do with it. Attractive, rich and vulnerable, she was surrounded by admirers who competed for her attentions, which she deflected by playing them off against each other. Annoyed, they gradually withdrew and, Edwina, knowing her little adventure was over, returned to the husband who had increasingly come to bore her.

CHAPTER 6

A Marriage Under Threat

Dickie had started at the signal school at Portsmouth at the end of September 1924. It was a tough few months with an examination every fortnight. After a day of polo, he would study all night in his barracks. Often the only entry in his diary was 'Work as usual'. His hard work paid off. When the final placing was announced the following summer, he had come top.[123]

Shortly before their American trip, the Mountbattens had taken a long lease on Adsdean, a large neo-Tudor house built of flint and stone, as a base near to Dickie's course in Portsmouth. It was to be their country home until Edwina inherited Broadlands shortly before the Second World War. The mansion, built in the previous century and covered in Virginia creeper, was situated in a wooded park of 50 acres on the Sussex Downs. With over 30 bedrooms, three tennis courts, 800 acres of shooting and 18 servants, it was ideal for their ambitious entertaining plans of a party most weekends.

Three days after Edwina returned from America, she had moved in and within a few days she had entertained her first guests – the Casa Maurys, Poppy Baring and Prince George, youngest son of George V. Henceforth, every weekend for the next 15 years, and whenever else Edwina was in residence, the house would be filled with friends and Dickie's naval colleagues.

Edwina decorated the house in her favourite colours of pink and cream and they added a nine-hole golf course, hard tennis court, a special pit for polo practice, a paddock and riding school, as well as a staff recreation room with radio, billiard table, darts board and table tennis; and plans were also made to build a private aerodrome – both Edwina and Dickie were learning to fly. The house was run with efficiency, not least by Dickie himself, who issued each evening a form in triplicate where guests needed to state what they wished to do the next morning and afternoon, which meals they required, the times they wanted to use the tennis court, and so on. Spontaneity was frowned upon.

He had first discovered polo whilst in India with the Prince of Wales and now he was to create his own team at Adsdean. Without ever being a good horseman, Dickie, as in everything he did, trained himself single-mindedly and systemically to be the best, substituting talent by focusing upon technique. He scrutinised slow-motion film of top players in order to analyse and improve tactics, developed a more ergonomically efficient mallet and regarded each chukka as just another naval engagement.

He created a polo pit of four sloping walls of chicken wire with a roof where, seated on a wooden horse, named Winston, he would practise hitting the ball again and again. He would strengthen his fingers by carrying a squash ball in his pocket and strengthen the muscles in his wrist by having a polo stick shortened and weighted with lead, which he would swing at every opportunity.

One young naval officer later complained that Mountbatten took all the enjoyment out of the game after he was invited to join the exclusive team. 'Life suddenly became rather real and earnest and no longer such fun. A weekly memo was sent to all the team members giving days to practise, days to play, ponies to play, diet sheets, dates for the weekly session on polo tactics using matchsticks on a card table at his flat in Guardamangia, and a reminder to be in bed by ten p.m. Of course, we won everything.'[124]

In September 1925, he was posted to the Naval College at Greenwich for the demanding Higher Wireless Course with its mix of algorithmic calculation and rote-learning, applied physics, advanced mechanics and pure mathematics. This was to be an important turning point, confirming to colleagues his ability in a rapidly expanding and important area of technical expertise, and his potential to rise to the very top of the Navy.

* * *

She called them her 'ginks', a dozen or so admirers, many of them Americans or from Dickie's polo circle, with whom Edwina went to parties and revues. They included Danish banker Aksel Wichfield; a Swiss friend of the Vanderbilts, Pierre Merillon; and the designer and former aviator, Deering Davis.[125] They might flirt and dance closely, but they seemingly posed no threat to the marriage.

At the beginning of 1925, however, Edwina stepped over that boundary. Her first lover was long-term friend, Hugh Molyneux, three years older than her, the heir to the Earl of Sefton and described as 'the best-looking man in society'. A former army officer, he had served as ADC to the Governor General of Canada immediately after the First World War and was a keen sportsman and racing enthusiast. The affair lasted for ten months before Molyneux was posted to India as ADC to the Viceroy.[126]

Almost immediately she took up with Stephen 'Laddie' Sandford, the heir to a $40 million fortune and champion polo player, whom she had first met on Long Island the previous autumn and had met again in July 1925, when he came to play for the Adsdean polo team. A few years older than Edwina, he had been educated at Yale and Cambridge, where he played number 1 in the polo team. Laddie was a glamorous figure – a big game hunter in Africa, who hunted regularly with the Quorn, Belvoir and Coltsmore packs. His most recent lover had been the socialite Doris Delevingne, whom he had set up in an apartment by The Dorchester Hotel and for whom he had bought a Rolls-Royce.[127]

In August, Laddie joined the Mountbattens for their annual holiday at Deauville and from then on, he and Edwina were inseparable. Dickie suspected nothing for many months until in December, the Prince of Wales told him. Even then he refused to believe it. 'Went to see David . . . He had a queer story about Edwina.'[128] Sandford was to remain one of Edwina's principal lovers throughout the interwar period, and the Mountbatten guest books at Brook House and Adsdean and the diary of her friend, Jean Norton, are filled with references to him.

Jean Norton was Edwina's best friend. Slender ,with large blue eyes and wavy golden-brown hair, she closely resembled Edwina. Married to the film producer Richard Grantley, she, too, was having an affair – with the newspaper proprietor Max Beaverbrook, owner of the *Daily Express*. Rare amongst Edwina's friends, she had a job, working at the New Gallery Picture House in Regent Street, where it was hoped her social contacts would help box-office takings.

The two women had worked together on the switchboard, as street vendors and in the canteen at the *Express* during the General Strike, as well as serving at the YMCA canteen in Hyde Park, making tea and cooking sausages for volunteer lorry drivers. It was Edwina's first proper employment and, though exhausting, she loved it. For once she had some worthwhile purpose in life.

But Laddie was not Edwina's only lover. By September 1926, she had a new one. Mike Wardell was a tall, dashing ex-cavalry officer with a passion for hunting. He had lost an eye in a riding accident and wore a black patch, which only made him more attractive to women. A close friend of Oswald Mosley, he owned Craven Lodge, a 24-bedroomed mansion at Melton Mowbray and the centre of the hunting set around the Prince of Wales. He had just joined the *Daily Express* as circulation manager and Edwina had met him through Jean Norton. During the autumn of 1926, he and Edwina were constantly out at the theatre and supper parties and he was invited to Adsdean. It only added to Dickie's humiliation.

Hints were dropped heavily in gossip columns, especially that of Lady Decies, of Edwina out on the town escorted by a variety of men – Hugh Molyneux, Laddie Sanford or Mike Wardell. Edwina's social life now became of concern to the Royal Family, much to Dickie's dismay. 'A royal spanking for gay lady Mountbatten' ran a full-page story in the *San Francisco Chronicle* in October, referring to her dancing with Fred Astaire, and that Queen Mary disapproved of her socialising. 'For Lady Mountbatten wears her skirts just about as short as you see them anywhere on Broadway, and to the staid people present the sight of Lady Mountbatten's garters and lingerie was, no doubt, a shocking spectacle.'[129]

Dickie did his best to demonstrate, for all his faults, his love for his wife:

I want you to know that no action, however small, of yours, passes unnoticed by your spouse and that he is more grateful than he probably shows for the hundred and one little thoughtful acts by which you make life so very pleasant for him. The interest you take in my humble efforts at polo and the encouragement you have given me to play as often as possible . . . have made a wonderful difference in my life. If I could in any way alter my character and nature to be less selfish and more thoughtful I should be a very happy chap. Should like to be able to wait until you have gone to sleep at night, sleep without snoring, steal out of bed without waking you up, sit up late and dance late with you, knock off making plans, writing chits and discussing servants. I should love to feel I really wasn't a snob, and that I wasn't pompous . . . I wish I could drive a car like Bobby Casa Maury, play the piano and talk culture like Peter . . . shoot like Daddy . . . play polo like Jack. I wish I knew how to flirt with other women, and especially with my wife. I wish I had sown many more wild oats in my youth, and could excite you more than I fear I do. I wish I wasn't in the Navy and had to drag you out to Malta. I wish I had an equal share of the money so that I could give you far handsomer presents than I can really at present honestly manage. In other words – I would like to feel that I was really worthy of your love.[130]

Edwina kept the letter but never replied.

* * *

Dickie's course at Greenwich had ended in the spring of 1926 and he had marked time in the Reserve Fleet battleship *Centurion*. Now, at the end of 1926, he was posted to Malta and it was hoped this might provide a new start. He and Thorogood went out ahead with the polo ponies, just after Christmas, with Edwina following in the New Year, accompanied by her sister Mary and Peter Murphy, though two-year-old Patricia was left in London.

Their new home, Casa Medina, was a row of four small houses at the top of a narrow lane below the Valetta city walls. Friends came to stay, such as Jean Norton and her children, Nada and even the Duke and Duchess of York. Soon the Mountbattens had created a new circle of friends, many of them centred around polo, though Edwina found it difficult being the wife of a junior naval officer. Within a month, she had returned to London via Paris.

Dickie's new job was assistant to the Fleet Wireless Officer. He was working hard, often late into the night, preparing lectures for midshipmen and junior officers, but his playboy image followed him. With his servants, Rolls-Royce with silver signaller on the bonnet, speedboat, polo ponies, celebrity friends and huge parties, it was easy to see how such accusations could be made. 'No one will ever believe I work,' he wrote to his friend Andrew Yates. 'If I work like a beaver, people won't believe it, and if I am seen on the polo ground, they will say "I told you so".'[131]

'We always thought of him as having married millions of pounds and being mad on polo and pretty girls, and we thought he was a write-off as far as the Navy went,' recalled one of his colleagues, Peter Kemp. 'We didn't see why he should *bother* to work. If any of us had had such luck, *we* shouldn't have bothered. No, he was becoming the great playboy, and he acted like one. He wasn't going to go far, that's what we said.'[132]

At the end of the spring cruise, his new ship *Warspite* was anchored at Villefranche in the South of France. Dickie had arranged to meet up with Edwina, but she wired to say she had been delayed. In fact, she was already there with Laddie, who was pressing her to leave Dickie. She played for time, returned to Malta, but three weeks later she was back in London for her sister Mary's wedding.

Mary's mental health had always been fragile and Edwina had been very protective of her sister. In 1925 she had announced that she had fallen in love with Alec Cunningham-Reid, her father's parliamentary private secretary. On paper, Cunningham-Reid looked a catch. Tall, with a pencil moustache and matinee-idol looks, a godson of Sir Robert (later Lord) Baden-Powell, he had been a Royal Flying Corps flying ace, winning the Distinguished Flying Cross during the First World War, and been appointed flying instructor to the Prince of Wales and Duke of York. After the war, he had become a Conservative MP.

Given Mary was aged only 20, recently launched into society and only able to come into her share of her grandfather's inheritance on marriage, there were the same family concerns about fortune hunters that had bedevilled Dickie. It was decided she should be made a ward of court and the couple should agree not to see each other for the time being. Mary reacted by smashing up Dickie's bedroom and accusing one of his guests of being a brain specialist in disguise. Paranoid and violent, she had to be nursed for several months at Adsdean and then sent to a sanatorium in Italy.

Eventually, in October 1926, the family relented and after a man-to-man discussion between the suitor and Dickie, conducted in the Burlington Arcade, it was agreed permission would be granted if Alec could show he was worth £10,000. He did so immediately by simply borrowing it. In May 1927 the two of them, described as 'England's wealthiest girl and handsomest man', married with Patricia as a bridesmaid and a reception for 1,000 guests at Brook House. Dickie was not amongst them.[133]

It was not only Mary's wedding that had brought Edwina to London. Laddie was back with his polo team, The Hurricanes. Each weekend at Adsdean, the lovers would argue about their future. Hugh Molyneux was also around, having returned from India after a broken love affair with a Maharani. A further complication was Mike Wardell, who had been included in a party, which also included Jean and Winston and Clementine Churchill, on a yacht that Beaverbrook had chartered to tour First World War battlefields and cemeteries.

Panicking, Edwina fled to Paris and then back to London before

being persuaded to return. 'Lunch with Hugh at the Berkeley Grill
. . . Had dinner on a tray and Mike came to see me,' read one
diary entry. One night it would be 'long talk with Hugh', the next
'long talk with Mike'.[134] In mid-October 1927, Laddie returned to
London to add to her troubles.

She suffered headaches and dizzy spells and had trouble with
her eyes and teeth. X-rays suggested further investigations were
required. Instead of staying in London, where she had had a small
gynaecological operation the previous year, she chose to go to a
nursing home in Paris, where she was joined by Jean. She had had
an abortion.

Early in 1928, a divorce action was threatened in the United
States, in which Edwina was to be cited as a co-respondent by
Adelaide Chaqueneau. Edwina had been conducting an affair with
Adelaide's husband Julien, known as 'Jack' Chaqueneau, grandson
of the founder of the American Locomotive Works in Paris. The
solicitor Sir Charles Russell was retained in Britain and Beaverbrook
was brought in to help on the American end.

'It is imperative that we should know in the first instance if this
threat is serious. If not we don't propose to do anything,' he cabled
the American lawyer Paul Cravath. 'If threat is serious, it is a matter
of utmost importance that suit should be stopped. Our immense
social influence in support of plaintiff. Please throw all your
personal interest into this case.'[135] It seems to have worked. The
Chaqueneaus, who had separated in January, divorced quietly in
May 1928. He later remarried and became a well-known theatrical
agent and president of a New York perfume company.

The affair with Laddie continued to rumble on. After a visit to
Paris in the spring of 1927, Laddie had pressed her to leave Dickie. At
the end of June 1927, he returned to America, their future together
unresolved, but was back in mid-October and they were at the Ritz

in Madrid in April 1928, when she also briefly saw Dickie. In June 1928, instead of spending the day with Dickie on his birthday, she pleaded toothache and drove to London with Laddie.

The next week, Laddie was one of the guests at a dinner Edwina held at Brook House for King Alfonso of Spain, which was followed by a showing of *The Gaucho* lent by Douglas Fairbanks. A hundred and sixty were invited to the reception and 68 for dinner, including Diana and Duff Cooper, Prince Serge Obolensky – a new admirer, the Admiral of the Fleet, David Beatty, Admiral Sir Roger Keyes, and the Duke and Duchess of York. (The evening was enlivened when guests in evening dress chased two burglars disturbed by a night watchman in an adjacent house.)

In August 1928, Laddie and his sister were with the Mountbattens in the South of France, and Edwina and Laddie were photographed together in the *Star*. Edwina could see how she hurt Dickie and felt guilty. 'I feel I've been such a beast,' she confessed to her husband. 'You were so wonderful about everything, and I do realise how hard it all was for you, altho' I know you think I don't. I feel terribly about it all.'[136] New attempts were made to patch up the marriage and try for another child. 'I am in Paris for a couple of nights so that Edwina can see her doctor, as it seems such a good opportunity,' Dickie wrote to his mother in mid-August from the Ritz.[137]

At the beginning of September 1928, Edwina left for New York escorted by Peter Murphy. Ostensibly she was staying with Grace Vanderbilt on Fifth Avenue and in Newport. Certainly, that's what Dickie thought. 'Edwina has written me the sweetest letter of our life & honestly, Mama dear, I can't see what there is to worry about,' he wrote to his mother. 'Almost as soon as she arrived in New York, she went on with the Vanderbilts to Newport, which she would hardly have done if Laddie meant very much to her. Anyway I couldn't be happier.'[138]

It was not Laddie she was seeing but Sophie Tucker, a Ukrainian-born American singer, comedian, actress, and radio personality, nicknamed 'The Last of the Red Hot Mamas', known for her stentorian delivery of comical and risqué songs. Tucker, who performed with the Ziegfeld Follies, had been a fellow passenger on the *Berengaria* in August 1924 on a previous trip to the States, and Edwina had recently heard her sing at the Kit Kat Club and Alhambra in London. The plan was that Tucker, who ran her own club, Sophie Tucker's Playground, would act as Edwina's escort around the clubs of Harlem, Tin Pan Alley and Greenwich Village. There were even intimations in the press that they were sharing an interconnecting hotel suite.

Peter Murphy was quick to correct the story, telling the *New York Mirror*, 'Lady Mountbatten did not come to the United States with Miss Tucker. She met her on the boat by chance. Miss Tucker has greatly exaggerated her friendly relationship with Lady Mountbatten. She has overdone it. There is nothing more to say.'[139] It was not a story the press believed. The caption of the two photographed onboard ship read:

> 'Just chanced to meet.' Rah-lly folks, this was only a chawnce [*sic*] meeting on shipboard between Sophie Tucker (right) and Lady Mountbatten. Enterprising photographer got them to pose together for this picture but – as for Lady Louis going into a nightclub to be opened by Sophie, why the very idea![140]

'She took me up in London society,' explained Sophie to a local paper, 'and I was the pet of the mob.'[141] As she was to learn, the Mountbattens could be ruthless about people they felt might be using or embarrassing them.

Tucker had shown Edwina the night spots of New York and, in

particular, Harlem. Edwina, since her trip to India in 1921, had found herself drawn to people of colour. This was not simply because she delighted in confounding prejudice or because, with her Jewish blood, she was sympathetic to the outsider and the oppressed – though that was part of it – but because she found darker skins, whether dusky Indian or jet black African, attractive. She liked black art and music, especially negro spirituals, soul, blues and jazz, and she enjoyed the easy banter and lack of deference of black people. This American visit was to mark her increasing involvement with people across the colour bar.

After two weeks in New York, Edwina joined Laddie on Long Island, where she discovered she might again be pregnant. She saw a doctor, who was guarded, and told Laddie. He now forced the matter to a head, asking her to choose between him and Dickie.

CHAPTER 7

Divergent Paths

Overnight Edwina made her decision, told her maid to pack and returned to London. Back not to Malta, but to a further series of tests to see if she had had a miscarriage, had merely suffered some obstetric problem, or was indeed pregnant. The answer came quickly. Her second child was due in May.

There was, however, time for one more adventure. Dickie's posting came to an end in June and they would be leaving Malta. When he left in mid-March for the Mediterranean and Atlantic Fleet's combined manoeuvres, she packed up Casa Medina and, having said goodbye to Patricia, not for the first time, motored with Ainsworth the chauffeur and her maid Harding in the Hispano to Algeciras, where Dickie, Georgie and three naval friends, Teddy Heywood-Lonsdale, Tom Hussey and Charles Lambe were waiting.

Over a few days' leave they explored Morocco, where they were received by the Sultan, before chartering a tug to make the five-hour crossing to Gibraltar. As the Fleet sailed, Edwina, eight months pregnant, and Ainsworth took it in turns to drive the 165 miles over rough roads to Ronda and on through the mountains to Malaga, where they caught a train to Madrid and then Barcelona to rendezvous with Dickie at the Ritz.

On 19 April, shortly after she arrived, Edwina suddenly went into labour. She was five weeks early, a shock to Dickie, who was a stickler for correct timekeeping. The child was named Pamela Carmen (after a close friend, the Duchess of Peneranda) Louise (after Dickie's younger sister). Writing to his mother shortly afterwards, Dickie explained, 'She came to within 5 minutes & asked for me & her first words were "I'm so sorry it isn't a boy" and though at any other time I should have been disappointed I was so truly thankful all was well that I could tell her in real truthfulness that I didn't care what the baby was so long as they were both well.'[142]

It had not been an easy birth, but it had helped bring the couple together. 'I think it takes sometimes a crisis like this to make one realise just how much one cares for a person,' wrote Edwina to her husband. 'I don't think there can be anything seriously wrong if we feel like I think we both did, during this last week.'[143]

Whilst Dickie remained in Malta, Edwina returned to London, where her health continued to be uncertain. In June 1929, she spent three weeks being treated at a spa in Normandy, where Dickie joined her. They also took the opportunity of looking, as Dickie wrote to his mother,

> at a rather nice looking tiny flat Edwina is thinking of taking under the enormous impression that it will be cheaper than always stopping at the Ritz. Actually I do not think this will be the case but as she goes to Paris for 3 or 4 days quite 8 or 9 times a year it will be much more comfortable for her & enable her to do her shopping without perpetually having to dine out.[144]

But further troubles lay ahead. The following month, the High Court heard a petition for divorce from Marjorie Hall Simpson against Henry Anthony Simpson, naming Lady Edwina Mountbatten as the co-respondent and alleging that he had 'frequently committed adultery with Edwina Cynthia Annette, Lady Louis Mountbatten', including in October 1926 at Brook House and December 1928 at the Ritz Hotel in Paris.[145]

Tony Simpson was a naval colleague and friend of Dickie's in Malta. Awarded the Distinguished Service Cross in 1917, he was a lieutenant commander serving as a naval aviator. It was simply blackmail, as Simpson had not lived with his wife for some time and she was, in any case, having an affair with an Italian aviator, Colonel Luigino Falchi. Eventually, again through Charles Russell, Simpson's wife was paid off – Beaverbrook and Marjorie Brecknock acted as intermediaries – and in November the petition was dismissed: but it had cost Edwina £13,000 with the legal expenses. Simpson was embarrassed and offered to pay back the Mountbattens, but for Dickie the money was immaterial. It was the scandal which counted, and Edwina seemed unconcerned about that.[146]

In the summer of 1929, Dickie was posted to Portsmouth as the Signal School's chief wireless instructor, where he showed himself to be a natural and conscientious teacher, able to convey complex ideas in a straightforward manner.[147] He updated the curriculum, created a single definitive instruction manual from a series of previous handbooks in loose-leaf form so it could be updated with clearer electrical diagrams, introduced sub-focal flashing lamps to speed up Morse transmission, and typewriter keyboards to complete the mechanisation of semaphore signalling. When the Admiralty claimed coloured illustrations were unnecessary and expensive, Dickie bought a colour-printer and produced his own.

'He had a marvellous way of clearly explaining things on this somewhat complex subject and he took the greatest possible trouble,' remembered one of his students. 'He also made it amusing and fun, which was a great thing in a course which was a hard grind for the students.'[148] It was a view shared by the captain of the signals school: 'Full of ideas, most of which are excellent . . . He has a great future in the service.'[149]

* * *

In August 1929, Edwina was again off on her travels. Beaverbrook had taken a shine to her, paying for a stay in Paris and including her in his fiftieth birthday party in May, when he had given his five principal female guests – Sheila Milbanke, Venetia Montague, Diana Cooper, Jean Norton and Edwina, £100 – some £6,000 in present value. Now he invited her to join him on the *Arcadian* for a Baltic cruise. The party included Jean Norton, Arnold Bennett, Venetia Montague and Mike Wardell. It was the first passenger ship to visit Russia since the Revolution and the Russian government did all they could to create a warm welcome. The party saw the Winter Palace in Leningrad and met the politician Maxim Litvinov, whose wife, Ivy, noticed Beaverbrook 'purring around' Edwina.[150]

In February 1930, Edwina sailed to New York with Marjorie and her husband Brecky, criss-crossing the country via Chicago to California and Mexico to New Orleans and Florida.[151] She now had two new film-star admirers, Ronald Colman and a good-looking friend of Douglas Fairbanks, called Larry Gray. Gray was then at the height of his career as one of Hollywood's leading men, playing opposite Louise Brooks, Clara Bow, Marion Davies and Norma Shearer, and it was he, rather than Colman, who captured Edwina's heart and accompanied her when she stayed with Randolph Hearst – whose mistress was Marion Davies – at his fantasy home, San Simeon. 'Italian villas, French chateaux and Greek Temples all thrown into one,' as Edwina told Dickie.[152]

She returned to Britain in April energised by the stimulus of a new country and social circle, but it had all been too much. Dining one night with Laddie at Brook House, she collapsed and started haemorrhaging. Her consultant concluded she had a severe internal infection, that there was a risk of septicaemia and that, without an operation, she might die. Dickie raced up to see her – but she refused to see him.

Septicaemia was avoided, but neuralgia and pernicious anaemia were diagnosed. After three weeks in bed, the Royal Family's doctor, Lord Dawson of Penn, was summoned but he 'talked a lot of nonsense', Edwina decided. 'So I took matters into my own hands and sent to Paris for a doctor.'[153] The French doctor gave her a transfusion and prescribed a diet of raw liver to cleanse her blood. After another month in bed with electrical treatment, ray therapy and massage, she was able to manage some public appearances – but it was not until Christmas 1930 that she was fully recovered.

Dissatisfied with her family life, Edwina continued to crave new experiences and excitements – but social life no longer held the same attraction. Now partly in search of winter sun and partly in a spirit of adventure and inquiry – she had become interested in archaeology – in January 1931 she joined Marjorie, the Duchess of Sutherland and Lady Mary Grosvenor on a cruise to the West Indies. In Havana, the party joined up with Geordie Sutherland and Larry Gray, but it was another member of the group, the handsome Spanish-speaking Ted Phillips, six years Edwina's junior, who caught her eye and replaced Larry in her affections. In the photos taken in Mexico City, Ted sits with one arm around Edwina, whilst Larry has been relegated to sit at her feet.

From Mexico City they moved on to the Yucatán Peninsula, studying Mayan art and civilisation, and Guatemala and Honduras. They visited Indian villages, archaeological sites, pyramids, temples and floating gardens. From there she returned to New York via California, where she saw Laddie. 'Lunched in town with Larry very late having driven in with Ted at 90 miles an hour and been arrested on the way . . . Laddie came for dinner . . . to the Cotton Club and only got to bed very late.'[154] Edwina's behaviour on their travels had shocked the Brecknocks and Brecky felt he had to write to Dickie. Back in London, Mountbatten pondered what to do, had a 'long and vital heart to heart' with Peter Murphy, and wrote in his diary: 'Worst night since Papa died.'[155]

There was worse to come. One of Edwina's stops had been Cuernavaca, a resort south of Mexico City, which allowed divorcing couples to speed up the qualifying period of separation, and the newspapers had jumped to their own conclusions. For months, papers had been hinting that Douglas Fairbanks and Mary Pickford would separate, with Edwina as the other woman. Now they declared Edwina was seeking to divorce Dickie. 'Heart to heart afternoon,' Dickie wrote in his diary after greeting Edwina on her return, but she did not want to face up to the reality of her marriage.[156] After cocktails with Peter, Brecky and Mike Wardell, she left to spend the evening with Laddie. The following nights were spent with Laddie at Ciro's and Hugh at the Embassy. Then she left for Paris.

Dickie had finally had enough of her infidelities and his humiliation. After taking advice from his mother, Peter Murphy, Teddy Heywood-Lonsdale and Jean, he decided to confront Edwina. As she sat weeping in the bath, she told him that she accepted they had to part. Dickie had finally stood up to her and discovered, as he told her, 'you had lost that devastating ability to frighten me which only resulted in my being meek or rude.'[157] He agreed to leave the next morning. Later that night, she made an excuse to come to his bedroom and return a book.

The marriage had been saved.

That weekend at Adsdean, they discussed the past and their future together. 'I offer you all my sympathetic understanding about Laddie, and will really . . . try,' Dickie told her, adding that he had been 'the cause of pretty well all the unhappiness I have known.'[158] In future he asserted that Laddie would no longer be welcome at Adsdean or Brook House. 'I suppose my affairs with Hugh and Laddie were what you would call serious,' she confessed, 'but as they never in any way altered my affection and respect for you I don't myself think of them as such.'[159]

In early June, Dickie tried to map out the future. 'I want you to be as great a friend to me as I am to you, easy going and with no secrets,' adding the most interesting person he knew was 'the lovely Edwina Mountbatten . . . I find her quite different to the Edwina Ashley I knew, the girl I idealised for 9 years: but I find her far more fun, far more sweet and can understand why all the world loves her.'[160] Edwina was moved:

> No one could have been sweeter or more tolerant of me than you during the last years and you'll never know how much your devotion and long sufferingness have meant to me. Now that we understand each other better and are such true friends I feel sure things will be so much easier and I feel so much happier about everything. I do too feel you're my best friend in all the world and a good deal more.[161]

They came to an arrangement. She would support him in his career and he would recognise her need for emotional and physical fulfilment elsewhere, as long as she was discreet. They would stay together, but in an open marriage. Edwina's infidelity and accusations of failure had deeply upset Dickie, but the unhappiness in his private life had at least one consequence – to spur on his ambitions in public life.

CHAPTER 8

A Terrible Scandal

In August 1931, Dickie returned to Malta as Fleet Wireless Officer, against the backdrop of the deepening sterling crisis and formation of Ramsay MacDonald's National Government. On 15 September, sailors of the Atlantic Fleet at Invergordon mutinied in protest against cuts in pay, but the Mediterranean Fleet had already commenced its autumn cruise, making communication between ships more difficult.

Dickie, responsible for monitoring communications and any sign of unrest, was later to claim that he had prevented the Mediterranean Fleet following suit by stopping all communications and warning Sir Ernle Chatfield, the C-in-C's chief of staff, of murmurings of discontent; but if true, Chatfield made no reference to it in his memoirs and it looks like the myth-making to which Dickie was increasingly prone in old age.

As the fleet wireless officer, Dickie was responsible for radio communications throughout the 70 ships of the Mediterranean Fleet. Based either aboard the Fleet's flagship or in the Castille on Malta, he set up a sophisticated communications centre, which allowed all wireless communications of the Fleet to be monitored and analysed, and created a system whereby all ships were able to acknowledge receipt of a message within a minute. He recognised that efficient communications remained essential to any naval operation and that in signals intelligence, wireless discipline was essential in evading detection, and to coordinating a large strike force.

He improved training, insisted that ships were constantly tested in decoding and that pay was improved. Above all, he fostered a strong *esprit de corps* and personal loyalty amongst his telegraphists, whom he regarded as the unsung heroes aboard ship. He made a point of visiting every ship in the Fleet – uniquely in his own private motorboat – and for each ship and individual he kept a card of successes and failures, encouraging competitiveness through a series of competitions. At weekends, he would take groups of midshipmen out on his boat to swim and generally relax.

One of his stunts was to ensure all 70 ships were able to hear King George V's first address to the nation on Christmas Day 1932. It encouraged him to press for all the silent-film projectors in the Fleet to be converted into sound projectors, so that they could show sound films, designing a loudspeaker system himself that was cheaper and therefore financially possible.

Another was a demonstration staged over several days to every officer based in Malta on the importance of wireless communications. Linking the high-powered transmitters from the naval station in Rinella and the receivers on the roof of the Castile to the lecture room, the lecture culminated in a simulated Fleet action with the messages distributed to the audience as they might be to the Admiral's staff on a flagship. There was even an officer on an imitation destroyer bridge, who added to the excitement by receiving orders from the captain and relaying them to an imaginary flotilla of destroyers. This was Dickie in his role of showman, a role he was to play many times over in his career.

Whilst Dickie settled into his new job, Edwina remained in London. Now that Dickie was prepared to turn a blind eye to her lovers, they did not hold the same attraction. She broke off the relationship with Hugh, and Laddie returned to America. But soon there was a new man in her life. Bobby Sweeney was ten years younger, a six-foot-three American Rhodes Scholar at Oxford, who had just been selected with his brother Charles to play golf for the university – he would win the 1937 Amateur championship. With his easy charm, movie-star looks and wealth – he divided his time between homes in London, Palm Beach and Long Island – he was an important catch.[162]

It was not only in her love life that the chickens had come home to roost. Years of unsustainable profligate spending, coupled with a drop in investment income, meant some tough decisions had to be taken. It was not helped when Britain came off the Gold Standard in September and the pound dropped in value by more than a quarter. 'Things very gloomy,' noted Edwina. 'Doing everything possible.'[163] She promptly went out shopping. It was clear that she would have to become a tax exile for the next two years, if she was not to pay 60 per cent of her income in tax.

One of the largest drains had been Brook House, with running costs of £16,000 over the previous year. This included 27 indoor and two outdoor servants when the Mountbattens were in residence, and even 17 when they were away. They looked with envy at Mary's house around the corner with its latest gadgets, spot-lit squash court over the garage and cocktail bar in the cellar, and yet was far less expensive to run. There was no real emotional attachment to what sometimes felt like a gloomy museum. Selling it and its contents would produce, after tax, £7,500 a year – plus a saving of £1,000 on staff. A problem was that Sir Ernest's will had forbidden such a sale, but eventually a way was found and the sale was announced in October 1931.[164]

Some items Edwina wished to keep but, rather than pay to store them, she offered them to the Prince of Wales who was furnishing his new home. So her jade, Van Dycks, Romneys and Raeburns found themselves temporarily at Fort Belvedere. He was 'absolutely *thrilled*, like a child, and is going round in circles arranging where they are to go.'[165] The house itself, however, found no takers and after 18 months of standing empty, it was pulled down. In its place arose an eight-storey block of flats, with the two upper floors an enormous penthouse that Edwina had reserved for herself. Sir Ernest's wishes had been complied with.

In November 1931, Edwina set off for Malta with her daughters, Pamela and Patricia. The Mountbattens were to be a family again. Dickie was pleased. 'Lovely to have the old girl back,' he wrote in his diary that night.[166] He was able to report to his mother of the improved marital relations:

It's funny, but until this year I've never really discussed my married life with anyone at all. I really just kept things to myself, principally because I was aware of Edwina's intense dislike of being discussed & felt it would be disloyal to speak about her. Actually being able to talk things over has helped so much and really improved the situation with Edwina so very much. It's funny but now that I see her as she is (& not on this old-fashioned pedestal I had put her on) I'm really ever so much more fond of her. She is so very, very sweet when one can talk freely with her and see all her difficulties & laugh her out of them. I do feel we're going to be happy – happier really than we've ever been.[167]

Edwina made the best of her new life, entertaining her husband's colleagues but also her friends – Ted Phillips stayed at the beginning of June. As part of the economy drive, their boat *Shrimp* had been sold to the son of the composer Giacomo Puccini, but the Cunningham-Reids had lent them their yacht *Lizard* and there were frequent expeditions and picnics around the coast. Dickie had taken up water-skiing and became so proficient he used to water-ski to shipboard parties in full mess dress tie, his shoes and socks around his neck. Soon Edwina began to enjoy herself. She was proud of her husband, whose career flourished, but the idyll couldn't last.

On 29 May 1932 in the Sunday newspaper, *The People*, under the heading 'Society Shaken by Terrible Scandal', an anonymous gossip columnist had written:

I am able to reveal today the sequel to a scandal which has shaken society to the very depths. It concerns one of the leading hostesses in the country – a woman highly connected and immensely rich. Her association with a coloured man became so marked that they were the talk of the West End. Then one day the couple were caught in compromising circumstances. The sequel is that the society woman has been given hints to clear out of England for a couple of years to let the affair blow over, and the hint comes from a quarter which cannot be ignored.[168]

It was clear the article referred to Edwina and the quarter that could not be ignored was Buckingham Palace. 'I hear that that vulgar Socialist Sunday paper "The People" has published what Norman Birkett (the KC Edwina had over the Simpson Divorce business) calls a "particularly outrageous form of libel" about Edwina & the black man,' Dickie wrote to his mother.[169] The Mountbattens were unclear what to do. 'We both don't want to add to the publicity by a notorious libel case, but cannot allow her to be thought guilty by taking no action.'[170]

After taking legal advice, and under pressure from the Palace, they decided to press ahead with court action against *The People* and its owners, Odhams Press. The case was heard on 8 July with the well-known barristers Norman Birkett acting for Edwina and Patrick Hastings for Odhams. It was held at the unusually early time of 9.30 a.m., without any advance notice to the press, so there was little reporting, and both Edwina and Dickie were unusually allowed to give evidence. Edwina claimed she had 'never in the whole course of my life met the man referred to' and the Lord Chief Justice, Lord Hewart, ruled in her favour. Odhams made a full apology and Edwina, claiming to be satisfied, did not press for damages.[171] Suspicions remained that a deal had been done.

That night the Mountbattens celebrated with a party at the Café de Paris and, as a mark of solidarity, the King and Queen entertained them to lunch at Buckingham Palace the next day and the Prince of Wales threw a party on the eve of their departure for Malta. There were, however, no winners. The Palace and Dickie were unhappy about all the publicity and it only strengthened Edwina's republicanism, furious that she had been forced to submit to this public indignation. Henceforth, she swopped the *Daily Herald* for the *Daily Worker*.

The black man was supposedly Paul Robeson, whose Othello had recently taken the West End by storm, and whom Edwina was to claim both in court and in her diary, 'I have never met.'[172] *The People* supposedly spent £25,000 trying to find evidence that the two had met at least once, but with no success. Dickie's official biographer Philip Ziegler argues:

> Even if one accepts that she lied in her private diary and that she was prepared to perjure herself, it seems inconceivable that none of the many fellow-guests who must have witnessed Robeson's presence was ready to testify to that effect in court.[173]

According to Edwina's official biographer, Janet Morgan, 'Every guest who came to Brook House or Adsdean, every entertainer of significance who performed at her house, was mentioned in her daily diary; there, for her own records, was a note of every outing with every lover. Robeson's name did not appear.'[174] She further pointed out that even Robeson's wife did not believe the story. 'It is most incredible that people should be linking Paul's name with that of a famous titled English woman, since she is just about the one person in England we don't know.'[175]

However, there is no reason that Edwina would commit everything to her diary and even Morgan admits that Edwina doctored her writing in case Dickie read it.[176] Equally, there is no reason Robeson's wife knew everything about his private life. The writer Marie Seton, who knew all parties concerned, said Robeson had told her that he did 'go to bed once' with Edwina, that she had been the seducer and he had accepted she had never met him, but it 'jarred inside him'.[177] The black singer Leslie 'Hutch' Hutchinson told a friend, Bill Pilkington, that Edwina and Robeson had had a brief affair.[178] Edwina's sister Mary later told the Mountbatten biographer Richard Hough, 'Edwina admitted that she had lied in court.'

Long after, Edwina made the same admission whilst having dinner with Catherine Courtenay and her husband in Kandy, Ceylon. Mountbatten talked openly of 'the whitewash in the court case with Robeson. Edwina just stayed silent, until she said, "It's over now. What else could I have done?"'[179] According to Hough, the figure most deeply affected was Paul Robeson. 'For Edwina to stand up in court and declare that she had never met him when their relationship had been so close, and when he had been invited to her house frequently and been seen there by dozens of her friends, deeply wounded him and he never got over it.'[180]

If the 'coloured' man wasn't Robeson, could it have been someone else? She certainly knew the other best-known black entertainer of the period, the singer and pianist Leslie 'Hutch' Hutchinson. He had played in private concerts at the homes of many of her friends, including Marjorie Brecknock, and she had presented him with a gold cigarette case engraved with her name and supposedly a loving message. 'Whenever she gave a party, Hutch played for her,' explained Edwina's daughter Pamela. 'It was the habit of society women to give the entertainers presents rather than pay them.'[181]

Hutch had been born in Grenada in 1900, but left as a teenager to study medicine in New York. A musical prodigy, he quickly switched to music and started performing in the clubs of Harlem, where he was taken up by the Vanderbilts. Through them, Edwina had most probably first seen him perform in Harlem and Palm Beach, and in 1924 she had recommended him as a piano teacher to the children of King Alfonso and Queen Ena of Spain. The affair between Queen Ena and Hutch was an open secret.[182] The writer Lesley Blanch later remembered, 'Lunch alone with Lady Mountbatten at Buck House, her infatuation for the pianist Hutch was a hushed-up scandal.'[183]

According to Hutch's biographer Charlotte Breese, 'Edwina and Hutch may have become lovers in Harlem in 1925, then he went off to Spain and they met up again in Paris.'[184] Hutch often performed at Zelli's in Paris, where Edwina was a regular visitor. She brought him over in the autumn of 1926 to play at a reception in Carlton House Terrace, given with a socialite friend, Lady Gibbons, and he played in London venues that the Mountbattens and their circle frequented, such as the Café de Paris and Chez Victor.

'At Chez Victor, he used to sing directly to Edwina Mountbatten who, on one occasion, took off her chiffon scarf and put it round his neck and kissed him while he was playing,' remembered Joan Vyvyan, a young socialite. 'He sang "The Man I Love" to her. He was madly attractive and intelligent. How we envied her!'[185]

The 'compromising circumstances' that had occasioned the gossip article were supposedly: 'Hutch and Edwina being inextricably united through vaginismus, a rare and temporary medical phenomenon; and having to be taken in *flagrante delicto* by ambulance from the Mountbattens' home at Brook House to hospital.'[186]

'I was at a grand party. Edwina interrupted Hutch playing the piano,' the BBC producer, Bobby Jay, recalled. 'She kissed his neck, and led him by the hand behind the closed doors of the dining room. There was a shriek and, a few minutes later, she returned, straightening her clothes. Hutch seemed elated, and, before he returned to the piano, told me that, with one thrust, he had flashed her the length of the dining-room table.'[187]

The bandleader, Alfred Van Straten, noted in his diary a night in the early 1930s, when Dickie came in to Quaglino's very drunk and sat with him. '"I am lonely and drunk and sad," he complained. "That n*gger Hutch has a prick like a tree trunk, and he's fucking my wife right now."' In the hearing of one socialite, Joan Vyvyan, Mountbatten exploded, 'If I ever catch that man Hutch, I'll kill him.' In both cases, the violence of his language has the ring of truth and speaks of pent-up pain and jealousy.[188]

Edwina had much in common with Hutch. Both promiscuous and uninhibited about sex, they were charming, funny and did not mind if they shocked people. Each gave the other an entrée to worlds that intrigued them, but that they could not enter alone. Hutch had far more to gain socially from Edwina's company and contacts, but through him, she could relax in a milieu that amused her, away from the responsibilities and restrictions of her marriage. The affair with Hutch was to continue off-and-on for the next 30 years. His other lovers would include many of those in the Mountbattens' social circle, including Merle Oberon and Princess Marina of Kent, Cole Porter, Noël Coward and Ivor Novello.[189]

* * *

It was in 1932 that Dickie was to have his own first affair, with a woman who would become his principal mistress until his death over 40 years later. Yola Letellier was in her twenties and the third wife of Henri Letellier, one of France's most successful newspaper owners and a man 40 years her senior. The owner of *Le Journal*, then the world's third largest-selling newspaper, and co-developer of both Deauville and Cannes, Letellier was one of France's most powerful men, reputed to own 1,260 suits, 11 motor cars, a champagne marque, a racing stable, Mexican oil fields, and 'real estate scattered throughout Europe and South America'.[190]

Mystery continues to surround Yola. Born Yvonne Henriquet, probably in 1904 – she gave dates ranging from 1900 to 1907 – she also used the names Henriques and Henriquez, whilst the dates of her marriage to Letellier vary between January 1926 and 1928. With her heart-shaped face, freckles and long legs, she was chic, animated, attractive, intelligent, undemanding and affectionate. Her aunt had been a friend of Colette and supposedly Yola was the inspiration for Colette's 1944 novella *Gigi*, filmed five years later, about a young girl who falls in love with a much older man.

Dickie had first met her playing polo in Deauville in 1928, and then again in April 1932 whilst staying with friends in Cannes.[191] Dickie was thrilled to discover that another woman found him attractive. 'Told her news,' Dickie wrote in his diary. 'Amazing heart to heart.'[192] Edwina was furious. She was allowed lovers but not her husband, and immediately left for Paris to confront her. 'Your girl is sweet,' she wrote to Dickie, 'and I like her and we got on beautifully and are now gummed and I am lunching with her at her house on Tuesday!!!'[193]

CHAPTER 9

Playing to Win

Restless and bored, Edwina now decided to go travelling. In August 1932, she and Jean holidayed on the island of Brioni, in the Northern Adriatic, before joining up with Nada at Wolfsgarten and going on to the Middle East, taking in Istanbul (where they stayed with the British Ambassador), Jerusalem, Damascus, Akaba, Baghdad and Tehran, travelling only with basic camping equipment and a change of clothes, and using local guides. When his ship docked in Haifa, Dickie joined them at Baalbeck.

In Transjordania, Edwina chartered a light aeroplane for crossing the desert, in Damascus she bought a car and drove the 600 miles to Baghdad, and at the buried city of Persepolis she spent a week with the archaeologist Ernst Herzfeld. At the end of November, the two women dined with King Faisal in Baghdad before returning home for Christmas. In the course of three months, they had covered 6,000 miles by plane and 4,000 by car. 'Divine having the old girl back,' Dickie wrote in his diary.[194]

Within three months, feeling depressed, Edwina was off again – this time to stay with Yola outside Paris. Diagnosed with malaria and jaundice, Edwina dieted and tried to gain her strength. In April, the two women left for Cannes to meet Dickie's ship, but Edwina remained weak and it was Dickie, not Edwina, who now danced the night away. Her spirits were only raised when a six-foot, blond, blue-eyed Hungarian count, Anthony Szapary, whom she had met a few months earlier in Budapest through Yola, arrived from Tuscany and took her to see the Grand Prix in Monte Carlo. Szapary, a few years younger than Edwina, an accomplished tennis player and well-known ladies' man, became Edwina's new lover. She now resolved to go to the Clinic Loew in Vienna for her troubles. It had the added benefit of being close to Hungary for weekend visits to Szapary.[195]

Edwina and Yola stayed in Vienna for two months as every possible treatment was tried to restore Edwina's health. 'My gall bladder, liver etc, don't work at all as they should, neither does my stomach or intestine.'[196] The experts pronounced she was suffering from a sort of Mediterranean parasite and only further rest in Vienna would cure her. She continued to enjoy her time with Szapary, but other rumours circulated. During the summer of 1933, Douglas Fairbanks and Mary Pickford divorced. Rumours began to fly with Fairbanks 'openly betraying his irritation as he was questioned about his friendship with a woman of title . . . He has been a frequent escort of Lady Edwina Mountbatten . . .'[197]

* * *

At the beginning of September 1933, Dickie began his four-month naval interpreter's course in Paris, renting the flat of Jean's sister-in-law Kay Norton in the Place du Palais-Royal. It was meant to provide a relaxation from naval duties, but Dickie, as always, took it very seriously, with all reading, writing (including his diary) and speaking to be in French. The result when he took his interpreter's examination in January was predictable. He had come top.[198]

Edwina, who was bilingual, was due to spend the autumn with him, but after three days announced she and Yola were returning to

Budapest to continue her treatment. Dickie stayed on, alone, lonely and miserable. 'I do hope you're not jealous,' she wrote after telling him that she and Yola were sharing a room.[199] He was jealous and told her not to interfere. 'If you get into that sort of mood,' she warned him, 'think first before writing as it's asking for trouble.'[200] When Dickie's French teacher, Madame Callede, announced she would be taking an autumn holiday near Biarritz, Dickie followed her to combine his lessons and see the Prince of Wales, who was also staying there. It was in Biarritz that Dickie and Edwina were reunited and where at a polo match Edwina was to meet the great love of her life.

Harold Phillips was eight years younger than her, the younger brother of Ted Phillips, a six-foot-five, square-jawed Guards officer with a private income. A fluent Spanish speaker – his mother's family, the Bryces, came from South America – he was also an excellent rider and held a pilot's licence. Where Dickie did everything with fanatical purpose, Bunny – so-called because of his long legs and back – was effortlessly competent. Where Dickie was exhausting, Bunny was easy-going. It was just what Edwina needed and he now took on the role in Edwina's life that Yola had played in Dickie's – a reassuring presence for all the family.

'We loved having Bunny in our home,' remembered Lady Pamela Hicks:

> Quite simply, he made my mother easier to be around and he genuinely loved being with my sister and me. He had the imagination for wonderful games into which she would also be drawn. When he was away, he wrote us warm, affectionate letters addressing each of us 'The Weewaks', one of many pet names he invented for us . . . Bunny brought great joy to our lives and I loved him deeply. He was a core part of my rather

eccentric family, and although he was our mother's lover, they never displayed more than a friendly affection in public. He would stay with us for long periods of time and, to us children, he was just a part of our everyday life.[201]

It was time for another expedition. Adsdean and the children were in good hands, Dickie was focused on his career and Yola, Brook House was still being built, and Edwina wanted time with her new man. At the end of January 1934, she set off with Bunny to explore South America accompanied, as chaperones, by Marjorie Brecknock and Jack Evelyn. Travelling by train to Lisbon and then boat to Brazil – during which Edwina was so drunk from the captain's planter's punch, she was only able to present the prizes for the games tournament after some fortifying cups of black coffee – in time for the Rio Carnival. From there they flew to Porto Alegre and Buenos Aires.

They crossed the Andes by horse, sleeping rough before returning up the coast of Chile, where they caught a train to La Paz in Bolivia. Here, they became caught up in a local uprising, when cadets from the military college took over the police headquarters and they were besieged in their hotel. 'Sat gloomily inside playing games until they had forgotten about us and we were able to emerge again,' wrote Marjorie in the diary she kept of the trip.[202]

It was then on to the Inca ruins at Machu Picchu before returning to the Mayan civilisation in the Yucatán, where they came across Katharine Hepburn. 'Very disappointing off the screen, with very untidy, lanky, reddish hair,' noted Brecknock disapprovingly.[203] 'We have covered 5,771 miles in the air up the West coast of South America, across Central America and from Merida to Miami, and about 1,500 miles down the East coast from Rio to Buenos Aires, making 7,271 miles in all,' was one triumphant entry in Marjorie's diary.[204]

* * *

In the spring of 1934, Dickie had achieved his first command, the very modern destroyer HMS *Daring*. He was well prepared, having learnt by heart details of the full crew of 140, so he was able to speak to every man as if he knew him intimately. He proved to be 'a fine seaman, of tireless energy, intense curiosity and unremitting drive,' one former officer remembered. 'In addition, he was very human and approachable . . . We were a thoroughly happy Wardroom under him and this atmosphere radiated throughout the ship, so that not only were we a happy ship but an intensely active and confident one.'[205]

Peter Murphy (who had just opened a Communist bookshop in London) and Noël Coward had come out in June with King Alfonso of Spain and a 13-year-old Prince Philip. They went out in *Lizard*, water-skied, swam and picnicked on the rocks at Gozo. The flirtatious, slightly camp, relationship that Coward maintained with Dickie is apparent from his thank-you letter:

> Dear dainty Darling,
> I couldn't have enjoyed my holiday more . . . Please ask Peter
> not to foul the guest cabin in any beastly way because I do
> so want to use it again . . . Please be careful of your zippers,
> Dickie dear, and don't let me hear of any ugly happenings at
> Flotilla dances, Love and kisses, Bosun [*sic*] Coward.[206]

* * *

In August 1934, Edwina was off again, this time to South East Asia. First stop was Canada with Noël Coward, where they stayed with the Governor General, before being reunited with Bunny and Ted Phillips in California. Edwina pretended in her letters to Dickie and her diary that she was part of a larger party.[207] In fact, she and Bunny travelled alone, visiting ruins and temples and the ancient site of Angkor Wat, watching Cambodian dancers and riding in rickshaws. In Hanoi, they rented a Chinese junk for a three-day cruise, swimming by moonlight and sleeping on deck. From Bali and Java, they flew to Singapore and from there caught a ship to Borneo and Sarawak. Then it was back via Bangkok, Calcutta, Jodhpur, Baghdad, Cairo and Budapest, where she caught up with Szapary.

It was not only the Mountbattens who had their personal problems. Edwina's father Wilfrid and younger wife Molly had never been that compatible. Having served as Minister of Transport, Wilfrid had been elevated to the House of Lords as Lord Mount Temple and accordingly was less busy. He now wanted to leave Molly, but Edwina backed her stepmother and told him he should stay.

Nada and George also had their difficulties. In October, a custody battle, *Vanderbilt v Whitney*, opened in New York. It centred around who should have responsibility for the ten-year-old heiress, Gloria Vanderbilt. On one side was Gertrude Whitney, on the other her sister-in-law, also called Gloria Vanderbilt and the child's 29-year-old mother. The six-week trial was a fascinating window into the lives of the ultra-rich in Depression-stricken America. Young Gloria's father, Reggie Vanderbilt, had died of cirrhosis of the liver when she was one, leaving nothing except debts. The young child had been brought up by her mother, who had moved in the same circles as her twin sister, Thelma Furness, mistress of the Prince of Wales.

During the trial, a chauffeur had testified about the elder Gloria Vanderbilt's several lovers, whilst her maid had given testimony that she had seen Gloria 'in bed reading a paper, and there was Lady Milford Haven beside the bed with her arm around Mrs Vanderbilt's neck and kissing her just like a lover.'[208] Gertrude was awarded custody.[209] Rumours had long circulated about Nada's colourful sex life and her love of lesbian bars in Paris and the South of France, but here was public evidence. Gloria had been a frequent visitor to Nada's home, Lynden Manor, near Bray, and of course Nada was close to Edwina.[210]

* * *

The same month, the end of October 1934, Dickie left for Singapore as part of a plan to improve the quality of destroyers serving on the China station, where he would exchange *Daring* for a much older destroyer, HMS *Wishart,* launched in 1919. Accompanying him was his pet tortoise, Andrew, and Peter Murphy. Initially disappointed, Dickie began to look on the positive side, telling his crew: 'Our ship is called after the Almighty himself to whom we pray every day: "Our father Wishart in Heaven . . ."'[211]

One of his first tasks was to restore the morale of his men, which he did with on-board competitions, shows, a band led by Peter Murphy, a ship's newspaper and films. He set the challenge of winning every prize at the flotilla's annual regatta in September 1935, most notably by setting a shorter, faster stroke of 38.5 strokes a minute in the rowing, which he did, being declared 'Cock of the Fleet'. It was not an approach that won him much favour in other ships. 'He took all the fun out of Fleet Regattas,' one former colleague remembered, 'because he never left anything for the other chap. He had to have every trophy and then crowed about it.'[212]

He encouraged the value of gunnery practice as a means of relieving the tedium of long periods at sea. Rather than rapid but unfocused firing, Dickie stressed the importance of conserving ammunition and precision targeting. He invented a new torpedo-grab, replacing the previous system of a sling, and the 'Mountbatten

Station-Keeping Equipment' that helped ships keep their distance when advance abreast, which was eventually installed in three classes of destroyer.

His tactics were not always regarded by other ships' companies as playing by the rules and suspicions remained about his wealth and playboy lifestyle. But Dickie always stressed he played simply to win, and his own crew loved him all the more for it. Few other commanders knew everyone's name, kept chameleons and a bear in his cabin – Edwina had picked up a black female honey bear, Rastus, on her travels for him to collect in Singapore – or asked for a jazz accompaniment to hymn tunes on Sunday mornings. A hard taskmaster and disciplinarian with the highest standards for himself and the company, he enthused the company with his own will to win. His innate qualities of leadership and initiative were at last being given full rein.

* * *

Edwina continued on her travels. After seeing her husband off at Sheerness, she left the next day for four months in the South Seas with Bunny, their third long trip together, returning via Java, New Zealand and Australia. To avoid any press comment they travelled separately, arranging to meet up in California, where they stayed at Pickfair and met Clark Gable, Loretta Young, Charlie Chaplin and Fred Astaire.

Edwina invented a story of travelling with two couples, the Tobins and Robinsons, who were planning to charter a copra boat and sail round the Marquesas and the other Society Islands, mapping and doing survey work. As mail was difficult and cables expensive, Dickie should not worry if he did not hear from her for a while. It was a story Dickie chose to believe to avoid any more scenes.

Bunny and Edwina pottered around the South Seas for three

months, living off sea snails, lobster, fish and sharks that they could spear or shoot. 'I think the Pacific a perfect Paradise,' she told Dickie in the second of only two letters sent to him between December 1934 and March 1935.[213]

By the end of April, she was back in Malta, having been one of the first commercial passengers to fly the Sydney–London route. She had been away six months. 'Lovely having the old girl back,' Dickie wrote in his diary. 'Looking sweeter than ever.'[214] But Edwina was restless. 'Malta saps all our energy and ambition,' she wrote in her diary, 'particularly in this weather and we all become completely gaga!'[215] She disliked entertaining Dickie's colleagues and hankered after the freedom of the South Seas. Soon afterwards she disappeared to Rome with Bunny.

Though they were reunited for their thirteenth wedding anniversary, Dickie was soon on his own again. At the end of the summer, worried about the growing political crisis in the Mediterranean – Italy had left the League of Nations over her territorial ambitions – Edwina decided to take the children to Hungary, where she thought they would be safer. At Kekes, 100 kilometres from Budapest, she found a hotel amongst pine trees and mountains that she thought suitable and, having settled them in with Nannie and their governess, drove to pick up Marjorie in Rome and bring her to Malta for a holiday.

'The place is thick with barbed wire entanglements and the ships at war stations, with warheads on their torpedoes,' Edwina wrote in the autumn of 1935.[216] Two rooms in Casa Medina were made gas-proof and, on 2 October, the Mediterranean Fleet was placed on a war footing after Mussolini invaded Abyssinia. Whilst most of the Fleet left for the less vulnerable harbour of Alexandria, Dickie remained as part of a small defence force. Edwina refused to be evacuated and, at the invitation of the Port Wireless Officer, was invited to read the London news bulletins. She quickly warmed to her task, combining it with trips to polo matches and cocktails. She was beginning to feel that she could contribute and compete with her high-achieving husband.

At the end of November, alerted by the hotel owner that it was closing for the winter and the bill needed to be paid, she and Yola set off to pick up the girls, still in only their summer clothes, having forgotten exactly where she had left them. As the Abyssinian Crisis worsened, she decided not to bring them back to Malta, but send them to stay with Uncle Ernie in Darmstadt.

From Darmstadt, she left for China. In Germany, she told Dickie, she had met 'some charming people called Ritter', who had invited her to accompany them to Moscow, and were persuaded to join her and Bunny in a luxury car on the Trans-Siberian railway to China. 'I tell you all this as I like you to know and you're so understanding,' she added.[217] Dickie knew the truth and teased her that his German professor had met some Ritters in London. 'They must be impostors,' she retorted.

'It's fascinating being here again and seeing the progress everything has made since 1929,' wrote Edwina to Dickie at the height of Stalin's purges. 'It's gone ahead by leaps and bounds . . . I gather shorter hours, higher wages, *and* lower prices (not only from what Intourist tell one!) and the people on the whole are contented, and the young ones happy and enthusiastic.'[218]

From Manchuria, Bunny and Edwina wound their way to Peking, before catching a ship from Shanghai to the Philippines. For seven weeks they travelled on small cargo boats, calling at Bali and Java, returning via Hong Kong, Japan and the west coast of America. She had been out of Britain for almost two years. Alone in Malta, Dickie's poignant diary entry for Christmas Day read: 'Had a bit of the servants' Xmas dinner on a tray.'

* * *

Dickie accepted his wife's wanderlust, her desire to pack in experiences of people and places, her need to escape domesticity and him – her unplanned arrangements were in direct contrast to his meticulous plans and, in some ways, he preferred it, leaving him alone with the children, free from her jealousies. 'She was very prickly, and we all had to be very careful of what we said in her company,' remembered her younger daughter:

> Sometimes it was as if we were treading on eggshells – she would be hurt by the most unlikely things and then sulk for hours afterwards. In contrast you could say anything you liked to my father, and I adored sharing a house with him once more. He was so inventive, constantly thinking up things that would make Patricia and me happy.[219]
>
> Daddy was in a particularly happy mood, sharing memories of his own childhood days in Malta when my grandfather was commander-in-chief of the Mediterranean Fleet. We explored the island with him and he showed us the beautiful blue lagoons where we could swim, and he gave me a donkey to ride. My sister and I were also given a chameleon each. I named mine Casper and could watch him for ages, endlessly fascinated as to how he changed from yellow to dark green.[220]

By June 1936, the Mountbattens were back in London and able to move into their new penthouse above Brook House. Designed by Edwin Lutyens, with interior decoration by their friend Mrs Joshua Cosden, their new home had 30 rooms, and was served by a high-speed lift from a tiny private entrance hall on the ground floor. At the top were Edwina's and Dickie's bedrooms, bathrooms, dressing-rooms and private sitting-rooms looking out over Hyde Park, with rooms for staff and visitors on the side.

The floor below comprised a morning-room, drawing-room and dining-room, again facing the park, linked with doors that could be opened for cocktail parties, a ball or to be used as a cinema. On the south side was the children's wing, on the north the kitchen and more staff quarters, together with offices for Stella Underhill and her deputy Nancie Lees. There were balconies on three sides, floodlit at the touch of a switch, the lower one accommodating 120 guests, the upper one taking half that number.

The two floors were linked by a double curved staircase in glass and polished chrome. Edwina's bedroom had been decorated by Rex Whistler, who had created 60 panels painted on canvas with fruit, flowers, cupids and goddesses, in grisaille against a background of delicate greyish blue, as well as representations of Broadlands, Adsdean, the old Brook House, Dickie on a polo pony and a naked Venus, with Edwina's features, watched by Father Time.[221]

In July, after two months leave, Dickie had joined the Naval Air Division in the Admiralty as Assistant Director, the first of his jobs in Whitehall. He had first learnt to fly in 1918 and had always been a proponent of the importance of air power for the Navy and he was delighted.

A primary responsibility was to bring full control of the Fleet Air Arm, shared since 1924 with the RAF, back to the Navy. Mountbatten enlisted the help of Winston Churchill, now the most important figure outside the government, sending him an 11-page memorandum on the subject in March 1937. His lobbying was successful, with the Navy achieving almost all it wanted – Coastal Command remained with the Air Force. In July 1937, a Fifth Sea Lord was created to head the Naval Air Service. Though the decision was a political one, Mountbatten had played an important part in making the case.

Another campaign was to persuade the Navy to adopt a new quick-firing anti-aircraft gun, designed by Anton Gazda, and constructed at the Swiss Oerlikon Works. The Oerlikon gun could fire a shell able to penetrate the armour of a U-boat. Dickie had first recognised the potential of the gun against dive bombers, especially the Stuka dive bombers, in 1937, but the Gunnery School Experimental Department remained wedded to the British-made Vickers multi-barrel, two-pounder pom-pom, seeing Gazda as just another foreign arms dealer. Dickie took Gazda round Whitehall, including to the First Sea Lord, Sir Roger Backhouse, but it was only in 1939 that the Admiralty ordered 500 of them – alas too late for the Norwegian campaign and Dunkirk evacuation.

He also advocated that the Navy should, like the Royal Air Force, use Typex enciphering machines, which were faster and more secure than the ones they currently used, though it was not until 1942, under American pressure, that Typex was widely taken up. His experience on *Daring* and *Wishart* had stimulated an interest in improving destroyer design and he had become friendly with the naval designer A.P. Cole. Now at the Admiralty, Mountbatten was able to lobby for changes that included an all-covered bridge across the ship with a deep drop covering the catwalk, a slanting roof and a windscreen, which meant, for the first time, those on the bridge stayed dry.

He had always realised the morale-boosting benefits of being able to show films at sea and many ships, partly through his efforts, now had sound projection, but the supply and quality of films was erratic. It was clear an organisation was needed to source and supply films and so in April 1939 was born the Royal Naval Film Corporation. He had already deployed Noël Coward around the Mediterranean and Home Fleets to establish the sort of films the men wanted to see, and now he used his various connections to ensure they received them. The Duke of Kent was brought in as Patron and a series of lunches held at Brook House to introduce the Naval hierarchy to film distributers and producers such as Alexander Korda and Darryl Zanuck. The result was that many now offered films for free.

At the end of his posting in June 1937, Dickie was promoted to Captain. He was 37, over five years younger than the average age for such a promotion. It was clear he was heading for the top.

CHAPTER 10

Problems in the
Family

In January 1936, King George V died, and Dickie's best man was finally the King. They met after the funeral: 'Talked with David til 3 o'clock in the morning . . . very satisfactory,' Dickie had noted in his diary.[222]

Mountbatten had stayed in touch with his old friend and would often visit him when in Britain. Edward's Windsor home, Fort Belvedere, was only an hour's drive from Adsdean and during the first part of 1934 Dickie had visited at least twice a month, often staying for dinner and the night. When Edward came to inspect the shell of Brook House in October 1934, it was Wallis who came with him. The couples had briefly been neighbours at Bryanston Court a few months earlier.

The Mountbattens did not like the new woman in Edward's life. They had been appalled at the callous way Freda Dudley Ward had been abandoned, when the switchboard was simply instructed to no longer put her calls through. Neither did Wallis like the Mountbattens. In Dickie she recognised a fellow careerist, whilst she was jealous of Edwina, with her upper-class charm and natural beauty.

In spite of that, Dickie and Edwina saw much of the new king and Wallis Simpson that year. In late May, they had dinner at York

House with the Simpsons, the Duff Coopers, the airman Charles Lindbergh, Stanley Baldwin and their wives. In June, Wallis stayed for several nights at Adsdean (bringing a cold chicken from Fortnum & Mason as a present, much to the chagrin of the Mountbattens' cook, Brinz). In July, they were together at a weekend party at Trent Park, Philip Sassoon's home just north of London.

In mid-August the Mountbattens, along with the Duff Coopers and Hugh Molyneux, accompanied the King and Wallis as they cruised the Dalmatian coast for ten days in the yacht *Nahlin*. Edward's attempts to travel inconspicuously as the Duke of Lancaster were doomed to failure by the presence of two escorting British destroyers and a Yugoslav torpedo boat, as well as repeated 21-gun salutes. The trip was marred by various mishaps, from crashing into a bridge in the Straits of Chalkis to Edward falling out of a motorboat.

A consolation was that a professional golfer, Archie Compston, was on hand with 3,000 golf balls, most of which ended overboard, to help the new king's pitching and driving. After seeing King George II of the Hellenes on Corfu, they sailed on to Athens and Istanbul, before returning by train through Bulgaria and Yugoslavia. At the end of September, they were at Balmoral with the King. The Simpsons were divorced at the end of October and the Abdication Crisis began with manoeuvring between the King and his staff, Stanley Baldwin, his Cabinet and the Church. An inside source on the Abdication Crisis as it played out during the autumn was Charles Lambe, whom Dickie had inveigled as Edward's equerry.

On 25 November, the day the King put his morganatic marriage proposal to Baldwin, Mountbatten approached Claud Cockburn, editor of an irreverent paper, *The Week*, offering 'certain "inside information" of a particularly sensational character' from Edward.

Cockburn agreed to hold *The Week*'s presses and waited all night, until early next morning a messenger arrived with the news: 'The situation has developed too fast.'[223] One version of events is that Mountbatten and John Strachey, then a Communist, had decided to release the story of Wallis's affair with the car salesman Guy Trundle to Cockburn, 'forcing the King to give up any idea of marrying her, and thus keeping him firmly on the throne as the "people's monarch". But at the last minute, the conspirators panicked and backed off from the plan'.[224]

As late as 7 December, Dickie presented himself as a loyal supporter:

> I can't bear to be sitting here doing nothing to help you in your terrible trouble. Do you realise how many loyal supporters of all classes you have? . . . If you want me to help you, to do any service for you or even to feel you have a friend of Wallis to keep you company you have only to telephone. I don't want to be a nuisance but I hate to feel that there is nothing I can do to help except to bite people's heads off who have the temerity to say anything disloyal about their king – and there are practically none who do so – at any rate in my presence.[225]

Edward's three brothers, Dickie, and the King's legal adviser Walter Monckton met at Fort Belvedere on 10 December. 'Dickie down at the Fort all day where chaos reigns,' wrote Edwina in her diary. 'Everyone completely sunk except the King who remains fairly calm and cheerful.'[226] Dickie's feelings were torn. Whilst loyal to his old friend, he could see his faults and unfitness to rule. He also had a growing respect for Bertie and recognised that his more low-key qualities, his decency and sense of public service might actually make for a better king. The next day Edward announced he was abdicating in favour of his younger brother George. The crisis was over.

In January, Dickie was appointed the new king's Personal Naval ADC and invested with the GCVO. 'Tea with Queen Mary at Marlborough House,' Edwina wrote on 9 February and 'cocktails with the King and Queen at Piccadilly. They only move to Buckingham Palace next week.'[227] Princesses Elizabeth and Margaret came to tea at Brook House. 'Showed them Mickey Mouse films after as we were trying out the cinema,' confided Edwina to her diary.[228]

The Mountbattens were quickly adapting to the new regime, whilst also trying to keep in with Edward, now the Duke of Windsor. In March, after seeing Yola in Paris, Dickie flew to see Edward, staying at Schloss Enzesfeld near Vienna with Fruity Metcalfe. 'Talking with David and Fruity nearly all day . . . Important talk with David, and possibility of return,' Dickie confided in his diary.[229] 'Very sad saying goodbye, on both sides.'[230] Returning in the aeroplane, he was sick.

'Thank you so much for the very pleasant 2 day visit to Scholss Cuzesfeld [*sic*]. It was very nice seeing you again & it felt quite like old times, you, Fruity & I being alone together,' wrote Dickie to Edward on his return, giving him some of the Coronation plans. 'I went & saw Bertie today & he was very friendly & delighted to have good news of you.'[231]

Dickie would later claim that he had twice offered to be best man, but Edward had hoped to have his two youngest brothers, in royal tradition, as supporters. He had certainly given the impression that he hoped to attend. 'You will have heard that although I succeeded in fixing a date for your wedding that suited Bertie, George etc that other people stepped in and have produced a situation that has made all your friends very unhappy,' Dickie wrote to Edward. 'I have made several attempts to get matters put right but at present I cannot even accept your kind invitation myself. I haven't quite given up all hope yet, though my chances don't look too good. I will write again when I know finally.'[232]

It appears that he and the royal brothers were warned off by royal courtiers, but Dickie sent three Old English pieces of plate, a 1633 wine flagon, a 1718 and 1731 tankard as wedding gifts, writing: 'I thought so much of you to-day and the great joy it must be to you to be with Wallis again.'[233]

* * *

Edwina, who hated the British winter and had suffered a series of colds as well as neuralgia, now announced she was off to Africa with Bunny, Jack and Nada. Hiring an open Buick with a Ford van for the luggage, they toured Uganda, the Belgian Congo and Kenya, where they mixed with the Happy Valley set. She returned from East Africa in time for Pamela's eighth birthday on 19 April, bringing with her a three-month-old lion cub. 'His name is Sabi . . . his mother was shot in the Transvaal for attacking a man and poaching cattle. We simply had to bring him back with us.'[234] The cub joined the menagerie of other animals at Adsdean.

In 1936, Bunny had commissioned a three-masted schooner from a Cornish boat builder, which he and Edwina called *Lost Horizon* after James Hilton's bestselling novel. By November it was ready and Bunny with crew left to take it via Lisbon across the Atlantic and from there to the Caribbean. The plan was that the Mountbattens and Yola would join him in the West Indies in January, where Dickie was captaining an English team in an international polo tournament.

No sooner had they arrived than Nada rang with the news that Georgie had been diagnosed with bone marrow cancer. 'I am so utterly wretched and heartbroken – I haven't been able to think of anything but poor dear Georgie since Nada telephoned,' Dickie wrote to his mother. 'I've been just like a baby – cry myself to sleep almost every night – a thing I haven't done since Papa died. Edwina has been a perfect brick . . . Oh! Why does God punish the good & sweet people of this world like George & let the cads & swines like Bobby Cunningham Reid flourish!'[235] It was clear that Edwina could not continue her holiday with Bunny. The Mountbattens returned to Britain.

Georgie died on 8 April. He was 45. Dickie was devastated: 'The sweetest natured, most charming, most able, most brilliant, entirely lovable brother anyone ever had is lost.' Eight years younger, he had worshipped his brother, with his charm, quick intelligence and an engaging sense of humour. He had inspired Dickie's own interest in a career in the Navy as well as in electronics and film. He was the sort of person who, instead of reading detective stories, would 'read problems of higher calculus and solve them in his head'.[236] Reputedly, he did *The Times* crossword in ten minutes.

In spite of being one of the youngest commanders in the Navy, Georgie, deciding he needed to make some money, had left the service in 1930. After a period working in a brokerage house on Wall Street, he became chairman and managing director of the British Sperry Gyroscope Company – an electronics company specialising in advanced aircraft navigation equipment – and director of Electrolux (where his brother-in-law Harold Wernher was chairman), Marks & Spencer, and various other companies.

His chief interest, however, was his model railway system, with its two miles of track, built in a converted barn at his home Lynden Manor, near Maidenhead, which was finished in 1929. He spent over £60,000 on it, with hills of papier mâché, goods sheds, forests and mountain ranges made from imitation ice. He had also inherited from his father one of the most comprehensive pornographic book collections in Europe. The library contained albums of photographs of various individuals and groups having sexual intercourse in every possible position, as well as books on sadomasochism, bondage, whipping, thumbscrews, and racks.[237]

Georgie had hitherto largely been responsible for the education of his nephew Philip. Now the duty of looking after him fell to Dickie. Philip's father, Prince Andrew of Greece and Denmark, had gone into exile in France in 1922, shortly after his son's birth. In 1930, Philip's mother Alice had been diagnosed with schizophrenia and sent to a Swiss sanatorium, where a fellow inmate was Vaslav Nijinsky, the ballet dancer and choreographer. Though eventually recovered, she had separated from her husband (who preferred the company of his mistresses in Monte Carlo).

Philip had been sent to prep school just outside London, before going to Gordonstoun in the north of Scotland. He had hitherto divided his holidays between his grandmother Princess Victoria, Georgie, Harold Wernher, and sometimes Dickie. 'Dickie was very good at that time, too,' Philip remembered. 'I used to see a lot of him, though he was often away for a long time.'[238] It was he who persuaded Philip to join the Navy rather than the Air Force. 'Philip was here all last week doing his entrance exams for the Navy,' Dickie wrote to Edwina. 'He had his meals with us and he really is killingly funny. I like him very much.'[239] This was the son Dickie had never had.

* * *

The winter of 1938–39 saw Mountbatten embark on a series of fast-track staff courses at the Royal Naval War College at Greenwich and the Higher Command Course at Aldershot, studying alongside seven major-generals and Claude Auchinleck of the Indian Army.

For years, he had been socialising with senior naval officers and politicians, but the course provided a more structured opportunity to network with senior personnel across all the Armed Services.

Though, on paper, only a junior captain, Dickie wielded influence that was disproportionate to his rank. Not only did he socialise with senior service officers, but also important politicians, notably Anthony Eden and Alfred Duff Cooper. He had never been shy about using his connections to promote his own career, but increasingly now it was directed at shaping government policy. He had congratulated Eden when he resigned in February 1938, in protest at the proposed settlement with Mussolini over Italy's invasion of Abyssinia, and a few months later Eden drove to Broadlands to discuss a letter he was intending to send to *The Times*.

When Duff Cooper resigned as First Lord of the Admiralty over the Munich Settlement, Dickie, a critic of Appeasement, wrote to congratulate him: 'I fear this is a long-winded letter, the first I have ever written on a political event, but your behaviour has been a real inspiration to me,' though he couldn't help adding, 'Next time I see you I must ask you who is likely to the next C-in-C in the Mediterranean, as I hope to go out there next year.'[240]

* * *

The worsening political situation in 1938, with growing tensions in Germany and Italy, had galvanised Edwina – who had rewritten her will after Munich. Her travels had opened her eyes to the suffering in the world and she increasingly wanted to do something more useful with her life. She started to learn first aid and approached the Red Cross about turning Adsdean into a hospital 'and running it as commandant myself'.[241] She joined the Red Cross Committee, run by her friend Eileen Sutherland, did six months' auxiliary nursing in wards, theatres and the out-patients' department of the Westminster Hospital, and passed her first-aid examinations. Dickie had his vocation, and now Edwina was finding hers, too.

Still she continued to travel – ten days with Bunny and Yola in October 1938 in Hungary, and then in February 1939 to Asia with Bunny. From Burma, they travelled to Northern Sumatra and Batavia, where they hoped to tour the islands in the Flores and Timor Seas, west of New Guinea. But when no boat could be found, she decided to drive along the new 700-mile road being built between Burma and South West China. Much of it could only be managed by lorry 'not more than 10 to 15 mph being possible for hours on end,' she told Dickie, 'bottom gear being used for long stretches.'[242] She would be the first woman to drive it.

At Batavia, she learnt that a small ship was leaving from Celebes to the islands in Dutch New Guinea, 'so cannot resist it as among the places are some I particularly wanted to go . . .' It meant she would be away for Pamela's birthday, Easter and the holidays, 'but having come *all* the way out it seems a pity to miss it . . .'[243] She returned at the beginning of May, bringing with her a pair of wallabies – Dabo and Bobo – to replace Sabi, who had died shortly before she left.

Almost immediately, she was faced by a family crisis. Her father Wilfrid, now in his seventies, announced he was leaving Molly to go off with a Frenchwoman. Again, Edwina counselled him to stay in the marriage, but what most shocked her was not his behaviour, but his appearance. He had Parkinson's disease and looked very ill. A few weeks later, he was dead.

'Terribly sad losing Daddy,' she wrote in her diary, 'and really heartbroken but feel for his sake it was for the best as he could never have stood a long illness and invalidism.'[244] She had never been that close to him, but she was now an orphan, and his death was a break with the past. It had brought on fresh responsibilities with the ownership and management of the entire Broadlands Estate.

* * *

Another family problem was her sister Mary, who now had two sons with Bobby Cunningham-Reid.[245] On marriage, they had moved to The Hall, Six Mile Bottom, with 8,000 acres, a swimming pool and tennis court, so they entertained widely – all captured on cine films – including Vivien Leigh, Laurence Olivier and Neville Chamberlain.[246] Bobby had set up Criterion Films with Douglas Fairbanks Jr, which brought a ready supply of attractive young women. This, and the fact that on their honeymoon Mary had insisted they share her wealth, because 'no decent woman likes to have a man live with her in charity', was to be the cause of their problems.

In December 1936, Mary had left Bobby, citing his adultery with three different women, and moved with her lady's maid, Elenor Smith, into Brook House. Thirteen months later, Bobby brought an action against his wife in the Chancery Court, claiming he was entitled to income under deeds signed when they had first married. Mary decided to go to court in order to revoke some of the arrangements. Cunningham-Reid defended the action, instructing the Labour politician Sir Stafford Cripps, whilst Sir Patrick Hastings acted for Mary. Eventually the case was settled, probably to save more dirty linen being washed in public. Cunningham-Reid became one of the first men to be paid alimony, receiving £10,000 a year, as well as the house in Upper Brook Street and the yacht. He did not, however, have it index-linked. In June 1939 they secured a *decree nisi,* made absolute in March 1940, not on the grounds of his adultery, but of hers with the French film star Henri Garat, in Antibes in August 1938. It is said Bobby himself had taken the incriminating photo.[247]

* * *

Throughout the spring and summer of 1939, refugees streamed into Britain. Edwina was keen to assist whom she could, enlisting Dickie's help to write letters to various British authorities. She sent money to various organisations and, in particular, the German-Jewish Aid Committee, the Federation of Czechoslovakian Jews and the Jewish Refugees' Committee, as she began to take a closer interest in her Jewish heritage.

In mid-August, Bunny had arranged to take his Talbot to be serviced in France and Edwina decided to join him. Friends thought them mad, but she felt there was time for one more adventure. They dropped off the Talbot in Paris, hired a Peugeot and meandered around the Loire, looking at châteaux and staying in small hotels. Suddenly Bunny, who had been appointed ADC to General Lloyd, was called up and they darted back. Whilst he took up his new responsibilities, she frantically arranged for valuables, including the Whistler murals from Brook House, to be sent to Broadlands, and herself moved from the vulnerable penthouse to Kensington Palace with her mother-in-law. The Rolls and Hispano were replaced by a more practical Austin Twelve.

On 3 September, war was declared. It would prove to be the making of both Dickie and Edwina.

CHAPTER 11

At War

Just before the outbreak of war, Dickie took command of his new ship, HMS *Kelly* – the first of the new 'K' class destroyers armed with six 4.7-inch guns and two quintuple torpedo tubes – and one that had been fitted out to his exact specifications, taking into account some of the designs he had discussed with the naval architect A.P. Cole. A particular feature was his cabin, a replica of his mock cabin at the Brook House penthouse, 'a large L-shaped room with a long desk equipped with a dictaphone and a multiplicity of gadgets along the end wall, or bulkhead . . . The walls of the cabin were pale green, the sofa and chairs covered with bright orange-and brick material, the carpet brown. An adjoining sleeping cabin and bathroom were decorated in the same pale green.'[248] On the bookcase were photographs of his father, brother, wife, daughters, Jean Norton and Yola Letellier.

The ship was still being prepared when in August the Nazi-Soviet non-aggression pact was signed, and arrangements for loading had to be quickened from three weeks to three days. The entire ship's company, including its captain, worked day and night, bringing on stores, fuel and ammunition, and painting the boat in a mixture of rose and lavender, called Mountbatten Pink, which Dickie thought best disguised its appearance from the air.[249]

War was declared on 3 September. Dickie, waiting for instructions in Portsmouth, was apprehensive. 'It is only when one faces the prospect of death,' he wrote to Edwina, 'that one realises how much one's loved ones mean.'[250] His first wartime duty was to collect his old friend Edward, Duke of Windsor, from exile in France, accompanied by Randolph Churchill in the uniform of a lieutenant of the 4th Hussars – the appearance slightly spoilt by the spurs being inside out and upside down.

Over the next few weeks the *Kelly* was engaged on convoy duties in the Channel and chasing U-boats – most of them, it transpired, imaginary – west of the Scillies. Then towards the end of October, Mountbatten was ordered to the Norwegian coast to engage the German pocket battleship *Deutschland* and pick up some captured merchant seamen from the *City of Flint*. He pointedly ignored the advice of his signals and navigating officers, plotting a course that left him missing the German pocket battleship. 'It is absolutely basic that in any intercepting situation like this you go to the position furthest on your target could have reached, and then work back,' the *Kelly's* signals officer, Edward Dunsterville, recollected. 'But Mountbatten would have none of this. He wanted to make a splash.'[251] The result was that 600 seamen spent five years in a German internment camp.

Returning, Mountbatten set a cruising speed of 28 knots, twice the safe rate given the weather conditions, leading to a seaman being swept overboard and the destruction of the starboard side when the *Kelly* hit a huge wave. Shortly after repairs were completed, he hit a mine after being ordered into the middle of a minefield in the Tyne Estuary to rescue a sinking British tanker. *Kelly* returned to dry dock for almost three months of repairs. It was ten days before Christmas and most men had used up their spare passes. Edwina offered to pay the return fares of any crew member who wished to go home for Christmas.

The episode was to provide one of the stories that would become part of the Mountbatten legend. All on board had felt the mine bumping under the bow, engine-room and ward room before it went off after touching the propellers. It had been too much for one of the stokers, who had deserted his post. The punishment for desertion was death but Mountbatten, addressing the lower deck, let the man off with a caution. 'One caution to him, and second one to myself, for having failed in four months to impress my personality and doctrine on each and all of you to prevent such an incident from occurring.'[252] No member of the *Kelly* crew ever again left their post and the stoker later won a gallantry medal.

In March, within a week of the repairs on the *Kelly* being completed, it collided with another destroyer, HMS *Gurkha*, requiring a further refit of six weeks. The following month it was despatched to embark the retreating forces in Norway and successfully rescued 229 French *Chasseurs Alpins* – its first useful contribution to the war effort in six months.

In May, Mountbatten first found himself isolated off the Dutch coast, fruitlessly chasing a U-boat, and then needlessly broadcasting his position by signalling with a bright Aldis light; one message read: 'How are the muskets? Let battle commence.' The immediate result was the *Kelly* was torpedoed, blasting a 50-foot hole in the starboard side, killing 27 and wounding many more but, though heavily damaged and with only emergency lighting, she had survived. All but six officers and 12 men were taken off, the torpedoes, depth charges, surplus ammunition and boats jettisoned, and the *Kelly* began its tortuous 91-hour journey across the North Sea to the Tyne, towed back in spite of considerable risk to the support vessels. It had been a feat of foolhardiness, but also courage and seamanship.

For most officers, it would have led to a court martial, but the heroic journey back had caught the imagination of the public looking for good news amidst the rapid German victories. It had not been calculated – Mountbatten simply wanted to save his ship – but it proved a morale-boosting propaganda coup. The Navy, seeing an opportunity, leaked the story to the *Daily Mirror*, whose centre-page spread paid tribute with plenty of references to Nelson and 'an epic story that will live for ever in British naval history'.[253]

Dickie, given a mention in Despatches, now lobbied hard through his royal connections – he had told George VI about his feat immediately when he returned – and Edwina for a Distinguished Service Order for bringing his ship home safely. In spite of Service objections to an award being given, when it was Mountbatten's stupidity that had caused *Kelly* to be attacked in the first place, his lobbying paid off. The naval action had also brought him to the attention of the man who would be his most important wartime mentor – the Prime Minister, Winston Churchill.

* * *

The war had brought the Mountbattens together, not least by giving new purpose to the rather aimless life that Edwina had hitherto been leading. 'I can never tell you what fun it has been,' Dickie told her in October 1939 after her fourth visit in six weeks, '. . . it has taken the war to realise all that you do mean to me – so at all events I have Hitler to thank for that.'[254] She gave him presents of a small gold identification disc, a kitten, and a scarf she had knitted herself, and sent clean clothes and food. This was the sort of tender affection that Dickie had longed for. 'We have had our ups and downs in our 17 years of married life,' he wrote, 'but I wouldn't marry anyone else if I had all my life over again – I can't say more.'[255]

There were also worries about Patricia and Pamela. With fear of German invasion, what would their fate be given their Jewish background and Dickie's royal relations? Edwina made plans to hire a skipper and some deckhands and sail to America via Madeira, until common sense prevailed – she booked them on a ship for New York with arrangements to stay with the Vanderbilts on Fifth Avenue.

Edwina had been trying to make her own contribution to the war effort, but no one wanted her. In turn, she was rejected by the Women's Royal Naval Service, the Women's Voluntary Service and the Women's Auxiliary Air Force, who remembered her pre-war, little-rich-girl-lost reputation. Eventually, in December 1939 she was interviewed by the Red Cross and the Order of St John, and the next month appointed Lady County President of the Nursing Division of London.

Edwina now threw herself into war work. In the autumn of 1940, she took a two-week Intensive First Aid Course and spent a month training on the wards at Westminster Hospital. Noticing the lack of coordinated organisation at the First Aid Posts at the shelters and in the Underground, she lobbied government ministers until proper arrangements were made. Now responsible for all St John Ambulance volunteers working in Rest Centres, Shelters and First Aid Posts, each night – oblivious to all dangers – she would set off in her car on a tour of inspection, so each shelter was visited at least once a fortnight.

'Did you hear of Edwina's exciting adventure with a time bomb that went off within 20 or 30 yards of her,' Dickie wrote to his mother in September. 'It knocked her down but her very closeness saved her as the fragments all passed over her head.'[256] Each morning would be spent organising the Nursing Flying Squad and interviewing prospective VADS, and afternoons at the Knitted Garments Depot.

She had learnt from her husband the importance of appearance and glamour. Her heels were higher, her hat worn at a jauntier angle and she had her uniforms specially tailored so that her skirts were shorter than those of her colleagues, and the jackets tighter-fitting. With her slim figure, high cheekbones and huge blue eyes, she looked more like a film star than a charity worker. More importantly, she rapidly demonstrated she could get things done. She was conscientious, hard-working and popular and, by January 1941, she was Acting Lady Deputy District Superintendent, only two places from the top position.

The couple were in unison, perhaps for the first time ever. Pressure brought out the best in them – their gifts of leadership, their organisational skills, their ability to use their connections, their meticulous preparation and command of their brief. Edwina had learned from her husband the self-respect that comes from working hard, indeed her equally competitive nature wished to outdo him. She would stay up later with paperwork, and drive herself harder in her daily tasks, to prove both to herself and to him that she could compete on equal terms. Her intelligence was at last being used.

Their increased closeness did not mean that the relationship was perfect. Edwina still found Dickie infuriating, self-obsessed and immature, but also increasingly recognised his affection and bravery. That said, she continued to see Hutch. In September, she joined the singer when he performed for the inmates of Dartmoor Prison at the end of a tour in Torbay. Mairi Craven standing outside remembered admiring a huge gleaming black car attended by a chauffeur, when Hutch swept through the gates, arm in arm with Edwina, 'looking beautiful, smiling, elegant and wearing a bandeau. A murmur ran through the wondering assembly. "It's Lady Louis".'[257]

Neither was the relationship with Bunny over, though he had told Dickie that Edwina did not enjoy love-making. It appears that

Above left: Dickie with his favourite teddy bear, Sonnenbeim, on the balcony of his parents' London home, 70 Cadogan Square.

© *Hulton Archive/Stringer/Getty*

Above right: Edwina pictured in *The Bystander* in 1909.

© *Illustrated London News Ltd/Mary Evans*

Below left: Mountbatten's parents. Prince Louis of Battenberg and Princess Victoria of Hesse and by Rhine.

© *Southampton University Archive*

Below right: Edwina's grandfather Sir Ernest Cassel at his estate, Moulton Paddocks, Newmarket.

© *PA/PA Archive/PA Images*

Dickie, the Prince of Wales and two officers of HMS *Renown* on the 1921 Royal Tour.

Dickie and his older brother George on their Douglas motorbikes, 1917.

Above left: Audrey James, the illegitimate granddaughter of Edward VII and the illegitimate daughter of Sir Edward Grey, 1st Viscount Grey of Fallodon, with whom Mountbatten fell desperately in love.

Above right: Peggy Peyton, the daughter of a retired colonel in the Indian Army, whom Dickie also thought he would marry.

Below: Mountbatten and Dick Curzon on the Vanderbilt's yacht *Venetia*, August 1921, when Dickie fell in love with Edwina.

Above left: The crowd in Parliament Square for Dickie and Edwina's wedding, 18 July 1922.

Above right: King George V and Queen Mary leaving St Margaret's, 18 July 1922.

Below: The newly married couple walking under the traditional arch of swords, 18 July 1922.

Above: The Mountbattens meeting Babe Ruth on honeymoon, October 1922.

Below left: Dickie and Charlie Chaplin making the film *Nice and Friendly*.

Below right: Edwina with Charlie Chaplin, to whom she supposedly made a pass.

The Mountbattens' interwar country house, Adsdean, on the Sussex Downs.

Mary Pickford and Douglas Fairbanks Jr. with the Mountbattens at Adsdean.

Edwina with her close friend Jean Norton, the mistress of Beaverbrook, working on the *Daily Express* switchboard during the May 1926 General Strike.   *© Southampton University Archive*

The Mountbattens as a young married couple.   *© Southampton University Archive*

The Mountbattens on RMS *Olympic* in 1925, the year a downcast Dickie first learnt of Edwina's infidelities.

Apic/Contributor/Getty

many of her affairs had been as much about asserting herself as about sexual frustration or high sexual drive.

* * *

In October 1940, Dickie was posted to Plymouth. The following month, whilst patrolling near Land's End, he blundered again and his ship HMS *Javelin* was torpedoed with the loss of 46 men and many injured. Dickie was heavily criticised by his superiors for failing to organise his attacking force correctly and open fire in time, but no action was taken. Here was a high-profile naval hero, whose supporters included the King and the Prime Minister.[258] The action had indeed caught the attention of Churchill, who summoned Dickie to Chequers, and offered him the post of Vice Chief of the Naval Staff, a huge promotion, with the intention he should become First Sea Lord later in the war. Mountbatten refused, saying he preferred to remain at sea.[259]

In May 1941, the *Kelly* was sent to Crete to bombard the airfield, which had been captured by the Germans. At dawn on 23 May, the ship was dive-bombed by Stukas and, still travelling at 30 knots, capsized.[260] The last view anyone had of Mountbatten, the first and last captain of the ship, was him standing on the bridge holding onto his Station-Keeping Gear. Edwina, knowing half the ship's company had been lost, anxiously waited for news of her husband's fate at Claridge's with Peter Murphy.

Picked up by HMS *Kipling*, Mountbatten was brought back to Alexandria, where he stayed for a few days with the Commander-in-Chief, Mediterranean, Andrew Cunningham, who was not a great fan. 'The trouble with your flotilla, boy,' he told another destroyer officer, 'is that it was thoroughly badly led.'[261] Many felt the problem with Mountbatten was that, for all his bravery and leadership abilities, he lacked judgement and patience, and was too much the showman where style triumphed over substance.

Johnnie Coote remembered the *Kelly* as 'the laughing-stock of the fleet' entering Scapa Flow:

> She looked magnificent, with her pendants streaming from her halyards, everything properly squared away, with her flamboyant CO prominently saluting as his piping party of four (usually one or two in wartime) sounded off. She was making 25 knots at the time. Her wash bashed all our boats against our armoured belt, doing some damage . . . MB had deliberately chosen 0900 as his ETA so as to be the focus of attention of every Flag and Commanding Officer in the Home Fleet. An hour earlier it would have been dark.[262]

In the autumn of 1941, Dickie was given command of the aircraft carrier *Illustrious*, currently under repair in Norfolk, Virginia, and ready to join the Mediterranean Fleet in November. The plan, supported by the Ministry of Information, was that he should go out in August, brief the American military, make some useful contacts and, as a well-connected and well-known naval officer, possibly help on the propaganda front. The couple saw it as an ideal opportunity to see their children, and Edwina also arranged to visit the States on a goodwill tour for the Joint War Organisation Committee, thanking organisations who had contributed to war charities and trying to rustle up more funds.

Edwina's tour of 28 states was a success, with lunches for up to 1,000 and scores of talks and visits across the country, including lunch with the Roosevelts at the White House. It was on this trip that the pattern was set for future tours – to test herself constantly by pushing herself to her limits. Partly this was a determination to cover as much ground as possible, to demonstrate, not least to her husband, what she could achieve; but there was also an element of punishment – a feeling she needed to make up for all those lost years of frivolity.

Initially nervous about public speaking, she discovered that she could be an effective speaker, after learning the speech by heart. Many Americans, embarrassed by their neutrality, were anxious to help. It had not all been work. She had seen more of Pamela and Patricia than probably at any time of their lives, also lunched with Salvador Dalí who had painted her five years before, and had a few days away with Bunny, who was now working for British Security Coordination in New York.

From the States she left for Canada, where she gave several speeches in French and stayed at Government House with Princess Alice, Countess of Athlone, who told Queen Mary, her sister-in-law, that Edwina was a changed woman:

> I think that she is a hard worker and clever, tho' one always feels that she has a hard streak in her character. But she certainly charmed everyone here and was more than nice with all the Old Trouts. This war has brought out a lot of good in all kinds of people one imagined merely butterflies and selfish ones at that.[263]

'I personally feel closer to you now than at any time during the previous ten or twelve years,' Dickie wrote to Edwina in Canada. 'I have been so immensely proud of the really wonderful show you have put up here and know that all the family – not only Mama but the King and Queen and George etc – will all be equally proud of all you have done when I tell them.'[264]

There was praise too for Dickie, who made good use of the connections throughout his career. Writing to the First Sea Lord,

Harold Stark, the American Chief of Naval Operations confirmed the need for closer cooperation between the two navies. Mountbatten had been:

> outstandingly helpful in every way . . . His knowledge of his profession, his keen observation of our methods, his frank statements of his thoughts of them, his telling us of the British Navy methods and comparisons with our own, his sincerity, frankness and honesty have not only won our liking but our deep respect.[265]

Dickie too travelled widely, staying with Douglas Fairbanks in California, dining with Norma Shearer and dancing with Rita Hayworth (whilst ostensibly thanking the studio heads for making films available free to the Royal Naval Film Corporation). He paid a visit to the American Fleet at Pearl Harbor, in Hawaii, where he was appalled by the vulnerability of the rows of aircraft parked beside the runway, the weak anti-aircraft defence, and the vulnerability of the ships and communication lines to an airborne attack. The Americans were implementing some of his suggestions when the Japanese attacked only eight weeks later.

Dickie had expected to stay in America until November, when he would sail back in *Illustrious* but, suddenly, on 7 October, he was summoned to the British Embassy in Washington and told he had a new job.

CHAPTER 12

Combined Operations

Combined Operations had been formed in July 1940 under Admiral of the Fleet Sir Roger Keyes to plan amphibious operations against the Germans. Keyes had already organised a few raids on the French coast and was training some 5,000 men in ten commandos, but his reporting responsibilities had been left vague. Was he responsible directly to Churchill as Minister of Defence, or to the Chiefs of Staff? The tensions between him and the Chiefs of Staff had come to a head in the autumn of 1941, when he was dismissed. It was clear a much younger, more dynamic leader was required – Keyes was almost 70 – with fresh ideas.

Mountbatten's principal task as the new head of Combined Operations was to prepare for the invasion of France, organise training areas and troops, develop weaponry and select an invasion site. As part of that preparation, he was to conduct a series of morale-boosting small raids to probe defences, destroy or capture key facilities and harass the enemy, and advise on larger raids under the control of the Chiefs of Staff. He also attended Chiefs of Staff meetings as 'technical adviser' when Combined Operations was on the agenda.

Mountbatten inherited a Combined Operations HQ of only 23, including typists and messengers, which required complete reorganisation and he immediately made changes to personnel and communications. He insisted that it was a totally integrated service with the first loyalty to Combined Operations and not to the parent service, and successfully arranged to work with overlapping organisations such as the Special Operations Executive. He created four separate areas on the operational side: planning, intelligence, training and communications. By the New Year, it had expanded from its single floor at Richmond Terrace to take over much of nearby Scotland Yard, and within six months the staff of COHQ had grown to over 400.[266]

Peter Murphy was brought in to look at the political implications of the various operations; Harold Wernher, George Milford Haven's brother-in-law, dealt with procurement; Micky Hodges, an old navy friend, was in charge of signals, and the Mountbattens' racing car chum, the Marquis of Casa Maury, made head of intelligence. Mountbatten always felt safest working with a close-knit group of glamorous friends – they came to be dubbed 'Dickie's Friends' – whom he could dominate and trust, but this was rarely popular or effective.

Robert Henriques, one of three novelists to serve in Combined Operations – (with Evelyn Waugh and Nevil Shute) was intrigued by Mountbatten's 'total inability to judge men correctly, whether they were his cronies or his subordinates, and yet with the power to command an uncritical loyalty from almost everyone . . . ?'[267] Hugh Dalton, the Minister for Economic Warfare, noted worries in his diary that Mountbatten had 'surrounded himself with a group of his personal friends, most of whom are not very good at their jobs.'[268]

Mountbatten, an inventor of gadgets himself, was one of the most technically highly trained naval officers of his generation, and he immediately saw the need to bring in Combined Operations scientists who, as he never tired of saying, did not 'have Staff

College minds'.[269] The crystallographer J.D. Bernal, biologist Solly Zuckerman, glaciologist and future winner of the Nobel Prize for Chemistry Max Perutz, and the eccentric Geoffrey Pyke all joined with instructions to think outside the box.

Though left-leaning – Evelyn Waugh joining them for lunch thought them 'a nest of Communists' – they proved to be a great success, not least at the Normandy landings, covering such diverse subjects as the use of drugs to prevent seasickness, how to improve night vision, ration packs for commandos, the physiological consequences of explosions and the minimum safe distance from an underwater explosion.[270]

Mountbatten, through a mixture of charm and ruthlessness, proved to be a decisive, forward-thinking commander with an ability to unite opposing factions in a common cause. He built up a good working relationship with the Chiefs of Staff, but it did not always make him popular. He had no hesitation in going above people's heads, often dropping the names of the Prime Minister and the King to achieve his ends, and his staff found he involved himself in unnecessary intrigue. He could not resist micro-managing and obsessing about minor detail and would delegate tasks that they would then find he had impatiently done himself anyway. It became known as 'doing a Lord Louis'.[271]

A whole series of raids had initially been considered by Combined Operations, only to be discounted as infeasible, from a landing on the south bank of the River Somme to allow a force of armoured cars to make a rapid dash to capture Paris, and the capture of the Cherbourg Peninsula, to landings in the Channel Islands. However, within weeks of his appointment, Mountbatten had organised the first of ten raids of varying sizes, which took place in the initial six months of 1942.

The first was a small raid at Vaagso, off the coast of southern

Norway, targeting enemy shipping and the destruction of fish-oil production and stores that the Germans used in the manufacture of high explosives. What made Operation *Archery* especially significant was that it was the first operation jointly planned and executed by all three services and it was in fact a 'pinch' operation to seize an Enigma machine.

In February, parachute troops were dropped onto the cliff top at Bruneval, north-east of Le Havre, demolishing the radar station and capturing key equipment. At the end of the month the dry dock at Saint Nazaire, where it was feared the German battleship *Tirpitz* might shelter, was destroyed by an obsolete destroyer packed with explosives being used to ram the lock gates, killing over 400 Germans. The raid has always been seen as one of the successes of Combined Operations – and one for which Mountbatten took full credit – but it came at a high price, with only four of the 18 coastal craft that sailed returning, over half of those who went ashore captured and a quarter killed, and many more seriously wounded. After the Fall of Singapore, and amidst Rommel's growing victories in North Africa, it was an Allied morale booster – five Victoria Crosses were awarded – but it bred a dangerous confidence at COHQ, which was to have disastrous consequences only a few months later.

These operations inflicted little damage on the Germans, but were important for morale and did much to enhance Mountbatten's reputation, not least with Churchill, who shared his buccaneering spirit and offensive attitude. In March, Churchill made Mountbatten, then a junior captain, Chief of Combined Operations with the acting rank of Vice-Admiral – the youngest since Nelson – and a Lieutenant General and Air Marshal. Much to Mountbatten's pleasure, only the King also held rank in all three services. He was also to sit as the fourth Chief of Staff and attend all meetings of the Chiefs of Staff Committee as a full member.

The Chief of the Imperial General Staff, General Sir Alan Brooke, was not impressed. 'Informed by the PM that I am to take over the chairmanship of the COS from Dudley Pound and that Mountbatten is to be additional member of the COS!' he wrote in his diary on 5 March. 'Rather doubtful how that business will run!', and adding:

> Mountbatten's inclusion in the COS was a snag. There was no justification for this move. His appointment as Chief of Combined Operations was excellent and he certainly played a remarkable role as the driving force and mainspring of this organisation. Without his energy and drive it would never have reached the high standards it achieved. However, the holding of this appointment was no reason for his inclusion in the COS, where he frequently wasted both his own time and ours.[272]

The appointment was, however, good news for Combined Operations – giving them influence at the centre of decision making.

* * *

At the beginning of July 1941, on his return from Crete, Mountbatten had seen Noël Coward and told him the whole story of the sinking of the *Kelly*. 'Absolutely heart-breaking and so magnificent,' Coward wrote in his diary. 'He told the whole saga without frills and with a sincerity that was very moving. He is a pretty wonderful man, I think.'[273] Coward, keen to make a propaganda film about the Navy, raised the idea a few weeks later with Mountbatten, who was very enthusiastic. At the end of July, the two worked up the idea at Broadlands and during August, Coward drafted a script. The film was originally to be called *White*

Ensign, but was later changed to *In Which We Serve* from one of the morning naval prayers.

'Drove down to Broadlands,' Coward wrote in his diary in December 1941:

> Quiet dinner, Edwina, Dickie and Lady Milford Haven. Long discussion with Dickie on general war situation and our naval losses. More and more convinced that he is a great man. His judgement seems to me to be sound and rational on every major issue. Discussed film script, which he has read. Was highly gratified that there were so few technical mistakes. Brief but hilarious lesson in naval deportment, salutes etc.[274]

The film was making great progress, though an official at the Ministry of Information raised objections to a war film showing a British ship being sunk – as if that was a unique occurrence. Mountbatten, who did much to bring the film in safely, immediately arranged to see the official. 'Dickie went off like a time-bomb and it was one of the most startling and satisfactory scenes I have ever witnessed,' Coward recalled. 'I actually felt a pang of compassion for the wretched official, who wilted under the tirade like a tallow candle before a strong fire.'[275]

The film was shot at the Denham Studio in Buckinghamshire between February and June 1942. In April 1942, the King and Queen with the Princesses Elizabeth and Margaret, and the Mountbattens, visited the set. 'The King took the salute and it was really very moving. It was charming of him to come in Naval uniform,' wrote Coward in his diary. 'I did the "Dunkirk" speech with the ship rolling and the wind blowing and a good time was had by all.' [276]

Mountbatten had shown a keen interest in every element of the film's production. The Lower Deck adviser was his cabin hand, who had been severely burnt when the *Kelly* was sunk, and he had personally arranged for 200 convalescent patients from the naval hospital at Haslar to be used as extras.[277]

In the first script, the captain was married to Lady Celia Kinross and living in a house even larger than Broadlands with a Rolls-Royce and driver. Mountbatten objected and it was changed. 'My Captain (D) is quite ordinary, with an income of about £800 a year, a small country house near Plymouth, a reasonably nice-looking wife (Mrs not Lady), two children and a cocker spaniel,' Coward now reassured Mountbatten.[278]

No one was fooled. The character was instantly recognisable by all as Mountbatten, down to his mannerisms and even verbatim speeches. Many of the scenes came from Mountbatten's own experiences, most notably when the stoker, played by Richard Attenborough, abandons his post and the captain blames himself for not having successfully inspired the young man with his own heroic values.

The film premiered in September 1942, the first time a premiere had been held on a Sunday, in aid of the Royal Navy Benevolent Trust, and attended by the First Lord of the Admiralty and the Mountbattens. Dickie was thrilled with it, seeing it twice more over the coming weeks – at a private performance for the King, the Queen and Mrs Roosevelt in the Buckingham Palace air-raid shelter, and at a special showing at Combined Operations headquarters – believing it to be a valuable booster of not only the Navy, but national morale at a time of few military victories.

It became one of the most popular films of the year, winning an Academy Award, with Dilys Powell in the *Sunday Times* calling it 'the best film about the war yet made in this country or in America'. It was one of Churchill's favourite films and he was only dissuaded from giving Coward a knighthood by concerns about Coward's recent court case on currency speculation. The film had done Mountbatten's career no harm either.[279]

* * *

The entry of America into the war after the attack on Pearl Harbor in December 1941 provided new opportunities and resources for Combined Operations. Having created a truly integrated headquarters of all three Services, with a virtual monopoly on amphibious warfare, Mountbatten realised that Combined Operations needed to embrace the Americans and Canadians. By the summer of 1942, nine staff officers, headed by a brigadier-general, were part of joint planning. It was a further example of how Mountbatten's outsider class status and easy familiarity with Americans made him stand out amongst his sometimes stuffy service colleagues.

The Russians, joining the Allies after the German invasion in June 1941, put new pressure on Combined Operations to hold down German troops on the Continent. By the spring of 1942, the Russians were pleading for a diversionary landing to divert forces from the Eastern Front.

Planning began for Operation *Sledgehammer* – a cross-channel invasion to take place in the autumn of 1942. Sholto Douglas (the head of Fighter Command) and Bernard Paget (the Commander-in-Chief, Home Forces) argued for a landing in the Pas de Calais. Not only was this the shortest crossing with the possibility of strong air cover, but it was the closest possible landing to the Rhine.

Mountbatten and the COHQ argued that the coast was too heavily defended, the ports too shallow and it would be easy for the Germans to bring in reinforcements. They suggested the less well-fortified Baie de la Seine in Normandy, with its open beaches and opportunity to establish a beach head more easily. The arguments raged on throughout the spring of 1942. Mountbatten was certainly one of the champions of the landings being in Normandy, but whether he was quite the lone voice he later claimed is debatable.[280]

In June 1942, General Dwight D. Eisenhower arrived in London as Commanding General, European Theatre of Operations (ETOUSA). He and Mountbatten were to work closely together, preparing for the invasion of Europe. The two men respected, trusted and liked each other, and Eisenhower pressed for Mountbatten to be put in charge of Operation *Sledgehammer* and the subsequent invasion. Throughout 1942, the arguments continued about the timing of the invasion – with Mountbatten arguing that the Allies did not have sufficient resources, especially landing craft, to succeed – but thought was now also being given to a smaller incursion as a holding operation politically. Its target was the French port of Dieppe.

The operation was to be one of the most controversial of Mountbatten's career.

CHAPTER 13

The Dieppe Raid

The Dieppe Raid was meant to address American and Russian demands for the opening of another front and as a modest substitute for Operation *Sledgehammer*. Its *raison d'être* was as much political as military, though sometimes sold as an exercise in the challenge of capturing a working port without destroying it in the process. Dieppe had the advantage of being reached from Britain under cover of summer darkness and was a prize target, given the number of ships sheltering there and a nearby radar station and airfield.

Preparations began in spring of 1942, but it was given fresh impetus by pressure from the Russians. The first plan was for flank landings of about 5,000 men several miles either side of the port, but this was quickly abandoned as taking too long for an operation designed to put troops ashore for less than 15 hours – and it would lose the element of surprise. Mountbatten accepted a revised plan of a frontal assault as long as there was a heavy air bombardment, but again concern was expressed about losing the advantage of surprise.

The bombardment was agreed by Churchill on 1 June, but then reversed four days later with the Commander-in-Chief of South-Eastern Command, Lieutenant-General Bernard Montgomery, in the chair, whilst Mountbatten was in Washington. The Force Commander, Major-General Hamilton 'Ham' Roberts, argued that bombing would create blockages and make it difficult for the tanks to traverse the narrow streets. Trafford Leigh-Mallory, the Air Force Commander, felt Dieppe was so small that bombs would either fall into the sea or inland, and the Air Force might be better employed on diversionary tactics. The only covering fire, therefore, would have to come from the sea. Mountbatten wanted a battleship, but the recent loss of the *Prince of Wales* and *Repulse* to air attack put paid to naval support.[281] Ditto it was regarded as too risky to send any cruisers. All that was on offer were some destroyers with guns of a modest calibre.

Mountbatten now learnt that a political decision had been taken to substitute highly trained Marines and commandoes for inexperienced Canadian troops. The plan was beginning to unravel, but the operation was taking on a momentum of its own, not least under the pressure to appease Ivan Maisky, the Russian Ambassador in London, and his masters. Mountbatten, naturally impatient and over-confident, took the decision to proceed with the operation anyway, picking the first suitable day after 24 June.

A dress rehearsal two weeks before did not augur well, with the darkness being blamed for troops being landed in the wrong place at the wrong time. The tanks arrived an hour after the infantry, and many of the troops suffered severe seasickness. In the end, on 7 July, bad weather led to the cancellation of a raid. Recent raids on Alderney and Bayonne had also been halted, and prudence would have been to leave alone (what had become known as) Operation *Rutter*, not least because the likelihood was that the Germans had now been alerted that Dieppe was a target.

Tom Baillie-Grohman, the Naval Force Commander, and 'Ham' Roberts sent Mountbatten a memo arguing that the operation should be abandoned for good. Montgomery wrote to his immediate superior recommending that no similar operation be contemplated in future, but shortly afterwards he was posted to the Eighth Army in North Africa. Dieppe was the only plan in the locker and for the sake of morale, and sustaining his own reputation for delivering high-profile attacks, Mountbatten felt something should be done.

Ignoring the warnings, he suggested the operation be resurrected under the name Operation *Jubilee*. Intensive lobbying took place over the coming days, until Baillie-Grohman was pushed out and the various doubting Thomases, such as Leigh-Mallory and Roberts, brought back on board. Admiral Bertram Ramsay's entreaties to Mountbatten to abort the raid on 25 July were ignored.

According to the new naval commander, John Hughes-Hallett, Mountbatten restated the case for rerunning Operation *Rutter* on 11 July. 'Nothing was put in writing, but General Ismay informed the Chiefs of Staff and the Prime Minister, who gave their verbal authority.'[282] Certainly, King George VI knew the next day, writing in his diary, 'Dickie gave me the latest news of the COS conversations . . . He is rearranging *Rutter* under another name for the end of August.'[283] According to F.H. Hinsley, official historian of British Intelligence in the Second World War, 'The Chiefs of Staff gave their approval to Jubilee on 12 August.'[284]

Churchill also appears to have known, telling Russian President Joseph Stalin on 15 August that 'there will be a serious raid in August, although the weather might upset it . . . It will be a reconnaissance in force. Some 8,000 men with 50 tanks will be landed . . . The object is to get information and to create the impression of an invasion.'[285] On the same day, he asked General 'Pug' Ismay, his chief military adviser, 'What is position about renewal of Rutter?'[286] To which Ismay replied the following day, '*Jubilee*, which is renewed Rutter *in all essential features*, is due to be carried out at first light August 18th' and then 'Jubilee has started.'[287] It is therefore not true, as is often claimed, that Mountbatten acted alone without the knowledge of his superiors.

Why was Mountbatten so keen to press ahead given all the reservations? Could it have been personal glory and the chance to lead the naval aspect of the D-Day invasion? Peter Murphy told General Dallas Brooks in an interview on 6 August 1942, 'the operation is considered very critical from the point of view of the CCO's personal career . . . If he brings this off . . . he is top of the world and will be given complete control.'[288]

Mountbatten always claimed that Churchill and General Sir Alan Brooke had supported Jubilee, but that for the sake of security, few others should be told. That included the Defence Committee, the First Lord of the Admiralty, the Vice Chief of the Imperial General Staff, the intelligence services and the Inter-Service Security Board. Nothing was committed to paper. Amidst the thousands of pieces of paper on the operation, there is not a single one signing it off. It also meant no more rehearsals.

In the early hours of Wednesday, 19 August 1942 – now slightly nearer daybreak to avoid naval collisions – an armada of 237 ships, ranging from destroyers and transports to MTBs and minesweepers – sailed for Dieppe. It included the first Americans to fight on mainland Europe and the future creator of James Bond, Commander Ian Fleming from the Naval Intelligence Department's Operational Intelligence Centre. The delay into August meant the raid had to take place over one tide, and not two, reducing the operation to a mere six hours.

The first signs of trouble came at 3.47 a.m., when German armed trawlers intercepted 3 Commando's boats, which included the naturalist Peter Scott, thereby alerting the Dieppe garrison and delaying the Commando's carefully synchronised landings. In spite of that, commandos, led by Lord Lovat, captured and destroyed a battery six miles to the west of the town, and to the east a similar attack gained its objective.

The main frontal assault, however, was a disaster, with the well-protected and armed German defenders picking off most of the troops on the landing craft or narrow beach with their heavy machine guns and 81 mm mortars, and the tanks unable to climb the steep shingle beach onto the promenade. Those tanks that did manage to surmount the beach found themselves trapped by debris in the streets. Ninety per cent of the Royal Canadian Engineers responsible for dismantling anti-tank obstacles lay dead or wounded, making any tank progress impossible.

Rather than pull back, the troops continued to be landed, even if many had to be forced off the landing craft at pistol point. Of the 6,000 soldiers and commandos who took part, over 900 were killed, 586 were wounded and almost 2,000 captured. The Royal Regiment of Canada suffered 97 per cent casualties in under four hours. Bodies kept being washed up on the beach for a week afterwards.

An informal inquiry held two days later revealed a shocking picture of panic, confusion and incompetence, including evidence that the beach master had refused to leave one of the two heavy-duty Landing Craft Mechaniseds.[289] A fuller, more sanitised, report in October concluded 'that a capital ship could have operated during the first hours of daylight without undue risk and could probably have turned the tide of battle ashore in our favour.'[290] Its recommendations included a higher proportion of military forces be held in reserve, tanks not to be landed until a beach head established, and the need for greater naval covering fire.

What new lessons were learnt for subsequent operations, such as the Torch landings in North Africa and even D-Day itself?

Clearly capturing a port without it being destroyed was going to be near impossible. The only option was to bring the port with you, stimulating the development of the portable 'Mulberry' harbours that were used at D-Day. In order to seize a port, it must be done from inland, which is exactly what happened on D-Day, when the Cotentin Peninsula was cut off and the port of Cherbourg taken from the rear.

Much heavier and more accurate covering fire than that provided by destroyers was essential, and also a much more highly trained, specialist naval assault-force with armoured landing craft would be required. At Dieppe, the Navy had been averse to sending in ships too close to enemy-held shorelines, but it was realised that as long as there was air superiority, then naval losses were likely to be minimal.

The radio navigation system used by the RAF, known as 'Gee', was subsequently adopted by the Navy, ensuring on D-Day the safe and timely arrival in the assault area, through the strong tidal streams of the Channel, of the armada of over 4,000 vessels. More communications headquarters ships were made available for the Normandy landings, as a result of the experiences at Dieppe, and there was greater integration of air support through a combined naval and landing force joint command.

The Dieppe Raid meant that the Germans had to commit greater resources to the west, which was part of the objective. In January 1942, there had been 33 German divisions in the west, which had increased to 35 by September and 52 by November. Unfortunately this did not alleviate pressure on the Eastern Front, where the number of divisions rose from 163 in January to 182 by September.[291] It did, however, lead them to concentrate on coastal defences in the belief that attacking forces could be destroyed on the beach – something which, as a result of Dieppe, was not tried again on D-Day.

Though often criticised, Mountbatten was justified in later years to say that lives on D-Day had been saved as a result of the knowledge gained at Dieppe, but it had still been a costly experience.

Who was to blame? Recriminations still continue over 70 years later. A case can partly be made for Montgomery. The decision to replace commandos with Canadian troops and to cancel the preliminary air bombardment was taken at the 5 June 1942 meeting chaired by him when Mountbatten was not present.[292] The Force Commander, 'Ham' Roberts, should have recognised that, without covering support from the Navy and Air Force, his troops were too exposed; but Canadian troops had been in Britain for two years without seeing action and the troops, their political masters and public opinion at home were hankering to be allowed to fight. The refusals of both Dudley Pound, the First Sea Lord, and Sir Charles Portal, the Chief of the Air Staff, to provide adequate gunfire and bomber support were also disastrous.

Mountbatten, or at least some of his appointments, were also at fault. German defences were stronger than intelligence estimates from COHQ had originally suggested. The man blamed was the head of intelligence at COHQ, Dickie's old chum Casa Maury, and he eventually resigned in February 1943.[293] The depth of the shingle on the beach had not been analysed, a failure of the scientists. The landing-craft crews, vital to punctuality and accurate navigation, were of uneven quality, especially for night-time, in-shore navigation – a failure of training.

Part of the problem was also down to organisation rather than individuals. 'My own feeling about the Dieppe raid,' Montgomery wrote in his memoirs, was that 'there were far too many authorities with a hand in it; there was no one single operational commander who was solely responsible for the operation from start to finish, a Task Force Commander in fact.'[294] Having three force commanders, each with their own planning team, plus Mountbatten and his staff, certainly meant there was no obvious channel of command or responsibility. There was also no contingency planning should things not go as intended, or for a breakdown in communications. In short, the problem with Dieppe was its objectives were never clear and its execution, after constant readjustments, faulty.

Mountbatten, for all his later attempts to distance himself from decisions or deflect responsibility, was the head of Combined Operations.[295] The buck stopped with him. If he had had reservations about the raid, he should have cancelled it. There were plenty of opportunities to do so, not least when air support and naval fire power were not made available and Canadian troops replaced Commandos and Royal Marines. He chose not to do so, overriding those who did raise objections. It appears the raid had taken on a momentum of its own, which few in real authority seemed prepared to question.

But could there be another explanation, given the obvious planning defects of the raid? David O'Keefe has argued that one purpose of the raid was to try and capture a four-rotor Enigma cipher machine used by the German Navy to encrypt its messages.[296] The British had captured a three-rotor machine, but with the introduction of the four-rotor machine in February 1942 they could no longer read German signals – the extra rotor multiplied already difficult odds against decryption another 26 times.

The codebreakers at Bletchley Park could no longer warn of submarine attacks and mounting merchant shipping losses in the Atlantic were threatening Britain's supply routes. This came to a head on 4 July, when the PQ-17 convoy was attacked, with only 11 of the 34 ships reaching Iceland. A week later, Mountbatten made his case for resurrecting *Rutter*.

Dieppe was a key link in the German Navy's signal chain and not only had the latest cipher equipment at its shore facilities, but the visiting vessels also held useful cipher material. A frontal raid makes sense if the purpose of the raid was really to seize the code books as quickly as possible from naval headquarters in the *Hotel Moderne*, and this would also explain the involvement of Fleming's Intelligence Assault Unit and the secrecy of the mission.

Throughout the battle, the focus of the raid remained resolutely to reach the trawlers and the naval headquarters, even when more attractive opportunities for advancing presented themselves, and it is clear that the Germans frantically attempted to drop overboard seven bags of Top Secret signals. The last bag failed to sink and attempts to make it do so with grenades led to the material being showered over the dock.

The minutes of one chief of staff's meeting read:

> Concerning the withholding of information that the Dieppe raid was to take place, Lord Louis Mountbatten explained that the necessary people had always been informed of previous operations and that there was no intention of withholding information in future from those whose duty necessitated their being so informed. On the particular occasion of Dieppe, however, he had received special instructions from the Chiefs of Staff that only certain individuals were to be informed of the intention to re-mount the operation. He had been compelled, in fact, even to mislead his own staff on this occasion.[297]

Mountbatten had always been a master of public relations, skilfully using publicity for an event or organisation to forward his own career, and the disaster was given a positive spin. At COHQ he had set up a news briefing system, which he would refine in all his subsequent appointments, and on his publicity staff were:

the former head of Twentieth Century Fox, Darryl F. Zanuck, who had been active in the Royal Naval Film Corporation; Jock Lawrence, Sam Goldwyn's publicist, and David Astor – already planning his relaunch of the *Observer*. This high-level galaxy of spin doctors ensured that, from the beginning, the Dieppe disaster was carefully controlled and presented as a success, a strategy that backfired when German news agencies began to present a very different picture.[298]

As the size of the losses sunk in, questions began to be asked in Whitehall about Mountbatten's future at Combined Operations. The Head of the Political Warfare Executive, Robert Bruce Lockhart, after lunching with General Dallas Brooks on 15 June, had already noted in his diary, 'There is considerable feeling against Dickie Mountbatten, both in the Royal Navy proper and in the Marines. The charge is that he is setting up a rival navy for a series of stunts which are useless unless linked with the general strategy.'[299]

Ten days after the raid, Sir Alan Brooke, dining at Chequers, raised his concerns about the raid with Mountbatten, occasioning the head of Combined Operations to respond: 'I was absolutely dumb-founded . . . when you made your very outspoken criticism of the manner in which the Dieppe raid was planned.'[300] He argued he had followed the proper procedures.

Brooke remained unsatisfied and in December, unimpressed by the invasion plans for Sardinia drawn up by COHQ, began to encourage Churchill to press Mountbatten on why Dieppe had failed so spectacularly. Dickie, skilled in the ways of Whitehall, deflected the blame onto Roberts, insisting that the planning, if followed properly, would have been successful and that, in any case, the lessons learned had justified the cost.[301]

Dieppe had, however, dented his reputation, 'I had a very heated discussion in the COS lasting about an hour, concerning the role and charter of Mountbatten (as Chief of Combined Operations),' wrote Brooke in his diary on 22 December. 'The suggestion being that he should command the naval forces for an invasion of France. Portal and Pug Ismay were supporting him, and Dudley Pound and I were dead against it on the basis that his job is one of an advisor and not of a commander. We finally shook the other two and went a long way towards making the point.'[302]

For all his problems at Combined Operations, Mountbatten had many successes with small landing operations. At the end of the year, Operation *Frankton*, which involved six canoeists fixing limpet mines to cargo boats in the docks at Bordeaux, took place. The operation, immortalised in the film *The Cockleshell Heroes*, damaged four ships but at a high human cost – only two of the 12 canoeists returned, having crossed the Pyrenees and Spain to Gibraltar.

The main priority were the Anglo-American landings in North Africa, Operation *Torch*, in November 1942, designed to open up a new front and use American forces that Combined Operations supported. This was followed by Operation *Husky*, the Allied invasion of Sicily, planned for the summer of 1943. With the creation of the new role of Chief of Staff to the Supreme Allied Commander (COSSAC), the role of COHQ had begun to shrink, but it continued to focus on planning for what would eventually become Operation *Overlord*, the D-Day landings. Its priority was to have ready 4,500 fully crewed assault ships and landing craft by 1944.

One of COHQ's great achievements was developing important innovations in modern warfare. These included: artificial harbours that could be towed across the Channel; PLUTO (Pipe Line Under the Ocean), which at its peak was allowing a million gallons of petrol to be sent to France each day; equipment to demolish underwater obstacles; waterproofed engines so vehicles could be driven ashore; and even a spring-loaded walking stick to test the hardness of a beach.

Mountbatten's experiences at COHQ had matured him into a very astute, if not always popular, political operator. He could still be impetuous, but he had learnt to be more calculating in his pursuit of power and manipulative in exercising it. The head of his secretariat, Captain N.T.P. Cooper, remembered:

A useful little device which I installed under his desk was an electric bell which, when he was tired of his current visitor, he could press with his knees which was the signal for me to go into his room to remind him of a very frightfully important appointment which was of course imaginary.[303]

Mountbatten's charm, strong work ethic and ability to work with others had been noticed. The broadcaster Arthur Marshall attached to Combined Operations remembered how, 'All officers in the HQ were invited, usually in pairs, to have lunch with the Mountbattens in their house in Chester Street. They could not have been easier or more welcoming and they made one feel that this had, for them, been the Treat of the Week.'[304]

He was much influenced by Maurice Maeterlinck's theory of 'the spirit of the hive' in his *The Life of the Bee* (1919), which argued the benefits of teamwork. A particular skill was 'man-management'. His deputy, Charles Haydon, upset about not being told about the remounting of the Dieppe Raid, proffered his resignation. But Mountbatten saw him immediately and the next day Haydon was writing, 'You are – you know – a very difficult person to deal with. Yesterday I felt angry, sore and hardly done by. Today I feel a worm for ever having harboured any of those feelings. I really do.'[305]

There are countless examples of his interpersonal skills winning round his opponents.

In April 1943, his punishing workload – often he worked 16 to 18-hour days with weekly tours of the units of his command – caught up with him and he came down with pneumonia. It was his first serious illness since adolescence. His doctor told him that if he had neglected his condition for another 24 hours, he might well have died.[306] For a month he recuperated at Broadlands, where he saw much of Edwina.

Her war work was also taking its toll on her. 'Felt terrible all day,' she wrote in her diary at the end of May, '. . . worked hard all the same . . .'[307] 'It was hard to believe that before the war she was reckoned to be one of the most beautiful women in England,' recalled a member of her staff. 'She was grey and haggard and lined. Even her beautiful eyes looked tired behind her thick spectacles.'[308]

In July 1942, she had been appointed Superintendent in Chief of the Nursing Division, the highest post a woman could hold. She was now responsible for 60,000 adult volunteers and 10,000 cadets. She continued to travel widely throughout the country, visiting convalescent homes, blood transfusion centres, hospitals and ARP posts, opening bazaars, presiding at auctions and inspecting Guards of Honour. Recognition of her work came with the award of the CBE in the New Year Honours list.

She had discovered that, like her husband, she had leadership qualities. She, too, could use her high-level connections to ensure things happened and was always well prepared. She had at last been given something useful to do and she had risen to the challenge, much to the pride of Dickie.

* * *

At the beginning of August 1943, Mountbatten, as a member of the Chiefs of Staff, sailed on the *Queen Mary* for Quebec, one of 150 officers going to the Quebec Conference. The meeting between Churchill and Roosevelt was to shape future grand strategy and especially discuss the invasion of Europe. It also gave Mountbatten an opportunity to demonstrate to the Chiefs of Staff a new invention for Combined Operations – an aircraft carrier 2,000 feet in length, made of frozen seawater and wood pulp called *pykrete,* which could be positioned as a refuelling stop for aircraft in the Atlantic. He chose to do so after a particularly acrimonious meeting in which the American Admiral Ernest King had punched a British officer, and the room had had to be cleared of most of the officials.

Mountbatten proceeded to produce two bits of ice – one purely consisting of water and the other *pykrete*. He then drew his revolver. Firing at the first, it shattered into a series of ice splinters. He now took aim at the second. Ricocheting off the block, the bullet buzzed around the room, grazing the leg of Admiral King before burying itself in a wall. There was a stunned silence and then from outside the room, a voice piped up: 'Oh God, they've started shooting each other now.'[309]

Dickie knew his time at Combined Operations was probably coming to an end soon, as others were brought in to command the larger planned invasions. He took every opportunity on board ship to press Dudley Pound for a date when he might return to sea. What he had not realised was that Churchill had other plans for him.

CHAPTER 14

Supremo

Mountbatten had first been suggested for the post of Supreme Allied Commander South East Asia by Leo Amery in May 1943, but concerns about his health – he had only just taken a month off work with pneumonia – and that 'he was not big enough' meant the suggestion was ignored.[310] It was only American pressure and Field Marshal Sir Archibald Wavell's poor working relationship with the American commander of the Chinese armies in Burma, General Joe Stilwell, that persuaded Churchill to change his mind. The job of Supreme Allied Commander in Europe had to go to an American – as the United States was contributing the majority of troops – much to General Sir Alan Brooke's disappointment as he had been promised the job. In return it was agreed that the South East Asian post should be filled by the British.

The first choice had been Air Chief Marshal Sholto Douglas, head of RAF Middle East Command, but he was vetoed by Roosevelt. The American Chiefs of Staff had then suggested Air Marshal Sir Arthur Tedder, but it was felt he could not be moved from his command in the Mediterranean. Sir Andrew Cunningham, commanding the Mediterranean Fleet, was next on the list, but he turned it down, keen to be appointed First Sea Lord instead. Six other Service chiefs were put forward and rejected. In the absence of any other obvious candidates, Mountbatten's name was again put forward and enthusiastically approved by the Americans, though there were still doubts amongst those who had worked with him closely. 'He will require a very efficient Chief of Staff to pull him through!' wrote Brooke waspishly in his diary.[311]

That Chief of Staff was to be Henry Pownall, formerly Chief of Staff to Archibald Wavell and presently C-in-C in Persia. Pownall had no illusions about the task that faced him:

Mountbatten, aged 43, will certainly have all the necessary drive and initiative to conduct this war. The difficulty will be to restrain him, or rather to direct his energies into really useful directions and away from minor details. He throws out brainwaves daily, some of them very good too, but not always timely. And he is obviously rather volatile. Most of his staff have already confided this to me, for they obviously rely on me to keep him on the rails, which won't be too easy. He also shows a distinct tendency towards creating a staff organisation which shall have places where his trusted colleagues and friends can fit in. Hardly the right way to go about it but I suppose Patronage, with a big P, is bound to be an element of the Blood Royal.[312]

With his experience of amphibious operations and on the Chiefs of Staff Committee, his ability to work with international forces, his close working relationships with the Americans, his energy and imagination and his diplomatic and public relations skills – Mountbatten was an inspired choice. Given the problems of jungle warfare, many of the military operations would have to be amphibious and here his Combined Operation experience would be invaluable.

Mountbatten knew he was not the first choice and it would not be easy, but he was delighted, writing to Churchill, 'I have never really thanked you properly for giving me the finest chance any young man has ever been given in war.'[313] To Edwina he was more open:

> I really don't know how I will be able to do this job without you. I've got so used to leaning on you and hearing your brutally frank but well-deserved criticism. But above all you have been such a help with all the people I have to deal with . . . Wouldn't it be romantic to live together in the place we got engaged in, and in a job which is really more important in the war than our host's was . . . Please don't think I underestimate the importance of your job – I am just being a very selfish husband who would like to have his wife with him![314]

In October 1943, Dickie left from Northolt for South East Asia, seen off by Patricia. As this was Bunny's last weekend at Broadlands, Edwina did not come to the airport to say goodbye.

The situation in South East Asia was dire. The Japanese had overrun the region as far as the India–Burma border and were menacing India itself. Mountbatten's orders were to defend India, drive the Japanese out of Burma and Malaya, and reopen land communications with China. His command stretched over sea, land and air to include Burma, Ceylon, Siam, the Malay Peninsula and Sumatra, but the chain of command had been left vague. Was Mountbatten simply chairing a collegial body of the Combined Chiefs of Staff, like Eisenhower in the Mediterranean, or was he, like the American General Douglas MaCarthur in the Pacific, the Supremo with his own planning staff able to direct his commanders-in-chief?

For example, he had no control over the American 10th Air

Force, until granted at the Cairo Conference in November, and Sir James Somerville, the C-in-C Eastern Fleet, was responsible for the protection of trade routes in the Indian Ocean, except when Mountbatten needed the ships for specific operations. This, together with childish squabbles regarding permissions to visit ships, was to be a source of constant friction until a truce was brokered by Charles Lambe.

'Supreme Commander means just that,' Pownall wrote in his diary shortly after Mountbatten arrived. 'He is not just the chairman of a committee.'[315] Perhaps, but in practice he had three powerful commanders-in-chief who were used to exercising power and were not going to surrender it easily, especially to someone younger and hitherto more junior.

Mountbatten arrived on 6 October and installed himself in Faridkot House, a maharaja's palace in New Delhi, where he immediately evicted the Naval and Army staffs to create room for his own expanding staff. It was a portent of what was to come. Many of the criticisms directed at him at COHQ followed him to SEAC. By December, Sir James Somerville, C-in-C Easter Fleet, was complaining to General Ismay that 'the machine has run away and is gathering momentum daily'.[316]

By December the staff had grown to 4,700. 'Dickie insists on duplicating everything. It's clear he wishes to have absolute control of everything in this theatre,' wrote Somerville to Ismay.

> I had a long talk with him yesterday about this . . . I admired intensely his enormous drive, grasp of facts and application, but that my brother C-in-Cs were most deeply concerned at what was taking place . . . He has great drive, personality and imagination but here lacks balance and is a most wishful thinker.[317]

There were the old complaints of chums being given posts. Amongst those brought out from COHQ were Micky Hodges and Peter Murphy, whilst the appointment of Johnny Papps, a former banqueting manager at the Dorchester Hotel, raised some eyebrows.

Mountbatten quickly built up an appreciation of the situation, discovering that advancing British forces constantly had to fall back to protect supply lines from Japanese troops, and air supply was hampered by lack of transport aircraft. He identified as his priorities morale, malaria and monsoon, of which the most important was restoring morale. 'I hear you call this the Forgotten Front. I hear you call yourselves the Forgotten Army,' he would tell them. 'Well, let me tell you that this is not the Forgotten Front, and you are not the Forgotten Army. In fact, nobody has even heard of you. But they will hear of you, because this is what we are going to do.'[318]

He made constant visits to the front line and hospitals, sometimes travelling hundreds of miles over mud tracks in his jeep with only two members of staff. Troops might not believe the visits were as spontaneous or unrehearsed as Mountbatten let them believe, that his stock phrases in the languages of his command were not learnt by heart, but it showed he cared. A newspaper, *SEAC*, with the former editor of the *Evening Standard*, Frank Owen, was set up together with Radio SEAC. SEAC news stories now appeared in the British press, and film showings were introduced. More mobile bath units were created, postal and leave arrangements extended and a programme of visits to the troops introduced. One of those to come out was Noël Coward.

Mountbatten lobbied Eden to create 'a political post within the Government, for the sole purpose of directing Far Eastern affairs'.[319] A brand logo was created of a phoenix, a symbol of rebirth, which the men soon dubbed 'pig's arse'. When General Ronald Adam inspected the command the following year, he was able to write, 'I can confirm the very high morale of your Army. In fact, I have not seen higher morale anywhere.'[320]

This improved publicity also served his own ends. Ralph Arnold, who handled Dickie's PR, remembered how:

Supremo's intense interest in everything to do with PR could be a bit awkward. As a start he took a keen interest in his own personal publicity, and made no bones about it. . . . Too much, or the wrong kind of publicity, embarrassed and annoyed him. Too little upset him. It was difficult to achieve the happy mean.[321]

In 1943, there were 120 sick for every battle casualty, mainly malaria, but also dysentery and other tropical diseases. By the following year it was 20 and in 1945 it was 10. Put another way, the number of men with malaria fell from 84 per cent to 13 per cent between 1943 and 1945. This rapid improvement in public health was achieved by introducing new techniques, drugs and methods of treatment and importing some 700 nurses, which Edwina had arranged in London. It meant his troop strengths were almost immediately multiplied. The battles with morale and malaria won, the third factor could be addressed. Hitherto there had been no fighting through the five months of the monsoon, May to October. Mountbatten decided that henceforth they would fight, giving the Allies the benefit of surprise and speeding up campaigns.

Henry Pownall provides a useful snapshot six weeks after his arrival:

The pace is pretty hot for Mountbatten gives neither himself, nor his staff, time for relaxation. His active mind is perpetually at work. Very often his push and drive are used in useful directions. But not always and he is apt to put urgency into matters which are not the least urgent, or subjects which ought to be carefully considered. He causes, too, quite a lot of unnecessary work by not consulting his staff, or asking how things stand from the staff officer concerned, before pushing out a Personal Minute on a subject on which he is not fully informed – because he has not asked for the information. But with all that, his energy and drive are most admirable features; for so young a man his knowledge is extremely good; his mind receptive; his experience of two years on the C.O.S. Committee stand him in admirable stead; he has a most attractive personality; and his judgement is good when things are put fairly and squarely to him. He doesn't always allow time for that latter item to happen.[322]

Though China was not in Mountbatten's command, it was to play an important role in his time at SEAC. China and Japan had been at war for seven years by 1943. Generalissimo Chiang Kai-shek controlled the central and southern provinces, with the Communists in control in the north. The Americans were determined to keep China in the war, as they added to the pressure on Japan in the region. This put Mountbatten in a difficult position as British policy was to recapture Burma, Malaya and Singapore, whilst the Americans, who supplied most of the resources, were only involved in the region as a means of supporting China. They had no wish to help SEAC – Save England's Asian Colonies.[323]

General Joe Stilwell, who was Mountbatten's Deputy Supreme Commander, was also the Chief of Staff to Chiang Kai-shek and commander of the Chinese troops in Burma and Assam with the responsibility of protecting Chinese interests. Already there was an inbuilt tension in his responsibilities, which were exacerbated by his directness, anti-British sentiment, his refusal to serve under General Giffard, the British Commander-in-Chief, and his plotting behind Mountbatten's back. At the same time Chiang Kai-shek, nicknamed 'Cash My-check', simply wanted to maximise aid from both the British and the Americans, and had no hesitation in playing them off against each other. It did not make for an easy life for Mountbatten.

'The Glamour Boy is just that,' wrote Stilwell in January 1944. 'He doesn't wear well and I begin to wonder if he knows his stuff. Enormous staff, endless walla-walla but damn little fighting.'[324]

The fighting was to come the following month with a Japanese attack on the 'Administrative Box', where large stocks of war stores had been established on the Arakan Front. Encircled, the British troops held on for 18 days, supplied by American aircraft diverted from supplying Chinese forces, and it was the Japanese who had to retreat. This first British victory was to be the turning point of the Burma Campaign.

The next month the Japanese counter-attacked the British supply bases on the Imphal Plain, just as Mountbatten was himself *hors de combat*. On 7 March, whilst driving his jeep, a bamboo stump had flicked into his face, damaging his left eye. For five days, whilst the battle raged, he was completely blind with both eyes bandaged, and he was not allowed to move his head or lie on his side. Nurses worked eight-hour shifts feeding, washing and reading to him until, at risk of losing the sight of his left eye, he ignored the doctor's protests and discharged himself.

Meanwhile at Kohima the garrison of 2,500, mainly non-combatants, had been surrounded by 15,000 Japanese troops. Between 5 and 18 April it saw some of the fiercest close-quarter fighting of the war and, at one point, the two sides were separated only by a tennis court. Eventually, the Allies' air superiority and reinforcements of an infantry division in 30 American transport aircraft (which Mountbatten had commandeered off the China supply route) meant the Japanese were finally on the retreat.

* * *

Mountbatten found life as Supreme Allied Commander lonely, as Peter Murphy had returned to London and Bunny Phillips was going back to Washington. 'The Rabbit and I parted very nearly in tears', Dickie wrote to Edwina; '. . . we used to ride together every evening when I could get away & used to talk & talk & talk. I always thought I'd get to like him very much once I really knew him & when he was with us you will agree that I didn't get much chance of seeing him alone!!'[325]

He wished she could join him and complained his hair was 'visibly greyer' and 'my middle-aged spread is increasing. I get tired fairly easily . . .'[326] She tried to reassure him, but his spirits were often low. There were continuing criticisms of his empire building, especially after he moved his headquarters to Ceylon and the imposing King's Pavilion at Kandy, formerly the governor's residence. By February 1944, his staff had risen to 7,000 and, soon after, was nearer 10,000. This, together with the galaxy of flags on the bonnet of his jeep, was all part of the showmanship – but it made him few friends.

'Dickie has many great qualities – indefatigable energy, great drive and lots of moral and physical courage,' wrote Ismay to General Claude Auchinleck, the C-in-C India, 'but there's an undue amount of ego in his cosmos and tact is not exactly his strong suit.'

I warned him not once but several times of the folly of setting up a huge staff and implored him not to repeat the mistake he had made as CCO (where incidentally he did a damn fine job of work); he in this respect is incorrigible. I also told him to lay off publicity as much as possible – until he has a victory or two to his credit. But here again my advice seems to have fallen on deaf ears. There doesn't seem to be much good in making mistakes, unless one is prepared to profit by them.[327]

There were also criticisms of the louche atmosphere. Mountbatten liked to be surrounded by beautiful women and both COHQ and the headquarters at SEAC were renowned for the glamorous female staff and relaxed atmosphere. General Oliver Leese was shocked when he arrived and was taken to a dance at the officers' club to see a pretty Wren kissing Mountbatten passionately. He wrote to his wife about the party, 'it was gay and full of life – full enough of drink – and very odd. Most girls were U's [Mountbatten's] and other secretaries and they seemed to spend their time sitting on the arms of U and others' chairs'.[328]

One of those women was Sally Dean, then in her early twenties, whom he described as 'my favourite and prettiest American signal officer'.[329] Dean had been brought up in France and Jersey and, after the outbreak of the war, briefly worked in the American Hospital of Paris, before dramatically escaping and enlisting in the Women's Army Corps and being posted to SEAC.

However, the person with whom Mountbatten had truly fallen in love was Janey Lindsay. Beautiful, tall, blonde, elegant, fluent in French and German, she had come out to join Mountbatten's personal staff at the end of 1943. The granddaughter of the Duke of Abercorn, her closest friend had been John F. Kennedy's sister, Kick Kennedy, and both Kennedy and the actor David Niven had been suitors. Her three-year-old marriage to Colonel Peter Lindsay, a colonel in Force 136 – the South East Asian equivalent of SOE – was already in difficulties, and she and Dickie were immediately attracted to each other. It was an affair that was to last until the end of his time in South East Asia and continue as a friendship until his death. He was later to write to her:

> It was a true godsend when I found you in Delhi and asked you to dinner in Faridkot House. At the time in the Purdah Court, the moment I touched your hand and you squeezed mine in return a new private life opened up for me in which I could throw off all worries and responsibilities and recuperate in your unfailing love. In two years we never really had an angry word. The week-ends we were able to go up to my bungalow – our bungalow – at Dimbula were sheer heaven and however utterly exhausted I was I always went back refreshed and full of courage.

He and Bunny had attended a Christmas Eve party at her bungalow at Meerut, where Mountbatten remembered:

> We sat till the small hours of the morning playing the gramophone and telling stories. I had never realised what a relief it was to get away from one's staff, however much one likes them, and go to a private house and spend an evening with friends of one's own set.[330]

The affair was sufficiently well advanced that he had given her a present of a dress for her twenty-third birthday on 15 January. They had then stayed together with the Nawab of Rampur in late February, where they had visited his jewel house – an honour usually reserved for the Viceroy – to see his collection of 250 radio sets. 'After dinner we sat around at the little tables in the night-club while His Highness played the trap-drums in his band, and finally forced me to do the same though I had not played the drums for over 20 years!'[331]

In April, he joined the Lindsays at their bungalow at Yahalatenna, eight miles outside Kandy, where they played a record of the musical *Oklahoma!*, until Mountbatten accidentally dropped it. The following month, Janey came to dinner to meet his nephew, David Milford Haven, 'as I thought David might like to see some pretty girls.'[332] Mountbatten felt isolated and lonely. 'I only have one friend I can gossip with about non-serious matters and that is Jane,' he confessed to Edwina at the beginning of May.[333]

Christmas Eve 1944 was again spent with Janey, together with Prince Philip, and his new chief of staff, Lieutenant General Frederick 'Boy' Browning. 'The cook had gone mad and started roasting the turkey a couple of hours too late,' Mountbatten recollected, 'so we had an inverted dinner, with the sweet, savoury, fruit, coffee and cigars before the turkey!'[334]

* * *

Edwina was also in love.

At the beginning of 1944, Bill Paley, who in the 1920s had developed a series of radio stations that would eventually become CBS (the Columbia Broadcasting System), arrived in London in the rank of colonel as Chief of Broadcasting within the Psychological Warfare Division at SHAEF (Supreme Headquarters Allied Expeditionary Forces) and took a suite at Claridge's complete with valet. His role was to arrange broadcasts into Germany and Occupied Europe and eventually to broadcast during the Allied invasion of France.

He had previously met Edwina when he was in London in August

1942 to see how government restrictions on news broadcasts might affect the CBS radio network, and he had taken her to dine at Beaverbrook's country home, Cherkley Court. Now, after a brief affair with Pamela Churchill, the wife of Randolph Churchill, he took up with Edwina.³³⁵ From February they spent most of their free time together, dining out in London and spending lazy weekends at Broadlands, until the affair came to a natural end a few months later.³³⁶

'She wasn't in love with Bill, but she liked him, much as she liked the other boys,' said Stuart Scheftel, one of Paley's colleagues.³³⁷ He seems to have felt the same. Daphne Straight, a friend of the couple, wrote to Duff Cooper that 'from his point of view anyway, this was on a strictly temporary basis, and he now appears to be coming up to breathe again'.³³⁸ The two, however, remained friends and he continued to send her presents of perfume, lipstick and other luxuries.

Meanwhile Edwina's relationship continued with Bunny, although, now he was on Dickie's staff in SEAC – where he too was having an affair with Janey Lindsay – they had seen little of each other.³³⁹ In July 1944, Bunny had returned and one weekend at Broadlands broke the news that she had always dreaded – he was engaged.

His new bride was Gina, the niece of Nada and daughter of Harold and Zia Wernher, and Edwina had partly been responsible for bringing them together, after she had sat them next to each other at a dinner party.³⁴⁰ Three times that day, Bunny came to Chester Street to explain, but neither Edwina nor Dickie, back on leave, could take in what had happened. Indeed, Dickie, who had been a close confidant of Bunny, had been on the point of offering Edwina a divorce so she could marry him. He delayed his return to Kandy and they spent his last few days at Broadlands, where it poured with rain and she took the dogs for melancholy walks.

Lady Pamela Hicks remembered:

My mother took the news very badly and there were times in the ensuing weeks, as she took endless dismal walks alone down the river path, when my father and my sister feared she might drown herself. It was no good bringing up Bunny's departure with her directly – she was never open to any conversation about relationships or feelings and had trained herself as a child to be self-sufficient.[341]

Dickie did his best to comfort his distraught wife:

I must tell you again how deeply and sincerely I feel for you at this moment when, however unselfish you may be about A's engagement, the fact that it is bound to alter their relationship – though I feel convinced not the friendship – which has existed between you, is bound to upset you emotionally and make you feel unhappy. You have however still got the love and genuine affection of two chaps – A and me – and the support of all your many friends. You have only one more bad patch in front of you – the week A gets married. After that they will presumably live a year or two abroad, and when next you meet I feel the difficulties will have disappeared & you will find a new firm and lasting friendship based on your 11 years' happiness . . . A always knew that I had accepted the fact that after the war you were at liberty to get married and I could not let either of you get the impression that anything I had ever done had stood in the way.[342]

Edwina was touched. 'As well as helping so tremendously at what must be a difficult time in my life,' she wrote, 'it has made me realise more than ever before how deeply devoted I am to you and what very real and true affection as well as immense admiration I have for you.'[343]

She continued, 'I know it is all for the best and hard though it is bound to be temporarily to readjust one's ideas and one's life, I have always felt that Bunny needed so much his own little home and family, and if I wouldn't give it to him, it was so important for him to find someone sweet like Gina who would.'[344]

'I shall not be gloomy and silly I promise you – I have my ups and downs!! But the latter are on the ascendant – and even though as you say there will be another trying time when Bunny comes over next I think I can now cope with that too! . . . It was wonderful to have you holding my hand just at the bad time . . . I have an angelic family and such marvellous friends and what more *can* one want?'[345]

Bunny's marriage had brought Edwina closer to her eldest daughter, Patricia. After spending time together at Broadlands, she had written to her father, 'the first really heart to heart I have ever had with Mummy.'[346] Rather tactlessly, Pamela had been asked to be a bridesmaid, 'but my mother told me firmly, without looking at her diary, that I would be at school that day and it would not be possible.'[347]

In her grief, Edwina threw herself into her work. In September, she joined a Medical Civilian Relief Unit in France, having travelled over in a converted bomber sent by Eisenhower. Accompanied by Joe Weld, part of the SEAC Rear Link in London, she inspected Ambulance Columns and Red Cross stores and visited welfare workers, doing her best to deal with the homeless, hungry and POWs awaiting repatriation.

In Paris, she checked that Peter Murphy's flat had not been damaged, dined with Bill Paley, saw the Duff Coopers at the Embassy and picked up some gold earrings she had ordered at the jeweller

Boucheron in 1939. There had been no news of Yola since 1941, so discovering she was now at Beauvais, 50 miles north of Paris, Edwina set off in a car, provided by Eisenhower, for a reunion. 'All quite unchanged and as enchanting as ever,' she wrote to Dickie.[348]

By the next month, Dickie had arranged for her to come out to SEAC as the official representative of the Joint War Organisation to inspect hospitals, casualty clearing stations and welfare centres. Her hosts had suggested she visit one establishment a day, but she insisted that by starting early and working late she could manage two. 'It was here she was first to exhibit the personal approach to vast numbers of wounded men that was to seal her fame,' wrote one of her biographers:

> She was not just another distinguished visitor. Every man as he lay in his cot became convinced of her burning interest in his personal welfare. Tirelessly she went from ward to ward, shaking hands, murmuring the appropriate word of encouragement, perhaps changing a dressing, undertaking to forward some message to his home. She performed the astonishing feat of speaking to every patient, every nursing orderly and every doctor in every hospital she visited . . . There was an abiding impression of personal interest and warmth and a positive electric charge of encouragement.[349]

The last day of the year was spent packing. 'Delighted to see the end of the old one!' she wrote in her diary.[350]

CHAPTER 15

Relief Work

Edwina set off at the beginning of 1945 on a three-month inspection tour, which would take in Cairo, Baghdad and India. She was accompanied by Nancie Lees, the former assistant of Stella Underhill, and Major Bryan Hunter from Dickie's staff. Hunter had ambitiously brought his golf clubs in the belief there would be some downtime. He should have known Edwina better.

After a long day inspecting medical and welfare establishments, the party would then write thank-you letters, compile reports of the day's activities, chase up issues that had arisen during the day (such as missing drugs or equipment), and even make new visits not already part of the programme. Edwina met the heads of medical services, Lady Wavell, who ran the Red Cross, and various generals. No issue was too small to be addressed, from the right food for patients with jaw injuries to army boots that chafed the feet of Indian and African troops.

In Madras, she visited the Joint War Charities Supply Depot, reviewed a parade of 600 St John Ambulance members and toured several hospitals. In Bombay, there were inspections of five hospitals, WRNS quarters, an ambulance train and a hospital ship. In Poona, she saw some eye, ear, nose and throat wards, blood plasma centres and a centre that fitted artificial limbs. The comedienne and actress Joyce Grenfell, in India entertaining the troops, remembered:

> Edwina Mountbatten was among us for two days and I took my hat off to her. She looks chic and attractive and never stops working. Hospitals all day, Indian and British, meals in messes with sisters, and one night she came to No 17 officers' ward to watch us do our stuff and the next night saw her at the BORS' dance where we all took the floor solidly for three hours . . .[351]

In Delhi, Edwina visited the Viceroy's House which, she told Patricia and Pamela, 'is immense with endless marble floored corridors and rooms so huge one is exhausted walking to one's bath and Lulu next door. Not my cup of tea at all . . . All rather stately and pompous.'[352]

From there it was north-east India and the Burma coast. She returned with a series of conclusions. Nursing staff was under strength, there were huge pay differentials between British and Indian nurses, and practices varied considerably between hospitals.

At the end of February, she embarked for the front, which gave her a thrill. 'Drove out to forward areas to within 500 yds of Jap positions with stench and debris of yesterday's fighting . . . Live shells and booby traps still strewn around,' she wrote.[353] In China, she paid visits to hospitals, orphanages, the Institute of Health, a blood bank and delousing station. She insisted on travelling third class on a leave train to see conditions for herself, travelling in the luggage rack. From there it was Ceylon, where she saw convalescent depots, clubs, dental surgeries, hospital ships, inspected parades and addressed the WRNS, VADs and various hospital and canteen workers.

By mid-April she was back in Britain, reporting to the Joint War Organisation, lobbying the War Office, Ministry of Health and India Office. She lunched with Churchill in an attempt to persuade him to send out more VADs and trained nurses, and saw the King and Queen. A month later she left on a month's tour of Italy, Greece and the Middle East, visiting sick and wounded troops. One of her biographers later wrote:

> Nothing pleased her more than to be invited to a party. She would have one drink; if she could get her favourite, rum and orange, she might have two. But she would talk to everybody and talk their heads off. If there was dancing, she would dance with every man at the party.
> She was an immediate success with the Americans in Burma. Entering wards in their hospitals, she would be greeted by wolf whistles. At Bhamo she autographed the plaster cast on a GI's leg and caused a riot.[354]

General Sir Philip Christison, one of Mountbatten's generals, remembered how she 'flew over to Sumatra where she hobnobbed with some Communist republicans and visited refugee camps and gained much intelligence from the Japanese. Dickie was exceedingly angry at the risks she had taken and the political implications that might follow. But her brave actions could not have been done by a man. He would have been murdered on the spot.'[355]

* * *

Mountbatten's affair with Janey continued throughout 1945. Edwina was well aware of it and did not mind. In March, she had arranged a lunch party for her husband and included Janey and Teddy Heywood-Lonsdale, and the following month Teddy and

Peter Murphy had given a small party with dancing and Janey had been invited. As soon as Edwina returned to Britain, Mountbatten joined Janey for a weekend at her bungalow at Yahalatenna. Edwina seemed accepting of Janey. 'I am so glad that you felt as happy as I did about our new-found relationship,' wrote Dickie.

> I have always wanted to have you as my principal confidante and friend, but so long as A was yours – it made it literally impossible for me. I hope you didn't mind my mentioning about my girl-friends – it was only to show you that they never have meant to me what A means to you, and so can never come between us, provided you no longer make difficulties about my seeing them, within reason, as you were apt to do in the old days.[356]

In May, Janey, after spending her last two days with Dickie, returned to Britain. She left him her Siamese cat, Sikri. 'Your going has left a horrible hole in my life,' he wrote to her in October:

> I have so many memories under every sort of condition & they're very pleasant & happy. Sikri is a constant reminder of you, sweet and affectionate. When you left she produced a load of kittens and I kept one . . . I miss you more than I would have thought possible. My sweet and lovely Janey, Bless you & much love, darling, Dickie.[357]

On 7 May 1945 Germany surrendered, but the war continued in the Far East. In March, Mandalay had been captured, and in May, Allied amphibious forces had entered Rangoon to discover the Japanese had already left, but Malaya, Singapore, Siam, Sumatra, the Dutch East Indies, Borneo and Indo–China remained under

Japanese occupation. Now that landing craft, shipping and aircraft were available, a huge amphibious operation – Operation *Zipper* – was being planned to recapture Malaya and Singapore.

In July, Mountbatten was back in Britain as the Labour election win – forecast by Peter Murphy – was announced. Edwina was delighted. She was now more tolerant of Dickie's girlfriends. 'The sweetest change,' he wrote to her, 'is the way you have conquered what we all thought was an unreasoning jealousy . . . You can feel easy in your mind that there is real safety in numbers & that I won't do anything silly.'[358]

Later that month, Mountbatten attended the last of the Inter-Allied Conferences at Potsdam, *en route* to being reunited for the first time since the beginning of the war with Yola. At Potsdam he met the new American president, Harry S. Truman – Roosevelt had unexpectedly died in April – and was let into the secret that the atomic bomb was about to be dropped on Japan. On 15 August, six days after the second bomb was dropped, the Japanese surrendered. Operation *Zipper* was cancelled.

On 5 September 1945, Allied Forces retook Singapore. A week later, Mountbatten accepted the surrender of 680,879 Japanese men in South East Asia, insisting that senior commanders hand over their swords in a public loss of face. He described the event in his diary as 'the greatest day of my life'.[359]

How does Mountbatten's record at SEAC stand up? His instructions had been to wage war with landings by sea, but none took place. His efforts were constantly rebuffed or frustrated and he was frequently denied requested troops and supplies, because of demands in other theatres of war, or because the Americans wanted to minimise British influence in the region.

The Chiefs of Staff thought a proposal to cut Japanese communications in eastern Burma was premature. Operation

Culverin, a plan first mooted at the Quebec Conference, to recapture the northern tip of Sumatra, was continually delayed and then abandoned. It was replaced by Operation *Buccaneer*, an amphibious attack on the Andaman Islands, which held important Japanese naval bases and airfields, but that was abandoned in the summer of 1945 as the war drew to an end. Operation *Zipper* had to be cut back after the British Government, for domestic political reasons, speeded up demobilisation.

Mountbatten did not handle his generals well, but then many were difficult and temperamental, suspicious of a man much younger and hitherto more junior to them. The demotion of General William Slim as commander of the Fourteenth Army by Oliver Leese, the Commander, Allied Land Forces South East Asia, and the subsequent replacement of Leese by Slim on Sir Alan Brooke's orders was an embarrassment showing the weakness of his authority.[360]

Personality differences between Mountbatten and Joe Stilwell, Mountbatten and James Somerville, the breakdown of the relationship between Chiang Kai-shek and Stilwell and differing views over wartime goals and post-war plans made SEAC less effective than it might have been. The British wanted to restore the British Empire, with self-determination to follow, whilst the United States' focus was on China. The fact that most of the money and resources came from America meant their objectives, especially the emphasis on the Burma Road supply line to China, took precedence.

What, then, were his achievements? Firstly, the improvement in morale, which contributed to the new military success. Though Slim and other generals should take credit for the victories from 1944, it was Mountbatten who created the framework and support that allowed them. Success at Arakan and Imphal was in large part due to his persuading the Americans to release aircraft from their trips over the 'Hump' to China to bring in extra troops and supplies. Perhaps, most importantly, and in difficult circumstances, Mountbatten largely kept the various competing factions in check.

Henry Pownall, who had seen Mountbatten at close hand, wrote a shrewd analysis of his strengths and weaknesses:

> One of his best points is his way with troops; that is quite admirable. He looks the part; he says the right things, and he's the King's cousin – at heart the troops are snobby to that extent. He has plenty of moral courage, yet not enough to allow him to face calmly an unpleasant interview . . . He is too fond of 'quarrel by proxy'. For he hates a row and wishes to be popular and well thought of, and is indeed almost pathetically surprised when he learns that there are people who do not care for him and his ways. His strongest point is his resilience. With all his natural advantages and the experience he is now getting, he will surely play a big part in the post-war Empire and he is qualified to do so.[361]

Mountbatten's Command with the end of the war was now extended to include French Indochina, Java, Borneo and the Celebes Sea, adding another half a million miles to the million square miles for which he was already responsible. There were 125,000 Allied prisoners-of-war and civil internees to be rescued, as well as 750,000 Japanese to be sent back to their country. Apart from the devastation of war, civil administration had broken down and the resulting power vacuum was being filled with a variety of nationalist groups. His 'Post-Surrender Tasks' were to restore the rule of law, regenerate the economy and either restore old governments or open the way to fresh elections. A complication was reconciling the interests of the former colonial powers, the indigenous movements, and the United States – who was now an important regional player.

His response was pragmatic. He did not have the resources to put down these nationalist uprisings, so he had to work with them. It might not be popular with some of the old guard, but he recognised that the popular aspirations released by the war could not be cast aside. Brian Kibbins, who served with Mountbatten in the new headquarters in Singapore, was aware that some thought him 'too inclined to the left, too ready to listen to upstart leaders in the emergent liberation forces. It would be fairer, I think, to say that he recognised more quickly than many that the old status quo could never be restored.'[362]

This was especially true in Burma, where he worked with Major-General Aung San, leader of the 'Burma Independence Army', which had been set up and controlled by the Japanese. Mountbatten's aim was to postpone the reimposition of indefinite direct rule in favour of an independent Burma, within the British Commonwealth, but his plans were thwarted by the British Cabinet and when the pre-war governor, Sir Reginald Dorman-Smith, was reinstated.

In Malaya and Singapore, ethnic conflicts, together with Communist influence, created an even more difficult situation. Here, Mountbatten kept civil order whilst again promoting moves towards independence within the Commonwealth, until in the spring of 1946, Malcolm MacDonald took over as Governor-General of the two countries. Siam (Thailand) continued as an independent country, but the problems of Indo–China proved more intractable.

Mountbatten controlled the country south of the 16th parallel with Chiang Kai-shek in charge above. Before the French could restore their colonial empire, Ho Chi Minh and his Viet Minh movement declared the independent Republic of Vietnam. Attempts by Mountbatten to persuade the French to come to terms with the Viet Minh were rejected and he was relieved shortly afterwards to surrender responsibility for the area.

The job of locating and rescuing these POWs and internees was called RAPWI (Recovery of Allied Prisoners of War and Internees) and was one where Dickie and Edwina worked together. The exact location of the POWs and internees had to be established, together with numbers and the extent of their needs, and arrangements had to be made for medical staff, supplies and transport. A key member of Edwina's staff was to be Elizabeth Ward.[363]

Siam, still regarded by the generals as too dangerous to visit (with 150,000 fully armed Japanese at large) was Edwina's first stop. At the Nakhon Pathom hospital camp, where almost 20,000 prisoners had died in 1942 and 1943, she found thousands of men suffering from TB, malnutrition, gangrene and dysentery. Climbing onto a wooden platform, which served as a communal bed, to rousing cheers, she gave them words of comfort. Always direct – she told one set of prisoners they smelt – modest, good-humoured and sympathetic, she immediately tried to improve their quality of life in all sorts of practical ways, such as insisting that relief parcels include packets of condoms as well as calling for magazines, books, playing cards and toys for the children.

In Singapore, she spent hours below deck in the hot and crowded hospital ships, ensuring she spoke to as many of the 600 patients as possible, and at a Leper Hospital she had no inhibitions about shaking hands, touching arms and stroking foreheads. Allied troops had not yet reached Sumatra but, guarded by ex-POWs with rifles but no ammunition, she flew there and toured the camps, as always bringing comfort and hope.

One of those accompanying them was Tom Driberg, a Labour Member of Parliament who, on the recommendation of Frank

Owen, had come out to write a few articles for *Reynolds News* and then been taken on as a temporary adviser. He remembered a formal dinner at Government House, with 40 senior officers in their white mess dress, when Mountbatten had also included four recently repatriated prisoners from Changi Jail (one of them the artist Ronald Searle, later best-known as the creator of the cartoon strip on St Trinian's School), all still in their shabby prison garb. They were the guests of honour and Mountbatten ensured at the end of the evening they were driven back to their camp.

> This incident, I thought, showed the best side of Mountbatten's character – his lack of pomposity, his curiosity about people, his keen sense of the effective gesture, perhaps of public relations. I found him and his wife an unusual and interesting couple: both were extremely good at their jobs – so much so that there was almost a kind of competition between them. At breakfast they would compare the total numbers of British prisoners in the camps whom each of them had spoken to and shaken hands with.[364]

At the end of November, Edwina returned to London. She had made a huge difference and her husband was incredibly proud of her. 'If you weren't my wife, I'd offer you permanent employment in a very high rank on my staff,' he wrote to her for her birthday, 'and I know of no other woman I'd say that to.'[365] In the New Year's Honours list she was awarded a DCVO on the recommendation of the King and Queen. She could now look Dickie in the eye.

Mountbatten was himself offered a barony in the New Year's Honours list, which gave him a seat in the House of Lords. For most people this would have been an offer that could not be refused but Dickie, already of higher precedence as the son of a marquess, was playing for larger stakes. Both Alexander and Montgomery had been made viscounts and he saw no reason why he should not be awarded one as well. Indeed, he argued disingenuously, it was simply downgrading his particular theatre of war. He was also worried that accepting a barony would make the subsequent offer of a viscountcy more difficult. In any case, he pointed out, he would much prefer the Garter or Order of Merit.

Edwina was despatched to bend George VI's ear. 'I have most decided views, which I would prefer her to discuss with you verbally if you can spare the time to see her,' Dickie wrote to him. 'Personally I don't want a peerage & above all would hate to lose the "Louis" from my name.'[366] Another argument was that he did not feel he could accept an honour 'whilst my men are still losing their lives in French Indo China and the Netherlands East Indies. I fear my job is by no means completed.' [367]

The King's private secretary, Tommy Lascelles, was infuriated by Mountbatten's 'somewhat film-starrish attitude towards his proposed barony':

the really fatal blunder would be to omit the name of SACSEA (Supreme Allied Commander, South-East Asia) from a victory honours' list, when the men of SEAC already feel themselves neglected, and that all the credit for victory is being given to 8th Army etc. But his protestations have revived the King's wish that he should have a viscountcy, and I had to go and see Attlee again this afternoon. But Attlee was adamant, basing his view, I am certain, on the advice of the Services, in the persons of Andrew Cunningham and Pug Ismay.[368]

Edwina was again deployed to make Dickie's case to the King, briefed by Peter Murphy. 'Dickie has thought it over and thought it over, and has discussed it with me unendingly; and I think that the attached "A" and "B" really represent his final thoughts on this subject,' Murphy wrote to Edwina from Singapore.[369] In the end, Dickie was offered a viscountcy and took it 'in the National Interest, subject to minor conditions, such as continuing to call myself Lord Louis Mountbatten'.[370]

* * *

In mid-March 1946, Jawaharlal Nehru, as a leading member of the Indian National Congress, was invited to Singapore to meet Indian troops and study the conditions of the large Indian community in Malaya. The British authorities, nervous that he was out to cause trouble, did not feel he should be officially received nor allowed to meet Indian troops. Mountbatten recognised that he might well be India's first Prime Minister and if he was not treated well that British actions would only further ferment anti-British feelings. He insisted that he would meet him at the airport and accompany him into town in his open-topped limo to a St John Ambulance Indian welfare centre, where Edwina would be waiting. What could have been a public relations disaster was turned into a celebration of Anglo-Indian friendship.[371]

All went well until Nehru's arrival at the centre. The delighted crowd rushed him, knocking Edwina over in the process. Jayanto Chaudhuri, a brigadier on Mountbatten's staff, tried to help:

> Trying to be chivalrous, I knelt down beside her and said: 'Lady Mountbatten, can I help you up? Let me give you a hand getting up.' She said: 'Don't be a mug. This is a friendly crowd. If you start giving me a hand, they will all give me a helping hand and they will pull all the clothes off my back, I might tell you that in this heat I have not got very much on.'[372]

Mountbatten and Nehru linked arms and charged the crowd to rescue Edwina, who had 'crawled between the people's legs and had come out at the far end of the room, got on a table and shouted to us that she was all right'.[373] A door was kicked in and eventually the party escaped the mob. It had been an unusual introduction to what would become a crucial relationship. That night, the Mountbattens and Nehru dined together. 'We talked about everything under the sun,' Mountbatten later remembered, 'and that is where our friendship started.'[374]

Mountbatten's time at SEAC had now come to an end. From Singapore the couple flew to Australia, where Dickie had meetings with the Australian Chiefs of Staff to discuss the handover to Australian garrisons in SEAC. When Dickie had last visited 25 years earlier, it had been as an aide to the Prince of Wales. Now he and Edwina were the star attractions, with cheering crowds, civic receptions and countless speeches. Dickie had always enjoyed this sort of attention. Edwina now found she did, too.

In May, they were back in Singapore for the winding up of SEAC, and swearing in of Malcom MacDonald as British Governor-General of the Malayan Union. At their farewell party, a baby elephant appeared carrying an illuminated sign that read 'Goodbye Supremo'.[375]

What were the Mountbattens to do now? The Duke of Gloucester had suggested his cousin succeed him as Governor-General of Australia; George VI thought he might become a Chief of Staff to the Minister of Defence; whilst an old friend, the Maharaja of Bikaner, was keen for him to succeed Archibald Wavell as Viceroy of India, but Dickie's ambitions were still focused on his naval career. 'I really want to go back to the Navy, as you know,' he told Edwina, 'and don't like the idea of governing . . . but if it ever became unavoidable I know that you would make the world's ideal Vicereine!'[376]

CHAPTER 16

Love and Marriage

In the summer of 1946, the Mountbattens returned to London for leave. They were fêted in Paris, where Dickie was invested with the Grand Cross of the Legion of Honour and Croix de Guerre and driven in an open car with outriders up the Champs-Élysées. In London there was another open carriage drive, when he received the Freedom of the City of London. Cambridge gave him an Honorary LLD and Christ's College an Honorary Fellowship, Oxford awarded him a DCL, whilst St Andrew's asked him to be Rector, which he declined.

Further happy news was the engagement in July 1946 of Patricia to one of Dickie's ADCs, John, the 7th Lord Brabourne. John Brabourne's father had been Governor of Bombay and Bengal and briefly served as India's youngest Viceroy in 1938. He had died the following year and the title inherited by John's elder brother, Norton, but he had been executed in 1943, whilst trying to escape from a prison train in Italy.

John Brabourne had been educated at Eton and Oxford and joined the Coldstream Guards aged 17. He had fought in France, been one of the extras in the film *In Which We Serve*, before becoming an ADC to first General William Slim and then Mountbatten. It was in Delhi, where Patricia had been posted with the Wrens in 1943, that she had met her future husband. He had proposed several times until she finally accepted. Even then she had her doubts.

'Subconsciously I suppose I was worried by the fact that my parents had had a difficult marriage for many years and I did not want the same thing to happen to me,' she later explained. 'I desperately wanted a marriage that would last and certainly I did not want to get married thinking if it didn't work out we could simply get divorced, which is what happens a lot of the time now.'[377] She told her father about her reservations, that she cared for Brabourne, but was not 'madly in love' with him. Mountbatten advised her to see it through – they remained married until Brabourne's death in 2005.

There was another complicating factor. The relationship between daughter and father was intense and it would have been difficult for any man to seek to replace it. John Barratt, Mountbatten's secretary, was later to describe how Mountbatten's 'feelings towards her verged on the unhealthy: he worshipped her'.[378] Patricia had early on taken the place of Edwina in his affections. Edwina found it difficult, because of her own childhood, to bond or communicate with her children and would often walk straight past the nursery door at night. Dickie was always there chatting about the day's events or their problems, or reading *Emil and the Detectives* or the Babar books in French, especially to his eldest daughter.

His easy relationship with his children only further stimulated Edwina's jealous nature. As a result, theirs often had to be a furtive relationship, hidden from his wife. A letter written on New Year's Eve a few years later encapsulates the intensity of his emotions about Patricia:

It is close on midnight. Most people are out at parties . . . but I have just finished work and my mind, as always, turns to you. You, yourself, know pretty well all that you have meant to me for the past thirty years, for I have never disguised my feeling from you, but in the years to come, after Mummy and I have both 'passed on' as the euphemistic term goes, I would have liked to feel that there was some record in the bottom of your 'Black Box' of the part you play in my life.

I have sometimes regretted that you turned into such a very lovely and attractive woman because I would certainly have loved you just as much, and very possibly more, if you had remained the ungainly, lanky creature with odd teeth and slightly receding chin that you presented when you first went to school. Physical attraction (by no means unknown to Freud between parents and children) has hardly ever entered into our very remarkable friendship . . . the attraction which you have had for me from the day I first saw you in April 1924 was an almost mystical feeling that you were really a part of me living on in the world.

I wanted a boy, not a girl, as you well know, but I am certain if you had a brother he could never have taken your place because from the day I saw you first as a two month old baby and was allowed to help with you, I have never really had eyes for anyone else.

You know how basically fond I am and always have been of Mummy, you know pretty well about my girlfriends, but none of them have had that magic 'something' which you have . . . . Of course, the miracle of our relationship is that you make me feel truly unselfish and wanting only your happiness. Why else should I have done so much to induce you to marry John when you were wavering? . . .

I have grown so fond of Pammy, few fathers could be fonder of a daughter or miss her more than I miss Pammy now, but the mainspring of my love is that she is *your* sister and *you* love her. Every achievement in life since 1924 has been achieved for you and because of you . . . If in years to come history takes the view that I did well in my jobs, the credit must all go to you. There is always one woman in a man's life and darling – she is you. Bless you always. You'll never really know how much I love you.[379]

Patricia and John Brabourne finally married in Romsey Abbey in October with Princesses Elizabeth and Margaret as bridesmaids, Philip as an usher, the Archbishop of Canterbury officiating and various members of the Royal Family in attendance. The only hiccup was when the bridegroom was temporarily refused entry as he had not been issued a ticket. As always, Mountbatten organised it like a military operation, with a special train from London that served lunch, committees to handle the traffic arrangements for the almost 400 close friends and relations invited to the wedding breakfast at Broadlands, part of it still being used as a hospital, plus the 600 at the reception in Romsey.

It was at the wedding where Princess Elizabeth's closeness to Philip became clear, when a newsreel shot caught a tender glance between the two.[380] Mountbatten had long encouraged the relationship between his nephew and his cousin's daughter. In July 1939, when the Royal Yacht cruised along the south coast and dropped anchor at Dartmouth, it was Mountbatten who had arranged for his nephew (then an 18-year-old cadet at the naval college) to escort the royal party and join them for tea the next day. When the yacht departed, escorted by a collection of sailing, rowing and motorboats, the last to obey the signal to turn back was a young, solitary rower – Philip.

He was to be a regular guest at Broadlands throughout the war, often bringing down his girlfriend of the moment, Osla Benning, a beautiful Canadian-born debutante who was sharing a cottage with Dickie's goddaughter, Sarah Norton, whilst working in a wartime aircraft factory and later in the naval section at Bletchley.[381] It was Mountbatten who had asked Sarah, daughter of Jean Norton, to matchmake for the young prince.

The Conservative MP 'Chips' Channon had noted in his diary in January 1941, 'He is to be our Prince Consort and that is why he is serving in our Navy . . . but I deplore such a marriage. He and Princess Elizabeth are too inter-related.'[382] Three years later, Dickie was writing to the King:

> Personally I hope you can persuade him to stay in your Navy & not go mixing himself up in Greek affairs. He can't even talk Greek & his outlook & training are entirely English. I don't believe Greece will remain a monarchy for long – they never have – & an exiled Greek Prince is a sorry sort of a job (look what it did to Andrea!) particularly for an outstanding young man like Philip. He is happy in the RN & can easily rise to the top on merit as my father did.[383]

One of the reasons Dickie was keen his nephew should serve in the Royal Navy was to help anglicise him. The plotting and romance continued. In April 1944, Philip was taking soundings from family members on whether he should propose; the following month, after Dickie and Edwina had dined with George VI, Mountbatten wrote:

> I think your plan of going ahead now with Philip's British nationality & a permanent commission in the Royal Navy excellent from every point of view as it leaves the question of Lilibet open. I have drafted out a paper, which I enclose, & from which I suggest you re-draft a paper of your own. Will

you please let me have a copy of the final paper & decision before I go so that I can talk to Georgie about this in Cairo & Philip in Ceylon when I leave in a week's time. I take it that the First Lord as well as Foreign Secretary & Pm will have to be consulted.[384]

By August, however, the King was getting cold feet. 'I have been thinking the matter over since our talk and I have come to the conclusion that we are going too fast.'[385] He felt the schemers should concentrate simply on nationality for the moment. 'I am sure this is the best way of doing this particular operation, don't you? Though I know you like to get things settled at once, once you have an idea in mind.'[386]

Mountbatten continued to push, writing to the King later that month after he had seen Philip in Cairo and he had 'signed the application for British Nationality and revocation to the throne of Greece':[387]

Thus the preliminary steps have all been taken and only the legal formalities now remain to be completed. I am quite sure that all this must be through & completed before the Armistice with Germany to ensure the minimum publicity & the best 'reception', but I am NOT trying to hurry you this time.[388]

'Philip entirely understood that the proposal was not connected with any question of marrying Lilibet,' wrote Mountbatten to his mother. 'Bertie had insisted on this – & Philip was quite happy about it . . . though there is no doubt that he would very much like to one of these days & I think realised that until this preliminary step had been taken he could not even be considered.'[389]

Eventually, having sown the seeds, Mountbatten and the King

realised they should let the relationship between the couple take its course. 'The young people appear genuinely devoted and I think after the war it is very likely to occur,' wrote Mountbatten to his mother in February 1945, 'but any "talk" now would undoubtedly make the situation much more difficult for Philip.'[390]

* * *

The Mountbatten marriage dynamics had now returned to their pre-war position, with Dickie as busy as ever, but Edwina searching to fill her time. Having experienced the satisfaction of a busy and useful life, she was now at a loss. She had outgrown her pre-war friends and life and had no role nor close intimates. Bunny was married and Jean Norton, one of her closest friends, had died unexpectedly in the spring of 1945. Into the vacuum came a new lover.

Edwina had met the conductor Malcolm Sargent in the 1930s, but the relationship had only developed during the war. Six years older than her, funny and quick-witted, always immaculately turned-out and attractive to women, he had become a well-known and popular public figure through his appearance on the BBC's *The Brains Trust* – it is estimated that almost 30 per cent of the population listened to the radio programme – where a panel of guests answered questions put by the listeners.

As conductor of the London Philharmonic, he had made a tour of ten cities, 'the Blitz tour', and it was at one of these concerts at the Albert Hall in January 1941 that Edwina had met him again. Sargent, unhappily married and mourning his daughter, who had died aged 18 in 1944, had a penchant for society women – and the two lonely souls became occasional lovers.[391]

Sargent became her new project. She attended all his concerts and helped raise money for his charities. He, in turn, provided the emotional support that Dickie, focused on his own activities, not least writing his report on his time as Supreme Allied Commander, could not always give her.

Dickie was now all set to resume his naval career. In the New Year, he was due to start the Senior Officers' Technical Course at Portsmouth in preparation for a new posting to Malta. Arrangements were being made to rent a house, when in December, shortly after being admitted to the Order of the Garter, he was summoned to Downing Street with the offer of a new job – the most important of his whole career.

CHAPTER 17

A Poisoned Chalice

On 17 December, George VI wrote in his diary amidst concerns about the current Viceroy of India, Wavell:

> The PM is wondering who to send there as Viceroy instead &
> suggested Dickie M who he said has tact & gets on well with
> people. I told Attlee DM must have concrete orders as to what
> he is to do. Is he to lead the retreat out of India or is he to
> work for the reconciliation of Hindus & Muslims?[392]

Indian self-rule had been promised by the British Government since 1917, but it had been slow to come. The Government of India Act 1935 had increased the number of voters to 35 million and created 11 British–Indian provinces with limited autonomy as the first step towards a federal India, to include the 565 Princely States who owed their allegiance to the British Crown.

The plan had always been for a united subcontinent, but from 1936 a sectarian element entered the equation. The leader of the All-India Muslim League, Muhammad Ali Jinnah, once a believer in Muslim cooperation with Congress, began to argue for a separate Muslim 'nation' to ensure the protection of the Muslim minority. This new state of Pakistan would be made up of the five Muslim majority provinces: the Punjab, Afghan frontier, Kashmir, Sind and Balochistan.

The Second World War further complicated matters. Congress taking advantage of British vulnerability decided it would not support the British war effort, withdrew its representatives from the 11 provincial governments, and mounted a campaign of civil disobedience. Into the vacuum stepped Jinnah's Muslims, who agreed to support the British war effort, thereby consolidating the Muslim League's position at the expense of Congress.

In the summer of 1945, Labour came to power determined to withdraw from India. The following March, a Cabinet Mission arrived against the backdrop of recent elections where Congress had won seats in the largely Hindu provinces and the Muslim League had taken seats in Muslim areas. It proposed a federal India, but with powers at the centre covering defence, foreign affairs, communications and the currency. Accepted by the Muslim League, it was rejected by the Congress Party.

On 16 August 1946, the Muslim League had called for a 'Direct Action Day' to protest against Hindu refusal to accept a federation. The four days of communal rioting that followed led to 20,000 deaths or serious injuries in Calcutta alone, and revealed the inability of the British administration to keep order and the impossibility of a united India.

'I have tried everything I know to solve the problem of handing over India to its people, and I can see no light,' Wavell told Mountbatten. 'I have only one solution, which I call Operation Madhouse – withdrawal of the British province by province, beginning with women and children, then civilians, then the army.'[393] Without another four or five divisions, he told the Cabinet, he could not hold India for much longer. He envisaged withdrawal by March 1948. 'Wavell was tired, and could make no progress,' John

Christie, Wavell's private secretary, later noted. 'He had maintained the political dialogue, but he lacked the flair, the zest and perhaps the imagination to break the deadlock.'[394]

It was against this backdrop that the decision to replace Wavell was taken with a new face and policy. Mountbatten had first been mooted in 1943 as one of four possible candidates – Anthony Eden, R.A. Butler and Archibald Wavell. 'Winston wouldn't have RAB because he said (in rather coarse language) that he didn't have the right appearance to carry off the position of Viceroy,' Julian Amery told Mountbatten. 'Your name was certainly considered but my father told me that it had been decided that you were to go to another job of the greatest importance in the war.'[395]

Stafford Cripps, who had been part of the 1946 Cabinet Mission, had hoped to be appointed himself and Pug Ismay, Churchill's wartime Chief of Staff, had also been considered. In January 1946, Mountbatten was again suggested, this time by a former Vicereine, Lady Willingdon, and also Stafford Cripps, probably at the suggestion of the secretary of the India League in London, Krishna Menon.

Mountbatten had several obvious attractions: his royal connections would appeal to the Princes and he had already established good relations with Nehru; he was young, dynamic, imaginative, charming, apolitical, had knowledge of India from his time at SEAC, looked the part and his pragmatic and liberal policies dealing with the nationalist risings in South East Asia appealed to Attlee. The Prime Minister wrote in his memoirs, 'he had imagination, sympathy and tremendous drive. I knew, also that he had, in Lady Mountbatten, a wife who would admirably assist him.'[396]

Mountbatten, keen to resume his naval career, was worried that a further delay in resuming it would put an end to it and felt he was being handed, after SEAC, another poisoned chalice. Edwina wanted to concentrate on her relief work, and on restoring Classiebawn, a home on the west coast of Ireland she had inherited from her father, and had no wish to be separated from friends and family again. She had had a partial hysterectomy at the end of February that left her suffering from neuralgia, which was exacerbated by plane flights. Her diary often had comments such as 'feeling like death'.

This reluctance allowed Mountbatten to lay down a series of conditions – perhaps not as many as he later claimed, but still more than his predecessors – before he would accept: his naval career must not be jeopardised by the new appointment; he must go at the invitation of the Indian politicians, rather than be imposed on them; the present Secretary of State for India, Pethick-Lawrence, should be replaced by Billy Listowel; he must have continued use of the York MW102 aeroplane that he had used at SEAC, and he must be able to choose his own staff.[397]

The most important choice was Pug Ismay as, in effect, his *Chef de Cabinet*. Others included Sir Eric Miéville, who had been private secretary to Lord Willingdon as Governor-General before becoming assistant private secretary to George V, and several former colleagues from Combined Operations and SEAC: Ronald Brockman as personal secretary; Alan Campbell-Johnson as press attaché, Vernon Erskine-Crum as conference secretary, and Peter Murphy as general adviser and speech writer. Edwina brought with her two women with whom she had worked during the war, Elizabeth Ward and Muriel Watson.

Whilst these negotiations were going on, Wavell had not been told by Attlee that he was to be replaced. Only on 13 February, two days after Mountbatten finally accepted the offer, was he informed. He plaintively wrote that his daughter's wedding with 800 guests was the following week, asking if the announcement could be made afterwards. On 20 February Mountbatten's appointment was announced to both Houses of Parliament.

On 18 March, the Mountbattens held a farewell cocktail party at the Royal Automobile Club – Dickie was president – for 700, followed by a dinner with the Brabournes and Prince Philip. Noël Coward, who attended, wrote in his diary, 'I wonder if they will come back alive. I think that if it is possible to make a go of it in the circumstances they will, but I have some forebodings.'[398] It was a concern Mountbatten himself shared: 'We shall be incredibly unpopular and the odds are we shall end up with bullets in our backs.'[399]

Two days later, the Mountbattens, including Pamela, were driven to Northolt, where they were seen off by, amongst others, Prince Philip and Malcolm Sargent. 'It is the definite objective of His Majesty's Government to obtain a unitary Government for British India and the Indian States if possible within the British Commonwealth, through the medium of a Constituent Assembly, set up and run in accordance with the Cabinet Mission's plan,' Attlee had told him. 'The date fixed for the transfer of power is a flexible one to within one month: but you should aim at 1 June 1948 as the effective date for the transfer of power.'[400]

On 22 March, the Mountbattens arrived in Delhi and were driven to the gates of the Viceroy's House, where they transferred to an open landau and continued with a cavalry escort. Awaiting them on the steps, along with bagpipers of the Royal Scots Fusiliers, were the Wavells and a dismounted Sikh Bodyguard in black and gold turbans, scarlet uniforms with white breeches and shiny black thigh boots.

The first night was spent with Wavell briefing the Mountbattens. 'The problems are quite horrifying,' Dickie wrote to his mother the next day, 'but I feel we shall find a way of surmounting them

& that Edwina will be a real help to me in this task.'[401] She quickly sought to become châtelaine of her new manor. 'No detail was left unexamined or unquestioned,' her daughter Pamela later remembered, 'the timing and cost of meals, the state of the servants' quarters, the condition of the linen and plate, the management of the house, the gardens, the stables, the school, the clinic and I would most often accompany her.'[402]

It was a major undertaking. Sir Edwin Lutyens' Viceroy's House, which had only been completed 18 years earlier, had 377 rooms, one and a half miles of corridors and occupied five acres. It consisted of a central block and four wings on four floors and every sort of Indian marble and stone or variety of wood had been used. In the basement was a fully equipped cinema and theatre, a modern printing press, pump-room for the air-conditioning machines, carpenter's and electrical workshops, storerooms and a laundry. The four large gardens covered a further 175 acres and included gardens in the Moghul and Italianate style, waterways, cricket grounds, a nine-hole golf course, a freshwater swimming-pool and a pack of hounds of the Royal Delhi Hunt, who were accommodated in kennels adjoining the Viceregal stables. Almost 6,000 people worked in the house or in the four large gardens.

Dickie worked from a small study, which he had painted light green with an inscription framed in leather on his desk:

There are four kinds of officers: hard-working and intelligent; lazy and intelligent, lazy and stupid and hard-working and stupid. The first are fit for top staff appointments, the second for the highest commands, the third can be tolerated, but the fourth type could prove dangerous and should be instantly removed.[403]

He never said which he considered himself.

On 24 March, Dickie was sworn in as the 45th and last Viceroy, accompanied by Edwina, in the magnificent Durbar Hall with its 180-foot dome supported by tall yellow-marble columns. The two walked in slow procession towards the two gold-and-scarlet thrones standing on a semi-circular dais at one end of the hall, Dickie wearing the pale-blue ermine-trimmed robe of the Grand Master of the Star of India over the full-dress uniform of a vice-admiral, Edwina in a long gown of ivory brocade, across which was the delicate pink ribbon of the Crown of India.

As they took their seats, trumpets and artillery sounded, and in every British garrison throughout India the 31-gun Viceregal salute was fired as the Viceroy's flag was hoisted atop the dome. Dickie chose to speak briefly. 'I am under no illusion about the difficulty of my task,' he told the assembled audience. 'I shall need the greatest goodwill of the greatest possible number and am asking India today for that goodwill.'[404] The whole ceremony, the first to be filmed and photographed, had lasted 15 minutes. Within half an hour of its start, the Mountbattens had shed their finery and were at work.

Alive to the need for pomp and circumstance, they had also decided to adopt a more informal style than their predecessors. Court circulars now simply announced the people they had seen. 'It's not by words or pompous notices that one keeps up the prestige of the Crown and one's country,' Edwina announced, 'but I think by behaviour and example.'[405]

Every week the Mountbattens held two garden parties, three or four luncheons for 30, and two or three larger dinner parties, each comprised of at least 50 per cent Indians with their dietary preferences indicated by a different coloured ribbon on the back of their chair.[406] Indians were now appointed as ADCs. Notes were kept of every meeting and circulated daily.

There were long 18-hour days, which began at dawn when Dickie and Pamela would ride together on the ridge above Delhi with a couple of armed bodyguards, sometimes with Mountbatten practising his polo swing along the way. His younger daughter had become his new confidante, with Patricia now married and living in the Chester Street house.

Edwina was now going through the menopause and Dickie found himself the butt of her various mood swings. Often he would spend hours in the evening trying to soothe her. 'My father would try to comfort her, but he just didn't know how,' Pamela recalled. 'He was very patient with her, but he couldn't cope with tears and – like a bull in a china shop – he always seemed to say the wrong thing and put his foot in it, when all he really wanted to do was help.'[407] Edwina had hoped for a quieter life after the war. 'My neuralgia has been frightful, but I still hope for the best,' she confided to her diary.[408] She told Pamela she realised, 'it's a great adventure, which it is, and I love the work and my Indians and a lot of the interest, but how I long for lovely Broadlands and sweet little Chester Street and the cosy and simple life.'[409]

She had identified women and welfare issues as an area she would support. One of her priorities was to win the trust of influential female figures such as: Gandhi's secretary, Rajkumari Amrit Kaur, who would become the first woman to hold Cabinet rank as Minister of Health after the transfer of power; Patel's daughter, Maniben; Jinnah's sister, Fatima; and Nehru's sister, Mrs Vijaya Lakshmi Patel. Pamela meanwhile worked two evenings a week in the Allied Forces Canteen, but also accompanied her mother to visit schools and hospitals.

Many Indians remained suspicious of the new Viceroy. 'Mountbatten said that he was forced to accept the Viceroyalty of India by His Majesty the King. There can be no bigger untruth,'

wrote Shahid Haid, Sir Claude Auchinleck's private secretary, in his
diary on the day of the swearing-in:

> It is common knowledge that he wanted it badly to enhance
> his political standing and he worked towards it. He established
> close contact with Nehru knowing that he would one day
> become the Prime Minister of India. It was the efforts of
> Krishna Menon which further cemented their friendship
> . . . According to common gossip, Mountbatten has come
> to partition India as quickly as possible, irrespective of the
> consequences – sort out the Princes; take all possible measures
> to keep the two countries in the Commonwealth; ensure that
> Britain's strategic and mercantile interests in South Asia are
> not jeopardised and, finally, keep the Indian leaders under
> pressure and give them no time to think.[410]

Each morning Mountbatten's key advisers – Pug Ismay, Eric
Miéville, George Abell for the Punjab, Ian Scott speaking for the
future Pakistan, John Christie for Bengal and Vernon Erskine-Crum
– would meet to review the previous 24 hours and Mountbatten
would use them as a sounding board for his various tactics. They
were later joined by V.P. Menon, the Reforms Commissioner, who
would give an insight into 'Indian thinking'.

One of Mountbatten's priorities was to get to know and win
the trust of the key players – Nehru and Gandhi representing the
Hindu community, Sardar Patel of the Congress Party, and Jinnah
and Liaqat Ali Khan for the Muslims. Each was invited for a one-to-
one chat in his study, generally of an hour followed by 15 minutes
with a stenographer to take down the salient details.[411]

Mountbatten's first visitor was Nehru and, helped by the
Singapore meeting the year before, relations were good from the

start. Indeed, it was not only Dickie, but also Edwina who instantly warmed to the lonely and charismatic widower. Hamid noted in his diary within ten days of the Mountbattens' arrival that 'according to Menon, Nehru's relationship with Lady Mountbatten is sufficiently close to have raised many eyebrows.'[412]

The two certainly spent much time together during the first week and there is evidence of an immediate intimacy. Photographs of the time show her looking lovingly at him at a Red Cross meeting. At the Mountbattens' first garden party, Nehru sat cross-legged at Edwina's feet during a dance recital with too few chairs for guests, and after the party she returned to his house, unaccompanied by her husband but with her daughter, for a nightcap.[413]

The senior Congress politician, Maulana Azad, felt that whilst Nehru was 'greatly impressed by Lord Mountbatten . . . perhaps an even greater was the influence of Lady Mountbatten. She is not only extremely intelligent, but had a most attractive and friendly temperament. She admired her husband greatly and in many cases tried to interpret his thought to those who would not at first agree with him.'[414]

Nehru also made an immediate impression, not least on Pamela:

> not only by his beautiful speaking voice and impeccable dress, a white buttoned-down tunic with the famous Nehru collar, jodhpurs and a rosebud in his buttonhole, but also by his warmth and charm, which enveloped me from our first handshake. Watching him interact with others, I could see that he reacted to things instantly, was quick to laugh or make you laugh, and always interested in what you had to say. I realised that both Gandhi and Nehru were the most extraordinary people I had ever met.[415]

On 31 March, it was Gandhi's turn. Though he held little political power, he was an important influencer. His calculated gesture of putting his hand on Edwina's shoulder to steady himself sent out signals to India and the world that this was a couple with whom he could do business.

The Mountbattens, however, found it difficult to establish any sort of personal rapport with the austere and intransigent Jinnah, who they did not meet until 5 April and then made a point of seeing every day until 10 April. Dickie, never sure whether Jinnah's demand for five Muslim provinces was a negotiating play or non-negotiable, was to call him at various times 'a bastard, a dolt, a clot, a psychopathic and hopeless case, a one-man band, an evil genius, a fool, a cold and repressed person'.[416] Edwina encountered the same problem when she had tea with Jinnah's sister in late April:

> She seemed almost fanatical at times in her attitude . . . Like Mr Jinnah, she has, of course a persecution mania, and is obviously convinced that the Hindu intends to subjugate and dominate the Muslim completely.[417]

It quickly became clear that Jinnah would not accept the Cabinet Mission Plan and that transferring power in June 1948 would be too late. 'The situation is everywhere electric, and I get the feeling that the mine may go up at any moment,' wrote Ismay to his wife Darry within days of his arrival. 'It is not reason or logic that is at the back of it all, but sheer emotionalism, and emotionalism is the hardest thing to contend with. There is very little anti-British feeling, but the inter-communal hatred is a devouring flame.'[418] In the Punjab, Governor's rule had been imposed by Sir Evan Jenkins after Hindus and Sikhs had refused to cooperate with the Muslim

League. There was also violence in North-West Frontier Province, where direct rule was also being considered by the governor, Sir Olaf Caroe.

Ismay was later to write in his memoirs:

> I had thought before I left England that a period of fifteen months was far too short a time in which to complete arrangements for the transfer of power. But I had not been three weeks in India before I was convinced that so far from being too short, it was too long. The principal reason for this change of mind was the realisation that communal bitterness had grown to incredible proportions since I was last in India.[419]

He quickly realised that with independence and partition, the police could no longer be relied on to operate in a non-sectarian manner. Without a dispassionate police force, there was little hope of keeping order except through the British Army. Indian Political Intelligence was also now run by an Indian, who would not share it with the new Viceroy.

Ismay continued, 'A second reason for my conviction that we could not continue to bear responsibility until June 1948 was that the administration of the country was going to the dogs.'[420] There had been no recruitment to the Indian Civil Service since the beginning of the war and numbers had fallen from a peak of over 1,000 to under 500. The Coalition Government was divided on communal lines and refused to work together. The Muslim League was in charge of Finance and rejected every proposal put forward by the Congress members of the Executive Council. 'The only point on which there was agreement,' Ismay noted, 'was that the British should quit India as soon as possible':[421]

They were torn with suspicions of each other and of the British. They read sinister motives into the most innocent proposals. They worked themselves into ungovernable rages with anyone who disagreed with them. They did not hesitate to wreck any plan that was not in entire accord with their own desires, but admitted no responsibility for finding any practical alternative.[422]

'The scene here is one of unrelieved gloom,' Mountbatten reported to Attlee on 1 April:

The country is in a most unsettled state. There are communal riots and troubles in the Punjab, the North-West Frontier Province, Bihar, Calcutta, Bombay, UP and even here in Delhi. In the Punjab all parties are seriously preparing for civil war, and of these by far the most business like are the Sikhs. I am convinced that a fairly quick decision would appear to be the only way to convert the Indian minds from their present emotionalism to stark realism and to counter the disastrous spread of strife.[423]

To the King the same day he concluded, 'that unless I act quickly I may well find the real beginnings of a civil war on my hands.'[424]

CHAPTER 18

A Tryst with Destiny

Even before Mountbatten had arrived, Indian politicians had accepted that partition was inevitable, not least because of Jinnah's insistence on a separate Muslim state and the paralysis in the Executive Council. Mountbatten's challenge was to find a plan that all would accept. On 11 April, Ismay sent V.P. Menon 'the bare bones of a possible plan for the transfer of power' asking him to make comments, 'put some flesh upon it' and 'work out a rough timetable'.[425]

'Plan Balkan' argued for the partition of Punjab, Bengal & Assam (a separate plebiscite in the North-West Frontier Province), with the provinces working out their own constitutions and with a Central Government dealing with defence, foreign affairs and communications. Mountbatten argued that it had to be the Indians themselves who would take the final decision on their future.

A few days later, the provincial governors met to discuss the plan. They agreed the transfer of power must be quick to avoid the country disintegrating and accepted, with regret, there was no alternative to partition. Sir Olaf Caroe, Governor of the North-West Frontier, and Sir Evan Jenkins, Governor of the Punjab, warned Mountbatten that once partition was announced it would be 'followed by an immediate blow-up. There was therefore a military problem of considerable magnitude.'[426]

Against these threats, British administration was breaking down. Sir John Colville, Governor of Bombay, said he had only 22 ICS officers to manage a province of about 30 million people and estimated there were 12 private armies operating, which numbered more than 400,000, from the 7,000 in Abdul Ghaffar Khan's Red Shirts to the 100,000 in the Hindu Mahasabha, the nationalist movement that proclaimed India should be for Hindus.

The North-West Frontier presented a particular problem, as 90 per cent of its population were Muslim, but it had elected a Congress government in 1945. Both factions therefore laid claim to it. At the end of April, Mountbatten decided he should visit it – one of only two provincial visits he would make during his Viceroyalty. The evening before, Government House had been invaded and a shot fired through a window. A crowd of Pathans, all supporters of the Muslim League, awaited his arrival. Caroe requested he should make an appearance to try and diffuse the situation. Edwina insisted on accompanying him.

From a railway embankment, hand-in-hand and silhouetted against the sky, the couple looked down on 70,000 people, any of whom, they were aware, could have killed them with a bomb or bullet.[427] By chance, they were dressed simply in bush shirts, the green matching the Pakistan national colour. 'I neither spoke nor waved to them but simply stood there,' Mountbatten later reported.[428] There was a moment's silence and then cries of 'Mountbatten Zindabad!' (Long Live Mountbatten!) The shouting was too great for a speech, so for nearly an hour the Mountbattens simply stood waving to the crowd.[429] The situation had been defused – but for how long?

Whilst Dickie and Pamela returned to Delhi, Edwina stayed on for four days, travelling 1,500 miles by air, jeep and on foot to see for herself the extent of the damage from the disturbances. In one town, Kahuta, a Moslem horde had overwhelmed the town, raping the women before killing them and burning the town down. For Dickie it was confirmation that independence needed to come quickly, for Edwina an indication of the challenges that might soon be faced in terms of humanitarian aid. She was immediately galvanised into action, writing to officials recommending various practical measures, including setting up health clinics in refugee camps. She had found a role for herself again, no longer simply as an appendage to her husband.

Dickie had no illusions about the problems that lay ahead, not least 'a great deal of trouble on the Frontier'.[430] He continued:

The more I look at the problems of India the more I realise that all this partition business is sheer madness and is going to reduce the economic efficiency of the whole country immeasurably. No one would ever induce me to agree to it were it not for this fantastic communal madness that has seized everybody and leaves no other course open.[431]

At the beginning of May, Ismay therefore presented the new plan in London. It allowed for each of the 11 provinces to decide their own future, Bengal and the Punjab to choose being split between India and Pakistan, to join one country entirely, or go it alone. Within a week, it had been approved by the Cabinet. The aim was to release the text 24 hours before Indian leaders next met on 17 May, thereby reducing the amount of time they could suggest amendments.

On 6 May, Dickie, Edwina, Pamela and Peter Murphy left to spend a few days relaxing in Simla – Edwina had suffered from bad neuralgia on the North-West Frontier and Dickie was 'recovering from a bad go of Delhi belly'.[432] Three days later, they were joined at the Viceregal weekend house, another 1,000 feet higher near the village of Mashobra, by Nehru, who entertained them by standing on his head and showing them how to walk backwards uphill.

Encouraged by the relaxed atmosphere and keen to have Nehru's views on the plan, Dickie gave Nehru his proposed plan to read as he was going to bed. His response was immediate and negative, arguing that the plan would 'Balkanise' India, creating a series of independent states at loggerheads with each other. Mountbatten thought Nehru had accepted the plan; Nehru claimed he had never properly been shown it. 'It is clear the whole of this sorry postponement has been due to over-trustfulness and impatience,' wrote John Christie in his diary on 14 May.[433] It had been a humiliation – Mountbatten had told the Cabinet the plan was acceptable to the Indian leaders – but at least he had averted a greater embarrassment. Soon Dickie, who could well have been finished, was congratulating himself that he had followed his hunch.

V.P. Menon now came up with a solution, one which saved face for both countries and Britain. Power would be handed over to two central governments, each with dominion status and a governor-general, and each with its own constituent assembly. If both countries were members of the Commonwealth, then some form of unity would be preserved. It would make independence smoother and encourage British civil servants and soldiers to stay on. It would also reassure the Princes and bring them to the negotiating table. According to Auchinleck's secretary, there was also a strategic element for the Chiefs of Staff:

In case of war with Russia, they could have strategic bases and other facilities in the North-West of the subcontinent. Besides, it will allow them the use of the Muslims' manpower and the goodwill and support of the other Muslim States. It will also ensure the independence and integrity of Afghanistan. At the same time it will have a stabilising effect on India and keep her on the right path.[434]

The plan, now labelled 'Plan Partition', ticked all the boxes providing for an early transfer of power, retained the essential unity of India and gave Jinnah his desired Pakistan. Edwina was not part of the discussions, but her persuasive powers were deployed by Dickie to bring round Nehru, who saw membership of the Commonwealth as at odds with his view that India should be a sovereign republic. 'We have made real friends with him and whatever else happens, I feel this friendship is sincere and will last,' wrote Dickie about the four days Nehru had spent with them.[435] Edwina had saved her husband's career.

Mountbatten won approval of the new plan and left to sell it to a bemused Cabinet – so much for his claimed plenipotentiary powers – who felt they had only recently agreed another plan. Whilst Dickie saw various ministers, especially Churchill, who as opposition leader was crucial to support the new legislation through Parliament, Edwina caught up with Malcolm Sargent and spent a few days at Nada's villa in the South of France. The plan now cleared by the Cabinet, the Mountbattens returned to sell it to the Indians.

At 10.00 a.m. on 2 June, a few days after returning to Delhi, Mountbatten called the Indian leaders together and gave out copies of the 'Immediate Transfer of Power', asking for their reactions by midnight. With minor quibbles, Congress, their dream of a united India in tatters, agreed but Jinnah, who had achieved his separate if 'moth-eaten' Pakistan, was reiterating his demands: a Pakistan with Punjab and Bengal undivided, and an 800-mile corridor linking East and West Pakistan. He said he needed a week to secure the support of the Council of the All-India Muslim League.

It looked like the plan would be defeated yet again, as Congress had only accepted on the basis that the Muslim League would simultaneously agree. Mountbatten then asked if Jinnah, who appeared prepared to lose his dream of Pakistan, would allow the Viceroy to say he had his support. The Muslim League leader nodded imperceptibly.

On 4 June, Dickie announced his plan at a news conference for 300 journalists. Speaking without notes for 45 minutes, Mountbatten outlined the plan and answered questions. The message was clear. Indians had wanted independence and partition. They must make it work themselves. Asked when Independence might come, he paused for a moment and then almost casually – this detail was not included in the summary sent to London – said 15 August.[436] It left 72 days to take the required bill through Parliament and divide a continent.

Francis Ingall, an Indian Army officer, was at dinner with the Mountbattens when Partition was brought up:

'It all seems so sudden . . .' someone remarked. There was a silence; everyone was waiting for the Viceroy's reaction. Lord Mountbatten smoothly agreed that it was perhaps rather 'sudden', but went on to say that in his experience that was the best way to get things done. 'You give your staff a plan,' he said, 'and ask how long they need to put the plan into operation. Let us say they estimate four weeks. Then you tell them, "Do it in two!" Everyone is shocked into action and you surprise your enemy.' Whereupon Ingall's voice was heard to say, 'And who is your enemy, sir?'[437]

The Indian Independence Bill created two separate Cabinets and administrations for the two countries. All the government posts, including the police, army, judiciary, postal system and civil service, would have to be split between the two countries and their assets divided – but for Pakistan it was the greater challenge, as everything had to be created from scratch. There were almost a million people working on Indian railways, with over 150,000 who wanted to transfer between the countries. There was no way this could be done in the time available.

Apart from dividing human resources, there was all the equipment that had to be split, down to who received the last trombone in the Lahore police band. The cash balances and public debt had to be apportioned, with the relative contributions and responsibilities between the two countries much disputed. Banking had always been the preserve of non-Muslims, principally because the lending of money for profit is forbidden under Islamic law. It was agreed the Reserve Bank of India would handle Pakistan's financial affairs until October 1948 and the existing Indian currency would remain in use in both countries until March 1948 – but by December 1947 the system had broken down as a result of a series of disputes.

The Andaman Islands in the Bay of Bengal were used as a penal colony. Congress felt that they belonged to India, the Muslim League wanted them as a refuelling point between East and West Pakistan, whilst British service chiefs argued for them remaining a Commonwealth naval base. And what would happen to assets overseas, such as India House and the treasures of the India Office?

Shahid Hamid, like many, could see the problems of this speeded-up transfer:

The pace is unrealistic. I think he is prepared to accept bloodshed and human miseries. Everyone can see the tragedy looming. Strangely enough, Mountbatten does not see it. Maybe he could not care less. One has a feeling that he wants to please his bosses in the United Kingdom and get out before a greater mess is created. Then he can blame all the politicians for the disaster . . . Mountbatten is impetuous and a hustler and gives decisions on the spot. He possesses incurable optimism and is over-sensitive to criticism which hurts his vanity. That is his weakest point. He is not prepared to listen . . . Jenkins, the Governor of Punjab, has sent hair-raising reports of the disorders which may follow. Mountbatten is paying no attention to them.[438]

Amongst those also telling him that the transfer could not be achieved in that time were Nehru, Congress politicians, and Mountbatten's own staff, such as Eric Miéville, Pug Ismay and Claude Auchinleck. The Viceroy ignored them. Could there have been a more personal reason for his rush? Marital relations with Edwina by June were even more strained than ever. She was anxious to leave India and ever more critical of her husband. 'Perhaps, if he could carry out the transfer of power swiftly and efficiently enough,' Alex von Tunzelmann has suggested, 'he might still save his marriage.'[439]

One of the biggest headaches was splitting the Indian Army. Clearly, each country had to have its own army, but to divide it in such a short time would be almost impossible – the Commander-in-Chief, Claude Auchinleck, thought it would take three years – and it did mean that, should there be communal violence, there was no independent body to maintain law and order. Ismay was concerned that 'these magnificent units were to be mutilated' and argued:

Why not divide the Army on numerical lines in the first instance, India getting two-thirds and Pakistan one third? Later on, when things were more settled it might be found more expedient to transfer the Hindu element in the Pakistan

Army to India and vice versa . . . Jinnah was adamant. He said he would refuse to take over power on 15 August unless he had an army of appropriate strength and predominantly Muslim composition under his control.[440]

The Joint Defence Committee to monitor the division of the armed forces was therefore set up on 30 June under Sir Chandulal Trivedi, a former secretary of the War Department and a Hindu, but also a close friend of Liaquat Ali Khan of the Muslim League, so it had Muslim support. The decision was made to split along religious lines, but that ignored personal wishes. There were, for example, many non-Muslims who considered provinces allocated to Pakistan to be home. Many could not decide or succumbed under communal pressure. And then there was the question of British troops, many of whom could not wait to be demobbed.

'My own view is that we should withdraw them immediately the transfer of power,' wrote Mountbatten in June to Archie Nye, Governor of Madras:

There is no reason to anticipate a movement specially directed against the British after the transfer of power and a handful of British troops would be no special security against sporadic disturbance in difficult parts of the country due, perhaps, to a general weakening of the administration.[441]

Edwina's role was to ensure that all the medical and social welfare organisations were prepared once the British had left. Throughout June and July, she brought various groups together, ensuring that facilities were ready, finances sorted and priorities identified. There was an appeal for nurses and midwives and a campaign to recruit over 14,000 health visitors to deal with tuberculosis. A major achievement was ensuring, through an appeal to Nehru, that the Nursing Council Bill, which regulated nursing care and gave nurses an honours degree from the College of Nursing (and had been stuck in the Legislature since 1943), was passed.

On 18 July, Dickie and Edwina celebrated their silver wedding anniversary, where they were presented with an inscribed silver salver by their staff. Ninety-five people came to dinner, including Nehru, Jinnah, the Cabinet and various Princes, and there was Indian music and dances. The strains of the heavy workload and Edwina's menopause, however, meant the marriage remained strained.

Another concern for Mountbatten was the future of the 565 Princely States. They covered some two-fifths of the subcontinent, made up a quarter of the population and were the direct responsibility of the British Crown, rather than the Government in Delhi. The citizens were not British subjects like other Indians, but 'British protected persons'. In return for acknowledging British 'paramountcy' through individual treaties, their defence, foreign policy and communications were the responsibility of the British.

Within their own borders, the Princes wielded absolute power over the lives of their subjects, making and enforcing their own civil and criminal laws, directing their own administration, levying their own taxes and customs, frequently minting their own currency and issuing their own stamps, but they varied enormously in wealth, size and importance. Many had preferred to spend their riches on women, horses, cars and gambling, rather than their states, with the result that many Princely States remained like medieval kingdoms, whilst others, like Mysore, were progressive and efficient.

The Princes had destroyed the central government provision of the 1935 Act by refusing to enter a federation and they remained a problem, one which Mountbatten had ignored until the date of transfer had been fixed. The Cabinet Mission Plan, arguing that British obligations lapsed at independence, had simply left them to strike their own arrangements with any successor governments or governments. Now with an Independence date set, some of the states declared that they would opt for individual independence, which would destroy the administrative infrastructure.

On 25 July, the Chamber of Princes assembled in Delhi – some 25 rulers and 74 representatives of the lesser states. Dickie, resplendent in full uniform with all his decorations, in a meeting capped at two hours, worked all his charms to bring them on board. When one representative claimed not to have received instructions on what to do, Mountbatten theatrically picked up a glass paperweight, looked into it and after a dramatic silence announced that the Maharajah had asked him to sign the Instrument of Accession. Three days later, Mountbatten gave a party for the Princes. Those who had not signed an instrument of accession were very publicly taken aside for a 'friendly' chat with the Viceroy.

Though the option of becoming independent was offered, the Princes were encouraged, through a mixture of charm, bribes of ambassadorships and threats, for the sake of an integrated India and Pakistan, to join either India or Pakistan, whilst the continent remained under British rule. An extra sweetener was that the two countries would be part of the Commonwealth, that the Princes could retain their privileges, properties and privy purses and that the new central governments would only control the functions previously exercised by the British – defence, external relations and communications.[442] The Princes had little choice, knowing that the new countries would otherwise simply seize their assets.

Privately, Mountbatten, though he was happy to take advantage of their hospitality, thought the Princes were anachronisms, referring to them as a 'bunch of nitwits'. He knew that the guarantees of local self-government and privileges offered by India and Pakistan would not be honoured for long – as they were not – but his job was to deliver 'a full basket of apples' to the two new countries before independence and that is largely what he did.

It left a residual bitterness with many. The Maharawal of Dungarpur told his political agent, Charles Chenevix Trench, that:

> By making them sign the Instrument of Accession, the Viceroy perpetrated the rape of the States. Had the Princes been left alone, Congress could never have got them to sign away their powers and heritage within a fortnight. No, never. Being a member of the Royal Family, many Princes took Mountbatten as a friend. Nothing could be further from the truth . . . the Princes expected justice and fair play, not lies and half-truths to beguile them into a snare.[443]

Two states, however, presented particular problems. The largest, Hyderabad – it was the size of France and had a population of 16 million – was predominantly Hindu and entirely surrounded by India, but ruled by a Muslim heavily influenced by a fanatical movement. In Kashmir, almost completely bordered by Pakistan, a Hindu dynasty ruled a mainly Muslim state. A further complication was that Nehru's family came from Kashmir and he had a strong emotional attachment to the state.

Dickie flew to have talks with the Maharajah Hari Singh, who found any number of displacement activities – from all-day fishing trips, where Mountbatten shocked staff by sunbathing in the nude, to bear hunts and visits to exhibitions of carpet-making and papier-mâché work – to avoid addressing the problem. In neither state had a decision been made when independence came, but Mountbatten's achievement was to have corralled all the others into making a choice by 15 August.

Dickie had expected to be Governor-General of both Dominions after Independence, to ensure a smooth transition and impartiality in overseeing the division of assets, but he had not counted on Jinnah's unpredictability, nor his distrust of the Viceroy – he thought him 'flash and second-rate'.[444] Rather than take the perceived more powerful position of Prime Minister at the beginning of July, Jinnah insisted on becoming Governor-General himself. It placed Mountbatten in a difficult position and further increased suspicion of him taking sides. He unsuccessfully lobbied Jinnah through the Nawab of Bhopal, the leading Muslim prince, and dithered on whether he should then solely accept the Indian role.

It had been a betrayal, a challenge to his authority and his reputation, and for several days Mountbatten threatened to resign. Ismay and Campbell-Johnson were sent to canvass opinion in London. Only personal messages from the King, Attlee and Churchill persuaded Mountbatten to stay, but 'From this stage on,' the Pakistan writer and politician Muhammad Ali remembered, 'there was a noticeable change in Mountbatten's attitude toward the problems of partition and toward Pakistan. Mountbatten had barely tolerated Jinnah in the past; now there was active hostility.'[445]

Mountbatten wrote to his eldest daughter despondently:

I've made a mess of things through over-confidence and over-tiredness. I'm just whacked and worn out and would really like to go. I'm so depressed darling, because until this stupid mishandling of the Jinnah situation I'd done so well. It has certainly taken me down many pegs.[446]

On 9 July, Edwina noted in her diary:

> Overwhelming opinion however that we should stay . . . Also
> to take on Chairmanship of Joint Defence Council. Decided
> therefore no alternative. Many misgivings. Morally, logically
> as well as personally feel it's wrong but that D has been faced
> with such a position that he cannot refuse.[447]

On 8 July, the barrister Cyril Radcliffe arrived to act as chairman
of a Boundary Commission to define the 3,800 miles of borders of
the Punjab and Bengal. Mountbatten had known Radcliffe during
the war when, as Director General of the Ministry of Information,
he had been responsible for running government censorship and
propaganda. A stocky, fastidious man, known at Haileybury as
Squit Radcliffe, he had taken a first at Oxford and was a fellow of
All Souls. The fact he had never been to India was regarded as a
strength rather than a weakness.[448]

Radcliffe had been given an impossible task, given his lack of
knowledge, the limited timescale, and the scant resources at his
disposal – he was working with a census that was six years out of
date – and the fact that his Hindu and Muslim colleagues on the
Commission divided on sectarian lines, requiring him to make
decisions alone. Amongst the factors he had to take into account
were river courses and irrigation systems, balancing assets between
the two countries, ethnic population divisions, natural boundaries,
the integrity of forests and communication networks – all in just over
a month.[449]

When Radcliffe recommended that disruption to Punjab's
intricate canal system could be minimised by India and Pakistan
jointly operating the head works, Jinnah replied that, 'he would
rather have Pakistan deserts than fertile fields watered by the courtesy

of the Hindus,' while Nehru 'curtly informed (Radcliffe) that what India did with India's rivers was India's affair.'[450] It was an indication of what was to come.

By 9 August, Radcliffe was ready to announce his deliberations. This presented Mountbatten with a dilemma. Knowing that the boundary decisions would be unpopular in some quarters, did he make them public immediately and overshadow the Independence celebrations, or did he kick the ball down the road, so it became the problem of the newly independent countries rather than the British?

'It is said that he is terrified to announce it before the Independence celebrations as disturbances may ensue on a large scale which would be his responsibility and that of His Majesty's Government to handle and control,' Hamid wrote in his diary on 9 August. 'This he is not prepared to face.'[451]

Sir George Abell argued for immediate release, so troops could be moved to the affected areas, but Mountbatten ignored his advice, possibly wanting to savour the day without recriminations, and chose to wait until Independence to announce the arbitration. It was a decision that was to have disastrous consequences.

The pressures of impending independence were beginning to take their toll on the Mountbatten marriage. '. . . the last two days have been pretty good Hell,' Ismay wrote to his wife at the beginning of August. 'Both Dickie and Edwina are dead tired, nervy as they can be and right across each other. So that in addition to my other troubles, I have been doing peacemaker and general sedative . . . it's very wearing for them, and for me.'[452]

In the past, the two had been able to manage separate lives. Now they lived and worked together. Naturally competitive, Edwina was jealous of her husband's new priorities, suffered from the heat and felt unsettled. These domestic tensions only added to the pressures Mountbatten faced.

On 13 August, the couple flew to Karachi for the Pakistan Independence celebrations. All did not go well. At dinner, Jinnah and Mountbatten argued over Mountbatten's decision not to arrest the Sikh leader Tara Singh – the Viceroy felt it would only further inflame the situation and in any case it was difficult to access the holy courtyards of the gurudwaras where he hid – and the delay in announcing the boundaries, which Jinnah argued only increased the possibility of violence. Jinnah made a short speech. Mountbatten, according to Hamid who was present, 'indulged in a long oration which was not in keeping with such an occasion,' then discussed why he had brought forward the transfer of power:

> He drew a childish smile by saying that the best way to teach a youngster to cycle was to take him on top of a hill, put him on the seat and then push him down the hill. By the time he arrived on the flat ground below he would have learnt to cycle. Thereupon somebody whispered that there was also the danger that he might break his neck![453]

A plot by the RSS (Rashtriya Swayamsevak Sangh) had been uncovered to throw a bomb into Jinnah's car during the three-mile state procession the next day, so Mountbatten had volunteered to ride with him. Sitting side by side in an open Rolls-Royce, Jinnah and Mountbatten braced themselves for the attack. As the procession ended without incident, Jinnah allowed himself to place his hand on Mountbatten's knee and congratulate him on bringing the Viceroy home safely.[454]

Back in Delhi, the Mountbattens dined alone and then spent their final hours in office watching Bob Hope in *My Favourite Brunette*. One of the Viceroy's final acts was to make the wife of the Nawab

The birth of the Mountbattens' eldest daughter Patricia, February 1924.

Dickie, Edwina, Patricia and Pamela in 1939.

Above left: Edwina between her husband and her lover, the polo player 'Laddie' Sandford.

Above right: Edwina's first lover, Hugh Molyneux, 7th Earl of Sefton, described as 'the best-looking man in society'.

Below left: Edwina with her lover, the Hollywood actor Larry Gray, in 1930.

Below right: Michael Wardell, one of Edwina's early lovers, an ex-cavalry officer who lost an eye in a riding accident.

Above left: The actor Paul Robeson, whose affair with Edwina was the subject of a court case in June 1932.

Above right: The singer Leslie Hutchinson, with whom Edwina had an affair for 20 years.

Below left: The Hungarian Count Anthony Szapary, one of Edwina's lovers during the 1930s.

Below right: 'Bunny' Phillips, Edwina's main lover during the 1930s.

Dickie between Edwina and his long-term mistress, Yola Letellier, supposedly the inspiration for *Gigi*.

Edwina with Bunny on her Africa trip, spring 1937. © *Southampton University Archive*

Right: Edwina with the lion cub, Sabi, at Adsdean, 1937.

Below: Edwina, the first woman to travel the 700-mile road between Burma and South West China, in 1939.

Helen Fitzgerald, Hugh Sefton, Wallis Simpson, Dickie and the Prince of Wales at Cannes, August 1935.

Right: The hallway of
the Mountbattens' new
penthouse, a 30-roomed
flat above Brook House,
designed by Edwin Lutyens
in 1936.   © *Country Life Picture Library*

Below: Broadlands, the
Hampshire country house
which Edwina inherited
from her father in 1939.

© *Southampton University Archive*

of Palamour a Highness, which the Colonial Office had refused, in spite of her popularity, because she was Australian.

Just before midnight, Nehru addressed the Constituent Assembly:

> Long years ago we made a tryst with Destiny and now the time comes when we shall redeem our pledge, not wholly or fully, but very substantially. At the stroke of the midnight hour, when the world sleeps, India will awake to life and freedom.

As midnight struck on 15 August, Nehru with Rajendra Prasad, President of the Constituent Assembly, arrived at Viceroy's House to formally invite Mountbatten to be India's first Governor-General and give him an envelope with the names of Ministers to be sworn in later that morning. When opened, it was empty. Such had been the excitement, they had forgotten to put anything inside.

At eight-thirty the next morning, the Mountbattens – Edwina in a long, gold lamé dress with a wreath of gold leaves on her head – entered the Durbar Hall for their second swearing-in in five months. Dickie became the first Constitutional Head of the new India.

That afternoon they were taken by carriage to a children's fête and to watch the new Indian flag being unfurled. Thirty thousand people had been expected, a quarter of a million had come. Escorted by their mounted bodyguard, the Mountbattens were stuck 25 yards from the flagstaff with the crowds trying to climb into the carriage. Mountbatten reported, 'we ended with four Indian ladies with their children, the Polish wife of a British officer and an Indian press man who crawled up behind.'[455] The planned parade and speeches had to be abandoned. All they could do was give orders to hoist the flag and fire a salute.

A state banquet for 100, speeches and at 9.15 p.m., in the State drawing-rooms, the Mountbattens received almost 3,000 guests, each of whom was presented to the new Governor-General and his wife. Outside the Moghul gardens sparkled with coloured lights. For Mountbatten it had been 'the most remarkable and inspiring day of my life'.[456] Congratulations arrived from around the world, including a telegram from Attlee:

> My warmest thanks to you on this day which sees successful achievement of a task of an unexampled difficulty. The continual skill displayed in meeting every difficulty has been amazing. Your short tenure of Viceroyalty has been one of the most memorable in a long list. In this message of thanks, I include Edwina, Ismay and other helpers.[457]

Mountbatten was raised in rank, taking the title Earl Mountbatten of Burma.[458]

The Mountbattens had done it together, a fact Dickie acknowledged, writing to 'the person who helped me most . . . Thank you, my pet, with all my heart.'[459]

Radcliffe, Jenkins and other officials had already left, not wishing to be part of the celebrations.[460]

CHAPTER 19

Governor-General

The next day, the new Earl Mountbatten of Burma handed copies of Radcliffe's report to the Indian and Pakistani leaders, who were given two hours to study it before a meeting at Government House.[461] The response was predictable – everyone was unhappy. Pakistan objected to Calcutta and the symbolically and strategically important Gurdaspur – India's only route to Kashmir – going to India; India that the Chittagong Hill tracts with only a three per cent Muslim population were now in Pakistan.[462] Mountbatten and Radcliffe's hope that the two countries would work together after Independence to solve some of the more difficult infrastructure problems had proved optimistic.

One of the criticisms directed against Mountbatten is that he favoured a strong India against a weak Pakistan. One example, often quoted and therefore worth examining in detail, was the tehsil – an administrative area of some 400 square miles – of Ferozepur, which was equally divided between Indian and Muslim populations. It was the main arsenal of the Indian Army, with an important bridge over the Sutlej River. The headwaters, vital for the irrigation of Bikaner, had been awarded to Pakistan.

It is claimed that Radcliffe may have had pressure put on him by Mountbatten after the Maharajah of Bikaner, learning of the decision, saw Mountbatten and threatened to accede to Pakistan unless the decision was changed.[463] How did outsiders know about the boundary decisions? Most probably through Rao Sahib V.D. Ayer, assistant secretary to the Boundary Commission and a Hindu, who leaked to V.P. Menon, a close associate of Nehru.[464] Certainly, many of the boundary decisions had leaked out early. Auchinleck's private secretary, Shahid Hamid, noted in his diary on 9 August:

> Everyone is talking about the impending Boundary Awards . . .
> Most of its salient points have already leaked out through the
> staff of the Boundary Commission and (Mountbatten's) own
> staff . . . It is common talk that Mountbatten is busy changing
> it, giving India . . . the Ferozepur headworks.[465]

In early August, the Governor of the Punjab, Sir Evan Jenkins, had been sent a map by George Abell showing the Ferozepur salient awarded to Pakistan, and this had been changed two days later after he received a cryptic telegram 'eliminate salient'. Decisions, even at this late stage, were still provisional, and it is possible Radcliffe simply changed his mind, feeling that the Sutlej River was a more natural boundary than the principle of 'contiguous Muslim nationalities', but it did nothing in the feverish atmosphere to reassure the Muslims.

Sir Francis Mudie, who was staying with Evans in early August, wrote in his unpublished memoir about the boundary change which he felt was not just about irrigation:

> This meant that Ferozpur was to go to India just depriving
> the Pakistan Army of most of its weapons. No explanation
> of why this sudden change was made at the last moment was

given or has ever been given, but I find it difficult to believe that it was not the result of pressure put on Lord Radcliffe by Mountbatten and his Government. This of course, has been strongly denied.[466]

In Ismay's papers there is a reference to a meeting between Mountbatten and Radcliffe in which they discussed the problems surrounding irrigation issues. They agreed that if Ferozepur was given to India, then there must be equal favours to Pakistan, such as the Chittagong Hill Tracts in Bengal, which was better than the Punjab given the complicating extra factor of the Sikhs.[467] This was probably a lunch on 12 August, when Ismay invited Radcliffe and Mountbatten but pointedly did not include Radcliffe's deputy, Christopher Beaumont.[468]

Mountbatten was under constant pressure to interfere and there is evidence he may have done so, though whether it was always in India's favour is more debatable. On 9 August, John Christie wrote in his diary, 'H.E. is in a tired flap and is having to be strenuously dissuaded from asking Radcliffe to alter his awards.'[469] Certainly, Radcliffe seems to have been susceptible to pressure. Philip Noel-Baker, the Secretary of State for Commonwealth Relations, told Attlee in February 1948 that Radcliffe had revised his decision, 'but we have no knowledge that this was done on the advice of Lord Mountbatten.'[470]

The immediate response to the boundary decisions was panic and a flood of refugees, as Muslims and Hindus escaped what they perceived might be violence, confiscation of property, persecution and religious discrimination in each respective country, even though Jinnah had insisted that the rights of minorities would be protected. The situation was further enflamed by Sikhs threatening to create a separate Sikh state through terror. By 27 August, it was estimated over ten million people were on the move in the Punjab alone. It also brought a cycle of violence as each atrocity was countered by another in revenge.

At the end of August, the train on which Wenty Beaumont, one of Mountbatten's ADCs, and his fiancée Sarah, daughter of Pug Ismay, were returning to Britain was ambushed and 100 Muslims killed. Only Beaumont's bearer, whom they had hidden under their seat, survived. The following day, the Viceroy's Treasurer and his wife were murdered in another train to Delhi *en route* to their son's funeral, also killed in the communal violence. This violence, which had never really gone away since the Great Calcutta Killings of August 1946, now became widespread and especially vicious, with a particular emphasis in the Punjab, with Sikhs and Hindus killing Muslims, and Muslims retaliating against Sikhs. Large gangs, often 600-strong, roamed the area, systematically raping, mutilating and then killing.

The charge sheet against Mountbatten is that he did not sufficiently anticipate the communal violence, especially the dangers posed by the Sikh community; that even when it took place he did too little too late; and that by rushing independence, preparations that might have alleviated the violence were inadequate. It is worth considering each charge.

* * *

The creation of the new state of Pakistan meant the isolation of the Sikh community, who in March 1947 called for their own state, Khalistan, between the rivers Chenab and the Jamna. The problem was that the Sikhs were not in a majority in any part of the Punjab, which made their demand for a state of their own, to include Simla and even Lahore, difficult. A further complication was that neither Hindus, nor more importantly Muslims, would have agreed to live in a Sikh state.

Mountbatten and his staff had repeatedly been warned by Evan Jenkins that if the Sikhs, a warrior sect, did not have certain holy shrines and at least one canal system, there would be violence. Jenkins also pleaded with Mountbatten to announce the partition decisions before 15 August:

> To stop panic and the mad hurrying to and fro of populations ... I believe that if the representatives of the future Dominions can make it clear now that there is no question of a chaotic changeover, that they mean business, and that they are sending an imposing organisation here to protect the people, with appropriate publicity, it will do much to steady the Punjab.[471]

On 27 July, Mountbatten was told that if the holy shrine of Nankana Sahib was not awarded to East Punjab, there would be violence. Already the Sikhs had amassed arms and the Muslims had made counter-preparations. A suggestion from V.P. Menon that the shrine should be made a separate state, like the Vatican, was noted, but nothing happened.

Mountbatten did consider arresting Sikh activists and banning the kirpan – a small dagger that Sikhs must carry as an article of faith – but was then advised by Jenkins and his two successors, Sir Chandulal Trivedi and Sir Francis Mudie, that to do so would only inflame an already tense situation. In any case, even if Tara Singh had given grounds to be arrested, others would have taken his place. There was also a concern about being seen to discriminate against a particular community.

That said, Pandit Pant in the United Provinces had arrested the more extreme Hindu Mahasabha and the RSS leadership and had little trouble. In his final retrospective report on his viceroyalty, Mountbatten accepted that he should have arrested communalist activists, but he lacked good intelligence because the Indians now controlled the Intelligence Bureau. The benefit of hindsight.

It has been argued that there were insufficient British troops and they were, in any case, keen to return to Britain, but British troops were available. Some 30,000 British troops and 35,000 Gurkha soldiers remained after independence, who were not due to be demobbed until the end of the year, and if used could have saved lives. There were 18 British infantry brigades, five artillery regiments, three armoured regiments and various support units stationed near or in the Punjab, but they were never utilised. There were also eight squadrons of Tempest fighter-bombers, which could have spotted trouble spots in open country and protected trains and railway lines, but a decision had been taken in July 'at the highest political and military levels' that they should not be used offensively.

In July, Sir Arthur Smith, Chief of the Indian General Staff, had published an order 'NOT to be divulged to Indians' that British troops were not to be used in communal disturbances except to protect British lives.[472] Now that Britain had granted independence, it had no wish to be drawn into a civil war that risked British casualties and losing goodwill on one side or the other, or both. Nehru had made plain his position. 'I would rather have every village in India go up in flames than keep a single British soldier in India a moment longer than necessary.'[473]

If there had been a longer timetable for the transfer of power, would the authorities have been better prepared for the violence? According to Mountbatten's successor as Indian Governor-General, Chakravarti Rajagopalachari, 'If the Viceroy had not transferred power when he did, there could well have been no power to transfer.'[474] Equally, Mountbatten's official biographer Philip Ziegler has argued:

Once the principle of partition had been accepted, it was inevitable that communalism would rage freely. The longer the period before the transfer of power, the worse the tension and the greater the threat that violence would spread . . . delay could only have provoked a far worse catastrophe.[475]

We will never know but, in any case, the authorities thought they were prepared. The Punjab Boundary Force, under General Pete Rees, had been created at the beginning of August to police the 12 most 'disturbed' districts, but the authorities had underestimated the scale of the violence. It had to police 37,500 square miles, 17,000 villages (many not linked by road) and a population of 14.5 million in 212 districts. At its peak, it had only 25,000 men – which meant less than two men per square mile. Jenkins had recommended that at least 100,000 troops were required.[476]

They did their best, but they were unable to operate within the territory of the bordering Princely States, such as Faridkot, Patiala and Nabha, where gangs often sought refuge. The Force received little support from the local civil authorities, especially the police now riven with communalism, or the new governments. Neither India nor Pakistan liked troops operating on their soil who were not responsible directly to them. General Sir Francis Tuker had advocated an all-Gurkha force, but ten of its 17 battalions had been raised from the Punjab and the soldiers quickly succumbed to the very communalism they were supposed to fight. By the end of August, against the wishes of Mountbatten, Auchinleck and Rees and on the instructions of Nehru and Jinnah, it was wound up.

In his report sent to King George VII at the beginning of September, Mountbatten expressed regret at the disbandment of the Punjab Boundary Force, which:

over-ride military considerations by political ones . . . and the assumption, by the Governments themselves, of direct military control in their respective areas. I was much opposed to this step at first – and am still opposed to it from the purely military view-point, because of the obvious lack of liaison and consequent risk of actual clashes between entirely separately controlled armies . . . But it gradually became apparent that the political leaders of both Dominions felt that their hands were tied until this step was taken.[477]

Within two months, order had been restored to the Punjab and the refugee crisis had abated, but it had come at an enormous and shameful cost – it is estimated that probably about a million people had died, with many millions horrifically injured and homeless.[478]

How far was Mountbatten personally to blame? He was certainly taken by surprise at the scale of the migration and violence – but so were many others, including Nehru and Jinnah. He should not have been, as Sir Evan Jenkins and many others had passed on countless warnings as soon as the Mountbattens arrived. Sir George Cunningham, a former governor of the North-West Frontier and private secretary to the Viceroy, felt that 'if the Punjab had been given time (say eight or nine months) to sort out their services properly, the terrible massacres of August–September–October would never have happened on anything approaching the scale that they did assume.'[479]

Certainly, if the governors had received advance warning of the boundaries, troops would have been deployed in readiness for any trouble. Mountbatten's decision not to arrest the Sikh leaders, on the advice of Nehru and the governors-designate of East and West Punjab, Sir Chandulal Trivedi and Sir Francis Mudie, now also looks the wrong call.

Mountbatten's defenders argue that the violence was largely

confined to the Punjab for a limited amount of time and could have been far worse. His critics point out that where preparations were taken with the presence of troops and agitators taken out of circulation, as in Calcutta, there was little trouble. The defenders respond that sometimes an assault on a large refugee column might consist of over 600 men. Against such force, there was nothing the authorities could do. The debate continues.

* * *

On 4 September, V.P. Menon telephoned Mountbatten asking for his help. The Mountbattens immediately returned from their break in Simla and within 48 hours Dickie had set up an Emergency Committee. He now exercised more power than he had ever done as Viceroy. Transport was requisitioned, trains provided with protection, dead bodies picked up in the streets, and cholera injections administered. Finally, some positive action was being taken.

Edwina now came into her own, setting up her own organisation, the United Council for Relief and Welfare, coordinating 15 separate relief organisations and two government ministries, providing medical supplies, food, clothing, shelter and water. Her first action was to ensure the protection of the families of the Muslim retainers who worked at Government House. Another 5,000 were brought within the compound.

Working 18-hour days, it is estimated in the five months following partition that she undertook 11 tours in the Punjab visiting 78 refugee camps, 46 hospitals and countless convoy encampments, welfare centres, clinics, schools and other institutions. This was to be one of her finest hours.

The violence had brought Nehru closer to Dickie. 'He has come suddenly to see me alone on more than one occasion – simply and solely for company in his misery; to unburden his soul; and to obtain what comfort I have to give,' wrote Mountbatten to the King.[480] Perhaps more importantly, it had cemented the bonds between Nehru and Edwina. Both of them ventured fearlessly onto the streets attempting to stop the violence and always looking out for each other.

On one occasion, learning that he had gone out alone, Edwina, with Amrit Kaur, went out in search of him to discover him attempting to hold back a group of armed men. On another, he caught a taxi to avert an attack on a Muslim college outside Delhi, only to discover Edwina already there without guards talking down an angry mob.

A further problem, at the end of October, was that some 5,000 Pathan tribesmen moved on Kashmir in a pre-organised plan, thought to have the assistance of the Pakistan authorities, in response to a campaign of genocide against Muslim Kashmiris. The Maharaja, who had yet to commit himself to either India or Pakistan, requested assistance from India to prevent further looting and killing. Mountbatten, as chair of the Indian Defence Council, was drawn into the dispute. The Indians now argued that the state must accede to India before troops could intervene. In fact, they were despatched before the ruler had signed the accession to India and his signature only backdated after pressure from Mountbatten and Nehru. It appeared to be further evidence of how the Mountbattens were in the pocket of Nehru.

In retaliation, Jinnah ordered Pakistan troops to respond. It looked like within months of independence, the two countries, each army led by British officers, would be at war with each other. The situation was only saved when Auchinleck threatened to withdraw all British officers from the Pakistan Army and Jinnah cancelled his military order. Mountbatten, after the failure of talks, now placed faith in the United Nations and a plebiscite, which was never held, to rule on whether Kashmir should go to India or Pakistan, but both countries remained suspicious of the other's motives – a situation that remains to this day.

The Mountbattens were now being drawn into a political maelstrom, which for many Muslims – and others – suggested they were under the influence of Nehru, who was Kashmiri by descent and emotionally drawn to the region. Ian Stephens, editor of the British-owned *The Statesman*, who had been under pressure from Mountbatten to give a stronger pro-Hindu line in the paper, dining with the Mountbattens at the end of October was startled by their one-sided verdicts on affairs. They seemed to have:

> become wholly pro-Hindu. The atmosphere at Government House that night was almost one of war. Pakistan, the Muslim League, and Mr Jinnah were the enemy. This tribal movement into Kashmir was criminal folly. And it must have been well-organised . . . It was a thoroughly evil affair. By contrast, India's policy towards Kashmir, and the Princely States generally, had throughout been 'impeccable'.[481]

The situation in Hyderabad had also not been resolved by independence. The Nizam, one of the richest men in the world, continued to prevaricate about which country to join, partly in the hope he might be able to become an independent state. He himself recognised the country's best interests were served by joining India, but he was in hock to Muslim fanatics. The challenge was to convince him of joining India, but still make him believe he was independent. He was given until August 1948 to make up his mind, but he still refused to make a decision. Two divisions of the Indian army, in what was described as a 'police action', invaded shortly afterwards. Four days later, Hyderabad became part of India.

CHAPTER 20

A Deeper Attachment

'Edwina has been dreadfully tiresome lately,' Ismay told his wife. 'There have been daily scenes about Dickie's decision to go home for the wedding. Personally, I think it's advisable on every count. It's good for the Govt of India because it will show them that they can do without him: it's good for Pakistan because it will show them that he is not as they charge – the Supreme Commander of the Kashmir offensive: and it's good for Dickie himself as he badly needs a change.'[482]

The wedding on 20 November was that of Prince Philip and Princess Elizabeth, one which Mountbatten had long encouraged and at which Pamela was due to be a bridesmaid. In August 1946, Philip had secretly proposed to Elizabeth at Balmoral, informing his uncle the next day, and in October the King wrote in his diary, 'Dickie came to lunch when we discussed everything.'[483] The following month, Dickie saw the Home Secretary and Prime Minister to finalise the naturalisation papers and agree that henceforth, Philip would be known as HRH Prince Philip, and arranged for the young naval officer to meet three Beaverbrook newspaper executives at the Mountbatten home so as to brief behind the scenes.[484]

In January 1947, it was Mountbatten who confirmed to the

Home Secretary that his nephew would be taking his family name on naturalisation – Oldcastle had been considered but rejected as sounding too much like a brewery.[485] Mountbatten's interfering was beginning to irritate Philip, who felt he was perfectly capable of running his own life:

> I am not being rude, but it is apparent that you like the idea of being General Manager of this little show, and I am rather afraid that she might not take to the idea quite as docilely as I do. It is true that I know what is good for me, but don't forget that she has not had you as Uncle *loco parentis*, counsellor and friend as long as I have.[486]

In March, the naturalisation of Philip, who gave the Mountbattens' home at 16 Chester Street as his address, was announced in the *London Gazette* and in July 1947 the engagement was officially announced.[487]

One of those who had helped prepare the ground was the journalist and Labour MP Tom Driberg, whom Mountbatten had first met at SEAC and had used as a useful sounding board and contact in both Parliament and the media. It was Driberg, who having talked to other Labour MPs, had advised that the wedding be kept low-key and that Philip's financial allowances be kept modest. It was a view that Mountbatten challenged:

> You have either got to give up the Monarchy or give the wretched people who have got to carry out the functions of the Crown enough money to be able to do it with the same dignity at least as the Prime Minister or Lord Mayor of London is afforded.[488]

On 11 November, the Mountbattens arrived back in London and, as the Brabournes were using Chester Street, took a suite at the Dorchester Hotel. Edwina was keen to see her first grandchild Norton, who had been born a month earlier, attend the christening and prepare Broadlands, which was hosting the first part of the royal honeymoon. She also wanted to see her old lover Malcolm Sargent and he stayed for one of their two nights at Broadlands, whilst Dickie made himself scarce. 'Thanks for being so sweet and understanding during these days in England,' Edwina wrote to her husband after their return.[489]

At the end of November, the Emergency Committee was closed down and its responsibilities handed to the Indian Government. Dickie had resolved in his last few months in India to visit every Province and principal state and so now, free of day-to-day responsibilities, the Mountbattens were able to travel. They were joined by friends such as Kay Norton, Yola Letellier, Bunny and Gina Phillips, Marjorie Brecknock and Peter Murphy and, for Christmas 1947, John and Patricia. Apart from continuing humanitarian work, there were also the celebrations for the Maharaja of Jaipur's Silver Jubilee, visits to Benares, Calcutta, Cuttack, Puri, Assam, Travancore, Cochin, Udaipur, Mysore and Ootacamund.

Behind the public appearances of affability, however, the tensions in the marriage continued with frequent quarrels, including one so bad between Edwina and Yola that the latter had offered to leave early. Edwina was resentful of the demands of her husband's job, his female friends and his relationship with his daughters. As always, Peter Murphy was the peacemaker, writing to Edwina:

Poor old Dickie's become so rattled: he is now in the state of feeling that he *must* try not to do silly little things which are habits and second nature to him. It distresses me so that you ever imagine that you are not a very great deep love in his life. I have been his confidant off and on for 25 years: you know that. What it seems you *don't* know is the unfailing affection and loyalty that he feels for you and that he has spoken of so freely to me. There has never been a *moment* in the past, Edwina – *however* difficult things may have appeared and in circumstances when 99 men out of a 100 would have felt they no longer had any responsibility – that Dickie didn't put *your* happiness first. I think if you look into your heart and honestly remember how good a <u>friend</u> he had been to you, you will realise that what I say is true.[490]

Whilst Dickie was able to relax with morning rides with Pamela and evenings on his genealogical 'Relationship Tables', with its various codes for the interlocking branches of his family tree, Edwina remained tense. She suffered from insomnia, partly influenced by the menopause, which was only resolved by pills or playing Elgar's 'Enigma Variations' on the gramophone.

There was some relief in the New Year when Malcolm Sargent came to stay *en route* to a music festival in Turkey, but he quickly developed dysentery and Edwina saw little of him. 'But darling do please take care of yourself. We do mind a lot what happens to you – all of us,' she wrote to him. 'I have missed you so much. I hate not seeing you and not being able to consult you about things . . . You are very sweet and wise and human and I value your opinion very much as you know.'[491]

One of those who had kept the communal peace was Gandhi, who had fasted until he felt communal violence had abated. At the end of January, as he made his way to a prayer meeting at his Delhi home, supported by his two young great-nieces, a lone gunman fired at him, killing him instantly. Mountbatten rushed to the scene. As he got out of his car, someone in the crowd shouted out to him, 'It was a Moslem who did it,' to which Mountbatten instinctively replied, 'You fool, don't you know it was a Hindu?'[492] The fact was that no one knew. If it was a Muslim, then civil war was inevitable.[493]

Inside the Birla House, Mountbatten found most of the Cabinet almost incoherent with grief. Ever the opportunist, he seized the opportunity for good to come from evil. Beckoning Nehru and Patel, who had recently become estranged, he told them of Gandhi's wish that they should remain friends. The two men looked at each other and embraced in silence. Later that evening, they jointly broadcast to the new nation.

The next day a huge crowd, larger even than the one on Independence Day, followed Gandhi's body, placed on an army weapons-carrier, in a procession of over 5,000 troops on the nine-mile route from Birla House to the Raj Ghat, by the banks of the Jumna, where he was to be cremated. So large was the throng around the funeral pyre that it threatened to push the Mountbattens into the flames, until Dickie ordered everyone to sit down, and then quietly slipped away.

Gandhi's death had not just brought the politicians together, but deepened the existing affection with the Mountbattens. Nehru had refused their invitation to live at Government House to ensure his personal safety, but he now saw even more of the couple and, in particular, Edwina, who had written a comforting letter after Gandhi's death.

Dickie had always had a picture of Nehru on his desk. Now Edwina had asked for one as well: 'My dear J-Lal . . . I would love to have one, in fact two! I'd like a formal one and if possible an informal snap shot . . . Love ever, Edwina.'[494] Thanking him a few days later for 'the delightful snapshots and photograph', she offered to return the favour. 'My admiration for you increases each day. I'd love you to have a photograph and will send for one, as soon as I've found one you might like . . . Love ever, Edwina.'[495]

For Nehru, amidst the loneliness of high public office, here was someone he could trust and to whom he could confide. 'I want someone to talk to me sanely and confidently, as you can do so well,' he wrote to Edwina in April, 'for I am in danger of losing faith in myself and the work I do . . . What has happened, is happening, to the values we cherished? Where are our brave ideals?'[496]

In mid-May, Nehru joined the Mountbattens, at Edwina's invitation, for a few days at the Retreat at Mashoba, driving there from Ambala in an open-top sports car. 'Although we have come to know him pretty well during the last fourteen months, it was during these three days that we really succeeded in establishing strong personal bonds,' Mountbatten wrote to George VI.[497] Dickie worked on his family tree, Edwina and Nehru walked, talked or read companionably with each other. There were picnics and after-dinner games of cards. After the pressures of the last few months, everyone could finally relax. 'A perfect evening,' Edwina wrote in her diary and then after the others had gone to bed, '. . . a fascinating heart to heart with J.N.'[498]

Seeing the strong emotional bond between the two, Dickie and Pamela discreetly withdrew to give them time together. Six weeks before her departure, Edwina had finally, according to her younger daughter, found 'the companionship and equality of spirit and intellect that she craved.'[499] On the morning Nehru had to leave, she rose at half past six to see him off and, almost immediately afterwards, sent him a letter. 'I hated seeing you drive away this morning . . . you have left me with a strange sense of peace and happiness. Perhaps I have brought you the same?'[500] He had felt the same, writing in a letter that crossed with hers, 'Life is a dreary business . . . and when a bright patch comes it rather takes one's breath away.'[501] A few years later, he was more open about the moment:

> Suddenly I realised (and perhaps you did also) that there was a deeper attachment between us, that some uncontrollable force, of which I was only dimly aware, drew us to one another. I was overwhelmed and at the same time exhilarated by this new discovery. We talked more intimately, as if some veil had been removed, and we could look into each other's eyes without fear or embarrassment.[502]

Restless and difficult when apart, Edwina would become exhilarated at the thought of being together with the Indian leader. For Dickie, however, life was easier, as his wife's 'new-found happiness released him from the relentless late-night recriminations.' Pamela remembered how:

> In recent months, whenever he had left his huge pile of paperwork to go up to say goodnight to her, my father would find himself subject to a long string of accusations that he didn't understand: he was ignoring her, his behaviour had been rude and he didn't care about her. He was sympathetic and apologised, even though he did not understand what he had done wrong. These were the exhausted outpourings of a woman who always drove herself too hard and felt intellectually isolated. To my father's great relief, after our short stay in the mountains, these sessions ceased. Now when my father went up, he would find her studying her pocket atlas, and she would simply smile and wish him a cheery 'Goodnight, Dickie, darling.' He would then return to work through most of the night without a heavy heart.[503]

On the 11 June, Edwina and Nehru flew to the United Provinces to say goodbye to Sarojini, now Governor of Bareilly and an old friend of Edwina's mother. They walked in the gardens, drifted on a boat in the lake and next morning rode together in the mountains. 'This was the only promise we ever made,' Edwina wrote to Nehru later, 'on the road to Naini Tal – that nothing we did or felt would ever be allowed to come between you and your work or me and mine – because that would spoil everything.'[504]

As the date for departure loomed, Nehru tried to convince her to stay and continue her work with refugees but, torn as she was, she knew her place was with her husband. 'And so it will be and it has to be,' he reflected. 'How wise and right you are, but wisdom brings little satisfaction. A feeling of acute malaise is creeping over me, and horror seizes me when I look at a picture in my mind of your shaking thousands of hands on the night of the 20th and saying your final goodbyes . . . Dickie and you cannot bypass your fate, just as I cannot bypass mine.'[505]

'We dined with Jawaha and his family,' she noted in her diary, 'sat in the garden with full moon. Sadder and sadder.'[506] Finally, the last night came. After a farewell party for all 2,000 staff, the Cabinet hosted a State Banquet in Government House, where the Mountbattens were presented with a huge silver tray inscribed with the names of the Indian Cabinet, the Governors of the Provinces and President of Constituent Assembly. In return, they donated the Viceroy's gold plate service.

Nehru began by paying tribute to Dickie:

It is difficult for me or anyone to judge of what we have done during the last year or so. We are too near to it and too intimately connected with events. Maybe we have made many mistakes, you and we. Historians a generation or two hence will perhaps be able to judge what we have done right and what we have done wrong . . .'[507]

He continued that he believed, 'we did try to do right, and I am convinced that you tried to do the right thing by India, and therefore many of our sins will be forgiven us and many of our errors also.'[508]

He then turned to Edwina, who had been in tears:

To you, Madam . . . the gods or some good fairy gave . . . beauty and high intelligence, and grace and charm and vitality, great gifts, and she who possesses them is a great lady wherever she goes. But unto those that have, even more shall be given, and they gave you something which was even rarer than those gifts, the human touch, the love of humanity, the urge to serve those who suffer and who are in distress. And this amazing mixture of qualities results in a radiant personality and in the healer's touch. Wherever you have gone, you have brought solace, you have brought hope and encouragement.[509]

Early the next morning, Nehru appeared at Government House where he and Edwina exchanged presents. For him, one of her most valued possessions, an 18th-century French box of enamel and gold, and for her an ancient coin, a box of ripe mangoes and a copy of his autobiography. Then the Mountbattens left Government House for the last time, a bodyguard lining the steps and escorting the carriage. As they were about to move off, one of the horses jibbed. 'Even the horses won't let you go,' someone called out.[510]

Away from the crowds on board the plane, Edwina finally broke down in tears. Taking off something round her neck, she passed it to her personal assistant, motioning to her to leave the plane. It was her precious St Christopher that she wanted Nehru to have. 'The long flight home passed in sombre silence.'[511]

CHAPTER 21

Malta Again

The Mountbattens arrived at Northolt to be met by Patricia, Prince Philip, Clement Attlee and the Indian High Commissioner, Krishna Menon. Edwina, still emotional after her parting, made a short speech about what India meant to her. Her younger daughter remembered how:

> she began to falter, and she had difficulty in getting the words out, '. . . every . . . possible . . . feeling.' She stopped, blinked, then licked her lower lip until for a horrifying moment I thought she might break down. Then, as she turned to my father for support, he gave her a warm, confident smile and she regained her composure and found the strength to continue.[512]

For Edwina, life in drab post-war London after the vibrancy and energy of India seemed trivial and low-key. She fell into a deep depression, exacerbated by exhaustion and the loss of her beloved Sealyham terrier, Mizzen, who had had to be put down *en route* to Malta.

After the splendours of Government House, 16 Chester Street seemed claustrophobic. Only Broadlands provided the peace she now needed. She missed the pace of life, the status, the sense of purpose she had enjoyed in India, and tried to replicate it. 'I have resorted to very hard work as a possible solution to the present situation,' she told Nehru at the beginning of July, 'it has helped although it is really only a drug.'[513] 'Feeling quite awful,' she confided to her diary the following month, 'general exhaustion and depression, I think.'[514] 'Life is lonely and empty and unreal,' she confessed to him.[515] Above all, she missed India and Nehru.

She would write to Nehru each day, following Dickie's habit for confidential correspondence of enclosing her letter in a second envelope. At first this was marked 'Prime Minister' and later 'For Himself', numbering each letter so each could be accounted for. Nehru, in turn, would write using the diplomatic bag c/o the High Commission. Whereas Dickie's letters had been prosaic, Nehru's were like poetry, indeed often quoting poetry – either his own or Yeats, Swinburne, Auden, Joyce and Blake. When no letter was received, like a lovesick teenager, she would call India with the help of half a dozen operators.

People did what they could to cheer her up. Malcolm Sargent took her to see Laurence Olivier in *Hamlet*. In August, the whole family went to Classiebawn for five days, staying in the local inn, whilst they brought the house back to life. The fresh air and peacefulness helped restore her good spirits. 'Scrambled over the rocks and dabbled in the pools,' she wrote to Nehru, energised. 'Back by the beach of white sand . . . brilliant sun and sapphire and multi-emerald coloured seas and countryside with its white-washed thatched cottages . . . we shrimped off the rocks and sat about in shorts sunbathing.'

In September the Mountbattens, with Pamela, stayed with Henri and Yola Letellier in the South of France, where Dickie practised his water-skiing and they saw the Duke of Windsor.[516] But Edwina remained dissatisfied. 'I somehow seem to have grown out of all this, the people, the life, even the scenery,' she wrote to Nehru.[517]

For Dickie it was different. Though he had been offered various jobs, including Governor of Malta, Governor General of Canada, and Ambassador to Moscow and Washington, he just wanted to resume his naval career.[518] He had put together an eight-page document headed 'My Next Appointment', which laid out all the possibilities and he discussed this endlessly with Peter Murphy and Charles Lambe. His two main options were to go to Bermuda as C-in-C West Indies, generally regarded as a pre-retirement job; or to return to Malta, which might prove politically difficult, given the problems in Palestine, and embarrassing as he would be subordinate to the Commander-in-Chief.[519]

Whilst Mountbatten had received praise for the transfer of power, it had been at a price. Dickie recollected how, shortly after their return, Churchill came up to him at a Buckingham Palace reception – '"What you did in India, it's as though you struck me across the face with a riding whip" and he turned his back on me and he didn't speak to me for several years.'[520] Mountbatten, however, continued to take an interest in the subcontinent, especially as many issues from his time played out after his return.

On 11 September, Jinnah died of cancer, weighing only 35 kilos. The ambulance taking him to hospital broke down and for an hour he lay dying, parked on the roadside. Mountbatten later reflected that if he had known the seriousness of his illness, he might have delayed independence, and there may have been no partition.

In October, Nehru came to Britain for discussions on the Commonwealth, before going on to the United Nations in New York. Dickie tactfully left the reunited lovers alone for a midnight rendezvous *en route* from the airport. 'Too lovely,' Edwina noted in her diary.[521] Whilst Dickie initially stayed in London, the two spent several days at Broadlands, where Nehru entertained Patricia's sons by 'getting down on all fours in the drawing room and making lion faces at Norton and his new brother, Michael John, who roared back in absolute delight.'[522]

For the next week they were inseparable. They visited Jacob Epstein's studio, Edwina joined Nehru on the platform at a meeting at Kingsway Hall, they saw Euripides' *Medea*, jointly attended the Lord Mayor's banquet, a reception at the King's Hall and a dinner for Dominion Premiers at Buckingham Palace, and were photographed at a Greek restaurant in Soho after the press were tipped off by Krishna Menon.

At the end of October, the Mountbattens returned to Malta, Nehru seeing them off from Northolt and Edwina in dark glasses to hide her tears. Dickie, who had been appointed as Commander of the First Cruiser Squadron, now reported to Manley Power, who insisted on continuing to call him 'sir'. It must have been a huge adjustment, from having ruled a subcontinent to an island just over 300 square kilometres; from having given orders to now being a subordinate. Power, initially wary, grew to respect his new colleague:

We saw eye to eye on most important matters. I found him an endless source of entertainment with his peacock Mountebankery which kept popping up at unexpected moments in sharp contrast to his normal sane and statesmanlike person . . . By the end of my time with Mountbatten I had reached the conclusion that, in spite of several failings, he was a great man and a statesman. He was dynamic, easy to deal with and always open to argument, with a tremendous gift of charm and inspired leadership.[523]

Their old house, Casa Medina, had survived the war, but was now converted into flats, so they first stayed at the newly opened Phoenicia Hotel before moving, shortly after Christmas, across the road from the Case Medina to the Villa Guardamangia. Royal Marine Ron Perks was assigned as Mountbatten's driver and lived at the Villa Guardamangia whilst it was being decorated.[524]

Perks would often drive Mountbatten to his scuba diving or to polo practice, 'where he spent hours practising on a stationary horse in an enclosed area with the ball ricocheting round. You could be very relaxed with him. He never stood on ceremony.'[525] He recollected how once driving through a 40-mph area, Mountbatten, who loved to drive fast, told him to 'Step on it':

> I explained about the speed restrictions and he insisted we swop places which we did. A few minutes later the military police, who we called Snow Drops on account of their white helmets, stopped us. After saluting me in the back they proceeded to give the driver a bollocking until they realised who he was. We then swopped places again and I drove to our function.[526]

Whilst Dickie quickly threw himself into his new responsibilities, Edwina felt trapped. 'One feels one's brain and even one's energy shrinking to fit the tiny island,' she told Nehru.[527] She continued to work for St John Ambulance and Save the Children, and Pamela became a case worker for the Soldiers, Sailors, Airmen Families Association. Eventually she settled into a routine. 'You will be pleased to hear that Edwina has been quite relaxed & very sweet & we never have a cross word – more like 1928 than 1948,' Dickie wrote to his mother. 'Still I think it a very good thing that we should have good long periods apart for we have been on top of one another for too long'.[528]

Whilst he was away on a winter cruise from January to April, Edwina returned to Britain, where Malcolm Sargent joined her at Broadlands and she spent a night at Sandringham ('quite the ugliest house I have ever seen') to see Philip and Elizabeth's new baby, Charles. She felt out of place, telling Nehru, 'I always feel most bogus in this kind of circle . . . I always feel I am about to say something which will surprise and shock them most terribly!'[529]

Only in India did she now feel fully at home. In mid-February she returned for five weeks, chaperoned by Pamela, to stay with Nehru. She continued to tour refugee camps and hospitals, saw old friends and visited refugee settlement projects. Nehru took her, Pamela and various members of his family for four days to Orissa in eastern India, where the two lovers walked on the white sand at midnight and swam at dawn.

In the third week of April, Nehru was back in Britain for a meeting of Commonwealth prime ministers and, after a meeting with Attlee and lunch with George VI, was immediately driven to Broadlands where he stayed for the next two weekends.[530] 'You have brought me all I was yearning for,' she wrote to Nehru, 'happiness, balance, misery even! But we know the reason (and we would not change it) and there is infinitely more power and purpose to life.'[531] But deeply in love as she was, she knew her duty was to be with her husband. That did not make it any easier. Quite the contrary. She was feeling angry, trapped and resentful and took it out on Dickie.

In these moods, Dickie had no idea how to deal with her except to give in. A particularly furious row broke out in June 1949, after he told her of his promotion to Vice-Admiral and Fourth Sea Lord. He opened his heart to her:

Although I did not do anything unkind intentionally, I fear that my own misery made me a poor companion and a thoughtless one who must have caused you pain. Believe me, darling, I never want to cause you any pain because I always have been and I always will be far too fond of you for that.

If I have avoided having talks with you I am sure it is the sub-conscious wish to avoid another scene which has hitherto followed my attempt to 'have things out' . . . When we had that row in the boat yesterday . . . I became so violently unhappy that I really felt physically sick, and greedy, as I usually am, I could eat no lunch, and talkative, as I usually am, I could find nothing to say.

Let me begin by criticising myself. I am terribly self-centred and rather conceited and full of the vainglory of uniforms and decorations. I am bad with women as a whole and of course particularly bad with you . . . I believe that early failures caused me to despise myself – and to feel (perhaps without justification) that you shared this view of myself . . . please believe me when I say that the one thing I've always looked for is complete family love and friendship. That love and friendship can grow and become the most vital thing in the lives of the 4 of us provided we do not start trying to impose restrictions on one another or harbour unkind thoughts.[532]

He continued, addressing Edwina's jealousy of his girlfriends:

As for Yola, we are all such friends that it is fun being together – but there are times when it is fun being alone. Just as you wept with disappointment when circumstances meant that I was going to be home the first evening that you and Jawahar were going to be together, I sometimes also feel I'd like to be alone with Yola . . . I never minded your seeing Malcolm and Jawahar alone, as you know.[533]

Edwina had suggested they not meet in Cyprus when his ship docked.

> But then the old, old miracle happened: 'You pressed my
> hand and caught my eye and gave me that divine smile which
> I like to think you give to no one else and which I can assure
> you I get from no one else and I kissed the back of your hair
> and the old heart fluttered in the same ridiculous way in
> which it has fluttered for 28 years, ever since I first met you
> at that divine dance of the Vanderbilts, and I realised that
> if you came to Cyprus in that mood, my mood would meet
> you more than half way and we could have a wonderfully
> happy time.'[534]

And they did, Dickie writing to his mother that they had 'never had a happier ten days than our time in Cyprus & Rhodes.'[535]

In October, Nehru was back with Edwina at Broadlands. It was a relationship that suited them well. Politically, emotionally and intellectually compatible, they drew support from each other. He brought her small exotic gifts, welcome in a Britain still in the grip of rationing, such as mangoes from India, cigarettes from Egypt, a Gruyère from Switzerland, but he brought much more. Where Dickie had been too gauche, busy or casually dismissive, here was a man with whom she felt comfortable and an equal, who respected her mind and knew how to appeal to her feelings.

She had been able to channel her love in the past to her animals or strangers such as the sick, the dispossessed or poor. Now she had found a soul mate. For Nehru, the lonely widower and public figure bowed down by the pressures of office, here was a woman who asked nothing of him, with whom he could relax and who brought long-lost domesticity.

Each saw the relationship as pure, whether it was or not. 'I dislike vulgar stories and cheap books and films based on crude sex appeal,' she wrote to him. 'I am even rather disgusted by them and I know in consequence am thought sometimes to be rather boringly prudish!'[536] 'I think I am not interested in sex as sex,' Edwina wrote to him. 'There must be so much more to it, beauty of spirit and form and in its conception. But I think you and I are in the minority! Yet another treasured bond.'[537]

A few months later, she joined him in India where she continued her work with the Refugee Relief and Rehabilitation Committee, which she had set up after Partition, but also visited museums and galleries. 'He was so knowledgeable about his country's past, and on that trip he brought Indian history and art alive for us,' remembered Pamela Mountbatten. 'My mother seemed to flourish in his company, so happy and fulfilled in his presence.'[538]

The Mountbattens' finances had been stretched with all the entertaining and travel in India and they continued to give generously to charities, support family retainers and live extravagantly. In Malta they employed a staff of 19, including a butler, housekeeper, two housemaids, two cleaners, three cooks, six stewards, two drivers and a valet – which Dickie thought was 'not too grossly overstaffed'.[539]

However, with income tax and surtax at 19s 6d in the pound, Edwina's trust income from her grandfather had dropped from £45,000 in 1939 to £4,500 in 1948. Unable to touch capital – protection against unscrupulous husbands – her only option was a government bill to let her draw on capital. By March 1949, 'The Mountbatten Estate Bill' had successfully gone through three readings in the House of Lords with no opposition, but it then encountered opposition after a press campaign orchestrated by Beaverbrook. The obvious solution was to bring in a bill that covered all women in her position and the Married Woman (Restraint upon Anticipation) Bill duly became law in November.

From this point dates Beaverbrook's vendetta against Dickie, which was to last until the 1960s. 'I regard Mountbatten as the biggest menace to the Empire,' Beaverbrook told Tom Driberg. 'He has perpetrated one outrage after another. He was responsible for the present position in Burma. His conduct in Malaya is indefensible. He damaged the Dutch suzerainty in Indonesia, thus weakening the whole Middle East [*sic*] structure . . . He should never be given power or authority.'[540] His view henceforth of the couple was 'Mountbatten is vain, not clever. The woman is clever, not vain.'[541]

It was not just public opposition, but a very private fight. When Janey Lindsay, who had married Beaverbrook's son, wanted to make Mountbatten godfather of her first child, the press magnate refused. The *Express* journalist Graham McKenzie was tasked:

> to dig up dirt on Mountbatten. Graham recalled how he was dispatched with a photographer to stake out a rural hideaway that Beaverbrook believed Mountbatten used when meeting his lovers. Graham and the photographer hid in a ditch for days observing Mountbatten's comings and goings, but they failed to come up with any juicy material.[542]

A series of critical articles by Sefton Delmer were suppressed by a contact within the Beaverbrook camp on grounds of inaccuracy in the early 1950s, but many others followed, questioning Mountbatten's misjudgements on Dieppe, South East Asia and India. Finally, in 1953, Mountbatten, who had been collecting examples of his negative coverage, considered legal action, but was dissuaded by lawyers and Peter Murphy.[543]

Nevertheless, he continued to be irritated by the feud. Michael Wardell, Edwina's former lover and an *Express* journalist, was asked to intervene and reported back to Dickie with:

> a statement signed by A.J. Cummings, an independent journalist of high reputation that he had examined all the *Express* cuttings on you and found them fair comment . . . I begged Max to see you personally, and I asked you to come round to Arlington House to talk to him but you and Edwina both decided against this course.[544]

What was really behind this animosity? One Beaverbrook biographer, Tom Driberg, believed it was because Mountbatten had told Jean Norton to break a dinner engagement with the increasingly controlling Beaverbrook, whilst another, A.J.P. Taylor, thought, 'Something about Mountbatten touched Beaverbrook on a raw nerve.'[545] Yet another biographer, Anne Chisholm, felt it was more than that:

> George Malcolm Thomson reflected the view of people inside *Express* newspapers at the time when he said, with confidence, though forty-five years after the event, that the cause of the vendetta was personal. After Jean Norton's death in 1945 at her cottage on the Cherkley estate, Beaverbrook learned from her papers that, while she was his mistress, she had also had an affair with Mountbatten. This coincided with the view of Edwina Mountbatten's friends, who remembered an earlier time when both the Mountbatten marriage and the Beaverbrook–Norton relationship had been under strain, and the two had seen much of one another.[546]

It is a view that was shared by Jean Norton's daughter, Sarah Baring, Mountbatten's goddaughter and confidante, and also Beaverbrook's daughter, Janet, who later wrote, 'by far the most likely reason for their feud, was that Father found a stack of passionate love letters Lord Louis had written to Jean Norton.'[547]

* * *

The Duke of Edinburgh had joined the Mediterranean Fleet in October 1949 and for his first month stayed with the Mountbattens, though there were tensions as the young naval officer fought to establish his independence from his controlling uncle. Shortly afterwards, Princess Elizabeth came to Malta for a month and she too stayed with the Mountbattens whilst their home was being prepared. Edwina, who gave up her room and instead took Dickie's bedroom, wrote 'It's lovely seeing her so radiant and leading a more or less human and normal existence for once.'[548]

The young couple joined the Mountbattens on picnics, on the naval barge, at the polo and at various dances. In Malta, Mountbatten had taken up a new hobby of scuba diving with a harpoon gun and he had introduced Philip to it, as well as polo. When asked whether he preferred polo or scuba diving, he paused for a moment before answering, 'Well, polo is only a game.'[549]

Elizabeth's views of the Mountbattens had been shaped as much by her mother – who distrusted them, as her father – who accepted them. Dickie's former chief of staff, Boy Browning, whom he had helped place as Comptroller of Philip and Elizabeth's household, had warned a member of the royal party, 'Remember you've got Dickie – he'd always rather do something under the table than above.'[550]

Dickie was anxious to know what she had thought of him, as Philip had told him she had not liked him, but in Malta the two warmed to each other. 'She has done a lot of good functions & has gone down wonderfully with everybody here,' Dickie wrote to his mother. 'I'd never really known her before & have quite lost my heart to her; she is very sweet – and my word she is kind and thoughtful for Philip.'[551]

Mountbatten threw himself into his new job, making a point of entertaining extensively and going to sea every week, and he had quickly flown his flag in every ship in the Squadron. He also continued to demonstrate that he played by his own rules. During an exercise against the larger Home Fleet, he smuggled a Warrant Telegraphist ashore with a radio-transmitter, who proceeded to report the movements of the enemy fleet. When complaints were made, he replied that, 'when he played war, he played with no holds barred.'[552] His handling of ships also remained problematic. On one night-exercise, he ordered the torpedoes to position to fire to port and then directed the ships in a circle so they would have destroyed each other. One young officer could not help exclaiming, 'The man's mad!'[553]

His career, however, remained unaffected. In June 1949 he had been made a Vice-Admiral and the following spring his time with the First Cruiser Squadron ended and he was appointed to the Admiralty Board. 'Vice-Admiral Mountbatten is most versatile and remarkable in ability and energy alike,' began Power's final report. 'Ambitious and perhaps impetuous, but not rash. A tremendous asset to the service to which he is devoted.'[554]

There were Five Sea Lords on the Admiralty Board: the First headed the Navy, the Second was responsible for personnel, the Third handled the design and building of ships, the Fifth was in charge of the naval air service. Mountbatten, having hoped to be chosen to run personnel, was appointed the Fourth Sea Lord and was responsible for stores and pay.

He put a brave face on it. 'Well, having blown off steam,' he wrote to Patricia, 'let me tell you that if I am sent as 4th Sea Lord I should go very humbly and loyally and do my best. I accepted to go back and take my chance at carving out a naval career and I have such ludicrous self-confidence that I still think I can get to First Sea Lord.'[555]

There was much that needed to be done. There were insufficient uniforms for the 150,000 reservists available for mobilisation, the mine-sweeping fleet was under-resourced, and pay needed to be reviewed. Within a month, he had visited the five major naval depots and each office in the Victualling and Stores Department. Crucially, the job gave him added experience of the workings of Whitehall, which was to prove useful in his career.

* * *

In February 1952, George VI died just after the Mountbattens' annual visit to Sandringham. 'A real shock,' wrote Edwina to Nehru. 'How fit we had found him shooting and walking in spite of intense cold and arctic winds.'[556] He and Dickie had been close since their time at Cambridge together 30 years earlier, and had corresponded on a regular basis. Dickie had always been scrupulous about keeping the Sovereign informed and making him feel important. He had also never been reluctant to use the King's 'wishes' to secure his own objectives.

As at the start of George's reign, Dickie pushed himself forward, or made himself indispensable according to one's point of view. Together with Churchill and the Duke of Gloucester, it was the Mountbattens who met Elizabeth when she returned to Britain from a tour to Kenya as Queen on 7 February. At the funeral, he had asked if he could walk immediately behind the coffin, as his father had at the funeral of Edward VII, until rebuffed by the Earl Marshall, the Duke of Norfolk, who was in charge of the arrangements. The young Queen did so instead.

For Dickie, the new regime signified the triumph of the House of Mountbatten and at a dinner at Broadlands the day after the funeral, he gave such a toast. One of the guests, Prince Ernst of Hanover, reported it to Queen Mary who complained to Winston Churchill, pointing out that George V in 1917 had decreed the House of Windsor to be the Royal Family's name forever. Churchill immediately called a Cabinet meeting to discuss, aware that public opinion, so soon after two wars against the Germans, would be against such a link. No one quite knew the position given the Queen's married name was Mountbatten, and a new decree had to be made in April re-emphasising the position. Philip was furious that he could not pass on his own name to his children.[557]

Even so, there were continuing concerns about Mountbatten's Svengali influence over the Royal Family and his left-wing views. Philip and Elizabeth were regular guests at Broadlands, and there were rumours that he was plotting to have Philip made King Consort.[558] When the Duke of Windsor was over for his brother's funeral, he noted of Mountbatten that 'one can't pin much on him but he's very bossy & never stops talking. All are suspicious & watching his influence on Philip.'[559]

Dickie wrote to Edwina in February 1952:

Four different people have come to me in the last two or three days to say that London is buzzing with rumours and talk in the clubs, etc. that I was to be offered an immediate post abroad so as to remove us from being able to influence Lilibet through Philip. My own influence was viewed with apprehension, and there was also the view that I would be passing on extreme left-wing views from you! Of course you always tell me that I am very right wing and reactionary compared with you . . .[560]

The reason for the gossip was an article in an American newsletter, 'The Bulletin of the International Services of Information', run by former intelligence officer Ulius Amoss, under the headline 'A Red Aura Hangs Over the Mountbattens' – which, amongst many claims, accused Peter Murphy, a strong influence on the couple, of being a member of the Communist Party. It was sufficient for MI5 to conduct an investigation into Murphy and raise their concerns with Mountbatten himself.[561] The FBI also investigated and deemed Amoss a nutter, but this was just the sort of attention that a senior naval officer did not need.

The Mountbattens' politics were complex. As a serving naval officer and member of the Royal Family, Dickie always claimed to try and stay above party politics – though he had to be rebuked at one stage by the First Lord of the Admiralty. 'There is a feeling that in some of your conversations . . . you have approached rather too closely to the dividing line between legitimate naval interests and foreign policy.'[562] He was a technocrat, keen to get things done, and a pragmatist, but he was also a progressive when it came to national aspirations and his record in India had aroused suspicion in right-wing quarters.

Edwina's politics were certainly to the left of his. Dining with Edwina in September 1944, Chips Channon noted in his diary:

However, politically, she talked tripe, and pretended to be against all monarchy, she who is cousin to every monarch on earth. According to her, they must all be abolished. How easy it seems for a semi-royal millionaire, who has exhausted all the pleasures of money and position, to turn almost Communist.[563]

'My mother was genuinely left wing and my father would try and persuade her only to argue with those she could influence and not die-hard Admirals but that was, of course, much more fun,' remembered her daughter Pamela. 'She worked with Jennie Lee and the Labour Government . . . several times people said they had been persuaded to vote Conservative after being charmed by her on the assumption she was a Conservative. She was very annoyed.'[564]

Her travels and humanitarian work had opened her eyes to the suffering in the world and the failure of governments to properly address it. Idealistic, perhaps politically naïve, she was deeply critical of American foreign policy and Britain's post-war colonial policy, especially in Malaya and East Africa.

On the day before the Coronation, tensions between her and government ministers came to a head at a lunch at Buckingham Palace when she, Nehru and Oliver Lyttelton, the Colonial Secretary, got into an argument about British policing in Kenya. It was sufficiently heated for Lyttelton to complain to the Cabinet and for Mountbatten to receive a letter from the First Lord of the Admiralty that it would be prudent for her not to accompany him on a forthcoming official trip to Turkey. Edwina, who planned to visit hospitals and universities on the trip, was incandescent.

After letters to both the First Lord and Foreign Secretary, giving her own version of the conversation, the Admiralty relented – but Edwina was to provide a convenient whipping boy for Dickie's enemies for years to come.[565]

CHAPTER 22

Separate Lives

In the spring of 1952, Dickie's time as Fourth Sea Lord ended and he moved on to his next post, Commander-in-Chief of the Mediterranean Fleet, taking up residence in Admiralty House, a five-bedroomed house with a ballroom in a narrow street in the middle of Valetta. 'In the entrance hall the soaring staircase rose between great marble plaques that listed all the naval commanders-in-chief since Nelson,' remembered Pamela Mountbatten. 'The garden overlooked the ramparts and could be reached only through a tunnel beneath the street and a climb up a steep staircase. When the fleet was berthed in Malta, my father worked in an office overlooking Grand Harbour.'[566]

Edwina continued her tours for St John Ambulance, Save the Children and the Red Cross and her involvement with Naval Wives Voluntary Service, the Allied Wives' Club, the Service Families Nursery and Convalescent Home, Malta Memorial District Nursing Association, Sea Rangers and Girl Guides. She set up a scheme for a volunteer car service for hospital patients and a 'housewives mutual help service'.

Brian Smith was a young secretarial officer in the Commander-in-Chief's Office, responsible amongst other things for the printing office. When he was duty secretary, one of his tasks was to take

Mountbatten's correspondence from the Naval Headquarters to Admiralty House at about nine in the evening, and wait on Mountbatten whilst he went through the papers that Ronnie Brockman had weeded out as requiring his personal attention, which usually took about an hour:

He'd hardly acknowledge that I was there. In all the time I was doing this, I only remember one piece of conversation complaining that his biro was not working. His usual place of work was his office in the naval headquarters in Lascaris, overlooking Grand Harbour. He would work there in the mornings doing the routine work of the day and exchanging calls. Then in the afternoons he would usually play polo. He did not seem overly concerned with the day-to-day running of the Fleet. He left that to the Chief of Staff (Manley Power), his Secretary (Ronnie Brockman) and the Captain of the Fleet. He delegated well and made sure he was supported by able people, while he focused on the matters that interested him. At this time, he was very much concerned with the setting up of a NATO Command – Allied Forces Mediterranean – which would make him a senior NATO commander.

Whenever he visited any ship or naval establishment, he always insisted on being well briefed, in particular he wanted people to think that he remembered them, which was not the case, and he would get lists of people in the ship who had served with him so that he could surprise them by appearing to remember their names at a 'contrived chance meeting'; sometimes when it went wrong, there were embarrassing mistakes. One of his hobbies was keeping up to date and publishing his family tree and he was extremely upset to find that the printing office did not have the same typeface to match the original for amendments. Every day his daily programme was printed and circulated to both Service and Civil Authorities in Malta. He wanted people to know what he was doing.[567]

But Edwina was very different:

> He and Lady Louis seemed to lead separate lives, going about their various engagements on their own. They were not often seen with each other unless attending an official function where they had to be together. If she needed any printing done for the Naval Wives Organisation, she would ask me to go to Admiralty House to discuss it and if it was about lunchtime, I would be asked to have lunch, which was very informal and enjoyable. She would kick her shoes off under the table complaining of sore feet. She would always make you feel that you were important to her and would encourage you to talk. She was always very grateful for anything that was done for her.[568]

In September, the Mountbattens cruised for a month on HMS *Surprise*, the Commander-in-Chief's frigate for official visits, bringing with them Yola Letellier. Malcolm Sargent joined the ship in Naples, ostensibly to discuss arrangements for the following year's coronation concerts. Over the next two weeks he and Edwina, according to his private diaries, spent 'hours of bliss, lolling in the sunshine' on the Commander-in-Chief's private deck, played with dolphins in the waters off Capri, climbed Mount Vesuvius, and toured the brothel district of Algiers.[569]

Dickie was himself enjoying his own affairs. According to Mountbatten's private secretary, John Barratt:

> He met another of his favourite women friends when he was in command of the Mediterranean fleet in the 1950s. She was very pretty [but] . . . She was not popular with the staff at Broadlands, to whom she was off-hand and patronising; I heard her described as a 'snooty little bitch' and worse. Lord Mountbatten kept an occasional relationship with her through the sixties, but by the seventies it had faded out.[570]

One particular issue as part of his new job was the division of responsibilities between Dickie, based in Malta, and his American counterpart, Admiral Carney, Commander-in-Chief, Mediterranean in the North Atlantic Treaty Organisation, based in Naples, which was only resolved that winter when the jobs were combined and given to Mountbatten. An integrated naval/air headquarters staffed by admirals from Italy, France, Greece, the United States and Turkey was set up, which had so many flags in front that it was nicknamed 'Selfridges' after the London department store. As he had at SEAC, and would do again in the future, Mountbatten soon succeeded in persuading different services and countries to become a reasonably coherent international force.

In February 1953, Mountbatten was promoted to Admiral. His nephew, who had recently been appointed Admiral of the Fleet on retirement from his naval career, telegraphed his congratulations: 'Keep it up – you may catch up one day!'[571]

* * *

The fifties were spent with Edwina caught between her husband and the man she had given her heart to. Each spring she would go to

India, where she would stay at the Prime Minister's house, and most years Nehru would come to Britain. At first, they had written to each other every day, but within a year it was weekly and by 1954, it was fortnightly.

But the bond remained strong. It was a bond that Dickie accepted, not least because it kept relations harmonious, but which unsettled Edwina. Throughout the early and mid-fifties she often discussed divorce. 'I've never attempted to stop you or hold you and I never shall,' he told her. 'I don't want you to stay against your will. I am not that selfish.'[572] But she stayed. She stayed because of children and grandchildren, because she liked the life that Dickie gave her, because he loved and needed her and because, in her confused state of mind, she also continued to love him.

Shortly after George VI's death, Edwina, hospitalised with a haemorrhage and worried she might die, passed Nehru's letters to her husband for safekeeping.[573] Dickie, nervous of what they might contain, asked Pamela if she would look at them first. Edwina's confessional letter read:

> You will realise that they are a mixture of typical Jawaharlal letters full of interest and facts and really historic documents. Some of them have no 'personal' remarks at all. Others are love letters in a sense, though you yourself well realise the strange relationship – most of it spiritual – which exists between us. J has obviously meant a great deal in my life, in these last years, and I think I in his too. Our meetings have been rare and always fleeting, but I think I understand him, and perhaps he me, as well as any human beings *can* ever understand each other . . . It is rather wonderful that my affection and respect and gratitude and *love* for you are really so great that I feel I would rather you had these letters

than anyone else, and I feel you would understand and not in any way be hurt – rather the contrary. We understand each other so well although so often we seem to differ and to be miles apart. You have been very sweet and good to me, and we have had a great partnership. My admiration and my devotion to you are very great. I think you know that. I have had a very full and a very happy life on the whole – all thanks to you! Bless you and with my lasting love.[574]

Dickie waited a year to answer:

I'm glad you realise that I know and have always understood the very special relationship between Jawaharlal and you, made the easier by my fondness and admiration for him, and by the remarkably lucky fact that among my many defects God did not add jealousy in any shape or form. I honestly don't believe I've ever known what jealousy means – universal as it seems to be – and if it concerns the happiness of anyone I'm as fond of as you, then only my desire for your happiness exists. That is why I've always made your visits to each other easy and been faintly hurt when at times (such as in 1951) you didn't take me into your confidence right away. Considering how deeply fond we are of each other and how proud and admiring I certainly am of all your wonderful achievements, I cannot but be sad and worried that we should have had so many differences . . . I know I'm selfish and difficult but that doesn't change my deep and profound love for you . . . You have been my mainstay, my inspiration and my true companion for far more than half my life.[575]

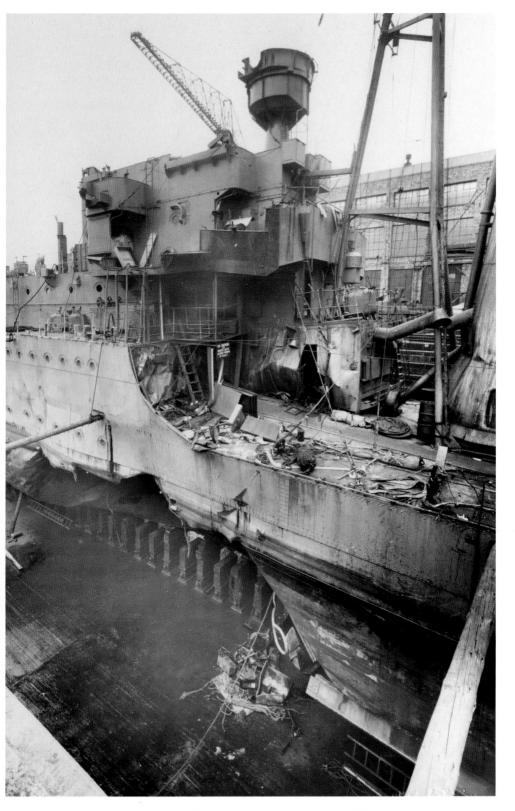

HMS *Kelly* after it was torpedoed in May 1940 with the loss of 27 crew.

The Royal Family watching the filming of Noël Coward's *In Which We Serve*, based on Mountbatten and the HMS *Kelly*, Denham Studios, April 1942.   © *AP Archive*

Mountbatten and Montgomery planning Operation *Overlord*.   © *Granger/Shutterstock*

Mountbatten, as Chief of Combined Operations, with Churchill and Roosevelt at the
Casablanca Conference, 14 January 1943.

Edwina receiving her CBE with Dickie at Buckingham Palace, 1943.

Above left: Mountbatten's lover at South East Asia Command, Janey Lindsay.

© *Southampton University Archive*

Above right: Bill Paley, the founder of CBS, and one of Edwina's wartime lovers.

© *Keystone/Stringer/Getty*

Below: Edwina on relief operations, 1946.

© *ANL/Collect/Shutterstock*

The Mountbattens after a civic reception, 1946.

Dickie, as Supreme Allied Commander South East Asia, accepting the surrender of Japanese forces, 12 September 1945, with Edwina on the balcony behind.

Above: The Mountbatttens
are sworn in as Viceroy and
Vicereine of India, 24 March
1947. *© Hulton Deutsch/Contributor/Getty*

Right: The Mountbattens
confronting 100,000 angry
Parthans, April 1947.

© Southampton University Archive

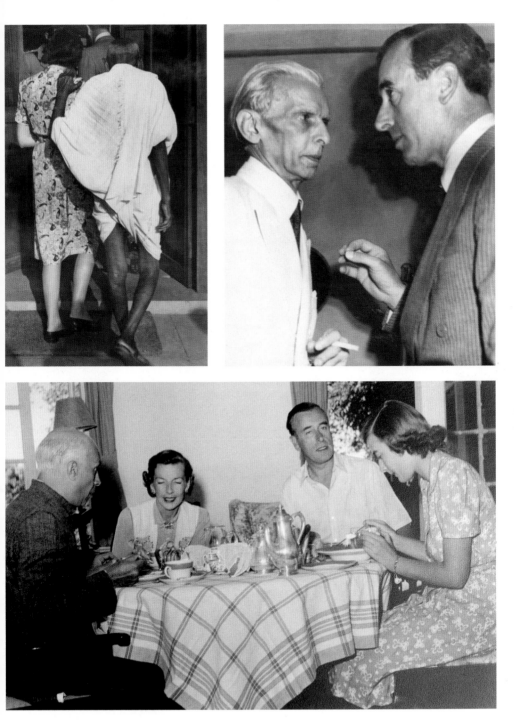

Above left: Gandhi's symbolic gesture showing he could do business with the Mountbattens, 31 March 1947.

© *Southampton University Archive*

Above right: The Muslim leader Muhammad Ali Jinnah and Dickie, a difficult personal relationship which had fatal political consequences, meeting on 5 April 1947.

© *Southampton University Archive*

Below: Nehru, Edwina, Dickie and Pamela having tea, Simla, 11 October 1947.

© *Southampton University Archive*

Edwina with her lover, the conductor Malcolm Sargent, and Walter Monckton's wife Biddy, Government House, 1948.

Edwina with Peter Murphy, a cross between court jester and *éminence grise*, Malta 1949.

What was the nature of the relationship with Nehru? Edwina's authorised biographer, Janet Morgan, has claimed, having talked to 'those who knew them well', that it was purer than a physical relationship, that Nehru respected Dickie and would not have abused that trust. 'To all her lovers she had given only the shell of herself. In exposing her doubts and hopes, she had exhausted herself to Nehru in a way that was more profound than a mere physical embrace. Nothing must be allowed to degrade the precious relationship.'[576]

She argues that the correspondence 'was rhapsodic but chaste, alluding only in general terms to the physical passion they denied themselves.'[577] According to Andrew Wilson, 'The highly charged, brittle and almost manic relationship which both Mountbattens had with Nehru seems to the eyes of hindsight to be much more explicable in terms of a non-consummated, sexual-emotional passion.'[578] Lady Pamela Hicks, interviewed for the publication of her memoir *India Remembered*, said it was platonic.[579] Philip Ziegler passes over it quickly: 'If there was any physical element it can only have been of minor importance to either party.'[580] Mountbatten's grandson, Ashley Hicks, claims Nehru's sister revealed that he was impotent and therefore there could not have been a physical relationship with Edwina.[581]

Yet Edwina writing to her husband refers to an element of the physical alongside the spiritual relationship. 'Others are love letters in a sense, though you yourself well realise the strange relationship – *most of it spiritual* (biographer's italics) – which exists between us.'[582] Richard Hough, the author of several books on the Mountbattens, and who interviewed Edwina's sister, later wrote, 'Mountbatten himself knew that they were lovers. He was proud of the fact, unlike Edwina's sister who deplored the relationship and hated Nehru for the rest of his life as a result.'[583] Marie Seton, a friend and biographer of Edwina, agreed: 'I really don't know about the physical side of their affair – I'd think probably yes.'[584]

Nehru was deeply attractive to women and had many lovers, including: the politician Padmaja Naidu, who threatened to commit suicide over the affair and whom he later appointed Governor of West Bengal; the actress Devika Rani; and Mridula Sarabhai, the General Secretary of the Congress Working Committee.[585] In May 1949, he supposedly fathered a son with a scholar of Indian scripture and mythology, in her early thirties, called Shardha Mata. The boy was brought up in a Christian Missionary boarding school.[586]

The writer Zareer Masani's parents:

> knew Nehru well, and they, and many others who did, thought he was 'highly sexed', as was the whole Nehru family . . . I do know that they wrote each other passionate love letters till she died and that he used to spend the night with her on trips to London as PM in the '50s (much to the chagrin of his Foreign Service minders, one of whom was my uncle and a future Foreign Secretary). It seems unlikely they didn't go to bed.[587]

There are countless references suggesting there was some sort of a physical relationship. Russi Mody, the son of the Governor of the United Provinces, later chairman of Tata Steel, on one of Edwina's early visits to India was asked to fetch Nehru and Edwina and bring them to dinner. Opening the door, he found the two embracing.[588] According to S.S. Pirzada, a former Foreign Minister of Pakistan, Jinnah was given several letters between Nehru and Edwina that had been intercepted. 'One said, "Dickie will be out tonight – come after 10 o'clock." Another, "I have fond memories of Simla – riding and your touch."' Jinnah returned the letters saying he had no wish to capitalise on them.[589]

Nehru's biographer, Stanley Wolpert, writes of seeing Nehru and
Edwina at the opening of New Delhi's Academy of Fine Arts:

And how like adolescent lovers he and Edwina behaved,
touching, whispering into each other's ears, laughing, holding
hands. 'The family line is that they are simply good friends,'
Lady Mountbatten's grandson Lord Romsey told me thirty-
five years later over tea in his sitting-room in Broadlands.
'Nothing more than that, you see.' But I had seen much
more, and Lord Mountbatten himself often referred to
Nehru's correspondence with his wife as love letters, knowing
better than anyone but Nehru how much Edwina adored her
handsome 'Jawaha', as she lovingly called him. That was why
Nehru's daughter Indira hated her.[590]

The author Charlotte Breese feels all the evidence points to a
physical relationship:

Henry Burdwan remembered that, when in Calcutta in the
1950s, Hutch used to hear that Edwina's relationship with
Nehru was 'complicated by his then reputed impotence'. At
this news, Burdman's father, who was 'very well informed'
and had known Edwina and Hutch in London for years,
used to roar with laughter. Many people in India believed
in Nehru's affair with Edwina and those still surviving (time
of writing, 1998) provide the evidence of their own eyes.
Furthermore, every year from 1950 until her death in 1960,
she went to see Nehru in Delhi whenever she could; and he
sometimes visited her in England. While I accept that the
impotence gossip is unproven, I find it strange of Morgan
to insist that Edwina and Nehru conducted an exclusively

affectionate and spiritual relationship . . . All else aside, given Edwina's character and physical needs, it is far more likely than not that she had a fully consummated affair with Nehru . . . There were many stories in Delhi and Kashmir of servants finding them in bed together.[591]

The official line has always been that the love affair did not begin until May 1948 and after the transfer of power, but rumours of their closeness had circulated from soon after the Mountbattens arrived in India. On 31 March 1947, Hamid was writing in his diary, 'Nehru's relationship with Lady Mountbatten is sufficiently close to have raised many eyebrows.'[592] A Balochistani politician, close to Jinnah, Yahya Baktiar claimed that by the summer of 1947 Nehru 'was having a roaring love affair with Lady Mountbatten . . . said to be with the tacit approval of Mountbatten.'[593]

Edwina remained as busy with her own humanitarian work, as ever driven by duty and competitiveness with her husband, but she also continued to support her husband in his career. She acted as charming hostess for politicians and naval colleagues at Wilton Crescent and Broadlands, she used her own contacts to put in a good word on behalf of her husband and she patiently put up with ceremonial events. He missed her when she was away.

'The house is very lonely without you,' he wrote in 1959. 'I shall hate passing your door in a few minutes when I go to bed, without looking in.'[594] Symbolically, that year her present to him was a wrought-iron gate for Broadlands – her monogram on one side, his on the other.

CHAPTER 23

Sea Lord

In 1954, Mountbatten's tour of duty in the Mediterranean ended. Now was his chance for the top job but, determined as Dickie was to be First Sea Lord, there were several senior naval figures equally adamant that he should not be appointed – the most important of whom was Admiral John Cunningham, who questioned his judgement. As so often, Edwina was deployed to use her charms to further her husband's career. 'I am sure you will be able to help, dear Pug,' Edwina wrote to Ismay. 'It would be heart-breaking if Dickie's remarkable personality and outstanding ability was to be wasted in these next vital years in a back yard.'595

Cunningham was soon persuaded that what the Navy needed was not necessarily the most respected or trusted figure, but someone who could fight its corner in Whitehall. In September 1954, the First Sea Lord, Sir Rhoderick McGrigor, offered the job to Mountbatten:

I want you to come here with your drive and powers of persuasion, experience and influence, to keep the Navy on its feet in the nuclear age, to give it a new look where necessary, and to keep up the confidence of the Service. I am sure you are the best man to do it, and it is essential for the good of the

Navy and of the Country that you should relieve me . . . I am sure at this time we need your prestige and qualities.[596]

He was not yet home and dry as Churchill, the Prime Minister, hitherto Mountbatten's greatest supporter, tried to block the appointment. His motives are unclear – perhaps rancour about India, perhaps a desire to have a more emollient First Sea Lord – but eventually he relented. Mountbatten had achieved his lifetime's ambition. On 18 April 1955, he arrived for his first day as professional head of the service to which he had committed his life, to his father's old desk in his father's old office, with a portrait of Prince Louis above the fireplace and his bust on a pedestal outside the door. Family honour had been satisfied.

Being Mountbatten, securing the post was not sufficient. He now intended to use his power, helped by the fact that his old friend and confidant Charles Lambe had been made Second Sea Lord. A Way Ahead Committee was set up to examine its purpose and priorities in the Atomic Warfare age. Amongst much else, it sought to improve recruitment by making the Navy a more attractive career, cut the size of the Reserve Fleet and Royal Marines, reassessed procurement and construction programmes, and concentrated research and development at Portsdown for surface and Portland for underwater weapons. Emphasis was now placed on adapting to the age of nuclear power with the development of the 'County' class guided-missile destroyers, Commando-carriers for amphibious operations and the use of helicopters.

Dickie was different to his predecessors in other ways. He had much larger staffs, including his own valet and stenographer, and insisted on travelling in VIP aircraft. He was also 'a born intriguer', remembered Manley Power. 'If there was a choice between open dealing and a corkscrew approach, he always chose the latter!'[597] Field Marshal Templer once told him, 'Dickie, you're so crooked that if you swallowed a nail, you'd shit a corkscrew!' It was a remark that Mountbatten liked to repeat – only with another recipient.[598]

But his manoeuvrings generally succeeded. He was persuasive, open to counterargument and the need to bring his colleagues along with him, hard-working, had a good political sense and excellent connections socially, regularly inviting politicians and senior naval officers for weekends at Broadlands. He remained a consummate PR man with newsletters to staff and charm offensives with the press. When budget cuts, for example, threatened the future of the Royal Marine band, he enlisted the help of the *Daily Mirror* who launched a successful campaign to save it. His vast experience of administration and politics, together with his technical training, were all brought to bear in the job he had sought all his life.

Dickie was stimulated and satisfied, but Edwina felt 'low and discouraged, like an animal in a trap'.[599] She hated the British weather and parochialism, yearned for the colours of India and the freedom of not being the wife of a public figure. It was on a trip to India in March 1956, Dickie's first since his time as Governor-General, that the tensions showed themselves to John Barratt:

> On an internal flight the photographer checked his equipment into the hold because the next stop was an informal one. During the flight a message was received that a reception committee awaited them. 'When Lord Mountbatten discovered that the photographer did not have his cameras with him, he flew into one of his monumental rages,' remembered John Barratt, 'insisting that the photographer be sent down to the hold during the flight to retrieve his equipment.'[600]

Another row took place because Edwina's special make-up had not been packed. 'I had long since realised who paid the piper in the Mountbattens' relationship: he went to enormous lengths not to upset her,' recollected Barratt. 'There was endless screaming going on, and the poor valet was shaking in his shoes, expecting to be shot at dawn.'[601]

In Burma, the couple stayed at Government House in Rangoon. Barratt later wrote how:

> The Mountbattens never shared a room, but had adjoining ones with her dressing room in between. One evening the maid came to me saying that she could not find the right gloves to go with Lady Mountbatten's outfit. I had the list of what was packed in which trunk, so I went along with her to find them. I knocked and walked in, went straight across to the trunks and retrieved the gloves. Then a voice behind me said, 'Did you find them?' and I turned round to see Lady Mountbatten sitting at her dressing table, stark naked. I was very young and didn't know where to look; she was totally unperturbed.[602]

Whilst Dickie was in India, the Commander Crabb case hit the headlines. On 17 April 1956, the Soviet leaders Nikolai Bulganin and Nikita Khrushchev had arrived in Portsmouth on the battleship *Ordzhonikidz*, on a visit to improve Anglo–Soviet relations. The Prime Minister, Anthony Eden, had given orders that there were to be no intelligence operations during the visit, but the instruction was misunderstood by MI6, who sent a freelance frogman for the intelligence services, Lionel 'Buster' Crabb, to study the underside of the boat.

That night the First Lord of the Admiralty, James Thomas,

dining with the Russian visitors, was asked about the frogman seen swimming around the battleship. There were furious British denials, promises of an inquiry, and the head of MI6, Sir John Sinclair, was quietly forced to take early retirement. Fourteen months later, a body was washed ashore, missing head and hands, which the government claimed was Crabb. This was refuted by his former diving partners and girlfriend and the mystery continues to this day about the fate of the frogman – with varying accounts of him being killed by Soviet frogmen at the time and being captured to live on in the Soviet Union until 1981.[603]

Mountbatten claimed that he knew nothing about the operation, codenamed Claret, and had even left instructions that, even if he had known, no operation should take place. But his own Vice-Chief of Naval Staff, Sir William Davis, gives a different version of events in his unpublished autobiography. He asserts that, contrary to Mountbatten's claim, he insisted that the First Lord of the Admiralty be told as soon as he, Mountbatten, learnt of the operation, and actually tried to hush up the story until it broke in the press. A suspicion was that Mountbatten had known all along and simply wanted to keep the operation quiet.

How involved in the operation was Mountbatten? There are accounts of him meeting Crabb at Cowdray Park shortly before the dive and that a naval team from HMS *Vernon* also inspected the Russian ship's hull the same day.[604] According to Sydney Knowles, Crabb's diving partner, Crabb had previously worked for Mountbatten in Gibraltar in 1943 and after the war 'on some type of secret work for Admiral Mountbatten in a research lab at Bushey Park.'[605]

Mountbatten, a keen diver, had a penchant for clandestine activities from his time at Combined Operations and SEAC, and certainly maintained close links with SIS and other intelligence agencies. When he retired, the head of SIS wrote to him, 'I have enjoyed working for you and how grateful I am to you for all the support you have given to our service.'[606] The previous October, Mountbatten had dined at the home of the SIS officer Bill Dunderdale, with the then head of SIS Sir John Sinclair, the writer Ian Fleming and the former naval intelligence officer Donald McLachlan. It is unlikely that he would not have been informed of the SIS operation. Whether he had any involvement in the Crabb mission remains a mystery. The relevant files remain closed.

In the summer of 1956, General Nasser nationalised the Suez Canal Company, which was the responsibility of the Anglo–French Suez Canal Company. The Prime Minister, Anthony Eden, was determined on seizing it back. The episode threatened to destroy Mountbatten's carefully planned career.

Mountbatten, as Acting Chairman of the Chiefs of Staff Committee, initially advised that two Royal Marine Commandos could within days seize Port Said and secure the first 25 miles of the causeway along the canal, but they would not have been able to hold it.[607] As planning progressed for what was called Operation *Musketeer*, he exercised doubts that strayed into the realms of politics, arguing that Eden's requested 'full-scale invasion' would involve bombing and bombardment and consequent civilian casualties.

Intervention was not only militarily difficult – the occupation of Egypt, even if it could be achieved, would tie down a large number of troops that were not even available – but, he argued, would destabilise the Middle East, undermine the authority of the UN, divide the Commonwealth, and diminish Britain's global standing

He alone amongst the military and political leaders seemed most aware of the diplomatic ramifications of intervention, most notably in the Commonwealth. He drafted a note, suggesting the first step should be economic sanctions combined with gathering international support to negotiate terms, which he showed first to the First Lord and then the Minister of Defence, both of whom advised him not to show it to Eden.

At the end of August, he drafted a letter of resignation to Eden, saying he was worried that military action was in breach of United Nations principles and risked provoking a thermo-nuclear war.[608] After sitting on it for 24 hours, he decided not to send it, but submit his resignation instead to the First Lord of the Admiralty, who advised further discussion with the Minister of Defence. They told him that, as a serving officer, he could not refuse to carry out orders.

In November, with an Anglo–French invasion force four days away from Egypt and the first parachute jump due in 72 hours, Mountbatten made another plea to Eden, fully expecting he might now be sacked. 'You can imagine how hard it is for me to break with all service custom and write direct to you in this way, but I feel so desperate about what is happening that my conscience would not allow me to do otherwise.'[609]

The situation was only saved when international pressure, notably from America, forced Eden to abandon his intervention and a United Nations Peacekeeping Force was sent in. 'Nothing that has ever occurred to me in time of peace caused me so much trouble, so much worry, so much pain and so much grief as the Suez fiasco,' Mountbatten was to claim when interviewed in 1972.[610]

Mountbatten's role during the Suez Crisis has excited much controversy. It is clear his conscience was troubled by the proposed British military action and the collusion with Israel and France but, as a serving officer, had he much choice except to obey orders? He kept threatening his resignation, but only finally did so after he had received his promotion to Admiral of the Fleet and a few days before the planned invasion, when it was unlikely it would be accepted – it wasn't. Was it really his place, as First Sea Lord, to resign simply because he did not agree with government policy, given no Cabinet Minister, apart from Monckton as Minister of Defence, did so? If he had been more prepared to sacrifice his career, would it have made a difference?

His final years as First Sea Lord were concerned with adapting the Navy to the age of nuclear weapons, managing demands for reduction in personnel, and defending the Navy against government cuts, especially its reduced role against the Army and Air Force and with the increased role of NATO. The latter he achieved with some success, cutting the civilian staff by 23,500 with the General List only pruned by 1,900 and pay increased. In May 1958, he was offered the post of Chief of the Defence Staff and was succeeded as First Sea Lord by Charles Lambe. After 40 years, his career in the Royal Navy was over.

* * *

On a snowy January day in 1960, Pamela married David Hicks, an interior decorator, at Romsey Abbey in what the press called 'The Wedding of the Year'.[611] The date had been picked to suit the Royal Family and most of them were in evidence. All except the Queen, who was expecting Prince Andrew. Princess Anne was a bridesmaid and Prince Philip proposed the toast. Amongst the guests were numerous crowned heads of Europe, Noël Coward, Douglas Fairbanks Jr, Malcolm Sargent, Clement Attlee, Bernard Montgomery and Harold Macmillan, many of whom had to get out and push the coach between Romsey station and the house when it became trapped in snow.

The main reception was held at Broadlands and was marked by a power cut and the appearance of a smartly dressed old lady wrapped in furs, who introduced herself as Princess Victoria of Hildenbergh, but who didn't appear on any list of invited guests. Bill Evans, who had just joined the staff as a valet, remembered, 'In the hall Lady Louis immediately took charge, kissing the old lady on the cheek and saying: "My dear how lovely to see you . . . You must be very tired after your journey, Your Royal Highness. Let me take you to your room to tidy up." The police were called and the old dear escorted off the premises.'[612]

Five days later, after a brief visit to Sandringham to see the Queen, Edwina left for a ten-week tour of Asia. 'I am off at dawn filled with trepidation and hardly dare even to *think* about my Tour, as it would be far too exhausting a process,' she wrote to her husband. 'I shall miss you a lot and think of you a great deal.'[613]

Edwina's punishing work schedule had already begun to take its toll. She constantly suffered from flu, tiredness, headaches and insomnia. In 1956, her doctor had diagnosed mild angina and warned she would be dead in three years if she did not slow down. Two years later, a growth in the parotid gland was surgically removed, giving her a lopsided cheek and drooping eye, and the impression she had suffered a stroke. In January 1959, she had caught chickenpox from a grandchild and the following year was told by her doctor that her angina had worsened and, without rest, she had only months to live. She had said nothing to her family and simply pressed on, as she was doing now.

After being reunited with Nehru in India, she flew on to Singapore and from there on 18 February to Borneo. After a day's rest, she threw herself into her programme, touring an army training area, watching a gymkhana and attending an eight-course Chinese dinner given by St John Ambulance. Robert Turner, the acting Governor with whom she was staying, later recollected that, though she picked at her food, she still managed to speak:

with complete assurance for some ten minutes without notes
. . . On reaching my house, she was preceding me up the
incline leading to the steps up to the entrance when she
suddenly caught the railing, and my wife took her arm. She
confessed that she had a headache and was tired but declined
offers of aspirin etc, thanked my wife and myself for a most
enjoyable day and went into her room. About an hour later
my wife noticed that the light in her room was on.[614]

Turner's wife knocked and asked if she was alright. 'She replied,
"Yes fine," and after exchanging good-nights she returned to her
room. The next day Edwina complained of a chronic headache and
a local doctor was summoned. 'He did not think there was anything
medically wrong, but that she might have the beginnings of flu or
even malaria,' Turner later wrote.[615]

After visiting a local hospital, she briefly attended a coffee
morning for representatives from local voluntary organisations and
then rested until the afternoon when, resplendent in white uniform
with a full row of medals, she inspected a police band, presented
some certificates and made a short speech, followed by a brief
appearance at an evening reception. Turner, concerned about her
health, suggested she should postpone her flight for the following
day, Sunday, until Monday. She smiled and 'said she would "see" in
the morning.'[616]

At 7.30 a.m. the next morning, her assistant, Irene Checkley, went
to her room to help her get ready for her departure for the airport.
The curtains had been drawn back, letting in the early morning
light. Edwina was still in bed. A touch of her cold cheek confirmed
she was dead, at the age of 59. Around her lay some of Nehru's
letters.[617]

The doctor who had seen her the previous day was summoned

and pronounced death from artery coronary thrombosis at 2.30 a.m. Dressed in her white St John uniform, after a short service conducted by an Assistant Bishop called from another Sunday service, she was driven to Government House where the air-conditioning was better, and placed under police guard. That evening her coffin, hastily constructed that day, was taken to the airport for the start of her sad journey home.

Dickie was at Broadlands and learnt of his wife's death from a phone call at 3.00 a.m. from Turner. 'It was a poleaxe blow. I simply couldn't grasp it.'[618] He had tried to ring her a few hours earlier and couldn't get through. 'He was waiting for her call when he received the news,' his daughter Pamela later remembered.[619] She, herself, was told of her mother's death at the airport as she arrived back in Britain from honeymoon.

'Miserable. I never realised how much I loved her and what she meant to me,' Dickie wrote in his diary for 23 February.[620] In spite of their marital difficulties, the two had become increasingly close in recent years. Edwina had remained restless and driven by her work, but the relationship was now marked by real affection, helped by the joys of being grandparents.

John Barratt was later to write:

Lady Mountbatten had become the faithful, devoted wife that he had craved – and missed – so much in the earlier years of their marriage. She had never lost her spirit, never been subservient, but they had spent more time together than they had previously, and the prospect of a comfortable and contented old age must have seemed both possible and enticing.[621]

Immediately Dickie's friends rallied around. Charles Lambe spent the whole next day with his former colleague. Some 6,000 telegrams and letters began to arrive, ranging from presidents and public figures, such as Cecil Beaton, to ordinary people whose lives she had touched.[622] Charles Smith's abiding image of the time was his employer, 'in the drawing room with one of these telegrams crumpled between his trembling hands . . . tears flowing from his eyes.'[623]

The condolence note from Ronald Brooke, who had served on Mountbatten's staff in SEAC and in Malta, was typical. He remembered: 'the remarkable way in which she so quickly knew everyone and remembered them as individuals' and that 'to her qualities of charm and gaiety she added a quite astonishing ability for organising and providing the driving force behind a vast range of activities, all of which were for the benefit of other people. The sum was an endearing and tremendous personality.'[624]

On 24 February Edwina's body arrived at Broadlands and was taken to Romsey Abbey, only a month before the scene of much family happiness, where overnight, 52 male members of staff took turns in pairs to stand guard over it in half-hour watches. Edwina had stipulated in her will that she wanted to be buried at sea and so the next day, after a short service of prayers, the hearse left for the 30-mile journey to the naval yard at Portsmouth. As the funeral cortège left, her butler Charles Smith took her white Sealyham terrier, Snippet, 'to catch a glimpse of the final departure of his mistress and the dog's instincts seemed to tell him what was happening. He stayed woefully in my arms and whimpered sadly.'[625]

Eight chief petty officers, to the sound of Bosun's Calls, carried the lead-lined coffin, covered by a Union Jack, onto the Frigate HMS *Wakefield* and laid it on a steel-grey bier on the Quarterdeck. Under pale, grey skies, the ship set out to sea. The Archbishop of Canterbury, Geoffrey Fisher, conducted a 15-minute service with no hymns or address. He ended with the traditional words 'we therefore commit her body to the deep' and the coffin was carefully tipped into the raging waters below as four Royal Marine buglers sounded *The Last Post* and *Reveille*.

Dickie, in full admiral's uniform, tears streaming down his face, gently kissed his all-white wreath and tossed it into the sea. A cable away on the Indian frigate the *Trishul*, Krishna Menon, Indian Defence Minister, dropped a farewell garland of marigolds from Nehru. Terry Cattermole, the Officer of the Watch on HMS *Wakeful*, remembered how:

> Lord Louis and the Prince [Philip], both in uniforms of Admiral of the Fleet, stood at the salute for a long moment as we slowly got underway. I noted in the Ship's Log 'Committed to the deep the body of Countess Mountbatten at 14.28 in position 50deg 36min North 0deg 57min West' and we turned back towards Portsmouth.[626]

CHAPTER 24

After Edwina

Edwina's death had made headlines around the world and scores of tributes poured in, of which Arthur Bryant's in the *Illustrated London News* was typical:

> She was a very great woman, one of those rare individuals, some famous and others not, who bear about them the unmistakeable hallmark of greatness . . . warmth of heart, the vitality and the splendid courage, selflessness and above all, humanity of this remarkable woman.[627]

On 5 March, a memorial service was held at Romsey Abbey attended by over 1,000 people, followed two days later by another at Westminster Abbey, the music arranged by Malcolm Sargent and attended by the Royal Family, Prime Minister and Cabinet. Hundreds of extra chairs had to be brought in for the overflow in the cloisters.

Edwina's death had brought even closer together the two men whom she had loved the most. It had taken almost a month, but on 18 March, Nehru wrote by hand to Dickie:

I was working in my office on the 21st February morning when the message about Edwina came through our naval headquarters. I was stunned and could not believe it . . . It was exceedingly difficult to connect Edwina with death. She was the embodiment of life and vital energy and joy . . . Edwina died as she had lived, a radiant figure, laughing her way through life's many troubles and bringing joy and healing to innumerable troubled hearts . . . It was our high privilege to have known her and had her love and friendship. In this rather dismal world, she came as a star brightening our lives and giving us generously and abundantly a bit of her rare and precious self. There is no way for me to express the depth of my gratitude for her.[628]

One of Dickie's virtues was his generosity of spirit. He had accepted Edwina's lovers during her life and he was not going to reject them now she was dead. Indeed, he felt a bond with anyone who had also loved Edwina. After her death he stayed in touch with them, called on their support for the Edwina Mountbatten Trust, which supported various nursing charities, and provided them with mementos of her life. Malcolm Sargent, for example, was touched to receive a 'very beautiful souvenir. I shall always cherish it and am most grateful for the gift'.[629]

Edwina's unexpected death changed Dickie's life in practical terms, with 80 per cent death duties with the remaining 20 per cent divided 7.5 per cent to each daughter and 5 per cent to him. He thought of selling Classiebawn and there were newspaper reports that a butler, chef, under-chef and parlour maid had been laid off. Douglas Fairbanks Jr wrote hinting that he could involve him in a land development plan in the Bahamas.[630]

'I shall not be able to do things on the scale which Edwina and I could do together in her lifetime, but I am not particularly keen on entertaining, or extravagant in my tastes,' Mountbatten replied. 'It is true that when I finish from this job, I might like to take on some business appointments to keep me occupied and to replace the very handsome salary and allowance which I receive in my present job. But that is still quite a way off, I hope.'[631]

In the end he decided to make Classiebawn pay its way, renting it out to rich Americans when not in use by family and friends. After Edwina's death, he made a point of going every August and most Easters. Edwina's death had drawn him closer to his daughters and their families, and Classiebawn became a place they could all come together, a place to recapture his own youth and where he could exert the authority and control that his character required.

Patricia by 1960 had four children – Norton (b. 1947), Michael John (b. 1950), Joanna (b. 1955), Amanda (b. 1957); Philip would be born in 1961 and Tim and Nicholas three years later. Overlapping them would be Pamela's children, Edwina (b. 1961), Ashley (b. 1963) and India (b. 1967).

William Evans had joined the staff at Broadlands in 1959 and was to remain with Mountbatten for the next decade. He has fond memories of his employer, but no illusions about him. 'Mountbatten was quite controlling. You had to know how to eat strawberries. They always had to have their husks. You would then make a hole in the sugar, fill with cream and swirl the strawberry. Ditto there were exact rules about how to eat a pear. Edwina just used to smile.'[632]

'He was very demanding. Just pressure of work. Everything was coded – telephones, the tooting of cars at the gate. Remember he was a signalman. We knew if the phone rang once it was for him or Edwina, twice for Patricia and three times for Pamela.'[633]

'He was always good fun especially with his grandchildren. One

Christmas he insisted I obtain a box of Beatles wigs for grand-children. The Managing Director of company had to drive down with a box. Mountbatten pranced around in the wig throughout Christmas Day.'[634]

Dickie found life as a widower difficult. 'I know you think that I ought to be able to live alone and spend my weekends alone,' he wrote to Patricia two years after Edwina's death, 'but I feel so terribly lonely without someone.'[635] Not that he was without admirers. He complained to a friend, Grace Stevens, that 'it is curious that at the very time I am living a fairly secluded, hardworking life, that so many people who knew Edwina, but who I hardly know, should be descending on me.'[636]

Amongst those who took an interest in him were two New York socialites, slightly older than him, Mary Hoyt Wiborg, a great-niece of the Civil War General William Sherman and Rhoda Tanner Doubleday, who had married into the publishing family. Another was Olga Stringfellow, a journalist at the *Daily Express,* whom he had first met in 1960.[637] Stringfellow had come to Britain from New Zealand in 1949, after marrying a naval draughtsman whom she later divorced, and was beginning to forge a successful career as an historical journalist. The two were sufficiently close for friends of hers to think they might marry. One of her presents to him was the tiller from Captain Bligh's boat.[638] Stringfellow later became a well-known faith healer, specialising in sportsmen. She died in her early seventies, having drunk herself to death.

Attending the wedding of the future King Juan Carlos of Spain in May 1962, Mountbatten found himself 'hotly pursued by a princess of considerable beauty and forty years his junior. She announced that she was madly in love and determined to marry him, and caused something of a scandal by rearranging the place-cards at the state banquet so that they were sitting side by side.' He was delighted:

'the whole experience was pretty good for the morale of a sixty-two-year-old widower.'[639]

But the person who had really captured his heart was a beautiful and vivacious Italian over 30 years younger. Blonde and with a stunning figure, which she showed off in very short minis, Sibilla Tomacelli was the daughter of the Duke and Duchess Della Torre and had recently married Columbus O'Donnell, nephew of the multimillionaire Huntington Hartford. Columbus' mother was married to Ivar Bryce, a former colleague of Bunny Phillips in the Latin American section of the wartime British Security Coordination, and Dickie had met them whilst staying with the Bryces on a visit to the West Indies at the beginning of the 1960s.

Throughout the next two decades, Sibilla and Dickie met regularly – sometimes alone and sometimes with her husband – on Mountbatten's annual trip to the Bahamas to stay with the Brabournes and Hicks at their holiday homes on Eleuthera, or on visits to London. 'He was such a glamorous person. I was flattered by his attention,' she later remembered:

> He certainly had a crush on me. He made his feelings very clear. He was very special. We would go scuba diving and riding. Everyone loved him. He was good company and a very easy guest. He had kindness, he was always trying to help people. If you needed help, he would do anything he could. I too admired and liked him hugely. He was a good-looking man, nevertheless, he was 30 years older and even though we had a very close relationship, it was never physical, and I was happily married.

At a family wedding of the time, whilst Sibilla was talking to Patricia Brabourne, Roald Dahl (whom both Sibilla and Patricia had not previously met) came up to Sibilla and remarked, 'I hear you are the girl that Mountbatten is in love with,' upon which, clearly seeing Sibilla taken aback by this comment, Patricia immediately added, 'Not only my father, but my husband and son too.'

After one such meeting, he wrote to her, 'I enjoyed your visit enormously, and so did Pammy & David. In fact, Pammy, who is apt to be critical of my friends, told Patricia that she had rarely found a girl so beautiful as you to also be so nice! I more than agree with Pammy & count myself as very lucky to have found such a gay & charming friend – we all miss you & send love.'

Two months later, he admonished her for not joining him for a weekend at Luton Hoo whilst the Queen was staying. 'The Queen wouldn't have eaten you & Prince Philip would surely have joined the ranks of your admirers! . . . I can never thank you enough for your sweet companionship and friendship which has meant a great deal in the life of a lonely man. Much, much love my dear from Dickie.'[640]

In February 1963, on a month's goodwill tour of Central and South America, Dickie stayed with the O'Donnells. Sibilla hired a speedboat and the two went to Rose Island, a short hop from Nassau harbour. 'She proved herself to be as reckless in a speedboat as in a motor car and presently succeeded in running us on to a coral reef,' he wrote in his diary. 'After that we had a lovely sunbathe on a completely deserted stretch of beach and embarked again in good time for lunch.'[641]

That evening they dined at the Casino and then danced until 1.00 a.m. in the Bahama Club. Sibilla remained on Mountbatten's mind and he wrote to her constantly on his trip. A postcard from Buenos Aires said it all: 'I miss you and all our fun in Nassau.'[642] Three weeks later, he wrote again:

Sibilla darling, Bless you for your very sweet letter which I found at Broadlands when I got back on 22nd – all alone and rather depressed and it cheered me up immediately. I loved my short stay at Galaxy very, very much – more than did I believe. I hated leaving. I miss you more than I should – I've not met anyone as lovely, loveable & sweet for very many years. Write to me again, Sibilla dearest & destroy this letter. All my love, Dickie.[643]

She returned his affections. Thanking him for a dress he had given for her birthday, in return for her having knitted a sweater for him, she wrote, 'My Darling Dickie. It's always fascinating to see what a man thinks a woman looks "smashing" in. The only thing I am sure of is that the length won't go much below the knee.' She continued discussing Patricia's refusal of some of her father's invitations:

I wish I was your daughter. I would never leave your side, not ever for a second. I was so sorry to hear about your gastric troubles and of the forthcoming hernia operation. I know of a wonderful nurse that would love to take care of you, highly qualified, her name Miss Sibilla. I miss you and I am looking forward to seeing you in April. All my love, Sibilla.[644]

Bill Evans remembered how 'he loved beautiful girls. He was especially close to Sacha Abercorn.' It was a view confirmed by John Barratt. 'But the only one he really deeply loved, apart from Edwina, was his goddaughter Sacha, the Duchess of Abercorn. He told me that if he ever married again, it would have to be Sacha.'[645] According to Brian Hoey, whose book was sanctioned by the Mountbatten family, Sacha Abercorn was, with Yola, the most important female relationship (besides Edwina) of his life and 'eventually became Mountbatten's closest companion'.[646]

Sacha Phillips was the daughter of Bunny and Gina Phillips, and one of Mountbatten's godchildren. Tall, slim and highly attractive, in 1966 aged 20 she had married James, Marquess of Hamilton, heir to the Duke of Abercorn, who had an estate a few miles over the border from Classiebawn. Hoey was to write:

> Mountbatten and Sacha had become close in the years leading up to her marriage but it was after she became Marchioness of Hamilton (before her husband inherited the dukedom) that the relationship blossomed into the deep and lasting love that caused Mountbatten to reflect to his secretary, John Barratt, that she was the only woman he could ever have contemplated marrying after Edwina. He had professed love for many women but said he had never considered marriage to any of them – except Sacha.[647]

Sacha Abercorn would later claim that if Mountbatten had ever proposed when she was single, she would have accepted. 'It was a huge physical and spiritual attraction on both sides,' she remembered, 'and the forty-five-year gap in our ages just melted away.'[648] They spoke each day on the phone and she would often visit Broadlands, where the two would walk in the grounds or ride. He took her to functions at Buckingham Palace, for a weekend to see Yola in Paris, or she would accompany him to social events. The artist Derek Hill remembered them at one of his openings as 'easily the most attractive couple in the room – though apparently, at first, few would have guessed that they were anything but what they appeared to be, an uncle with his favourite niece.'[649]

For her, 'It wasn't the great passion one reads about, but a mutual affection and respect.'[650] It lasted ten years from the mid-sixties, and she credits the relationship with giving her greater self-confidence. 'I know I became a much stronger person through knowing him.'[651] As with Sibilla, when her marriage ran into difficulties, Mountbatten took it upon himself to intercede and try and save the marriage, drawing on his own experience with Edwina. He saw nothing unusual in doing so. For him, a relationship with a married woman was safe. As Sacha Abercorn later reflected, 'He knew it could go only so far and that's what he wanted. No permanent commitment.'[652]

There were to be many girlfriends after Edwina's death. According to his daughter, Patricia, they tended to be:

> youngish, very pretty with long legs and a small waist – rather Victorian figures really. Girls didn't have to be intelligent either. He could be quite attracted to someone who wasn't that bright, if it was going to be just a minor flirtation, but all his real, serious girlfriends were intelligent.[653]

Many of the girlfriends were the wives of men who had served with him. The couple would be invited down to Broadlands for the weekend and the men then distracted by the offer of a day's fishing or shooting – or would have to return to work on the Sunday night and the wife would stay on until the following day. Sometimes the wife came down on the Friday to be joined later by her husband. On one occasion, the husband:

> Arrived a few hours earlier than we had anticipated, while his wife and Lord Mountbatten were upstairs together in one of the spare bedrooms. I could see the husband coming, so I dashed upstairs and tried all the rooms until I found one that

was locked. I called to Lord Mountbatten and explained the urgency of the situation, arranging to meet the lady at the side entrance. I found Lord Mountbatten's Labrador, Juno, and took her with me, so that the lady could slip outside with her and go round to the main entrance as though she had been for a walk with the dog.[654]

'All girls had their set dates,' recollected Bill Evans. 'We all knew where to be or not to be. He would go out riding then return to bath and change. He would put them in dressing rooms next to him. They were generally women in their thirties, young wives, very beautiful and always slim, the thinner the thighs the better. We knew to stay away. He had a settee bed in the guest room which linked through to his room. He liked his women small-breasted like Edwina. I could tell when he was in nookie mode.'[655]

John Barratt remembered, 'he liked slim-hipped women with flat chests, very like Edwina. His ideal woman was the young Jane Fonda: an all-time favourite film of his was *Cat Ballou*' and 'he loved riding with a woman, which was almost an obsession, a kink.'[656] 'His big turn-on was riding boots and jodhpurs, but only when they were worn by young women with long, slim legs,' according to Bill Evans.[657]

Part of Mountbatten's interest was voyeuristic. Barratt noticed that he kept a viewer and slides in his bedroom:

My curiosity was aroused – as soon as I had the chance, I looked at the slides. Every single one was of a young woman in riding gear, wearing high boots and spurs. There was nothing pornographic about them – the girls were fully dressed – but he obviously got a thrill out of seeing young women in boots spurring the horses. He also kept one or two magazines under lock and key: they were mildly pornographic, but nothing dreadful. He told me he was particularly fascinated by the story of a riding mistress who made her pupils sit astride a wooden horse and whipped them. Anything to do with riding turned him on.[658]

Another young woman to whom he became close was Mary Lou Emery. Aged 17, she had come to Broadlands as a groom in 1964 and would ride with Mountbatten several times a week – he had heart trouble and it was felt someone should always be with him – and take care of his dogs when he was away. He enjoyed her company – she was less deferential than other members of staff – and a similar age to his eldest grandchildren, and they remained close even after she married in 1969.

She and her husband accompanied Mountbatten to see Yola in France and he became like an honorary grandfather to her children, sending them postcards, arranging tickets for the Garter Ceremony, the Opening of Parliament and Trooping the Colour. Their closeness, and his generosity to her, aroused jealousy amongst the staff and even rumours that her son was Mountbatten's.[659]

The suggestion that he might be having an affair with Mary Lou was fed by:

the fact that, whenever he went out riding with Mary Lou or one of his girlfriends, he wore a French letter, and all his close staff knew this. He tried to be secretive, but he was hopeless at it. He kept his supply of washable condoms in a little wooden box by his bed, which always amused the servants and caused much speculation among them. He also always wore spurs when riding with a woman, and if he was going riding immediately after working with me in his bedroom on the mail, he would slip the spurs surreptitiously out of the drawer where he kept them – as though they were something to be ashamed of, and as though I didn't know about them.[660]

Another regular riding companion and visitor to Broadlands was Philippa de Pass, whose husband Robert had served on Mountbatten's staff.

'He also invited us to Classiebawn Castle, where our children had wonderful holidays with his grandchildren,' she remembered:

He was very good with the young and we all had such happy times together. Robert and myself took him to a Magic Circle evening and he caused quite a stir by producing an unusual pencil, which was in fact a pistol that I think was presented to him by Muhammad Ali Jinnah. He fired it into the floorboards on the stage and the poor lady at the piano had quite a fright! . . . We both have so many happy memories of Dickie. He was a remarkable man having had so many extraordinary careers – such good company and so interesting to talk to and be with. He always entertained us with great style.[661]

Mountbatten had a very old-fashioned, aristocratic view of marriage, partly shaped by his own marital experience, of it being separate from love. As long as one was discreet, anything was permitted. One of his girlfriends, at his request, even initiated a young member of his family into sex.[662]

Mountbatten was also a client of the celebrated Madame Claude. According to William Stadiem, who worked for her and later wrote her biography, Mountbatten:

was so discreet that the only place he would see her girls was in Baron Elie de Rothschild's private jet, circling the skies above

Paris as the two old friends enjoyed a *ménage à quatre*. While Mountbatten (whose military nickname was 'Mountbottom') had long been rumoured to have unconventional interests, Claude had no interest in 'outing' him.[663]

In the early 1960s, whilst visiting Los Angeles, Dickie had met the 30-year-old actress Shirley MacLaine through the producer Mike Frankovitch. She had been his escort to a dinner at Jack Warner's home and then they had seen the film of John Fowles' *The Collector* together. That evening Dickie wrote in his diary, 'I drove Shirley back in my car – she certainly is a very sweet girl.'[664] MacLaine, in an open relationship with her businessman husband Steve Parker, was then at the height of her fame after *The Apartment* and *Irma la Douce*, in which she played the part of a prostitute.

Another guest, Christopher Plummer, remembered, 'After dinner we were all marched into the screening room to watch a sneak preview of *Irma la Douce*. Mountbatten and Shirley were two rows in front of me. His arm was around her and tsk! tsk! Was it the boozy haze clouding my heavy eyes or did I not catch sight of them spooning in the dark?'[665]

Shortly afterwards at another dinner, which involved a party game of couples being tied up and then freeing themselves, MacLaine had been his partner and he confided to his diary, 'I must say Shirley is a very sweet and amusing girl and we got on like a house on fire.'[666] In July, she was one of his guests for a party at Broadlands alongside Douglas Fairbanks Jr and Rex Harrison, and was thrilled to meet Indira Gandhi.

According to William Evans, 'She was a very bright cookie. She often stayed at Broadlands or they would meet in New York and she became a good friend. She often acted as Dickie's hostess and could hold court with anyone from heads of state down . . . the affair went on for many years. They hit it off immediately and she was number 1 for a long time.'[667]

There were several beautiful and rich women to whom he was attracted. They included Cristina Ford, an Italian-born socialite, over 25 years younger than Mountbatten, who had married Henry Ford II, chairman of the Ford Motor Company, in 1965.[668] After he received a picture of her on her 1969 Christmas card, he wrote to Sibilla, 'She was wearing long slim black boots over the knees in the photo! She should join my Life Guards!'[669] Another was Lydia Melhado, a General Motors heiress married to Francis Farr, one of Wall Street's richest salesmen, over 30 years younger than Mountbatten, whom Dickie would see whenever he was in New York.

He also remained loyal to Barbara Cartland, who was completely in love with him, though her affections were not reciprocated. Dick Hough remembers how 'they met at least once a week and often spent the weekend together at Camfield Place or Broadlands. Barbara told me later, bubbling away, "We are terribly fond of one another – almost lovers." Then a shrill laugh. "But not bed, my dear. Oh no, no, no. We're both long past *that*."'[670]

William Evans remembered:

> she would call in for lunch or tea, in a mass of pink chiffon, then vanish, leaving behind her a pile of books on health and homeopathy and a quantity of new vitamin pills and elixirs to try. Down the years she recommended to him the remarkable proprieties of a great variety of elixirs, herbs, vitamin capsules and royal bee jellies. One of the elixirs, a brown syrupy honey, he took quite regularly.[671]

Mountbatten would respond diplomatically to her various gifts. 'I must say I am very touched at the expensive Christmas present you gave me of seven vitamin E pills. I gather they were Vita-E Gels with strength of 800 i.v.,' he wrote in 1961. 'I am in the midst of taking them and look forward to feeling terrific at the end of the week.'[672] At Christmas the next year he wrote to thank her for a book on acupuncture. 'I must say it is marvellous the way you find all these interesting medical theories.'[673]

Her biographer, Tim Heald, wrote, 'Barbara Cartland talks with huge affection and admiration of Mountbatten and claims that in later life they were much in love, spoke every day on the telephone, and that each morning to enable him to face the rigours of the day he used to play her the Royal Philharmonic Orchestra recording of *Love Songs, Sung Especially For You*.'[674]

Another platonic friend in love with him was Carola Rothschild, a wealthy Jewish widow – she was part of the Warburg family who had been business partners of Felix Cassell – with whom Mountbatten often stayed in New York. She was involved with United World Colleges, a charity in which Mountbatten played a prominent role as a member of the American committee and benefactor.[675] Pammy and Patricia had stayed with her at her home in South Carolina during the Second World War. Mountbatten had no compunction about taking advantage of her generosity, allowing her to pay for a swimming pool at Broadlands, costing $17,000, for his seventieth birthday and paying for his trips to America.

'Carola was very fond of him, and they would sit for hours holding hands, but he never felt for her the way she felt for him,' remembered John Barratt. 'In fact, while he was spending time with his girlfriend Sibilla Clarke, life in New York would be rather awkward because Carola was wildly jealous and would listen in to his phone calls – and even mine, because sometimes he got me to ring and make arrangements for him.'[676]

Mountbatten also kept in touch with his former girlfriends.[677]

Sally Dean, now married to John Connell, Chief of Staff of the American Air Force whom she had met at SEAC, visited Broadlands with him in 1966. She wrote thanking Mountbatten, 'Dearest Dickie . . . I hope to retain my shape until we meet again and trust that you will continue to be as handsome and fatally attractive as ever. Love to you as always, Sally.'[678]

Janey Lindsay had divorced Peter in 1946 and in August that year married Beaverbrook's son, Max Aitken. That marriage had not lasted and they had divorced four years later. The following year she married Robin Compton and she and her husband often saw Mountbatten.[679]

Looking back on their times together, Mountbatten wrote in January 1969:

Darling Janey, 25 years ago was the first time we celebrated your birthday together – so Wednesday is a sort of Silver Jubilee and I send you all very best wishes for your dear birthday. No other girl I know has retained her slim figure and youthful look so much as you and I think back to our two lovely years with undying gratitude for this memory. Bless you Janey darling and all my love, Dickie.[680]

CHAPTER 25

Retirement

Mountbatten had been determined to be a reforming Chief of the Defence Staff. His priority was to impose greater centralisation and standardisation across the three armed services, partly to achieve economies of scale and partly because he felt the armed forces would thereby operate more efficiently. He brought back Solly Zuckerman, with whom he had worked at Combined Operations, as Chief Scientific Adviser, who proved to be both a brake on some of Mountbatten's wilder ideas and a stimulating and forward-thinking confidant. And as part of the centralisation of power, he introduced a Director of Plans to run the Joint Planning Staff – reporting directly to him. But there were some concerns that this centralisation was as much to do with Mountbatten's own ambitions as the needs of the services. A campaign for the CDS to hold five-star rank in all three services, long an ambition of Mountbatten, was unsuccessful.

The new CDS had long been in favour of amalgamating the three armed services after his time in Combined Operations. He had been responsible for a paper in 1945, which had argued for a common entry and education, with some specialist training, for all officers with a year each at Dartmouth, Cranwell and Sandhurst and with all courses on an inter-service basis.[681] Now he began the amalgamation by creating unified commands in the Near East

(1960), Middle East (1961) and Far East (1962). In April 1964, the three separate Service Ministries were abolished and their staffs moved into a single building.

His thinking on nuclear weapons also took shape, influenced by Zuckerman. He accepted that they could not be un-invented or abolished, and that they were a deterrent, but saw no point in accumulating ever more stockpiles and launching sites, which he saw as a needless expense and simply created a greater risk. They must be a weapon of last resort and only used in conjunction with America and NATO. Far better, he argued, to concentrate on conventional forces, which were more likely to be deployed. In particular, and against conventional military thinking, he saw little value in tactical nuclear weapons with all the attendant problems of radiation and escalation.

From 1955, he had supported controlled disarmament and in that year produced a memorandum for the Foreign Secretary arguing that, given the Russians had superiority in conventional forces but not in nuclear weapons, 'a method must be found to give them an adequate feeling of security to induce them to go ahead on their proposed reduction of conventional forces.' He proposed each country make public the extent of its nuclear stockpile and additions be monitored in an attempt to preserve parity.[682]

Given Britain had to have a nuclear deterrent, he was determined it should be controlled by the Royal Navy and launched from a Polaris submarine, rather than the Skybolt long range-air-to-surface missile, controlled by the Air Force, which had encountered testing problems. In late 1962, Solly was duly despatched to Nassau, where at an Anglo–American conference the decision was taken to commit to Polaris. The Navy had won over the Air Force yet again, but it had not made Mountbatten friends in Whitehall.

Mountbatten's dealings with his American counterparts, from

President Eisenhower down, were helped by the fact he had known many of them during the war. Even Eisenhower's successor, Kennedy, had once been to a party at Brook House. His dealings with his colleagues as CDS, however, were more difficult, with suspicions about his love of publicity and his economy with the truth.

Edwin Bramall, later himself CDS, who worked with him in the early sixties, remembered him as an Italian Renaissance Prince:

> He was a larger than life character. He had glaring strengths and weaknesses. In a sense he was a genius. He could deal with things on two different levels. He could deal with the bigger picture, but he had an eye for detail and the big vision at the same time. He had an incredible capacity for work. Anything you gave him in the box one evening he would have back to you the next morning though he may have had a state banquet or dinner party. He had driving ambition, a determination to do all the things he wanted to do by fair means or foul. They don't come like that more than very occasionally in a generation, but he was a very circuitous person. He almost preferred the indirect to the direct approach . . . He wished to achieve his own visions, to get his own way. He used to use every trick in the book.[683]

Edward Ashmore, also a future CDS, worked with Mountbatten at the Admiralty during the sixties:

> He had a sense of humour and could laugh at himself, if necessary, but I thought him capricious and vain and felt that many of his manoeuvrings, usually unnecessary, arose from an inability to recognise early enough that he could, in fact, be wrong. He worked quickly, with a certain fitful brilliance,

but his high opinion of his own abilities made him a difficult colleague for the Chiefs of Staff.[684]

My feeling was that 'Dickie' with his wide experience, his connections, his butterfly approach, very often generated more heat than steam. He gave stimulus to an organisation which may well have been momentarily salutary, but . . . I felt that the restless brilliance did not emanate from any inner happiness or peace and so lacked stability, even conviction.[685]

The writer Alistair Horne noted: 'On several occasions Dickie reported decisions of the Chiefs of Staff to the Minister of Defence in terms quite contrary to what had actually been decided.'[686] His military assistant, Pat MacLellan, recollected how: 'He'd talk to the Minister before the meeting to ensure that he had his backing for the line he intended to take.'[687] Sam Way, the Permanent Secretary of the Army, thought him 'the most mistrusted of all senior officers in the three Services for his ambition and his motives.'[688] Sam Elworthy, the Chief of the Air Staff, called him a liar and a cheat to his face.[689]

Mountbatten had always been susceptible to hearing what he wanted and this tendency was to become even more exaggerated in later life. When in June 1963 it was mooted that Mountbatten's term of office be extended, the Permanent Secretary at the Ministry of Defence explained this would be unpopular, as Mountbatten was 'widely disliked and distrusted'.[690]

In July 1965, Mountbatten retired as CDS. He had served his country for over 50 years in 35 different appointments, including over 20 years as a member of the Chiefs of Staff Committee. It was the end of what in defence circles had come to be called 'The Mountbatten Era'. Mountbatten was thrilled to be awarded the Order of Merit, claiming he was only the seventh sailor to receive it – in fact he was the twelfth.⁶⁹¹ The *Sunday Telegraph* in a profile by its defence correspondent, based on interviews with Mountbatten's colleagues, summed up his time as CDS:

> a top-grade organisation man; a practical, hustling executive ('he's a driver, not a leader') quick to seize on new ideas and gadgets, agile in their promotion . . . He set about changing the Navy, forcing through the commando ship concept, carrier task forces, guided-missile ships, nuclear hunter-killer submarines. By 1959 the Navy had been hurled into the modern age. But as the new Chief of the Defence Staff, raised above the other Service Chiefs, Mountbatten's difficulties were undoubtedly aggravated by his complicated and devious nature; his imperious assumption of precedence; his singular self-centredness ('He does everything for an audience of one') . . . His preoccupation with both the substance and the apparel of power, exasperated his fellow Chiefs. 'We'd go on for hours, trying to work out just how many guns ought to salute the Chief of the Defence Staff.' . . . But what caused even more concern among his colleagues was his infinite capacity for minor intrigue. He was clumsy at it; people compared notes. 'You could hear him a mile off, crashing about like some great animal in the jungle.' His fellow Chiefs suspected his advice to Ministers would vary from their own, and their suspicion was fuelled by the fact that he quite often did not deign to declare it to them . . . For 10 years he was the only constant presence on a scene disrupted by the passage of seven Defence Ministers. Of the closing stages of his career it can be said that more might have been done but for his extraordinary capacity to alienate people; that without him nothing might have been done at all.⁶⁹²

* * *

Mountbatten was not temperamentally suited for retirement. He was used to routine and hierarchy and still, in spite of some health scares, full of energy and determined to stay active rather than lead the quieter life of a more reflective man. He had little interest in the arts or music (except to dance to) and read little. Whilst he enjoyed shooting it was more for the social side, the opportunity to network and to test himself – a bag of over 1,000 birds a day at Broadlands was a long-held ambition. He generally rented out the shooting to rich neighbours, such as Donald Sopworth or Sir Donald Gosling, but would retain certain days for himself where he would invite Prince Philip, Prince Charles, King Constantine of Greece, the Duke of Kent or King Carl-Gustaf of Sweden. Each January, he would be invited to shoot at Sandringham, where he was regarded as 'a poor shot but a greedy one'.[693]

He continued to involve himself in a myriad of organisations – he was associated with 179 when he retired – from the Admiralty Dramatic Society to the Zoological Society. He continued to employ a staff of four to respond to a voluminous correspondence, all of it courteously and quickly answered, and to help draft the various speeches he was asked to make each week.

He spoke occasionally in the House of Lords, especially on defence matters, but he still desired to be more active in public life. An opportunity presented itself in 1965 when Rhodesia, a British territory in South Africa that had governed itself since 1923, threatened to declare Independence – the first unilateral break since the United States Declaration of Independence some two centuries earlier. After securing permission from the Queen, Harold Wilson approached Mountbatten to replace the existing Governor, Sir Humphrey Gibbs, who had lost his authority. It was hoped that

Mountbatten's proven skills of negotiation in India might resolve the situation.

After considering the offer, and on the advice of Solly Zuckerman, he turned it down, writing to Wilson that he believed replacing Gibbs would make little difference and at 65 he felt too old. 'But above all I had the world's most remarkable woman as my wife who was an indescribable help to me in contacts with people and a support and comfort to me when exhausted and facing terrible problems. I do not believe any Governor can do the job properly without a wife.'[694]

A month later, with the situation deteriorating, Wilson summoned Mountbatten to Downing Street, suggesting a special mission to invest Gibbs with a Knight Commander of Victorian Order. This time Mountbatten was prepared to go and proposed taking Sir Solly Zuckerman and John Brabourne, but courtiers, nervous of the constitutional implications, vetoed the trip. Rhodesia declared a Unilateral Declaration of Independence on 11 November, which was only invoked in December 1979.[695]

In August 1966, the Labour Foreign Secretary, George Brown, suggested he should join the Foreign Office as Defence Adviser, which he also declined. Then in October 1966 the Home Secretary, Roy Jenkins, asked if he would chair an inquiry into the prison escape of the spy George Blake. Mountbatten readily accepted, asking only that a scientist, retired prison governor and serving policeman should also be part of the inquiry. The policeman chosen was Sir Robert Mark, until recently Chief Constable of Leicester. The appointment was to bring Mark to the attention of Roy Jenkins, who appointed him Commissioner of the Metropolitan Police in 1972. It was also the beginning of a close friendship with Mountbatten, to whom he would become a useful ally.[696]

The 'Report into Prison Escapes and Security' was published

in December and Mountbatten was so pleased with it that he sent a copy to members of the Royal Family for Christmas. It proposed improving morale amongst prison officers with better conditions and more rapid promotion, better electronic security and the appointment of an outsider as Inspector General. His most controversial suggestion was for the construction of a maximum-security prison entirely for Category A prisoners on the Isle of Wight, which he felt with its enhanced security would allow the most dangerous prisoners more liberty than being contained within a conventional prison, but it was not to be.

He had always had strong associations with the Isle of Wight, having lived there as a child, been educated at Osborne and eventually having been elected (at the second attempt) to the Yacht Club. In 1965 he was invited to become Governor, a duty he took seriously, visiting at least every other month and in 1974, when it became a shire county with its own Lord Lieutenant – until then the Lord Lieutenant had also been responsible for Hampshire – Mountbatten was appointed as the first incumbent.

One of the appointments that gave him greatest pleasure was as Colonel of the Life Guards in January 1965, not least for the opportunity it gave him to dress up. Writing to Bob Lacock, he remarked, 'Only Angie (Lady Laycock) will fully appreciate my schoolboy delight at this unique honour, because she knows my weakness for uniforms.'[697] Whilst to Sibilla he was even more forthcoming, 'I am busy fitting my scarlet tunic, my white leather breeches, my very high jackboots, my helmet and my cuirass.'[698] He took his role in the Trooping the Colour each year very seriously, practising with his charger at Broadlands dressed in helmet, thigh boots and hacking jacket. He also took a great deal of pleasure in interviewing every prospective officer.

But his main focus was as chairman of the Council of World

Atlantic Colleges, to which he had been introduced by John Brabourne. The first Atlantic College had been opened at St Donat's Castle in Wales in 1962, a sixth form college drawing pupils from around the world based on Kurt Hahn's teachings on the importance of outside activities and community service, and where 70 per cent of the places were financed from scholarships.

Mountbatten's imagination was captured by its mission statement and its internationalist outlook and, until handing over to Prince Charles in 1978, he worked tirelessly on behalf of the organisation, travelling the world, fundraising by using his famous contacts – Jeffrey Archer, Bob Hope, Frank Sinatra, Noël Coward and Grace Kelly were all corralled into taking part in gala evenings – and setting up the second Atlantic College in Singapore in 1971.[699]

With his retirement, Mountbatten also began to give thought to ordering his archives – he had kept almost every piece of paper related to his life with the most sensitive entrusted to the 'black box' – and preparing a biography, which he saw not just as a way of shaping his legacy, but providing money for his grandchildren. He had always been keen to provide his own version of events in which he had been involved. To that end, he persuaded friends to return letters – not all of which were eventually made public – and to contribute reminiscences, and he began with a researcher, Robin Bousfield, to create tape recordings covering his life.[700] He would also specifically spend weekends discussing the past with close friends, such as Solly Zuckerman, in front of a tape recorder and then have the talks transcribed.

His secretaries, David Brice and Charles Nelson, had produced catalogues up to 1952 and 1959 respectively, but now Mollie Travis was brought in as a full-time archivist and a proper muniment room created. Amongst the collection was extensive correspondence with the Royal Family, especially Prince Philip, and King George VI.

'There is a treasure trove of letters from LL to King George V1 from 1920–1952,' wrote Bousfield to Travis. 'I had no idea they knew each other as well as they did long before the Abdication . . . I think it is vital that I should précis large chunks of them for our archives, as opposed to leaving them there "for future historians".'[701]

There were also some 55 letters that Peter Murphy had left to Mountbatten on his death in 1966. 'They are on the whole very intimate letters to his best friend; much more informative to an ultimate 21st-century biographer than the letters to his mother,' Bousfield told Travis. 'They exhibit the normal exuberant instinct of a very young man.'[702]

In March 1969, the trustees of the Broadlands Archives – John Brabourne, the writer and publisher Rupert Hart-Davis, and Charles Troughton, a director of WH Smith – signed an 'Undertaking by the Trustees of the Broadlands Archives Settlement', agreeing that the archives would be administered along the same lines as any material in the Public Record Office and that there would be no access to the papers without permission from the Cabinet Office.[703]

C.S. Forester, author of the Hornblower series, had been the first candidate as an official biographer. 'If ever there is to be a biography written about me (which God forbid),' wrote Mountbatten, 'there is no single writer I would be more willing to have as the author . . . since you undoubtedly succeed in capturing the spirit of the sea better than any other author I have read.'[704] Forester died in 1966 and the idea of an authorised biography was shelved, though almost 20 writers continued to approach him asking for his cooperation over the next two decades, including F.D. Roosevelt's son Elliott in 1976 and Denis Judd in 1977.[705]

In 1948, Mountbatten had allowed Ray Murphy to talk to colleagues for *The Last Viceroy*, authorised by the British Information Services, and had given two interviews himself.[706] The book was serialised in Beaverbrook's *Sunday Express* where, to Mountbatten's dismay, headlines and sub-editing emphasised the less attractive elements of his character.

In 1951, less than three years after the events, Alan Campbell-Johnson's *Mission with Mountbatten* about Mountbatten's time as Viceroy and Governor-General was published. Campbell-Johnson had kept a daily diary in India and had long been Mountbatten's preferred candidate as official biographer.[707] It was a version of events Mountbatten clearly supported – over 100 copies were sent out to family, friends and influencers on publication, and in 1972 Mountbatten contributed a foreword to a paperback reissue.[708]

Campbell Johnson had first tried to write a biography in 1944 and had been told there was 'a good chance of being accepted once the war is over', but the approach came to nothing.[709] There were discussions in 1958 about an official biography, but Mountbatten accepted that nothing could be published in his lifetime or that of his principal characters.[710] In 1953 Brian Connell's deferential study, *Manifest Destiny: A Study in Five Profiles of the Rise and Influence of the Mountbatten Family*, was published and six years later Mountbatten had contributed comments to *Supremo* by Christopher Maitland, the pseudonym of the writer George Baker.[711]

Edwina's reputation was also to be carefully curated. Initially, Nehru's sister, Vijiya Pandit, had been earmarked to write an official life, but it came to nothing.[712] In 1952 Dennis Holman's *Lady Louis: Life of the Countess Mountbatten of Burma*, described as 'the complete authorised biography of Edwina Mountbatten, written with her consent and cooperation after more than a year's research into her personal diaries, letters, records and interviews with her family, servants, friends and associates', had come out.

Six years later, Madeleine Masson published *Edwina: The Biography of the Countess Mountbatten of Burma*. Though billed as unauthorised, Edwina had given several interviews for the book, provided extracts from her diaries, and many of her close friends and colleagues had spoken to the author. 'She has omitted a lot of what I would have thought important things, and treated less important ones at length,' wrote Edwina to her secretary Elizabeth Collins. 'But it's her book thank God – not ours! . . . it's a pretty good attempt.'[713]

Masson later claimed that was not entirely the case and that 'when she had finished the book Mountbatten asked to see the manuscript – and altered it in his own hand, using blue pencil, the traditional tool of the military censor. In Madeleine's words, "He rewrote history by taking out anything, however petty, that did not show the Mountbattens in a good light, and inserted new information." Horrified, she summed up his uniquely annotated version as "lies, pure lies".'[714]

Then the year after Edwina's death, her childhood friend Marjorie Brecknock brought out *Edwina Mountbatten: Her Life in Pictures*, a short illustrated book based on private albums to raise money for the Edwina Mountbatten Trust, which had been set up to raise funds for Save the Children and the St John Ambulance Brigade.

Mountbatten also contributed to scores of forewords to various books touching on his career. A good example was Michael Harrison's *Mulberry: The Return in Triumph* (1965), in which the first chapter is devoted to Mountbatten, who gave the author access to all the key figures in COHQ, taking the opportunity to settle some old scores with critics such as Field Marshal Lord Alanbrooke and Bernard Fergusson's history of Combined Operations, *The Watery Maze*.

After Leonard Mosley's *The Last Days of the Raj*, critical of

Mountbatten's role in India, had been published in 1961, supposedly under Beaverbrook's instruction, Pug Ismay had written:

> I have come reluctantly to the conclusion that there is a serious risk that history will do you a grave injustice unless very early steps are taken to establish the fact that there is no substance in the charge that your decision to transfer power in India as early as the 15th August 1947 was responsible for the carnage that took place . . . I was at great pains to explain that you had not been impetuous, but extremely wise, and that if you had not taken the initiative in a way that no one else could have done and driven the scheme through with all the drive at your command, there would have been no power to hand over: only bloody chaos.[715]

Ismay had suggested first an article then a book be written for the fifteenth anniversary in August 1962, with access to the key individuals involved on Mountbatten's staff, explaining the reasons for partition 'by someone with a gift of attractive presentation, such as Peter Fleming or Alan Morehead'.[716] Dickie was keen, 'I should be more than happy to give the fullest possible cooperation to you if you would be prepared to take the initiative.'[717] Both Fleming and Morehead refused, as did Cecil Woodham-Smith, who worried about libel and that it was not her subject area. Eventually, H.V. Hodson, a former editor of the *Sunday Times*, accepted in September 1963, and his book came out six years later.

Mountbatten was also able to control, to a certain extent, what was written about him by holding out the promise of an authorised version. Many publishers, such as Robert Lusty at Hutchinson, rejected any book that did not have the support of Mountbatten in the hope of being offered the official book. A good example was

Alden Hatch's *The Mountbattens*, a study of Prince Louis, Dickie and Prince Philip, published in 1966, which did not find favour with the family, largely because of its inaccuracies.

At the beginning of the seventies, Mountbatten supplied material, contacts and commented on a book originally called *While the World Slept*, which became a 1985 international bestseller and TV documentary *Freedom at Midnight*, after the Cabinet Secretary Burke Trend cleared his participation. He and his secretary John Barratt made extensive comments on the script, notably on criticisms of the Punjab Boundary Force and that Mountbatten had been unfair to the Princes, to the extent of producing completely redrafted sections.[718] As Philip Ziegler wryly noted, it was 'remarkable chiefly for the faithfulness with which it portrays the history of the period as Lord Mountbatten would have wished it to be seen.'[719]

* * *

Though Mountbatten had been adamant that no biography of him should appear in his own lifetime, he was persuaded by John Brabourne to tell his story in a series of very personal television films about his life and times. In return for his participation and the use of his archives, which included extensive photographs and cine film, he would own the subsidiary rights with monies going to the Broadlands Trust, which had been set up to benefit his children and grandchildren.

This alarmed the Government, concerned with what he might say, especially concerning India and Pakistan, as he might be seen to be personally profiting from the use of official documents, and secret material might have found its way into his private archive. Mountbatten was summoned to a series of meetings with the Cabinet Secretary, Burke Trend, who was insistent the Government should see the television scripts. He also suggested Mountbatten deposit his papers as Viceroy in the India Office Library on permanent loan, as 11 previous Viceroys had done, where they might be more strictly regulated.[720] His 'hot' papers were given to the Royal Archives, where they remain unavailable to researchers.[721] It was also agreed that his papers could not be sold or loaned without permission of the government and that proper arrangements needed to be made for safe custody.[722] For years afterwards, his papers were subject to repeated weeding by various government departments.[723]

In October 1966, the 12-part series was announced, to be produced and directed by Peter Morley, a former BBC current affairs producer, whilst the job of researching and scripting the series went to John Terraine, who had just written and produced a BBC documentary *The Great War* and its sequel, *The Lost Peace*.[724] Originally commissioned and then dropped by the BBC, it was eventually bought by the independent Thames Television. Filming took up much of the next two years and included contributions from Prince Philip, the Duke of Windsor, Dwight Eisenhower and Anthony Eden – some more enthusiastically than others.[725] The series was launched in December 1968 with a Royal Preview at the Imperial War Museum, attended by the Queen, Prince Philip and most of the Cabinet.[726]

The series ran every Wednesday from the beginning of January and was a critical and commercial success, being shown to over 300 million viewers in over 70 countries and sold to PBS in the United States, and shown twice more in the following decade. The programme was seen by 38 million people in Britain – 68 per cent of the population – and the tie-in book by John Terraine, which quickly passed over or omitted any embarrassing subjects, sold over 30,000 copies in hardback.

Mountbatten had long recognised the importance of television and film in promoting image – he had always had large publicity staffs at Combined Operations, SEAC, and as Viceroy focused on recording his every activity on film – and he collaborated with several sympathetic television programmes throughout the 1960s, including a documentary for CBS in 1963 (*Twentieth Century: Mountbatten Man of Action*) and a six-hour series in 1969 for PBS's Twentieth-Century Leaders series: *Lord Mountbatten: A Man for the Century*.

It seemed his legacy was safe.

CHAPTER 26

Fixer

In August 1967, Cecil King, Chairman of International Publishing Corporation, confided in his diary:

> Cudlipp had some talk a few weeks ago with Mountbatten at some dinner. Hugh asked him if it had been suggested to him that our present style of government might be in for a change. He said it had. Hugh then asked if it had been suggested that he might have some part to play in such a new regime? Mountbatten said it had been suggested, but that he was far too old (sixty-seven, I think).[727]

Here were the first references to one of the most mysterious and controversial episodes in Mountbatten's life. Harold Wilson's government, which had been in power since 1964, had been beset with economic problems and industrial unrest. There were concerns about cuts in the armed forces, a belief that public spending needed to be reduced to help interest rates and tougher laws needed against the trade unions.

Added to this, in 1964 Jim Angleton, the head of the CIA's Counterintelligence Division, had told MI5, Britain's domestic security service, that, according to a secret source which he would not divulge, Wilson was a Soviet agent. The case would henceforth become known under the code name 'Oatsheaf'. Whatever the merits of the accusation, it was certainly true that there was extensive Soviet penetration of the Labour Party. Various defectors had named a series of Labour MPs and trade unionists, including Joseph Kagan, a close friend of Wilson's.

For months, Cecil King had publicly been saying that Wilson should be replaced by a coalition government, and on 23 April he had dined with Oswald Mosley in Paris to sound him out as a possible leader of a national government. His other possible candidate was Mountbatten, and an opportunity soon presented itself for further discussion.

On Saturday, 27 April, Edward Pickering, Chairman of the *Daily Mirror*, was Mountbatten's guest at the annual reunion of the Burma Star Association at the Albert Hall – the *Mirror* helped with advertising for the event – and Mountbatten took the opportunity of discussing with him his concerns about the 'developing national crisis' of strikes and economic problems. He asked if he could meet Hugh Cudlipp, the paper's editorial director.

On the following Monday morning, Cudlipp, who had been sailing in the Solent at the weekend, saw Mountbatten at Broadlands, *en route* to London, noting in a memo to himself afterwards Mountbatten's concerns:

> Important people, leaders of industry and others, approach me increasingly saying something must be done (Mountbatten said). Of course, I agree that we can't go on like this. But I am 67, and I'm a relative of the Queen; my usefulness is limited: this is a job for younger men, and obviously talent and administrative ability which does not exist in Parliament

must be harnessed. Perhaps there should be something like the Emergency Committee I ran in India.[728]

Cudlipp told his host that Cecil King shared his views. 'The crux of the problem was that the nation had lost faith in Mr Wilson and the Socialists and still had no faith in Mr Heath and the Tories,' said Cudlipp. 'The head of a Coalition Government, whatever it may be called, would have to be a Labour Minister.'[729] He suggested Roy Jenkins or Denis Healey and Mountbatten expressed his preference for the former, adding, 'I certainly don't want to appear to be advocating or supporting any notion of a Right Wing dictatorship – or any nonsense of that sort. Nor do I want to be involved at my age. But like some other people I am deeply concerned about the future of the country.'[730] They agreed to meet the following week at Mountbatten's London house with King and, at the suggestion of Dickie, Solly Zuckerman, 'whom he described as now utterly disenchanted with Harold'.[731]

The four duly met at Kinnerton Street at 4.30 p.m. on the afternoon of 8 May. According to Cudlipp, King, after outlining his concerns about Wilson's government and the need for action, asked Mountbatten if he would:

agree to be the titular head of a new administration in such circumstances? Mountbatten turned to his friend: 'Solly, you haven't said a word so far. What do you think of all this?' Sir Solly rose, walked to the door, opened it, and then made this statement: 'This is rank treachery. All this talk of machine guns at street corners is appalling. I am a public servant and will have nothing to do with it. Nor should you, Dickie.' Mountbatten expressed his agreement and Sir Solly departed. Only a minute or two elapsed between

Zuckerman's departure and King's. Lord Mountbatten was, as always in my experience, courteous but firm: he explained explicitly but briefly that he entirely agreed with Solly and that that sort of role, so far as he was concerned was 'simply not on'.[732]

That night Mountbatten wrote in his diary, 'Drove back with Solly in Graham's car from Lincoln's Inn where we had dinner to 39 Montpelier Walk to discuss with John and Patricia meeting which Solly and I had with Cecil King and Hugh Cudlipp. Dangerous Nonsense.'[733]

Thirty-six hours after the Kinnerton Street debacle, and with Labour routed in the local elections, King published 'Enough is Enough', a front-page article in the *Daily Mirror* calling on Harold Wilson to step down as Prime Minister over his mishandling of the British economy. King blamed both Tory and Labour governments for Britain's failure to make the same post-war recovery as other nations, notably the defeated Japanese, Germans and Italians, and called on Wilson to resign.[734] But the fall-out from his provocative headline had unintended consequences. It was King, not Wilson, who was forced to resign. The man who took his place as chairman of IPC was Hugh Cudlipp.

Two years later, King returned to the issue. In July 1970 he wrote to Dickie, 'You may recall that about three years ago you asked me to come and see you. Since then events have moved, though slowly. I wonder if it would be helpful if I were to call on you at your convenience and continue our conversation.'[735] Dickie replied, 'I well recall our meeting but you will remember that at the end I definitely came to the conclusion that there was nothing I could do to help in this matter. I am afraid my views are unaltered.'[736] To Solly, Dickie wrote the same day enclosing his reply, adding

'As you can imagine, the last thing I want to do is to continue any conversation with him.'[737]

That might well have been the end of the matter, but for the fact that Cudlipp decided to refer to the episode in his memoirs. In November 1975, he therefore sent a draft of his recollection to Dickie:

> I have told the story of the meeting with you in a way in which it can do no possible harm to you and Solly . . . If you would like me to add anything, please be kind enough to tell me, and I will not approach Solly until you and I have agreed on what I say about you, but I will not, of course, mention Solly without his agreement.[738]

Mountbatten replied two days later: 'Your description of the interview is incomplete and inaccurate. I have discussed this with Solly and my Private Secretary, John Barratt, who was coming down from his office and had reached the landing next to my sitting room when he heard Solly make this statement. All three of us agree that Solly said words to this effect: "This is rank treachery. All this talk of machine guns at street corners is appalling. I am a public servant and will have nothing to do with it, nor should you, Dickie." I expressed my agreement with him. He then left . . . Not more than a minute or two elapsed between Solly's departure and yours. I was merely courteous and explained explicitly and briefly that I entirely agreed with Solly and that sort of role, so far as I was concerned, was "simply not on".'[739]

Cudlipp's book was published in October 1976 and serialised in the *Observer*. It created a media storm. 'There are various inaccuracies with which I will not bore you,' wrote King to Cudlipp on reading the book, 'but the interview with Mountbatten, at which I was present, had no resemblance to the one described in your book. The plans and ambitions attributed to me at the end of my time at the *Mirror* are primarily fanciful.'[740]

Suspicions of a planned coup refused to go away. On 29 March 1981, a story about the coup appeared in the *Sunday Times*. The following day, Zuckerman was interviewed on the *Today* programme. King responded a few days later by releasing his diary entry for the May 1968 meeting, which gave a rather different account of the meeting:

> Hugh and I called on Dickie Mountbatten at his request at his flat at 4.30. He insisted that Solly Zuckerman should be there. Dickie spoke of him as a man of invincible integrity and as one of the greatest brains in the world . . . Solly seemed embarrassed by this and hurried away as soon as he decently could. Dickie does not really have his ear to the ground or understand politics. After Solly had gone, Mountbatten said he had been lunching at the Horse Guards and that morale in the armed forces had never been so low. He said that the Queen was receiving an unprecedented number of petitions, all of which have to be passed on to the Home Office. According to Dickie, she is desperately worried over the whole situation.
>
> He is obviously close to her and she is spending this weekend at Broadlands. He asked if I thought there was anything he should do. My theme was that there might be a stage in the future when the Crown would have to intervene: there might be a stage when the armed forces were important. Dickie should keep himself out of public view so as to have clean hands if either emergency should arise in the future. He has no wish to intervene anyway.[741]

Cecil King said he had withheld this note from his published diary on the grounds that it was confidential, 'especially the part about the Queen'.[742] It was beginning to emerge that Mountbatten had shown far more interest than he, or the others, had earlier admitted.

In November 1975, whilst those involved had been straightening out their version of events, Zuckerman had added a diary note to his file on the episode: 'All I hope is that Dickie did not go beyond what we had agreed. The fact of the matter is – as Hugh Cudlipp knows only too well – that Dickie was really intrigued by Cecil King's suggestion that he should become the boss man of a 'government' . . . When I saw Dickie at Prince Philip's dinner party on 17th November, three nights after I started to dictate this note, he seemed very pleased with himself and thought the whole matter was settled – once again implying that his record of what had happened in an event would be the statement which history would accept.'[743]

In fact, Dickie in 1968 had put forward various names who might be 'useful' for such a national government, including: Zuckerman himself, the government's advisor on nuclear matters; Air Vice-Marshal Deryck Stapleton, a former Director of Defence Plans at the Ministry of Defence, who had retired that month as Commandant of the RAF Staff College at Bracknell; Duncan Lewin, a former Director of Plans at the Admiralty; Lord Beeching, famous for his report on the railways, a deputy chairman of ICI and director of Lloyds Bank; and the businessman Sir Charles 'Dick' Troughton, who would become chairman of WH Smith the following year.[744]

He also suggested Sir William Armstrong, the Head of the Home Civil Service; Sir Michael Cary, the Second Permanent Under Secretary at Defence dealing with the Royal Navy; and Jimmy Carreras, head of Hammer Film Productions – a 'great go-getter', whom Mountbatten had met through the Variety Club.[745] Political suggestions ranged from a former Labour Chief Whip,

Lord Aylestone, and Barbara Castle, to Roy Jenkins, Jim Callaghan, Reginald Maudling and 'Alec Home for Foreign Office'. 'The people trust him, perhaps alone of the politicians.'[746]

There was history here about Mountbatten's political ambitions. In June 1946, whilst receiving his honorary degree at Oxford, Mountbatten had talked long into the night with Zuckerman about the war, the enormous problems that it had left behind, and about what his future was to be. He wanted to return to the Navy, but other ideas had been mooted, such as his becoming Governor-General of Australia.

Zuckerman later wrote in his memoirs, 'The one job that he felt that he could have done was that of Prime Minister, but that office had been closed down to him because of his royal connections. He and Edwina would have known how to handle the settling of ex-serviceman, and so on and so on. He talked as though there was nothing that he could not do.'[747]

In December 1947, Orme Sargent, Permanent Under-Secretary at the Foreign Office, had confided his fears in Dickie's dictatorial ambitions to the journalist Robert Bruce Lockhart.[748] In 1951, Zuckerman and Mountbatten had met again at a cocktail party given at Admiralty House. 'He drew me aside, and we had a long talk about many things, but particularly about the sorry state of the country,' Zuckerman later wrote. 'Dickie was immensely worried, and I was not surprised when he again said that with all his political experience, he might have made a better job of leading the country than had Attlee.'[749]

The 1968 coup was only part of an ongoing battle, which continued throughout the seventies between politicians and, in particular, Harold Wilson and the 'Secret State', largely represented by MI5.[750] In July 1977, Zuckerman had run into Harold Wilson, who had unexpectedly resigned the previous year, at the Queen's Jubilee

Party at Buckingham Palace. Zuckerman was being interviewed the following day by Barrie Penrose and Roger Courtiour, who were writing a book about the plotting against Wilson.

Zuckerman 'immediately asked what it was all about: were they trying to "frame" Mountbatten?' No, it's not Mountbatten they are after, was the reply, but I knew that there was one section of MI5 which wanted to get at him, Harold Wilson, and Lady Falkender, and one or two others.'[751]

Courtiour and Penrose claimed to have a senior MI5 officer as a source who, with others, 'had told them that there was something much more substantial behind the story of a possible military takeover than people assumed. They then referred to Cudlipp's account of the meeting with Mountbatten and explained that their MI5 informant had told them that the danger of a military takeover had been real. As they saw it, Cudlipp had indicated this in his account of the meeting with Mountbatten.'[752]

Amongst those who had been approached was David Stirling, the founder of the SAS, who in the mid-seventies had created an organisation called 'Great Britain 75', recruiting members from the aristocratic clubs in Mayfair; mainly ex-military men (often former SAS members). The plan was simple. Should civil unrest result in the breakdown of normal Government operations, they would take over its running.[753]

According to the writer Charles Higham, 'One who took the plot seriously, perhaps too seriously was Marcia Williams, Harold Wilson's secretary, who apparently spoke to the press at a later stage, talking of Mountbatten as "a prime mover in the plan". She added, "Mountbatten had a map on the wall of his office showing how it could be done. Harold and I used to stand in the State Room at Number Ten and work out where they would put the guns."'[754]

There's no doubt that Mountbatten believed in strong leadership and that a national government might be required, was vain and flattered to have been approached and did not immediately reject the overtures, but the evidence that his own role went any further than a few conversations remains hidden.[755] *Private Eye* was later to claim that Zuckerman had talked Mountbatten out of it.[756] But Alex von Tunzelmann, drawing on private information from Buckingham Palace, has suggested the advice came from elsewhere. 'It was not Solly Zuckerman who talked Mountbatten out of staging a coup and making himself President of Britain. It was the Queen herself.'[757]

Mountbatten's relationship with the Queen was a complex one. She had known him since she was a child, he had become a father figure to her after the death of her own father, when she was in her twenties, and she regularly went to stay at Broadlands. She was fond of her husband's uncle, but she had no illusions about him and how he used her to further his own ends.

A standing joke in royal and army circles was how quickly he would make reference to 'my niece, the Queen' – often using her as an excuse for being late. According to her private secretary, Lord Charteris, 'The Queen's attitude was that he was her Uncle Dickie and she was very, very fond of him, but sometimes she wished he'd shut up. Once she said, "I always say yes, yes, yes to Dickie, but I don't listen to him."'[758]

During the seventies, Mountbatten had resurrected his old friendship with the Duke of Windsor. In February he had dined with him in Paris. 'We seem to have caught the old spirit really even more than in the 1930s,' he wrote in his diary, returning again the next month.[759] There was a purpose behind this newfound friendship, amidst concerns about the Duke's health and what would happen to his papers and possessions after his death.[760]

In May 1972 the Duke had died, and Mountbatten was asked to

greet the Duchess at the airport when she accompanied the body back to Britain for burial. She was nervous about meeting the Royal Family, especially the Queen Mother, but the visit passed smoothly. Mountbatten noted in his diary after he took her to see her husband lying in state in St George's Chapel:

> At the end she stood again looking at the coffin, and said in the saddest imaginable voice: 'He was my entire life. I can't begin to think what I am going to do without him, he gave up so much for me, and now he has gone.'[761]

Broadcasting a tribute, Mountbatten, with customary hyperbole, spoke of how the Duke had not just been his best man, but 'my best friend all my life'.[762]

Mountbatten now turned his attentions to ensuring the Duke's estate came back to the Royal Family, suggesting to the Duchess that she left everything in her will to the Royal Family, or to a charitable foundation in the Duke's name, which he and Prince Charles would administer. He was concerned that she had dismissed her English solicitor and that her French lawyer, Maître Suzanne Blum, was exerting her influence. Mountbatten offered to act as an executor of her will and to find another lawyer connected to the Royal Family.

There were claims by Blum that 'two individuals, authorised either by Lord Mountbatten or "some other person", acting upon what she alleged to be royal authority, had somehow obtained the keys to the Duke's boxes and confidential filing cabinet and burgled the contents . . . The contents included the Duke's private correspondence, the documents of divorce from Win Spencer and Ernest Simpson . . . and a certain amount of the Duchess's personal correspondence.'[763] There were also rumours that Mountbatten had arranged for correspondence between the Duke of Windsor and German, Italian and British fascists to be placed in the Royal Archives.

A friend of the Duchess, Linda Mortimer, visiting her shortly afterwards found her 'very angry. She said she had been thinking of leaving most of her things to Prince Charles, and some younger members of the Royal Family', but Mountbatten had been 'picking up boxes and swords and trinkets', saying, "This belongs to the Royal Collection."' Wallis told Mortimer that she had changed her mind and Mortimer tried to persuade her 'that's just the way Mountbatten is. He's never been known for his tact.'[764]

Tactful or not, Mountbatten did save the papers from being sold on the open market or given away and a large amount of material was indeed returned to the Royal Archives in three batches – 15 June 1972, 13 December 1972 and 22 July 1977 – all of it approved by the Duchess and her advisers.[765] Kenneth Rose, close confidant of the Royal Family, noted in his diary: 'I hear that the Duchess of Windsor has promised to leave Queen Alexandra's jewels back to the Queen – on condition that the Prince of Wales attends her funeral. Mountbatten arranged the deal.'[766]

Mountbatten enjoyed being the elder statesman of the Royal Family and had no hesitation offering advice to the Queen and to Philip – advice they sometimes took. It was Mountbatten who had suggested Prince Charles attend Trinity College, Cambridge, Dartmouth and then spend some time in the Royal Navy.[767] He was close to the whole family, but had become even closer to Prince Charles in the early seventies, when the Prince of Wales was posted to Portsmouth and would frequently come to stay at Broadlands, where a room was left permanently made up for him.

'It's lovely having him here,' Mountbatten wrote in his diary at the beginning of 1972. 'We've had so many cosy talks. What a really charming young man he is.'[768] In November, Mountbatten had written to him, 'I miss you a lot for there is no one whose company I enjoy more, as I expect you realise.'[769]

The relationship was reciprocated. 'As you know only too well, to me it has become a second home in so many ways,' wrote Charles after leaving Broadlands for a six-month cruise, 'and no one could ever have had such a splendid honorary grandpapa in the history of avuncular relationship.'[770] Mountbatten responded, 'I've been thinking of you – far more than I had ever expected to think of a young man – but then I've got to know you so well, I really miss you very much.'[771]

Not close to his parents, 'in his Uncle Dickie he found someone to whom he could open up, confess his mistakes and misgivings, and turn for advice,' felt John Barratt. 'Lord Mountbatten was never short of a few words of advice for anyone, and he particularly enjoyed having the boy who would one day be king turning to him for counsel.'[772] The royal biographer Sarah Bradford thought Mountbatten 'uniquely placed to instruct the Prince with authority and intimacy about the governance of Britain and to help him interpret the duties and opportunities which faced him. By the time Charles was twenty-three, Mountbatten had become his closest confidant and the greatest single influence of his life.'[773]

Just as he had allowed Philip, before he married, to use Broadlands to meet young women, so Dickie encouraged Charles to discreetly bring girlfriends, such as Georgina Russell (now Lady Boothby) to the house. One visitor that spring of 1972 was Lady Jane Wellesley, daughter of the Duke of Wellington, who was to be his girlfriend for the next year.[774]

According to the gossip columnist, Nigel Dempster:

Mountbatten set up a slush fund, administered by a British lawyer through a private bank in Nassau in the Bahamas . . .

to ensure that potentially troublesome conquests could be swiftly and handsomely paid for their silence. Certainly two, and possibly three, six-figure dollar contracts were signed between December 1974 and July 1979.[775]

Mountbatten's advice to his great-nephew was clear:

I believe, in a case like yours, the man should sow his wild oats and have as many affairs as he can before settling down, but for a wife he should choose a suitable, attractive and sweet-charactered girl *before* she met anyone else she might fall for. After all, (your) Mummy never seriously thought of anyone else after the Dartmouth encounter when she was 13! I think it is disturbing for women to have experiences if they have to remain on a pedestal after marriage.[776]

Mountbatten was not above pushing his own candidates including, in 1974, his 17-year-old granddaughter, Amanda Knatchbull, whom he told Charles was keen on. He drafted 'how to woo letters to Charles and even going to the lengths of enlisting his favourite goddaughter, the chic Sacha Abercorn, to take Amanda to Paris on a clothes-hunting trip to smarten her up.'[777]

Amanda and Charles saw much of each other over the next five years in London, at Broadlands and in the Bahamas. Sibilla O'Donnell hosted them twice at her home in Nassau. 'I was given strict instructions by Dickie to leave them alone as much as possible which I did, and then they went to Eleuthera . . . Dickie tried very hard to get them together.'[778]

Jonathan Dimbleby revealed in his authorised life of Prince Charles that:

Amanda had grown fond of Prince Charles, warming to his energy and enthusiasm, his sense of the ridiculous, and his kindness. She admired his immense seriousness, his understanding of the natural world, the fact that he had read *Small is Beautiful*, the seminal work on the environment by Fritz Schumacher, and that he could quote from Laurens van der Post. She was also touched by his love for her family, and especially for her grandfather.[779]

In 1978, when Prince Charles was due to visit India, Mountbatten engineered a visit for himself and tried to include Amanda in the trip – but both her father and Prince Philip objected, worried that Mountbatten's presence might distract from Charles' visit and put Amanda unfairly in the media spotlight. In spite of that, Charles did propose to her, but she gently refused. 'They liked each other, but they couldn't fall in love,' according to Sibilla. 'There was no chemistry. They had known each other too long, since they were children.'[780]

Mountbatten needed to be wanted and loved to feel he could act as an intermediary in other people's love affairs. Another relation he tried to matchmake for was his nephew Carl Gustaf, King of Sweden, first with Lady Jane Wellesley and then Lady Leonora Grosvenor, and when Prince Michael of Kent confided in him, alone of the Royal Family, that he had fallen in love with a Catholic divorcée, Marie Christine von Reibnitz, it was Mountbatten who encouraged the match and suggested they marry in Vienna.

His desire to involve himself in his family's life was not always welcome. In December 1977, after handing over responsibility for World Atlantic Colleges to Prince Charles, the latter wrote to him:

I agreed to take over as President from you on the under-standing (as I saw it) that you wished to cut down on your commitments, etc. From the way you have been tackling things recently, it looks as though you are still going to do too much as Patron. I hate having to say this, but I believe in being *absolutely* honest with you, and when I take over as President I may easily want to do things in my *own* particular way, and in a way which could conflict with your ideas. So please don't be surprised if, like the other evening at Broadlands, I disagree with your approach or appear to be awkward and argumentative. I am only taking a leaf out of your book after all.[781]

In April 1979, tensions flared up again after Mountbatten criticised Charles for breaking short his holiday with the Brabournes on Eleuthera, which had caused inconvenience for others:

I thought you were beginning on the downward slope which wrecked your Uncle David's life and led to his disgraceful Abdication and his futile life ever after. Of course you were legally right – the US Coastguards could recall a crew from Easter weekend leave if you really wanted them. An officer was on duty and had no claim for the extra 3 days with his fiancée. But how unkind and thoughtless – so typical of how your Uncle David started. When I pointed this out you flared up – so I knew you had seen the point. I spent the night worrying whether you would continue on your Uncle David's sad course or take a pull.[782]

Charles was shortly – as he now seriously contemplated marriage – to keenly feel the loss of the wise advice of his honorary grandpapa.

CHAPTER 27

Ireland

Classiebawn, the Mountbatten home in Sligo, had continued to be a haven though, given the costs of running it, attempts were made in 1975 to gift it to the Irish nation 'for use by the President, members of the Government or Official visitors to Ireland' on the understanding Mountbatten could use it in August, but the offer was declined on the grounds 'of the limited use the State would be able to make of the castle.'[783] The following year, Hugh Tunney, a local businessman, agreed to buy the castle subject to letting the family use it every August.

Mountbatten was a popular figure in Mullaghmore. A few years earlier, he had sold most of the property in Sligo town belonging to the Ashley estate. Accompanied by his Sligo solicitor Charlie Browne, Declan Foley recounts, 'Mountbatten personally called on each householder in John Street, Sligo. After he had introduced himself, he inquired how many years the family had been renting the house. Depending on the number of years, he quoted a price. One woman told me when she asked how much, he replied, "Would fifty pounds be okay?" Browne the solicitor interrupted, "But Lord Mountbatten . . ." That was as far as he got, when Mountbatten reminded him, "Mr Browne, you are my solicitor, I will advise you! Now please draw up the sale of this property and have it ready by the end of the week!'"[784]

Family had always been important to Mountbatten, and his grandchildren would join him every Christmas at Broadlands, each Easter at the Brabourne or Hicks holiday homes in the Bahamas, and every summer at Classiebawn – quite apart from annual trips to Trooping the Colour or the Royal Tournament, where his grand-daughter India Hicks remembered how he would invariably fall asleep and have to be pinched in time to take the salute. She fondly remembers the Mickey Mouse pen on his desk, how his shooting socks were used as Christmas stockings, and the tradition of fudge making:

> He was the centre of stage, he always dictated the agenda, not least because we always met in his homes with his staff . . . He always liked us to be busy and would say, 'Don't walk around like an envelope waiting to be posted' . . . He had a gift of making each of us feel special and unique.[785]

At Christmas, each grandchild would receive a stocking made up of various presents he had collected on his travels that year – elephant droppings from Africa, shark's teeth from New Zealand, Eskimo carvings from Canada, pieces of coral, or special menus from a grand function – all individually wrapped. This attention could be claustrophobic, because everything had to be on his own terms. 'He was a man who took over everyone and everything – very bossy, even down to deciding what everyone was going to have for breakfast,' recollects his granddaughter Edwina.[786]

He wanted to know about their friends and love lives, but his gift, according to her, was 'the ability to talk to you about anything under the sun: love, sex, school, nothing was taboo and he never talked down.'[787]

One of his grandsons' girlfriends, who stayed several times at Broadlands and Classiebawn, remembered how Mountbatten was:

A massive interferer but his family loved and respected him. He loved his grandchildren and was wonderful with them. They would rib him, but he liked people to push back. He was great fun. A terrible flirt. He'd put his hand on one's knee under the table at dinner. He thought it fitted the image of how he saw himself . . . The family were very unassuming and natural, especially in Ireland, but standards were still kept. Staff lined up to greet one when one arrived and when staying one's clothes were laid out or packed in tissue paper. Mountbatten liked to eat sardines in their tin, but they were still served by a butler with the top neatly rolled back.[788]

Part of his ability to relate to children was that he was childlike himself, not least in his sense of humour. His grandson Michael-John remembered he 'had the most wonderful giggle and he would love to sit with us and watch a Charlie Chaplin or Buster Keaton film. It didn't matter that he had probably seen it before dozens of times. He loved slapstick and Laurel and Hardy were also two great favourites.'[789]

Timothy Knatchbull writes of the train set they had at home:

It comprised three sets of interconnecting tracks and a large array of electric points. My grandfather would take the controls and post children around the table to operate the points. Under his command it ran much better. He got excited when the trains ran well, frustrated when they did not, and cross if a member of the team was negligent and let the side down.[790]

Knatchbull especially loved his grandfather's bus drivers' version of the Lord's Prayer, which he would recite:

Our Father which art in Hendon
Harrow be thy name
Thy Kingston come, Thy Wimbledon,
In Erith as it is in Hendon.
Give us this day our Leatherhead
And forgive us our bypasses
As we forgive those who bypass against us.
Lead us not into Thames Ditton
But deliver us from Ewell
For thine is the Kingston, the Purley and Crawley
For Esher and Esher,
Crouch End.[791]

Emma Temple, daughter of Robert Laycock and a godchild, remembers how he would regularly entertain her at Broadlands on Sundays when she was at boarding school. 'He was the most fantastic godfather. I adored him . . . He was such fun to be with. Of course, he was terribly pleased with himself, but one just accepted that. He was so charming, incredibly warm and young at heart, though my parents were less fond of Edwina because she was so cold and not very nice to him.'[792]

* * *

As the Troubles worsened throughout the sixties, security at Classiebawn became a more important issue. In the summer of 1960, a telephone threat to the Dublin office of the *Daily Mail* had been dismissed as a hoax, but the local Garda Superintendent in Sligo reported back to Dublin: 'While everything points to the fact that no attack of any kind on the Earl by subversive elements was at any time contemplated, it would, in my opinion, be asking too much to say in effect that we can guarantee his safety while in this country.'[793] IRA chief of staff, Ruairí Ó Brádaigh, later president of Republican Sinn Fein, claims he vetoed an IRA attack on Mountbatten in 1960 or 1961, because operations were not allowed outside Northern Ireland.[794]

It was not only the IRA who were a threat, but groups like the League of Empire Loyalists, 'as he is known to hold liberal views on the Partition question . . . Earl Mountbatten is very friendly disposed towards the Catholic clergy, particularly the Jesuits, and it is thought that this attitude is frowned upon in certain quarters, who are hiding behind the guises of concern for his safety.'[795]

His protection became a bigger issue in the seventies. On holiday in the summer of 1971, he had 12 policemen protecting him 'of which three have been on round-the-clock duty in the house, besides two police cars for escort duties. I think the Irish Government were afraid the IRA might try to kidnap me and offer me in exchange for some of their leaders who are now in internment in Northern Ireland.'[796]

In 1972 the advice was that he was safe, Arthur Hockaday of the Cabinet Office telling Mountbatten, who had reported an IRA activist in the village: 'If you had no IRA man on your estate, you would probably be the only landowner in the Republic of whom this can be said.'[797] The following year, protection was stepped up with a 15-man protection squad. After the 7th Earl of Donoughmore and his wife were kidnapped by the IRA as political hostages – they were released after a week – in June 1974, Mountbatten sought advice from his old friend, Sir Robert Mark.[798]

A raid on an IRA safehouse in Southampton, ten miles from Broadlands, had revealed that Mountbatten was one of over 50

IRA targets and a senior IRA intelligence officer confirmed there was a plan in the early seventies to attack Mountbatten as he left Classiebawn, but was called off to avoid 'civilian casualties'.[799] After discussing the risk with the Garda, Robert Mark wrote: 'We cannot show the white flag to the IRA and although we do not think there is any real danger, we feel obliged to assure you that as many men as are needed will be applied to the task.'[800] The August holiday, with a protection team of 28, was cut short that year.

In 1976, 20 members of the Garda were assigned to guard Mountbatten. Reviewing security in the spring of 1978, Scotland Yard decided that Mountbatten was also at risk in London and there were extra car patrols near Kinnerton Street. In August an attempt to shoot him on his boat was only aborted when choppy seas prevented the sniper lining up his target.[801] The same year a loosened bung was found in *Shadow V*. It was clear the IRA were narrowing in for the kill.

Early in the summer of 1979, the broadcaster Ludovic Kennedy went to Broadlands to record an obituary programme:

> Mountbatten looked much older than when we had last met, still handsome and alert, but with deaf-aids in both ears, wearing a blazer that now hung loosely on him, and in his walk the beginnings of old man's shuffle. He had kindly invited us to what he called a light lunch, which consisted of an egg dish, lamb cutlets, a pudding, cheese and a dessert of frosted red currants, all served by a bearded butler and two footmen in naval battle dress.[802]

After lunch, Mountbatten was filmed talking about his life and the funeral arrangements he wanted. 'Was all this . . . an act of consideration to pre-empt family arguments,' Kennedy wondered, 'or yet another example of his abiding vanity?'[803]

The summer was spent compiling a picture book to mark his eightieth birthday, *80 Years in Pictures*. The idea had been that of Barbara Cartland – John Brabourne was against it, to protect a projected authorised biography in which the family had a financial stake – and much of the work was done by John Barratt, but Mountbatten relished the opportunity to look at his life again. David Roberts, the editor on the book, remembers visiting Mountbatten at Broadlands to go through the proofs:

> The photographs I was looking through were much more interesting than snaps of Erroll Flynn or Chaplin. They had been censored to be sure, but there were still photos of Princess Anne in a grass skirt dancing on the Royal Yacht and intimate photos of Edward VIII. There were touching photographs of the Tsar's children who were slaughtered during the Revolution. The idea of Lord Mountbatten as a child playing with these doomed children was touching. There were lots of photos of Mountbatten's girlfriends of which he seemed proud and I did wonder if they were disguising other tastes . . . When he had nothing better to do, Mountbatten would come down to the photo archive in the basement to see how I was getting on and on one occasion invited me up to lunch with him. It was a beautiful day and we sat outside at a little table on the terrace overlooking the Test – the river whose course Capability Brown had changed so we could enjoy its serene magnificence from the house. The butler came to serve us with three frankfurters and Mountbatten solemnly cut one in half so we had equal shares.[804]

The book was ready in time for Christmas and Mountbatten was able to sign six copies just before he set off for his annual Irish holiday.

* * *

In March, Sir Richard Sykes, British Ambassador to the Netherlands, and the MP Airey Neave had been assassinated by the Provisional IRA. In June, NATO Chief General Alexander Haig had narrowly escaped an IRA assassination attempt in Belgium meant for a senior British army officer, and in July, two IRA suspects were arrested on Lough Ross some ten miles from the County Monaghan home of one of the IRA's top bombmakers, the Libyan-trained Thomas McMahon. Shortly afterwards, Mountbatten was advised not to go to Ireland by Chief Superintendent David Bicknell. 'But the Irish are my friends,' he replied. 'Not all of them, my Lord,' replied Bicknell.[805]

In spite of that, Mountbatten left at the beginning of August. Pamela, with two of her three children, would be there for the whole month and Patricia and her family planned to join them from their nearby holiday home, Aasleagh Lodge in County Mayo. However, security was stepped up, with 28 men providing a day and night guard at Classiebawn and a further 12 at Aasleagh.

One of those responsible for the family's security was a 21-year-old corporal with the SAS-trained 177 Provost Company, the Army's elite close protection unit, Graham Yuill, who had previously been personal bodyguard to General David Miller, commander of the Ulster Defence Regiment. At the end of July, he conducted a full risk assessment identifying *Shadow V*, which was often moored in the public bay and could easily be boarded unseen at night, as the most likely target.[806] What especially concerned him was:

a car registered in Belfast – I remember the licence plate to this day. It kept returning to the quayside. At one point I remember looking at its occupants through binoculars. He was looking towards the boat through binoculars to the water. He must have been 200 yards from the quay.[807]

Yuill claims that:

According to intelligence just a few days after the event that said vehicle was already known to the RUC and army intelligence as a vehicle frequently used by the IRA for gun running and transporting bombs for the IRA. What's more that vehicle had been bugged for months by British army intelligence tracking its movements.[808]

But Yuill's report was not acted on and shortly afterwards he was told his services would no longer be required, and the Garda would henceforth be handling security.[809] He was forced to sign a gagging order, which only expired in 2017.

The lack of security on the boat is confirmed in a letter from Robin Haydon, British Ambassador to Ireland, to the Foreign Secretary, Lord Carrington, explaining it was the first year the boat had not been guarded during the day nor searched before it sailed.[810]

* * *

Monday, 27 August, a Bank Holiday, was a gloriously sunny day. After days of rain the family had decided at breakfast that morning to drive the mile to Mullaghmore and go out in the 29-foot Donegal fishing boat, *Shadow V*, and lift the lobster pots they had set the previous day. Dickie's grandchildren, Edwina and Nicholas (known as Nicky), had been playing backgammon. She had decided to remain behind, but the young boy was keen to go, telling his cousin they could finish the game on his return. Setting off after a late breakfast, they were accompanied by their Garda protection, Kevin Henry, and a uniformed officer.

At 11.30 a.m. Mountbatten, his daughter Patricia and her husband John, his 83-year-old mother Doreen and Patricia's 14-year-old twins Nicholas and Timothy, together with 15-year-old Paul Maxwell (who holidayed in the village and helped with the boat) boarded *Shadow V*. With the two Garda detectives following the progress of the boat through binoculars from the shore, the boat cleared the harbour wall and headed for the open bay. Mountbatten, standing tall at the wheel, opened the throttle to gain speed. Also watching the progress of the boat through binoculars were another two pairs of eyes – belonging to members of the Provisional IRA.

At exactly 11.45 a.m., just as their boat reached the lobster pots, a few hundred yards away on the cliff top overlooking the bay, the PIRA team pressed the button, which activated the bomb they had planted on the boat, moored in the bay, the night before. Fifty pounds of gelignite exploded, sending showers of timber, metal, cushions, lifejackets and shoes into the air. Then, there was a deadly silence. Mountbatten's body, his legs severed and most of his clothes ripped off in the blast, except for a fragment of his long-sleeved jersey with the badge of HMS *Kelly* on the front, was found floating face downwards in the water. He had been killed instantly.[811]

Shortly afterward, the Provisional IRA issued a statement through the *Republican News* in Belfast to the Press Association that 'The IRA claim responsibility for the execution of Lord Louis Mountbatten.'

* * *

Arrangements for Mountbatten's funeral, code-named Operation *Freeman*, had been in hand since 1967 and regularly assessed and refined with the latest review in March 1979. In 1971, Mountbatten, who wanted a magnificent State occasion, had outlined exactly what he wanted from the funeral service itself through to his burial. After first considering the Isle of Wight with his parents, he had opted for Romsey.[812]

Claiming he did not mind what form the service took, he then gave specific instructions over eight pages and with a four-page appendix. In death, as in life, Mountbatten would be a stickler for detail and the proper etiquette. He wanted the State funeral to follow the format for his father and was anxious to know what he was entitled to as an Admiral of the Fleet. How large a naval gun crew might he have? Could extra Royal Marines take part, given he had been Colonel Commandant?[813] Should the French government send an official representative? Where should his coffin rest before the funeral and which organisations should send representatives? When the Lord Chamberlain, Lord Maclean, objected to ideas that were not in keeping with Mountbatten's position in the Royal Family, Dickie simply went above his head to the Queen.

The funeral took place on Wednesday, 5 September at Westminster Abbey with 1,400 guests including the Queen, the Duke of Edinburgh, the Prince of Wales, most of the crowned heads of Europe, Margaret Thatcher and four former Prime Ministers, and was televised in over 20 countries. As the funeral procession wound its way from the Chapel Royal to the Abbey, the gun carriage pulled by 130 sailors, it was watched by a crowd of over 50,000 spectators.[814] Alongside marched eight pall-bearers of four admirals, three generals and a marshal of the Royal Air Force.

In front was Lance Corporal of Horse, Keith Nicklin of the Life Guards, leading Mountbatten's charger Dolly with Mountbatten's shining black thigh-boots poignantly reversed in the stirrups. The symbols of his naval and military ranks – his Gold Stick as Colonel of the Life Guards, his three-cornered cocked hat as an Admiral of the Fleet, his sword – lay on the top of his coffin covered by a Union Jack. Six cushions were required to carry all his decorations. Walking behind were his grandsons Norton, Michael-John and Philip Knatchbull and Ashley Hicks, followed by the Duke of Edinburgh, Prince of Wales, Duke of Gloucester, Duke of Kent and Prince Michael of Kent.

Mountbatten had always joked about how sad he would be to miss his own funeral. His instructions had been carried out faithfully – a 19-gun salute from King's Troop Royal Horse Artillery, 'Eternal Father', 'I Vow to Thee My Country', 'Jerusalem', the prayer of Sir Francis Drake and Psalm 107, 'They That Go Down to the Sea in Ships', read by Prince Charles – following which he gave a 30-minute address.

From Westminster, the body was taken to Waterloo and by train to Romsey, where he was interred in a side chapel of the Abbey. Further services took place all over Great Britain and Ireland – two days later, an ecumenical memorial service at St Patrick's Cathedral, Dublin, attended by the Taoiseach and almost all the Irish Cabinet; a joint funeral for Nicholas and Lady Brabourne near the family home in Kent; and on 16 September, Stephen Roskill, not always a friend to Mountbatten when he was alive, spoke at a service opposite Mountbatten's old Cambridge college:

It is certainly the case that when Mountbatten was born a fairy godmother endowed him most lavishly with gifts: good looks and a fine presence, courage and determination, a very quick and original mind, and the capacity to win influential friends. Undoubtedly, he made the greatest possible use of these gifts.[815]

On 20 December, a memorial service was held at St Paul's for

2,000 people, where the Prince of Wales again gave the address. He remembered:

> a constantly active brain which was never allowed a moment's rest. There was always a new challenge to be overcome, fresh projects to be set in motion, more opposition to be defeated – all of which were pursued with a relentless and almost irresistible single-mindedness of purpose . . . Although he could certainly be ruthless with people when the occasion demanded, his infectious enthusiasm, his sheer capacity for hard work, his wit made him an irresistible leader among men.[816]

On Monday, 5 November the trial of Thomas McMahon, aged 31, a bombmaker with strong links with the PIRA's South Armagh Brigade, who had been behind a series of landmine attacks against British troops, and Francis McGirl, aged 24, a known PIRA activist, opened in Dublin. The two men, who had been acting suspiciously, had been taken in for questioning at a routine road check even before the explosion.[817]

The evidence against them was circumstantial – the men had traces of gelignite on them and McMahon had specks of green paint from *Shadow V* – but intelligence confirmed that the attack had been ordered by Martin McGuinness, later Sinn Fein's chief negotiator in the Northern Ireland peace process.[818]

It also emerged that a member of PIRA, who had taken responsibility for the Mullaghmore attack, had been a temporary member of staff during the 1978 holiday and *Shadow V* had been under surveillance until 18 August, when the local Garda had decided to henceforth rely on visiting patrols. There had also, it appeared, been an unsuccessful attempt on Saturday, 25 August – but the bomb had failed to go off. On 23 November, the court delivered its verdict. McMahon was sentenced to life imprisonment, but there was not enough evidence to convict McGirl.[819]

John Courtney, who led the Garda investigations, found several others connected with the assassination – McMahon and McGirl had been taken into custody before the bomb was detonated – but did not have enough evidence to bring charges.[820] They included an IRA leader from Monaghan believed to have orchestrated the attack – who was questioned and then released – the bomb detonator, and three women living in a caravan opposite Mullaghmore Harbour, who it was suspected had been watchers. Of those that came under suspicion, one still lives and works in Dublin as a journalist, another was released under the Good Friday Agreement, whilst a third became a member of the Forum for Victims and Survivors.[821]

'The Garda never closed the Mountbatten file, because they believed it was a wider conspiracy and they were hoping someone would rat out the people up the chain of command who ordered it,' says veteran Northern Ireland journalist, Martin Dillon. 'Like the Shergar episode, senior IRA figures did not want their fingerprints on it. This source says the Garda have been sitting for decades on a list of guys they would like to attach to the assassination, but no one is prepared to offer them up.'[822]

If the IRA had thought their 'spectacular', for which they were reputedly later paid £2 million by Syria, would help their cause, they were to be disappointed. Public opinion was horrified by the senseless killing of teenagers and the elderly on holiday. There were calls for the reintroduction of capital punishment and the withdrawal of troops. It was something the British immediately exploited, in particular with regard to cooperation over security issues with the Republic and IRA financing from America, though, as a briefing paper for Mrs Thatcher noted, 'the Dublin Government is short on resources and long on political inhibitions.'[823]

Amongst the options considered were the reintroduction of executive detention, the closure of 35 border crossings, increased use of the UDR and SAS, and improved cooperation between the RUC and the Army with more joint operations rooms.[824] One of the ironies is that Mountbatten had been sympathetic to Republican aims and even offered himself as a middleman negotiator, but had been refused by Ruairí Ó Brádaigh, president of Sinn Fein.[825]

The Provisional IRA had killed the wrong man.

CHAPTER 28

Rumours

During his life, and after his death, rumours circulated about Mountbatten's sexuality, encouraged by his friendship with well-known homosexuals such as Noël Coward and Tom Driberg, his close working relationship with Peter Murphy and his tactile behaviour.[826] It was a question that his official biographer addressed head-on:

> If Mountbatten was a practising homosexual, he was risking everything he valued most to indulge a fleeting appetite. In that case, his character was wholly different from anything delineated in this biography . . . All his naval contemporaries who have expressed an opinion on the subject – and some worked very close to him – state emphatically that they do not believe the stories to be true . . . Sex itself was not a matter of great importance to him . . . To suggest that such a man was actively homosexual seems to be flying not merely in the face of the evidence but also of everything we understand about his character.[827]

It was a view shared by his secretary, John Barratt. 'He certainly was not homosexual. The allegations that he "consorted" with young naval officers at his house in Kinnerton Street are preposterous . . . There is no possibility that he could have kept any homosexual activities secret from me in the intimate relationship that we had over the last fourteen years of his life.'[828]

It's an issue that Brian Hoey in his authorised book also dismisses, quoting evidence from Sacha Abercorn, John Barratt and Bill Evans – with the latter claiming that stories of bisexuality are: 'Absolute rubbish . . . Men and boys weren't his thing at all.'[829] Hoey concluded that 'the most convincing argument against Mountbatten being bisexual is that in the fifteen years since his death, no one has come forward claiming that he was his lover.'[830]

And yet rumours continued to circulate. Just after Mountbatten's death, *Private Eye* ran a story:

News that Lord Weidenfeld has signed up naval historian Richard Hough to write an intimate family portrait of Earl Mountbatten raises speculation as to just how 'intimate' a portrait this will be. Will it, for example, reveal that the old sailor, particularly in the last 19 years of his life following the death of his heiress wife Edwina Ashley, was also a raving queen? Residents living close to his London home at 2 Kinnerton Street, SW1 have hair-raising stories to tell of the rollicking all-male frolics held there by the ageing matelot. Lord Louis, it seems, had a preference for young servicemen. This worked to advantage both ways: doing a turn for Dickie could do wonders for a young officer's career, and in turn the former Chief of the Defence Staff could count on the discipline of service life to ensure discretion, and not have to monkey around with the disreputable and mercenary 'John Come Home' rent boys of Piccadilly.[831]

Writing of the Ziegler biography, the author Michael Thornton 'utterly disbelieved his insistence that there was no evidence to suggest Mountbatten was bisexual. My own knowledge of Dickie over the years suggested the opposite conclusion and Noël Coward, whom I knew extremely well for the last thirteen years of his life, told me it was "beyond doubt" and to his certain knowledge that Dickie had had male as well as female lovers.'[832] The entrepreneur, Jeremy Norman, whose business interests ranged from *Burke's Peerage* to the Embassy nightclub, and who met Mountbatten a couple of times, 'always thought he was gay; a crashing snob, interested in genealogy, loved uniforms and decorations – all typical of a gay man of that generation.'[833]

'There were rumours he was homosexual. I was surprised but not that surprised though I never saw any evidence,' remembered Derrick Meakins, who served on his staff in 1948. 'He was very manly. I had heard about friendships with other women. They were quite happy to go their own way.'[834] Hugh Montgomery-Massingberd, in his memoirs, wrote of Mountbatten's home in Kinnerton Street that 'The tiny mews house seemed awash with young, muscular and suspiciously good-looking Naval ratings bustling about the place to no apparent purpose.'[835]

Jackie Crier, who together with the casting director Celestia Fox worked in a clothes shop called 'Spice', owned by the Kinks' management, opposite the Kinnerton Street flat in 1964–65, often saw Mountbatten. He would flirt with them and joke about the strange clothes they were wearing, but then pretend not to recognise them if they saw him in Wilton Crescent, as if that was a different persona. 'He was hugely charismatic, always looked amazing with cheeky smile and eyes,' remembered Crier. 'I always thought, here's serious grown-up crumpet. He was very dashing, elegant, dignified with wonderful manners. But I couldn't help noticing the succession of handsome young men frequenting his flat through the day, including some rather shady characters. Sometimes they stood outside smoking. A sixth sense told me they were gay.'[836]

The journalist Nicholas Davies recalled that, 'In 1975 I helped write a series of articles for the London *Daily Mirror*, which revealed details of a homosexual ring centred on the Life Guards barracks in London. A number of young guardsmen informed me that Mountbatten was involved and they gave detailed, signed statements of alleged visits to his Kinnerton Street home. As a result of an internal investigation by the army, five Life Guards officers and thirty-six guardsmen were found guilty of homosexual activities and dismissed from the regiment.'[837]

Francis Wheen, the biographer of Tom Driberg and *Private Eye* journalist, had collected material on Mountbatten that was destroyed in a fire. 'It's so maddening that all my boxes of Driberg research went up in flames in the great shed fire,' he wrote, 'as I know the Mountbatten file included (for instance) a letter sent to me by a chap whom Mountbatten tried to seduce when he (my correspondent) was a 17-year-old rating.'[838] The 'young naval rating was lined up to "go on a picnic" with Mountbatten when the great man was visiting (I think) Malta. On the day, the youth was startled to discover that it was à *deux* – and that Mountbatten assumed that the sailor was to be served as a human dessert.'[839]

Charlotte Breese wrote in her acclaimed biography, *Hutch*, 'As for Lord Mountbatten's bisexuality, many of those I interviewed were convinced of it. When he was Supreme Allied Commander in South East Asia, several officers boasted of their liaisons with him. A naval friend came across him on an island, when he was serving in Malta, nude *in flagrante* with another officer . . . These and other stories that refer to Mountbatten's sexual proclivities have been consistently denied by their [*sic*] family.'[840]

'Lord Louis' homo leanings were not any secret in the XIVth Army messes, which I heard about on my return to Calcutta at the end of the war,' according to Philip Hindin, who served with Mountbatten in India and Burma:

> By then I had been commissioned in the field. One of my sergeants used to boast about it in his cups. The end of the war situation lessened the division between ranks especially in the East, and junior officers used to use the Sgt's mess in Fort William in k.d. (khaki drill) without the 'pips', as the food was better than any officer's mess. Jack Hawkins (then a full colonel in the entertainments section) squashed these comments whenever possible. [841]

The writer Elisa Seagrave remembered, 'My father always claimed that Mountbatten, whom he had met in the navy, was "a most frightful shit and probably a bugger boy!"'[842] According to someone in royal circles, 'They were divorcing just before he became Viceroy and he persuaded her to go. She enjoyed the starring role. They were living apart. He had men friends – often naval ratings – and she liked black men.'[843]

A banker seconded to Bombay in the seventies heard various stories about Mountbatten's homosexual affairs – a long-standing Indian staff member of the bank had reputedly been one of his lovers.[844] A Garda Special Branch officer heard stories about Mountbatten's assignations in India through the Indian High Commission in Dublin.[845]

James Lees-Milne recounts in his wartime diaries hearing from John Gielgud a story about 'MB who decoyed a young man into his Eaton Square house and made him strip MB and beat him. The young man laid on with such violence that MB screamed in agony and the butler appeared. When confronted with the scene, all the butler remarked was, "I thought you rang, sir."[846]

In his memoir, *To Kill and Kill Again: The Chilling True Confessions of a Serial Killer*, published in 2002, the conman and murderer Archibald Hall, also known as Roy Fontaine, claimed to have been Mountbatten's lover during the war. Hall wrote that through the bisexual Vic Oliver, who was married to Winston Churchill's daughter, he was taken up by Ivor Novello and at wartime parties in Novello's flat above the Strand Theatre, he met the playwright Terence Rattigan, Conservative peer Lord Boothby and Mountbatten.[847]

Paul Pender, who wrote a biography of Fontaine with his cooperation, asked him: 'You mean – you mounted Mountbatten?'

'No,' Roy replied, ever a stickler for detail, 'Mountbatten mounted me. He believed it is better to give than to receive.'

Pender then asked Fontaine what he called his royal lover, to which the butler responded: 'Most of Mountbatten's gay friends called him "Mountbottom".'

'Did you call him Mountbottom?'

'Of course not. That would have been disrespectful . . . I called him the Queen.'[848]

Whilst research in their papers shows Ivor Novello and Terence Rattigan were friends, there is no evidence that Mountbatten knew either them or Hall. Pender stands by Fontaine's claims, but Allan Nichol, in his biography of Fontaine, exercises caution: 'It is impossible to ascertain how many of Fontaine's recollections of early sexual exploits are true. If anything can be judged from his proven exaggerations elsewhere, it is fair to say that few of his boasted sexual adventures with the rich and famous of wartime Glasgow and London can be believed.'[849]

In September 1987, an article appeared in the New Zealand

tabloid magazine *Truth*, drawing on the testimony of Norman Nield, Mountbatten's driver between 1942–43, who now lived in New Zealand, and had decided to tell his story after reading *Spycatcher* and after the death of his wife. 'When I saw what all the fuss was about, I realised I had a better story to tell,' Nield said.

He claimed he 'was ordered to take young boys who had been procured for the admiral to his official residence in Lord Mountbatten's Humber car' and was paid £5 a week for his silence at a time when ratings were paid three shillings a day. According to Nield, Mountbatten, known as L.L., used brandy and lemonade to help seduce the boys, who ranged in age from eight to 12, and that once 'he saw Lord Mountbatten in bed with a prostitute and two teenage girls, who tried unsuccessfully to seduce him for more than an hour.' The prostitute, Barbara Harris, declared him unfit for 'the sandwich treatment'.[850]

'Barbara Harris always brought some clothing like that for a baby girl but outsize – large enough, in fact, for one of these boys to wear,' Nield said. 'Obviously it had been specially made and she would hand it to L.L. with the boy. In the beginning I didn't see what went on in the room, but one didn't have to be a genius to guess what was going on.'

Nield claims the link between Lord Mountbatten and Harris was London's fashionable wartime Pink Petal Club.

L.L. was a close friend of Noel Coward, who was also a patron of the club. Barbara Harris, through her notoriety in the early sex scandal, became friendly with L.L. and was a well-known face at the club . . . Twig warned me to be most careful about what I heard and saw. He said I was picked for the job because they believed I would be discreet. He later told me that L.L. was under a lot of pressure and released his tensions with his fondness for young boys dressed as small girls. He also told me that L.L. engaged in sex with men or even girls if they were youthful enough. He told me that L.L. was confused sexually and that I was being paid very well to keep my mouth shut . . . It all ceased when the admiral was taken ill.[851] On his recovery late in 1943, he went to south-east Asia as a supreme commander of Allied forces.[852]

There was no reason for Nield to make up the story, especially in so much detail – though certain details do not fit the conventional story. He says that at the time Mountbatten was living in a large house at Fareham near Portsmouth, but in 1942–43 Mountbatten was head of Combined Operations and based in London. However, Southwick House at Fareham was, from 1943, the location of the advance command post of the Supreme Headquarters Allied Expeditionary Force, which Mountbatten would have had cause to visit and he may have used a house nearby. Broadlands is about an hour's drive from Fareham.

Peter Thompson, a former *Mirror* editor, writing in *Diana's Nightmare*, told of how 'an informant came to Fleet Street to sell a story alleging deviant behaviour by Mountbatten . . . Maxwell bought the story and supressed it . . . It was a small but important favour.'[853] The cookery writer, Clarissa Dickson Wright, told Thompson that her uncle, Douglas Wright, as a Surgeon Commander, had served with Mountbatten during the Second World War.

Wright was summoned to Mountbatten's cabin and found him taking a bath. Dickie 'proceeded to make a pass at the doctor but was turned down':

'What about your career?' asked Lord Louis.

'You don't understand,' replied Dr Wright. 'I'm planning to make a career outside the Navy.'

When Mountbatten persisted, he was told: 'Just remember, I'm the doctor – the man with the needle.'

'Sure enough,' said his relative, 'Mountbatten got a dose of the clap in the Far East and Dr Wright had to treat him.'[854]

Anthony Daly, whose memoir *The Abuse of Power* recounts his experiences as a rent boy to the rich and famous during the 1970s, was particularly close to Tom Driberg, who told him that:

> He flew to Ceylon in a cargo plane. On arrival at Colombo, Mountbatten sent his private Dakota to pick him up and he was flown to HQ at a place improbably called Kandy. Tom said that after cocktails, one of Mountbatten's aides offered him a Burmese boy, whom everyone at HQ called Candy. Tom had sex with Candy in the Dakota – how could I forget that!
>
> Tom really did give me the impression that Mountbatten actually preferred men to women (wishful thinking on his part perhaps), and said they both had frank, not to say graphic discussions about homosexuality. They discussed the pornography they liked (Tom offered to show me his collection, but I declined). Tom said Mountbatten had something of a fetish for uniforms – handsome young men in military uniforms (with high boots) and beautiful boys in school uniform.[855]

Daly picked up gossip from the circles he moved in and was told, 'Mountbatten had a sexual preference for well-bred and well-educated young men of good standing (that would have ruled me out), from good families; or public school boys.'[856] He chose not to mention Mountbatten in *The Abuse of Power*, but described how Mountbatten had been courted by members of the National Association for Freedom, later the Freedom Association, who were plotting against Harold Wilson:

> The Mountbatten connection here, as told to me by Noel Annan (Lord), was that this group were very actively trying to enlist Mountbatten to their cause, and that their enticements included a position of power and prestige and to offer him various young men for sex.
>
> You may recall from the book that I endured a full night with Annan. It was he who led me to believe there was what I would now describe as an Anglo-Irish vice ring, with the landed gentry on both sides of the Irish border, abusing boys and young men. He told me that the venues for parties were the grand houses they owned. The young Grenadier Guard I was teamed up with for a pornographic photographic session told me he had been transported by helicopter to an elite gathering in a castle in either Belfast, or possibly just minutes over the border. Mountbatten's castle Classiebawn was just twelve miles from the NI border.
>
> Annan appeared to be very knowledgeable about all things Establishment and spy related, and their indiscretions. He told me Mountbatten was bisexual and had affairs with numerous young men, including an Indian prince![857]

The former Conservative minister Keith Joseph had 'said that Mountbatten had affairs with many young sailors whilst at sea – he said such liaisons were perfectly normal for men at sea; but he said that Mountbatten also bedded countless women . . . Mountbatten's sexuality seemed to be an open secret in the circles I moved in.'[858]

In 1980, an article appeared in *International Times* claiming that Cecil King was so annoyed at Mountbatten's failure to take part in his coup that he 'forever after spewed out low-minded and scandalous observations about his former idol to anyone who'd listen. Even when he was rung up from Dublin by a television journalist to discover his reaction to Mountbatten's execution by the IRA, he maintained that Mountbatten was a "sexual pervert" and that his wife Edwina had been a nymphomaniac.'[859]

That same year *Now Magazine* published an article under the headline, 'Mountbatten was part of a gay ring which was linked with Kincora', in which the Northern Irish writer Robin Bryans 'claimed that leading British establishment figures were in a vice ring which abused boys from the notorious Kincora Home in East Belfast . . . that the late Lord Louis Mountbatten, Captain Peter Montgomery, a former intelligence officer from Northern Ireland, Sir Anthony Blunt, the infamous homosexual MI5 traitor, and Peter England, a senior member of the British Secret Service (MI6), who served undercover at Stormont in the 1970s, were members of an old boy network which held gay orgies in country houses and castles on both sides of the Irish Border.'[860] It added that 'Mountbatten was a great one for boys in the first year of public school, like at Portora Royal, which was thirteen and fourteen.'[861]

In April 1990, *Now Magazine* returned to the subject with an article which claimed that, according to some Belfast journalists, Mountbatten lived a secret life both in Eire and, more particularly, Northern Ireland. 'Lord Mountbatten was interested in what homosexuals call "the rough trade" and liked to have contacts with working-class youths. He was particularly attracted to boys in their early teens.'[862]

Robin Bryans, also known as Robert Harbinson, a few months later made the same accusation in a private letter, claiming: 'Kincora and Portora Boys' Schools were used as homosexual brothels by many prominent figures, including Lord Mountbatten, James Molyneux . . .'[863] He went on to say of Mountbatten that, 'In the 1930s he had shared Anthony Blunt's butch lover, Alan Price.'[864]

The *Now Magazine* articles and Robin Bryans' claims were dismissed, but now a new person has come forward, who is using a pseudonym. 'Sean' was 16 years old when he says he was driven from the Kincora Boys Home in Belfast to Classiebawn in the summer of 1977. As the men who had brought them waited outside, 'Sean' remembers being taken into a darkened room where he was joined by:

a man who undressed me and then gave me oral sex. I was there about an hour. He spoke quietly and tried to make me feel comfortable. He was one of those men who wanted attention, wanted you to chase him . . . I think he felt some shame. He said very sadly, 'I hate these feelings.' He seemed a sad and lonely person. I think the darkened room was all about denial . . . He grabbed my hand and put it on his chest . . . I only recognised who he was when I saw on the news that Lord Mountbatten had been killed.[865]

Another 16-year-old boy from Kincora, who is using a pseudonym, remembers being brought to Mullaghmore during the summer of 1977. 'Amal' says he met Mountbatten four times that summer on a day trip from Belfast. Each time the encounter, lasting an hour, took place in a suite at a hotel by the harbour about 15 minutes from Classiebawn.[866] 'Amal' remembered:

He was very polite, very nice. I knew he was someone important. He asked if I wanted a drink or candy. He told me he liked dark-skinned people especially Sri Lankan people as they were very friendly and very good-looking. I remember he admired my smooth skin. We gave each other oral sex in a 69 position. He was very tender and I felt comfortable about it. It seemed very natural. I know that several other boys from Kincora were brought to him on other occasions.[867]

Hints at Mountbatten's bisexuality are provided by Ron Perks, who has spoken for the first time about an episode over 70 years ago. Perks, who served in the Royal Marines from 1944–57, was appointed Mountbatten's driver on his arrival in Malta in 1948. Mountbatten's predecessor commanding the First Cruiser Squadron, Rear Admiral R.V. Symons-Taylor, had told him, 'You are going to be the driver of my successor. I want you to find out all these places':

The Red House near Rabat was amongst them. It was an isolated, baronial-style building with a flat roof. One day as we were driving along, Mountbatten asked if I knew the Red House. I said I did and he asked if I would take him there, which I did. I never dropped him there, but he had his own car which he used often. He wouldn't have asked me for nothing. I didn't know what it was and only learnt after I came out of the service that it was an upmarket gay brothel used by senior naval officers. You're taught to keep out of trouble in the Navy and I've never said a word about the incident until now.[868]

The son of one of the ADCs on Mountbatten's staff said that whilst his:

father was posted at SHAPE in the mid-1950s (which was then located at Rocquencort next to Versailles), he remembered a succession of young men being taken up to Lord Mountbatten's suite in a hotel in Paris, which raised a few eyebrows at the time. I was particularly struck by my father's disapproval as he was not a particularly censorious person, and I think that it was the indiscretion of Mountbatten's behaviour which surprised him most.[869]

My father left no doubt that the young men were there for sexual favours and not part of the Army/Civil Service. I have always imagined that it was in the evening and would have been single men, but on a regular basis. The way my father told the story implied that a significant number of people knew about it, hence his disapproval.[870]

One of Mountbatten's most fruitful sources of young men was the Life Guards. Nick Best, who served in the Grenadier Guards, remembers that: 'It was said when Mountbatten was the Colonel of the Life Guards, he always took every new officer out to dinner to explore the homosexual potential.'[871]

The writer Nigel West is convinced Mountbatten was bisexual, giving three reasons:

1. My father worked for Mountbatten on the Joint Planning Staff at Kandy, and heard about the outrage when Mountbatten arranged for the transfer of the alleged boyfriend, Peter Murphy.

2. A good friend of mine [*name deleted*] was very shocked when he applied to join the Life Guards (or some similar smart cavalry regiment) and was offered an interview with Mountbatten (I think through a godfather), who then promptly propositioned him! [*Name deleted*] was appalled. Allegedly, at around the same time (late 1960s)

Nehru and Edwina on holiday in Simla.

Dickie at Prince Philip's stag night, November 1947.

Dickie and Edwina with Prince Charles and Princess Anne, Malta, April 1954.

Dickie, Queen Elizabeth ll, Prince Philip and Edwina on the steps of Broadlands, 6 April 1957.

Left: One of the last pictures of
Edwina, February 1960.

Below: Edwina's funeral, HMS
Wakefield, 25 February 1960.

Left: Sibilla O'Donnell with Dickie in the Bahamas.

Right: Yola Letellier at Broadlands.

Left: Sacha, Duchess of Abercorn, Bunny Phillips' daughter and Dickie's goddaughter who was his closest companion in later years.

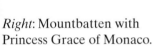

Left: Mountbatten with Clark Gable and Jayne Mansfield.

Right: Mountbatten with Princess Grace of Monaco.

Left: The actress Shirley MacLaine, who often acted as Dickie's hostess, with Rex Harrison and his wife Rachel Roberts at Mountbatten's retirement garden party, Broadlands, July 1965.

Above: Dickie and family having tea at Classiebawn, 1963.

Below left: Dickie playing with Patricia and his grandchildren in front of Classiebawn.

Below right: Mountbatten with his grandchildren, Philip, Amanda and Joanna at Classiebawn, 1963.

Above left: Mountbatten's bodyguard, Graham Yuill, who was relieved of his duties shortly before Dickie was killed.   © *Graham Yuill*

Above centre: Thomas McMahon, who served 19 years for Mountbatten's murder before being released under the Good Friday Agreement.   © *Maxwell Photography*

Above right: Francis McGirl, who was acquitted of Mountbatten's murder but died later in a mysterious tractor accident.   © *Irish Times*

Below: Mountbatten's funeral, which he had been planning for years, 5 September 1979.

© *Popperfoto/Contributor/Getty*

Federal Bureau of Investigation

United States Department of Justice

New York 7, N. Y.

February 23, 1944

FJM:RD

~~PERSONAL AND CONFIDENTIAL~~

Director, FBI

DECLASSIFIED BY SP6-BJafocke
ON 2/8/90

Dear Sir:

In a recent interview with LADY ELIZABETH DECIES in connection with an investigation being conducted by this Field Division in another matter, LADY DECIES volunteered the following information to Special Agent Francis J. McCarthy, Jr.

She has been an intimate of the British Queen Elizabeth, Queen Mary and her ladies-in-waiting. She states that in these circles LORD LOUIS MOUNTBATTEN and his wife are considered persons of extremely low morals. She stated that LORD LOUIS MOUNTBATTEN was known to be a homosexual with a perversion for young boys. In LADY DECIES' opinion he is an unfit man to direct any sort of military operations because of this condition. She stated further that his wife, LADY MOUNTBATTEN, was considered equally erratic and that it was known that PAUL ROBESON, Colored singer and actor, was her paramour. LADY DECIES said that she knew that LADY MOUNTBATTEN took PAUL ROBESON on a six-weeks caravan into the Sahara Desert a few years before the war began and that these two had six weeks of un-chaperoned association together. LADY DECIES added that LADY MOUNTBATTEN has a huge naked statue of PAUL ROBESON in her home.

The foregoing is submitted for whatever value it has to the Bureau.

LADY DECIES is the widow of the recently deceased BARON DECIES, a well-known British political figure. LADY DECIES is a member of the DREXEL family and ANTHONY DREXEL BIDDLE is her cousin. LADY DECIES is the owner of a $5,000,000 home in Paris, France and apparently has been in intimate contact with various members of European royalty including Queens WILHELMINA and MARIE and others. At the present time LADY DECIES is residing at the Plaza Hotel in New York and appears to have no special motive in making the above statements. With the exception of the fact that LADY DECIES is greatly worried about the safety of her Paris home, she appears to be otherwise normal.

EX-56

RECORDED

INDEXED   31 MAR

Very truly yours,

E. E. Conroy

E. E. CONROY
SAC

Part of Mountbatten's FBI file with its claims of his paedophile tendencies.

Mountbatten was caught with a Guardsman in St James's Park and the Palace declined to intervene when the Yard reported the incident.

3. When I worked at the BBC's General Features Department at Kensington House in 1978 (then headed by Desmond Wilcox), a neighbouring programme filmed an interview with Mountbatten, at his request, in which he acknowledged his homosexuality. The rumour was that the film, intended to be broadcast after his death, was suppressed by the Palace.[872]

When interviewed, the friend of Nigel West said that he had met Mountbatten for a very good lunch at White's Club:

He was very charismatic and attractive and wit and humour will get you everywhere. It was certainly true of Mountbatten. He was bloody funny. Age meant nothing to him. If you had a bit of gumption, he liked you. About two-thirds of the way through the lunch, his hand appeared on my knee and stayed there. West had warned me he was a switch-hitter and would bonk anything, so I wasn't worried. We just made a joke of it. 'Why do you think I'm Colonel in Chief of the Life Guards,' he said. 'We have such beautiful boys.'[873]

Mountbatten's male lover for the last eight years of his life is now in his seventies, but looks considerably younger. Handsome, smartly dressed and well-spoken, meeting for lunch he remembers his times with Mountbatten, a near neighbour, with great affection:

He was lovely and great fun. I saw him at least once a month, sometimes for a chat, sometimes for more. He was a great mentor to me, introducing me to all sorts of useful people, and we had lovely times together. He was perfectly relaxed about our relationship, in spite of the forty-year age gap, and certainly felt no shame. I was always up for sex, so happy to see him. He would ring to warn me when he wanted to pop round. John Barratt knew all about it and did not mind. His death was a great shock.[874]

Further evidence of Mountbatten's bisexuality comes from FBI files. In February 1944, the American writer and society figure, Elizabeth de la Poer Beresford, Baroness Decies, was interviewed by the FBI about another matter. But the FBI report reads:

She has been an intimate of the British Queen Elizabeth, Queen Mary and her ladies-in-waiting. She states that in these circles LORD LOUIS MOUNTBATTEN and his wife are considered persons of extremely low morals. She stated that Lord Louis Mountbatten was known to be a homosexual with a perversion for young boys. In Lady Decies' opinion he is an unfit man to direct any sort of military operations because of this condition. She stated further that his wife Lady Mountbatten was considered equally erratic and that it was known that Paul Robeson, coloured singer and actor, was her paramour . . . At the present time LADY DECIES is residing at the Plaza Hotel in New York and appears to have no special motive in making the above statements. With the exception of the fact that LADY DECIES is greatly worried about the safety of her Paris home, she appears to be otherwise normal.[875]

Ulius Amoss' accusations in 1952 against the Mountbattens had been dismissed by the FBI, but in November 1955 an FBI file was opened on Edwina, most probably because of her close association with Krishna Menon and her various political pronouncements on India and Africa and during the Suez Crisis. The FBI at the same time sent a report to the Department of Justice on Mountbatten's homosexuality.[876] In April 1957, the FBI produced a memo on allegations of an affair between Paul Robeson and Edwina and in September 1959 her file was again reviewed.

In May 1968, further accusations against Mountbatten were supplied to the FBI by John Grombach, who has been described as 'one of the most remarkable and yet least known intelligence leaders in American history.'[877] Grombach, a brigadier in the New York National Guard, under cover of a company called Industrial Reports, ran his own independent spy operation for J. Edgar Hoover 'known informally as the "Pond" that conducted espionage operations for the US government from 1942 to 1955.'[878]

An international fencer, who also claimed to have been a stunt double in Hollywood movies, Grombach had been educated at West Point and worked in the State Department during the war dealing with British Intelligence. He told the FBI: 'the person who furnished a report in 1953 regarding the alleged homosexuality of Anthony Eden, Earl Mountbatten and Anthony Nutting, was believed to be Lady Judith Listowell, née Márffy-Mantauno.'[879]

Born Judit Márffy-Mantuano de Versegh et Leno on the family estate in Hungary, the daughter of a Hungarian diplomat, Listowell had studied at Budapest University and the London School of Economics, where she met 'Billy' Hare, the future 5th Earl of Listowel and Viceroy of India, which gave her access to British social and political circles – her soirées in Belgrave Place during the war were famous. They had married in 1933, but divorced 12 years later, and she later served in the Hungarian diplomatic service and worked as a journalist and writer.[880]

Much of Mountbatten's FBI file, only part of which was released after Freedom of Information requests, remains closed. Some of the Kincora files at the British National Archives from the late 1970s and early 1980s are 'Temporarily Retained by Department', whilst others, which were due for release in 2018, were in August that year extended for a further period. One has to ask why.

Was Mountbatten perhaps abused as a young boy? The thirteen-year-old Dickie, recovering from whooping cough and bronchitis, spent several weeks alone at Bridport in Dorset in the summer of 1914 with a private tutor called Frederick Lawrence Long. Long, then in his early thirties, had left the Royal Navy to train for the ministry a few years earlier and was doing some private tutoring.

The friendship between Mountbatten and Long, which continued after their sojourn in Bridport, was close – Long was to officiate at Mountbatten's wedding – and is marked by some intense correspondence. 'Dear Kid, I have one special pupil now – Prince John de Mahe. He is about your age & a decent enough kid but you need not be jealous as you know there is only one Dick in the world for me & there never will be anyone before or anywhere near him in my affections,' wrote Long to Dickie in February 1916. 'It is hardly necessary for me to add that I would give anything to wipe the floor with you. Goodbye my best beloved & dearest kid. With all my love, ever yours affectionately, F. Lawrence Long.'[881]

Shortly afterwards, Long, who never married, wrote to his former pupil:

I don't expect you know how much I would have given for a line from you dear for several reasons, but don't worry yourself, and anyway, God bless you for the times of happiness we have had together and keep you always safe in body and soul . . . All my love to my best friend.[882]

Then, after Mountbatten had been the first to congratulation Long on his ordination later that month:

> You won't find that ordination makes me any the less yours or you any the less mine; although I think I understand just what you felt. However many things there may be to do & think about there will always be time to think about you – and in the way that will be of most use. The use of those envelopes is a sound idea – very as I always have had an idea you wished to say more, in some ways, than you cared to do . . . you are constantly in my thoughts. Best of love, your devoted, Lawrence.[883]

Quite apart from the familiarity of Long's letters, one has to question, given Mountbatten kept almost every letter sent to him and this was clearly a close friendship, why there is so little correspondence between the two men in the Mountbatten archives and why should a tutor and his pupil communicate through double envelopes. Even though Long officiated at his wedding, Mountbatten makes no reference to him in his letters to his family, nor does he appear in any book on Mountbatten. It is a relationship worthy of closer study.

CHAPTER 29

Legacy

After his death, various ideas were put forward to commemorate Mountbatten, including a statue on the extra plinth in Trafalgar Square, the foundation of a Chair of Commonwealth History with bursaries along the lines of the Rhodes Trust, and even that the August bank holiday be known as 'Mountbatten Day', though this was dismissed as 'it would be better to commemorate Lord Mountbatten through a memorial which related to his achievements, rather than one which drew attention to his death.'[884] Instead, the Mountbatten Memorial Trust was set up to support the charitable organisations with which he had been most associated, especially technological research and support for the United World Colleges movement.

Eventually it was also agreed to erect a bronze statue on Foreign Office Green, overlooking Horse Guards. In November 1983, Her Majesty the Queen unveiled the nine-foot memorial statue by the Czech sculptor, Franta Belsky, of Mountbatten as Admiral of the Fleet, standing holding binoculars with eyes fixed on the Old Admiralty Building.

In her speech she paid tribute to her husband's uncle:

Why was it that the moment Lord Mountbatten came through the door he seemed to fill the room? It was first and foremost the vitality and force of his personality, combined with an astonishing range of abilities. He could be farsighted with enormous breadth of vision and yet he could also concentrate on the minutest detail of any problem – a perfectionist who always mastered his subject. Add to this unfailing courage, immense charm and a never flagging determination to get his way, and you have a truly formidable character. Above all, he was a natural leader who managed to convey to those who worked with him his sense of enthusiasm and dedication.[885]

In July 1980, Dick Hough's biography appeared with a three-day serialisation in the *Sunday Telegraph*. Even though the book was a broadly sympathetic account and made little reference to his private life, the Broadlands Archives trustees, led by John Brabourne, took exception to Hough's claim that it was authorised – Mountbatten had given him many hours of interviews, but for a book on his parents – to protect the official biography by Philip Ziegler. They fought a High Court battle, which they won, requiring Hough to deposit all his material with them – material that is still not publicly available – and pay legal costs of £20,000. The final order was so secret that it was made in Chambers rather than Open Court and the affidavits kept secret. A penal notice prevented him from even discussing the settlement.[886]

Later in the year, Charles Smith's *Fifty Years with Mountbatten*, a memoir by his butler, and long discussed with Mountbatten, appeared. Smith had begun work as Edwina's travelling footman in 1930, before being made Dickie's valet in 1936 and becoming butler in 1954. Since his retirement in 1974, he had worked as an archivist and guide. It provided an affectionate portrait of the family and their guests and was never going to land him in the High Court.

In November 1980, Ludovic Kennedy's six-part television series, *Lord Mountbatten Remembers*, which had been filmed the previous summer with instructions that it should not be transmitted until after Mountbatten's death, was shown. Interviewed by John Terraine, he reflected on his life and career. Kennedy later wrote, 'A working title for it might have been "How I Got My Way and Was Proved Right in Everything I Did." Then I remembered Stephen Roskill telling me not to believe a word Mountbatten said or claimed unless it was corroborated from other sources.'[887]

He nicknamed the programme 'Firm Friends', because Mountbatten would always go above someone's head or threaten resignation, but having won, he would claim 'we became firm friends'.[888] This was Mountbatten at his most boastful and ingenuous. Reviewing it, Miles Kington observed: 'He reminded me, in fact, of the well-known singer who, when informed of Elvis Presley's death, said, "Poor Elvis. He was always my greatest fan."'[889]

The most controversial episode was the one devoted to Suez, because of its criticisms of the then Minister of Defence, Lord Hailsham, and the former prime minister, Harold Macmillan, who were both still alive. Robert Armstrong, the Cabinet Secretary, later known during the *Spycatcher* trial for himself being economical with the truth, noted in an internal memo, 'There are good reasons for thinking that Lord Mountbatten's account of the matter was in many respects some way from the truth – though I do not suggest that his own view of the matter at the time was other than as he describes it.'[890]

Armstrong had long sought for the programme to be deferred, arguing that it was in breach of confidential relationships laid down in the Report of the Privy Council on Ministerial Memoirs.

However, no one was persuaded, as the restrictions were limited to 15 years and Suez had taken place some 24 years earlier. There were also suggestions there could be 'untoward consequences while the situation in the Arab world is as critical as it is at present.'[891] But the situation in the Arab world in 1980 was not then critical and in fact Mountbatten had tried at Suez to dissuade Anthony Eden from attacking the Arabs.

Kennedy, exasperated, leaked the transcript to the journalist Bernard Levin, who then wrote up a major feature in *The Times*, which occasioned a letter from Hailsham refuting Mountbatten's version of Suez.[892] Further complaints followed about his version of other events, notably the sacking of Oliver Leese and the relations with James Somerville during his time as Supreme Allied Commander. Writing to George Howard, chairman of the BBC Governors, Somerville's son noted 'there was more than a touch of Baron Munchhausen about Lord Mountbatten.'[893]

Stephen Roskill summed it up, writing to Somerville's son:

I have done so much to contradict MB that there is I think a danger of me being regarded as a professional de-bunker of him. For instance, I don't know if you belong to the *Naval Review*, but in that journal I have recently disproved his claim to have been responsible for the adoption of the Swiss Oerlikon gun – and almost all who know the true story have supported me . . . I could give a dozen examples of his utter unreliability on historical issues. In fact, I tell everyone who comes to me on such matters NEVER to rely on his testimony unless it is supported by independent evidence. Perhaps the worst case is the story that at Second Quebec he was given authority by the COSS to dismiss any C-in-C in the SEAC on demand.[894]

Mountbatten's carefully nurtured reputation was beginning to be dismantled.

In 1985, after five years' research, Philip Ziegler's 800-page official life of Mountbatten, drawing on unrestricted access to all of the Mountbatten papers, was published. The book published by Collins, where Ziegler was editor-in-chief and one of the Broadlands Archives trustees, Charles Troughton, was a director, had been worth £300,000 to him and £300,000 to the Broadlands Archives Trust, with the *Sunday Times* paying £350,000 for eight instalments to serialise the book.[895] It is a generous and elegant biography, not afraid to pull its punches where criticism is due – Mountbatten's command of the *Kelly*, his vanity and mendaciousness – which comprehensively covers Mountbatten's public life, if perhaps hinting more about the private life than he is prepared to reveal.[896]

Capitalising on the publication of the official life and success of his own biography of Dickie, Richard Hough in 1985 published a life of Edwina, drawing on interviews with her sister Mary.[897] Six years later came the authorised biography of Edwina by Janet Morgan, commissioned by Philip Ziegler and published by Collins again. Though suffering from no footnotes, it is a shrewd and nuanced account of a complex woman.

Anthony Lambton's, *The Mountbattens: The Battenbergs and Young Mountbatten*, the first of a projected two-volume life, appeared in 1989, concentrating on Mountbatten's genealogy and arguing that shame at the illegitimacy in his family tree had shaped his character, most notably his vanity and insecurity. Further memoirs by members of staff followed in 1989 and 1991. William Evans had been Mountbatten's valet from 1959 to 1969. His book, *My Mountbatten Years: In the Service of Lord Louis*, provided a discreet but revealing insight into Mountbatten's life after the death of Edwina. Even more revelatory was John Barratt's *With the Greatest*

Respect, a memoir by his secretary subtitled, '*The Private Lives of Earl Mountbatten*', which recounted details of Mountbatten's lovers and voyeuristic tendencies.[898]

Further damage to Mountbatten's reputation came with Andrew Roberts' collection, *Eminent Churchillians*, which included a scathing essay, 'Lord Mountbatten and the Perils of Adrenalin', describing him as 'a mendacious, intellectually limited hustler. . . promoted wildly above his abilities, with consistently disastrous consequences', which argued for Mountbatten's impeachment over the partition of India.[899]

Within days, *Mountbatten: The Private Story* by royal writer Brian Hoey was published. The book had been commissioned by the Mountbatten family, who felt the Ziegler book had been rather too official. It benefited from interviews with Mountbatten's two daughters, his sons-in-law, eight grandchildren, Sacha Abercorn, King Constantine of Greece, Prince Michael of Kent and Prince Philip. Its main revelation was Mountbatten's love affair with his goddaughter, Sacha Abercorn.

The family have continued to provide their own version of events, downplaying the couple's infidelities, and drawing on their own related stories. These include Tim Knatchbull's moving memoir of the events of 1979, *From a Clear Blue Sky*, published for the thirtieth anniversary of Mountbatten's murder, and two charming memoirs by Lady Pamela Hicks, *India Remembered* (2007) and *Daughter of Empire* (2012).

Probably the most important of the specialist recent books on the Mountbattens has been Alex von Tunzelmann's critically acclaimed debut in 2007, *Indian Summer: The Secret History of the End of an Empire*, an examination of the transfer of power, arguing that Mountbatten's poor relationship with Jinnah and closeness to Nehru did affect the details of independence; and Adrian Smith's

Mountbatten: Apprentice War Lord, focused on Mountbatten's naval career up to 1943, which appeared in 2010.[900]

Many of these books have benefited from the extensive Mountbatten archives at Southampton University, donated on permanent loan in 1989 and purchased in 2010 for £2.85 million, with £1,993,760 alone from the National Heritage Memorial Fund. The archive comprises some 200,000 documents and 50,000 photographs, comprising letters to hundreds of figures, family correspondence, photograph albums and news cuttings (the Mountbattens at some stages of their lives were in the papers every day and all was dutifully recorded by press cutting agencies), household accounts, shooting game cards, files on each of the myriad organisations with which the couple were involved, letters of condolence, transcripts of the *Life and Times* television series and visitors books.[901]

Yet the couple's private diaries and letters to each other, plus the letters between Nehru and Edwina, available to the authorised biographers, remain closed to researchers. It appears there are still Mountbatten secrets to be revealed.

Like Churchill, Mountbatten wanted to be remembered and that reputation to be one which he had curated. Fame was to be important to him, not only during his own lifetime, but also afterwards. He was keen to do so because, as Pat MacLellan noted:

> his public image – far-sighted, imaginative, bold, dynamic, charismatic, and vigorous – was not shared by many of those who competed with him and who regarded him as devious, vain, imperious, unscrupulous and unprincipled. In fact, privately he was kind, charming, sentimental, witty and magnetic.[902]

Friends were deployed to support his version of events, later a role taken on by his family. 'The Mountbatten daughters seek to obscure three aspects of their parents: their mother's physical relationships with "men of colour", her perjury; and both their parents' bisexuality,' wrote Charlotte Breese in her biography *Hutch*. 'While I did not seek definitive proof of any of these, all three are evident from existing research in other books and from people I have interviewed.'[903]

The family, first daughters and now grandchildren, constantly denied Dickie's bisexuality and the extent and range of both their love affairs, though the story kept changing. Edwina's relationship with Nehru was impossible, first because it was platonic and then because he was impotent. Lady Pamela Hicks and the authorised Edwina biographer, Janet Morgan, suggest that most of Edwina's affairs were simply unconsummated romantic flirtations.

According to Pamela Hicks, her 'mother had at least eighteen lovers but my father, to my knowledge, only had one other.'[904] Yet Dickie's authorised biographer, Philip Ziegler, almost 30 years earlier had concluded:

> He conducted at least two protracted love-affairs outside his marriage, to the apparent satisfaction of both parties, but he was never promiscuous. Though he liked to imagine himself a sexual athlete, he seems to have had in fact only slight enthusiasm for the sport. He loved the company of women, sought their affection and had an almost irresistible urge to use them as confidantes, but his energies were channelled into his working life.[905]

He then devotes a single paragraph to his subject's mistress of 40 years with no reference to anyone else. According to John Barratt, his employer although 'he had quite a number of sexual liaisons, he seemed to be quite happy, even during the years he was married, with long periods of celibacy.'[906] Amongst the 4,000 files at Southampton University, there are few hints of the couple's extra-marital relationships.

Part of the control of the Mountbatten legacy has been exercised by withholding permission and material, much of which still remains in the archives at Broadlands or closed under a Ministerial Directive at the Hartley Library. Lambton, one of many writers to suffer from these controls, reflected:

> It made me draw the conclusion that every author who was not prepared to accept the Mountbatten myth would be starved of information. In the past the favoured few were fed with carefully selected passages.[907]

Dickie's wartime and post-war career remains controversial. Debate continues about his effectiveness at Combined Operations, South East Asia Command, as Viceroy, First Sea Lord and Chief of the Defence Staff. Was he over-promoted by his mentor Churchill and given jobs because of his connections and public relations skills, or was he an inspiring leader who could be trusted to get things done?

For David Cannadine, 'there was about almost everything Mountbatten did an element of the makeshift, the insubstantial, the incomplete, and the disingenuous, a disquieting gap between the promise and the performance that no amount of bravura on his part could ever quite conceal.'[908] To a naval colleague, however, he was: 'A single-minded enthusiast in anything he took up and endowed with boundless energy and ability, I am sure that no one in the Fleet, even in those early days, doubted that he would go right to the top and deservedly so on his own merits.'[909]

His record is not clear-cut. Dieppe may have been poorly planned, but it is unfair to blame Mountbatten entirely. Many of the fateful decisions were not his own. And though the Dieppe disaster overshadows his time at Combined Operations, it is generally acknowledged that he did build a totally inter-service organisation, which not only kept pressure on German forces but prepared the way, not least with his encouragement of technical developments, for the successful D-Day landings.

In spite of being deprived of the necessary resources to wage the sort of campaign he would have liked in Burma, he did restore the fighting spirit. Bill Slim and his generals were the military brains, but it was Mountbatten's leadership that allowed them to flourish. His appointment, with its confused command structure and diplomatic sensitivities, was a political rather than a military one, and on that score, he acquitted himself well. He may have fallen out with various of his generals, and relations with the Americans were strained at times but, in a difficult situation, he kept the show on the road.

The ends of wars are messy affairs. There are huge logistical problems of demobbing troops, rescuing prisoners of war, repatriating captured soldiers and rebuilding devastated areas. Both Mountbattens rose to the challenges and this was perhaps their finest hour, with Dickie's decision to work with nationalists, such as Aung San, proving to be pragmatic and far-sighted.

The rapid transfer of power, Indian Partition, the subsequent communal violence and problems in Kashmir continue to be debated. Faced with the instability of the Interim Government, the breakdown in British administration, the Indian impatience for independence, rising communal violence and a brief to hand over power with as much dignity as possible from a British government with other priorities, Mountbatten had little choice.

Rushing partition was tactical – to concentrate minds, demonstrate good faith and narrow options – but also if he had not rushed it, there would have been no power to hand over. It is certainly not the case that Mountbatten brought it forward so he could return to the Navy sooner. If that was true, he would not have stayed on as Governor-General. Indeed, his reputation might be higher now than if he had left in August 1947.

Yes, the Mountbattens probably did show favouritism towards Nehru and the Hindus, but Jinnah had not been an easy person with whom to deal. Mountbatten was charmed by the old Harrovian and fellow Cambridge alumnus, Nehru, whereas, in spite of a genuine effort, he was never able to establish the same close relationship with Jinnah. On such personal matters, history can be shaped.

According to the BBC journalist, John Osman, sitting next to Mountbatten in the officers' mess of the Life Guards at Windsor, and chatting about his time in India:

> Speaking with a frankness that surprised me, Mountbatten blamed himself, saying how he had 'got things wrong' . . . To this day his own judgment on how he had performed in India rings in my ears and in my memory . . . As one who dislikes the tasteless use in writing of the dictionary's 'vulgar slang' word, I shall permit myself an exception this time, because it is the only honest way of reporting accurately what the last Viceroy of India thought about the way he had done his job: 'fucked it up'.[910]

Is this fair? On the five criteria set for him on going out as Viceroy – unitary Government by June 1948, 'fair and just arrangements' for Princes, 'the closest cooperation with the Indians' and no 'break in the continuity of the Indian Army' – Mountbatten had failed. Over a million people had died in the

Punjab, in spite of repeated warnings from various government officials, and many might have been saved if the boundaries had been clear before independence. But he had delivered his brief.

Mountbatten's score card at the Ministry of Defence is mixed. He did integrate the three armed services and make tough choices about Britain's nuclear deterrent, but he was simply a public servant reporting to politicians who created policy. And he incurred unnecessary unpopularity along the way for his ruthless ambition and rather unsophisticated plotting. As Field Marshal Sir Francis Festing told Field Marshall Lord Carver, 'If the front door was wide open, Dickie would still prefer to come down the chimney.'[911]

Mountbatten was a man full of contradictions. Self-confident in public life, he was insecure when it came to his private life and relations with his wife. Able to think outside the box and see the big picture, he was obsessed with trivial detail – often to do with his own personal appearance or prestige. Always immaculately dressed and handsome in the correct uniform, he had no taste when it came to casual dress. With his lack of empathy and concern with detail – 'his eggs had to be cooked for exactly one and a half minutes after being plunged into boiling water' – there appear to be hints of autism and narcissism in his make-up.[912]

No one disputes the vanity born of his insecurity. Ludovic Kennedy, a fellow speaker at a naval dinner in Newcastle in 1975, having arranged to meet him at a local hotel:

> put my head gingerly round the semi-open door. There I saw an unusual sight: the admiral in shirtsleeves and braces sitting aside a very low dressing-room stool and gazing keenly at his reflection in the mirror, the ADC on his knees behind him brushing the curls at the back of his head.[913]

His obsession with uniforms and decorations was legendary. Harold Macmillan is supposed to have muttered to a courtier after a Silver Jubilee celebration lunch at the Guildhall, 'I hope you'll give us all a medal. Dickie will be so disappointed if you don't.'

John Festing, son of Field Marshal Frankie Festing, tells similar stories of Mountbatten persuading the Powers That Be to give him certain key jobs to his father's detriment, and inviting himself to memorial events when he had conspicuously not been invited. 'I suspect that he was a very unusual man and a bit more Germanic than he would like people to know.'[914]

Pat MacLellan, the former military assistant to Mountbatten, agrees:

> He was different because he was Hanoverian. He had a Teutonic determination. He never actually fitted in. He didn't play by the same rules as other naval officers. Above all he wanted to be accepted. How to prove you're better than everyone else is by getting to the top.[915]

As Mountbatten confessed to one of his wartime generals, Philip Christison, whilst trying to get him to take responsibility for one of his mistakes:

> Christie, you know how my father was treated when World War I came. Ever since that disgraceful episode, I have lived determined to get to the top and vindicate his memory. Nothing, and no one; I repeat, nothing and no one, will ever be allowed to stand in my way.[916]

What had driven him was partly the desire to avenge family honour, partly a deep insecurity that required constant adulation. 'Where his career was concerned, nothing else mattered,' thought his son-in-law David Hicks. 'He could be a complete bastard.'[917] It was something Mountbatten recognised himself. 'I know what I want and I go for it and I am ruthless. If anybody stands in my way, I circumvent them if I can't finish them off.'[918] Having achieved his lifetime's ambition, even when he retired, he was driven partly by a strong sense of public duty and *noblesse oblige*, partly by loneliness and a need to keep himself busy and wanted.

He had married one of the most beautiful and richest women in the world, yet it was not the great love match for which he had perhaps hoped – that was reserved for his eldest daughter. Part of the reason for the failure of his marriage may have been the dark secret about his own sexuality, unknown until now, but his sense of inadequacy in his private life found an outlet in his determination for public office.

The story of Dickie and Edwina Mountbatten is almost the story of the 20th century. Both were born at the turn of the century and their lives touched many of the greatest events of the period or intertwined with the dominating figures of the time. Their biographies have a neat narrative symmetry divided by the war. Until then, Edwina was a rich little girl lost, who sought release and escape with lovers and travel. Dickie was a hard-working naval officer, who may eventually have made flag rank. The war changed their lives irretrievably, catapulting them into positions of fame and influence.

Edwina's reputation is secure, universally admired and loved. An aimless youth was transformed into a middle age of lasting accomplishments as a humanitarian. Difficult, complex, determined to emerge from the shadow of her husband, she proved herself more than his equal in intellect and achievement, and her influence on him in public life has been underrated.

'She was quicker and more intelligent than her husband,' the politician Woodrow Wyatt remembered, 'and understood politics better.'[919] She had continually advanced Dickie's career, whether sweet-talking King George VI to give her husband a D.S.O. or a viscountcy, persuading Nehru to accept the Partition plan, or the Admiralty Board to promote him.

Her husband's reputation is less clear.

Mountbatten loved to portray himself as a player on the world stage who had changed nations. He wanted to take credit for events, inventions, operations to which he was not fully entitled and even when they did not always reflect well on him, such as Dieppe. Always desperate for attention, even if it was not always admiring, he skilfully used PR agents to promote himself at the expense of others and together with colleagues and family carefully curated how he would be remembered. Living longer than most of his wartime colleagues made it easier to shape the narrative as he wished.

The reality, especially as Supreme Commander and Viceroy, was that he was subject to wider underlying historical currents. Given America called the shots in South East Asia, there was little Mountbatten could do except abide by their wishes. Given the positions adopted by Congress and Jinnah, partition was inevitable even before Mountbatten arrived in India.

He was good at dressing up his role and spinning his apparent influence, but he was really just a front of house manager to make sure everyone remained happy. The irony is that the strings were being pulled elsewhere.

Acknowledgements

I am grateful to Her Majesty the Queen for permission to quote from material in the Royal Archives.

Lady Pamela Hicks kindly gave me an interview, as did her daughter India and son Ashley. Sibilla O'Donnell, a close family friend, shared her correspondence with Lord Mountbatten and generously had me to stay in the Bahamas. Philip Ziegler, Dickie's authorised biographer, saw me, and Janet Morgan, Lady Balfour of Burleigh, Edwina's official biographer, answered various questions.

Others who knew the Mountbattens personally and spoke to me included:

His gamekeeper Bernard Aldrich, who started working at Broadlands in 1956; John Attwood, who spent time on HMS *Kelly* in 1939; Mountbatten's personal pilot John Barnes; Pamela Baxter, a matron at a convalescent home for service children in Malta between 1952–54; Tim Benn, who was part of the funeral escort in 1979; David Bicknell, who advised Mountbatten on his security; John Blanten, who worked as a steward at Broadlands in the 1950s; Brenda Bury, who painted Mountbatten's portrait in 1965; Myra, Lady Butter, the sister of Gina Phillips; Alan Campbell-Johnson's daughter Virginia, who met the Mountbattens in India; Peter Carter, a steward at Broadlands during the 1970s; Terry Cattermole, the officer of the watch at Edwina's burial; Graham Chillingworth, a Life Guard during the 1960s; Rick Compton, son of Janey Lindsay; Jackie Crier.

The late Lady Ursula d'Abo; Robin Dalton; Edward Dawnay; Mary Lou Emery and Philippa De Pass, regular riding companions of Lord Mountbatten; Davinia Eastwood; James Ellery, a former ADC to Lord Mountbatten; Bill Evans, Mountbatten's valet 1959–69; Mike Goodyear of the Lifeguards; Peter Hames, who met Mountbatten in 1947 in Delhi; Mountbatten's godson Peter Heywood-Lonsdale; Peter Hinton, who served with Mountbatten during the 1950s; Michael Hodges; James and Priscilla Howes; Michael Hutton, who served with Mountbatten during the 1950s; Momin Latif; Freya Lomax; Julian Loring, who served on Mountbatten's staff in Malta; Barbara Cartland's son Ian McCorquodale; Mountbatten's military assistant during the 1960s, Major General Pat MacLellan; Derrick Meakins, who was on Mountbatten's staff in 1947–48; Janet, Marchioness Milford Haven; the Viscountess Monckton of Brenchley, who knew the Mountbattens in Malta in 1948.

Derek Oakley, Mountbatten's Royal Marines ADC; Columbus O'Donnell; Ron Perks, Mountbatten's driver in Malta in 1948; Kerry Pocock; David Roberts, who edited Mountbatten's *80 Years*; Sammy Rowe, who served on HMS *Glasgow* with Mountbatten; Martin Sands, who worked with Mountbatten during the 1950s; Brian Smith, who served in Mountbatten's private office, 1952–53; Mountbatten's goddaughter Emma Temple; Allan Warren, who knew Mountbatten well during the 1970s; Pam Williams, who served on Mountbatten's staff in 1964; and Graham Yuill, who served as Mountbatten's bodyguard in 1979 and spoke to me at length about the lapses in security.

My thanks also go to:

Richard Aldous for help with Malcolm Sargent; Rupert Allason;

Acknowledgements

Viscount Allendale; Ron Atkin for advice on Dieppe; Mary Aylmer for providing photocopies of *Private Eye* references; Jo Baddenham and her fellow trustees for access to the Derek Hill archive; Mandy Banton for help on the Borneo archives; Simon Baynes; Robert Beaumont for showing me his father Christopher Beaumont's papers; Sally Bedell Smith for material on Bill Paley; Nicholas Best for various introductions in Ireland; Michael Bloch for introducing me to Allan Warren; Colin Bonner; Richard Britten-Long, who spoke to me about Paula Long and shared his private photo collection; Alan Brodie and Freya Smith, who made some of the Noël Coward correspondence available; Christian Browning; Stefan Buczacki; Cathy and Charlotte Burnaby-Atkins for showing me parts of their father's diary; Dorothy Byrne for her introductions.

Cal Calvert; Duncan Campbell; Eileen and Robert Carron; Kim Cobbold; Marc Cole-Bailey; Richard and Juliet Cornwall; George Cruddas; Noel and Fiona Cunningham-Reid; Tony Daly; Sylvia Darley; Paul Davies; Georgia de Chamberet; Lord Decies; Anne de Courcy for some extracts from Edwina's diary; Martin Dillon; Patrick Dillon; Jane Dismore; Charles Doble, who supplied his father's correspondence with Lord Mountbatten; Frank Donald; Stephen Dorrill; Hugh Drake Brockman for information on Tony Simpson; Jeremy Dronfield for various editorial suggestions; Martin Duberman; the Earl of Durham; Rupert Earle and Clara Hamer for their legal advice; Piu Eatwell for help contacting Yola Letellier's family; Vera Fairbanks, Victoria Fairbanks and Anthony Fairbanks Weston for information on Douglas Fairbanks Jr's friendship with Lord Mountbatten; Clive Wigham Ferguson for information on Irene Wigham Richardson; Andrew and John Festing for talking to me about their father Sir Francis Festing's relationship with Lord Mountbatten; Peter Sutton Fitzgibbon; Declan Foley; Maurice Frankel for advice on Freedom of Information issues.

Patrick Gallagher, the butler at Glenveagh Castle; Sandy Gandhi for family stories about the Mountbattens; Melinda Gilbert for help with the Cabinet Office; Mark Girouard; Tommy Gorman; Jill Goulding; Lord Grantley; Elizabeth Haslam for research in Cyprus; Paddy Hayes for several Irish contacts and interventions; Judy Hough for making her husband Dick Hough's papers available; James Howard-Johnston; Cathal Hunter and Elaine Kelly of the Department of the Taoiseach; Shama Husain, daughter of Shahid Hamid; Brian Hutchinson; Mike Hutchinson; Richard Ingrams; Louis Jebb; Cathryn Keller; Kitty Kelley; Susannah Kelly; Janey Lindsay's half-brother Simon Kenyon-Slaley; Angus Konstam and Brian Lavery for some naval research; Harshan Kumarasingham; Robert Lacey; James and Emma Lambe for letting me consult Charles Lambe's private papers; Edward Laxton; Celia Lee; Fiona Lee; Ray Levine; Trudy Lomax.

Joe McGowan; Bridie McKie; Leo McKinstry; Adam Macqueen; Sue Marsh, Bruce Rawlings, Sally Martin and Jerry Smith of Friends of Sri Lanka Association; Zareer Masani; Hamon Massey; Roger Matthews for memories of Mountbatten's butler Eric Carmichael; Patrick Mercer for information on the Warrenpoint killings; Chloe Morse-Harding; John Morton; Lord Ivar Mountbatten; Idula Mukherjee; Nilanjan Mukhopadhyay; Dan Mulvenna, who put in various FOI requests to the CIA; Jade Neergaard; John Nield; Selene Obolensky; Gemma O'Doherty; Romaine Orthwein; Joanna Oswin; Mitchell Owens, who provided information on Eleanor Cosden; David Panter for various introductions in India; Paul Pender; Prudence Penn; Kate Buchanan Phillips; Rifat Pirzada and his father the late Syed Pirzada; Brian Pollitt; David Pratt, Marquess Camden, who generously lent me his mother's travel diaries; Clive Prince.

Merick Rayner for information on his mother Madeleine

Acknowledgements

Masson-Rayne; Jean Ritchie; Toby Rolt for insights into his grandfather Kip Bradford; Bertrand Ruillier and Philippe Savignac for background on Yola Letellier; Nayantara Sahgal; Roddy Sale; Victoria Schofield; Ritchie Self; Rashmi Seth; Desmond Seward; William Stadiem; Peter Steven; Giles Stibbe for various introductions in the Household Cavalry; Lord Strathnaver; Douglas Thompson; Peter Thompson for help with the 1968 Coup; Michael Thornton; Richard Thorpe; Neville Thurlbeck; Clifford Thurlow; Michael Tillotson; Phil Tomaselli; Hugo Vickers; Alex von Tunzelmann; Colin Wallace; Charles Wardell for photographs and information on his father Mike Wardell; Mike Welham for information on Commander Crabbe; Carinthia West; Francis Wheen; Captain Gordon Wilson for his paper 'Mountbatten – Signal Officer Supreme'; Malcolm Yorke; Felicity Yost; and in Malta, Roger Baldacchino, Peter Apap Bologna, Justin Camilleri, Susan Mompalao de Pino and Charles Gauci.

Very special thanks to the following:

Marie Black for her research in US archives; David Burke, with whom I had an enjoyable research trip in Ireland and who introduced me to senior intelligence officers in the IRA and Garda; Charlotte Breese, the author of a wonderful book on 'Hutch' and who introduced me to several useful contacts; Greg Callus, who generously and very skilfully acted pro bono in several Freedom of Information legal actions on my behalf; Glyn Gowans for wise pro bono legal advice over many years; 'Sean' and 'Amal' for so bravely speaking out for the first time about their experiences over 40 years ago; Amy Ripley for all her publicity tips; Susan Williams for sharing her Indian research notes; and my sister Helen Leatherby, who again read and commented on the first draft.

Part of the research was conducted whilst a visiting archives bye-fellow at Churchill College, Cambridge and I am grateful to the Masters and Fellows for the fellowship, Allen Packwood, Piers Brendon and Christopher Andrew for supporting my application and the archivists for all their help during my time there.

The research for this book has taken four years and involved dozens of interviews and research in countless archives around the world reflecting the wide interests of the Mountbattens. The most important Mountbatten archive is at Southampton University and I am grateful to the archivists there for all their help during four years of visits.

My thanks too to the archivists at: the National Archives, Kew; King's College London; the Baker Library, Harvard University; the British Library; the Howard Gotlieb Center at Boston University; Christ Church, Oxford; the Czech Security Services Archive; the Royal Air Force Museum; the Margaret Herrick Library, Los Angeles; the Tozzer Library, Harvard University; the Schomburg Center, New York; the Beinecke Library, Yale University; Howard University, Washington; the New York Public Library; American Heritage Center, University of Wyoming; Birr Castle, Ireland; Library of Society of Friends, London; BBC Written Archives Centre, Caversham; Cadbury Research Library, University of Birmingham; the National Records of Scotland; the Parliamentary Archives, House of Lords; Special Collections, University of Oregon; University Archive, The Open University; the Bodleian Library, Oxford; Cambridge University Library; the Imperial War Museum; the National Maritime Museum; Reading University; the National Archives in Dublin.

A particular thanks to Lynsey Gillespie at PRONI; Allison Derrett and her colleagues at the Royal Archives; Gillian Dunks at McMaster University, Canada; Bridget Gillies at the University of East Anglia; Louise Harrison of the London Metropolitan Archives; Alison

Acknowledgements

Harvey at Cardiff University Archives; Elisa Ho at the Jacob Rader Marcus Center of the American Jewish Archives; Micah Hoggatt at the Houghton Library, Harvard University; Roger Hull at Liverpool Record Office; Meirian Jump at Marx Memorial Library; Hayley Mercer of the Schlesinger Library; Nigel Taylor, the legal Records specialist at the National Archives; Bethan Hopkins Williams at the National Library of Wales; Catherine Williams of the Institute of Advanced Legal Studies Library; Miriam Cady of the Philadelphia Museum of Art; Dr Kevin Greenbank at Cambridge's South East Asia Centre; and Genevieve Maxwell of the Academy of Motion Picture Arts and Science Library.

Last, but not least, I owe a considerable amount to Bill Hamilton, who did a brilliant job agenting the book, and the enthusiasm and professionalism of Matt Phillips, Beth Eynon, Karen Stretch, Sophia Walker, Kate Parkin, Emily Rough, Lisa Hoare, Ali Nazari, Stuart Finglass, Nico Poilblanc, Jon Watt and Alba Proko at Bonnier, Barry Johnston, who has again very skilfully and cheerfully edited my text, as well as Nicole Patterson and Jane Donovan.

My wife Angela was the first person to read the biography and give comments and the book is dedicated with love to her and our two children, Robert and Alice.

I am grateful for permission to reproduce extracts from the following books: *Edwina* by Richard Hough; *Hutch* by Charlotte Breese. If any permissions have been missed, I would be happy to rectify the omission.

Selected Bibliography

BOOKS

Adams, Jad and Whitehead, Philip, *The Dynasty: The Nehru–Gandhi Story* (Penguin, London, 1997).

Ahmed, Akbar, *Jinnah, Pakistan and Islamic Identity: The Search for Saladin* (Routledge, London, 2005).

Aitken, Janet, *The Beaverbrook Girl: An Autobiography* (Collins, London, 1987).

Akbar, M.J., *Nehru: The Making of India* (Viking, London, 1988).

Aldgate, Anthony and Richards, Jeffrey, *Britain Can Take It: The British Cinema in the Second World War* (Blackwell, Oxford, 1986).

Aldous, Richard, *Tunes of Glory: The Life of Malcolm Sargent* (Hutchinson, London, 2001).

Aldrich, Richard, *Intelligence in the War Against Japan* (Cambridge University Press, Cambridge, 2000).

Alexander, Joan, *Mabel Strickland* (Progress Press, Malta, 1996).

Ali, Chaudhri Muhammad, *The Emergence of Pakistan* (Columbia University Press, New York, 1996).

Ali, Tariq, *An Indian Dynasty: The Story of the Nehru–Gandhi Family* (Putnam, New York, 1985).

Anon, *Demosthenes Demolished: A Record of Cambridge Union Debates, February 1919–June 1920* (Heffer, Cambridge, 1920).

Arnold, Ralph, *A Very Quiet War* (Rupert Hart-Davis, London, 1962).

Ashmore, Edward, *The Battle and the Breeze* (Sutton, Stroud, 1997).

Attlee, Clement, *As it Happened* (William Heinemann, London, 1954).

Azad, Maulana Abul Kalam, *India Wins Freedom: An Autobiographical Narrative* (Longman, Harlow, 1959).

Baker, George, *Mountbatten of Burma* (Cassell, London, 1959).

Baker, Richard, *The Terror of Tobermory* (W.H. Allen, London, 1972).

Bangash, Yaqoob Khan, *A Princely Affair: Accession and Integration of Princely States in Pakistan 1947–55* (Oxford University Press, Oxford, 2015).

Barnes, John and Nicholson, David (eds.), *The Empire at Bay: The Leo Amery Diaries 1929–1945* (Hutchinson, London, 1988).

Barratt, John, *With the Greatest Respect: Private Lives of Earl Mountbatten and Prince and Princess Michael of Kent* (Sidgwick & Jackson, London, 1991).

Bayley, Christopher and Harper, Tim, *Forgotten Armies: Britain's Asian Empire and the War with Japan* (Allen Lane, London, 2004).

Bedell Smith, Sally, *In All His Glory: The Life of William S. Paley* (Simon & Schuster, New York, 1990).

Bedell Smith, Sally, *Reflected Glory: The Life of Pamela Churchill Harriman* (Simon & Schuster, New York, 1997).

Bedell Smith, Sally, *Princes Charles* (Random House, New York, 2017).

Bloch, Michael, *The Duke of Windsor's War* (Weidenfeld & Nicolson, London, 1982).

Selected Bibliography

Bloch, Michael, *Wallis and Edward: Letters 1931–1937*
(Weidenfeld & Nicolson, London, 1986).

Bloch, Michael (ed.), *James Lees-Milne Diaries 1942–1954*
(John Murray, London, 2006).

Bond, Brian (ed.), *Chief of Staff: The Diaries of Lieutenant-General
Sir Henry Pownall, Vol. 2* (Leo Cooper, London, 1974).

Bradford, Sarah, *King George VI* (Weidenfeld, London, 1989).

Bradford, Sarah, *Elizabeth: A Biography of Her Majesty The Queen*
(William Heinemann, London, 1996).

Brecher, Michael, *Nehru: A Political Biography* (Oxford University
Press, Oxford, 1959).

Brecknock, Countess of, *Edwina Mountbatten: Her Life in Pictures*
(Macdonald, London, 1961).

Breese, Charlotte, *Hutch* (Bloomsbury, London, 1999).

Bristow, R.C.B., *Memories of the British Raj: Soldier in India*
(Johnson, London, 1974).

Brown, Judith, *Nehru: A Political Life* (Yale, New Haven,
2003).

Brownlow, Kevin, *David Lean: A Biography* (Richard Cohen
Books, London, 1996).

Bryans, Robin, *Checkmate* (Honeyford Press, London, 1994).

Bryans, Robin, *Blackmail and Whitewash* (Honeyford Press,
London, 1996).

Bryce, Ivar, *You Only Live Once* (Weidenfeld & Nicolson, London,
1975).

Buczacki, David, *My Darling Mr Asquith* (Cato & Clark, London,
2016).

Butler, David, *Lord Mountbatten: The Last Viceroy* (Methuen,
London, 1985).

Byrne, Paula, *Kick* (Collins, London, 2016).

Campbell, John, *Dieppe Revisited* (Frank Cass, London, 1993).

Campbell-Johnson, Alan, *Mission with Mountbatten* (Robert Hale, London, 1951).

Cannadine, David, *The Pleasures of the Past* (Collins, London, 1989).

Carey Evans, Olwen, *Lloyd George Was My Father* (Gomer Press, Ceredigion, 1985).

Carrington, Peter, *Report on Things Past* (Collins, London, 1988).

Carswell, John, *The Exile: A life of Ivy Litvinov* (Faber, London, 1983).

Cartland, Barbara, *The Isthmus Years* (Hutchinson, London, 1943).

Cartland, Barbara, *The Years of Opportunity* (Hutchinson, London, 1948).

Cartland, Barbara, Love *at the Helm* (Weidenfeld & Nicolson, London, 1980).

Cartland, Barbara, *I Reach for the Stars: An Autobiography* (Robson, London, 1994).

Carver, Michael (ed.), *The Warlords: Military Commanders of the Twentieth Century* (Weidenfeld & Nicolson, London, 1976).

Castle, Charles, *Noel* (W.H. Allen, London, 1972).

Catterall, Peter (ed.), *The Macmillan Diaries: The Cabinet Years 1950–57*, (Pan, London, 2003).

Cave Brown, Anthony, *Bodyguard of Lies* (Collins, London, 1975).

Chandra, Bipin, *India's Struggle for Independence* (Penguin, New Delhi, 1989).

Chaudhuri, Nirad C., *The Autobiography of an Unknown Indian* (Macmillan, London, 1951).

Chenevix-Trench, Charles, *Viceroy's Agent* (Cape, London, 1987).

Chester, Lucy, *On the Edge: Borders, Territory and Conflict in South Asia* (Manchester University Press, Manchester, 2008).

Chisholm, Anne and Davie, Michael, *Lord Beaverbrook: A Life* (Hutchinson, London, 1992).

Christiansen, Arthur, *Headlines All My Life* (William Heinemann, London, 1961).

Christie, John, *Morning Drum* (BACSA, London, 1983).

Clarke, Liam and Johnston, Kathryn, *Martin McGuinness: From Guns to Government* (Mainstream, Edinburgh, 2001).

Clement, Catherine, *Edwina and Nehru: A Novel* (Penguin, New Delhi, 1996).

Close, H.M., *Attlee, Wavell, Mountbatten and the Transfer of Power* (National Book Foundation, Islamabad, 1997).

Cockburn, Claud, *In Time of Trouble* (Rupert Hart-Davis, London, 1956).

Collins, Larry and Lapierre, Dominique, *Freedom at Midnight* (Collins, London, 1975).

Collins, Larry and Lapierre, Dominique, *Mountbatten and the Partition of India* (Vikas, New Delhi, 1982).

Colville, John, *The Fringes of Power: Downing Street Diaries 1939–1955* (Hodder, London, 1985).

Connell, Brian, *Manifest Destiny: A Study in Five Profiles of the Rise and Influence of the Mountbatten Family* (Cassell, London, 1953).

Connell, Brian, *Knight Errant: A Biography of Douglas Fairbanks Jr* (Hodder, London, 1955).

Cookridge, E.H., *From Battenberg to Mountbatten* (Arthur Barker, London, 1965).

Cooper, Artemis (ed.), *A Durable Fire: The Letters of Duff and Diana Cooper 1913–1950* (Collins, London, 1983).

Copland, Ian, *The Princes of India in the Endgame of Empire 1917–1947* (Cambridge University Press, Cambridge, 1997).

Corfield, Sir Conrad, *The Princely India I Knew from Reading to Mountbatten* (Indo British Historical Society, Madras, 1975).

Courtney, John, *It Was Murder. Murders and Kidnappings in Ireland: The Inside Story* (Blackwater Press, Dublin, 1996).

Coward, Noël, *Present Indicative* (William Heinemann, London, 1937).

Coward, Noël, *Future Indefinite* (William Heinemann, London, 1954).

Crook, Paul, *Came the Dawn: 50 Years an Army Officer* (Spellmount, Tunbridge Wells, 1989).

Cudlipp, Hugh, *Walking on the Water* (Bodley Head, London, 1976).

Cunninghan, Andrew, *A Sailor's Odyssey: The Autobiography* (Hutchinson, London, 1951).

Dalton, Robin, *One Leg Over* (Text, Melbourne, 2017).

Danchev, Alex and Todman, Daniel (eds.), *Field Marshall Lord Alanbrooke War Diaries 1939–1945* (Weidenfeld & Nicolson, London, 2001).

Das, Manmath Nath, *Partition and the Independence of India* (Vision Books, New Delhi, 1982).

Das, Manmath Nath. *Fateful Events of 1947: The Secret British Game of Divide and Quit* (Standard Publishers, New Delhi, 2005).

Davie, Michael (ed.), *The Diaries of Evelyn Waugh* (Weidenfeld & Nicolson, London, 1976).

Davies, Nicholas, *Queen Elizabeth II* (Carol Publishing Group, New York, 1996).

Day, Barry (ed.), *The Letters of Noel Coward* (Methuen, London, 2007).

Deacon, Richard, *The Greatest Treason* (Century, London, 1989).

Dean, John, *HRH Prince Philip, Duke of Edinburgh* (Hale, London, 1954).

De Chambeet, Georgia, *On the Wilder Shores of Love: A Bohemian Life* (Virago, London, 2015).

De Courcy, Anne, *The Viceroy's Daughters* (Weidenfeld & Nicolson, London, 2000).

Dempster, Nigel and Evans, Peter, *Behind Palace Doors* (Orion, London, 1993).

Dennis, Peter, *Troubled Days of Peace: Mountbatten and South East Asia Command 1945–46* (Manchester University Press, Manchester, 1990).

Donaldson, Frances, *Edward VIII* (Weidenfeld &Nicolson, London, 1974).

Dorrill, Stephen & Ramsay, Robin, *Smear! Wilson and the Secret State* (Fourth Estate, London, 1991).

Driberg, Tom, *Beaverbrook: A Study in Power and Frustration* (Weidenfeld & Nicolson, London, 1956).

Driberg, Tom, *Ruling Passions* (Cape, London, 1977).

Duberman, Martin, *Paul Robeson* (Bodley Head, London, 1989).

Dudley Edwards, Ruth, *Newspaperman Hugh Cudlipp, Cecil Harmsworth King and the Glory Days of Fleet Street* (Secker & Warburg, London, 2003).

Dutton, David, *Anthony Eden: A Life and Reputation* (Hodder Arnold, London, 1996).

Eade, Philip, *Young Prince Philip* (Collins, London, 2011).

Eccles, David and Sybil, *By Safe Hand: Letters of Sybil and David Eccles 1939–42* (Bodley Head, London, 1983).

Edwardes, Michael, *The Last Years of British India* (Cassell, London, 1963).

Eisenhower, Dwight, *Crusade in Europe* (William Heinemann, London, 1948).

Ellis, R.J., *He Walks Alone: The Public and Private Life of Captain Cunningham-Reid* (W.H. Allen, London, 1946).

Evans, Sian, *Mrs Ronnie: The Society Hostess Who Collected Kings* (National Trust, London, 2013).

Evans, Sian, *Queen Bees: Six Brilliant and Extraordinary Society Hostesses Between the Wars* (Two Roads, London, 2016).

Evans, Trefor (ed.), *The Killearn Diaries 1934–1946* (Sidgwick & Jackson, London, 1972).

Evans, William, *My Mountbatten Years* (Headline, London, 1989).

Faigot, Roger, *Nous Avons Tue Mountbatten!: L'IRA Parle,* (editions Jean Picolec, Paris, 1981).

Fairbanks, Douglas Jr, *The Salad Days* (Collins, London, 1988).

Fairbanks, Douglas Jr, *A Hell of a War* (Robson, London, 1995)

Felton, Mark, *The Final Betrayal: Mountbatten, MacArthur and the Tragedy of Japanese POWS* (Pen & Sword, Barnsley, 2010).

Fergusson, Bernard, *The Watery Maze: The Story of Combined Operations* (Collins, London, 1961).

Fjellman, Margit, *Louise Mountbatten: Queen of Sweden* (Allen & Unwin, London, 1968).

French, Patrick, *Liberty or Death: India's Journey to Independence and Division* (Collins, London, 1997).

Gandhi, Sonia (ed.), *Two Alone, Two Together: Letters Between Indira Gandhi and Jawaharlal Nehru 1940–1964* (Hodder, London, 1992).

Garewal, Sher Muhammad, *Mountbatten's Viceroyalty and the Creation of Pakistan* (Pakistan Study Centre, Karachi, 2011).

Garrett, Richard, *Motoring and the Mighty* (Stanley Paul, London, 1971).

Godfrey, Rupert (ed.), *Letters from a Prince* (Little, Brown, London, 1998).

Goldsmith, Barbara, *Little Gloria, Happy at Last* (Macmillan, London, 1980).

Grantley, Lord, *Silver Spoon* (Hutchinson, London, 1954).

Grove, Eric and Rohan, Sally, 'The Limits of Opposition: Admiral Earl Mountbatten of Burma, First Sea Lord and Chief of the

Naval Staff' in Sean Kelly and Anthony Gorst (eds.), *Whitehall and the Suez Crisis* (Frank Cass, London, 2000).

Guha, Ramachandra, *India after Gandhi* (Macmillan, London, 2007).

Hajari, Nisid, *Midnight's Furies: The Deadly Legacy of India's Partition* (Amberley, Stroud, 2015).

Hall, Roy Archibald, *To Kill and Kill Again: The Chilling True Confessions of a Serial Killer* (Blake, London, 2002).

Hamid, Shahid, *Disastrous Twilight: A Personal Record of the Partition of India* (Pen & Sword, Barnsley, 1993).

Hamilton, Nigel, *Monty: The Making of a General 1887–1942* (Hamish Hamilton, London, 1981).

Hampshire, A. Cecil, *Royal Sailors* (Kimber, London, 1971).

Harrison, Michael, *Mulberry: The Return in Triumph* (W.H. Allen, London, 1965).

Hart-Davis, Duff (ed.), *King's Counsellor: Abdication and War: The Diaries of Sir Alan Lascelles* (Weidenfeld & Nicolson, London, 2006).

Harvey, John (ed.), *The War Diaries of Oliver Harvey* (Collins, London, 1978).

Hashim, Raza, *Mountbatten and Pakistan* (Quaid I Azan Academy, Karachi, 1982).

Haslam, Nicky, *Redeeming Features* (Knopf, New York, 2009).

Hastings, Max, *Nemesis: The Battle for Japan 1944–45* (Collins, London, 2008).

Hastings, Selina, *Evelyn Waugh: A Biography* (Weidenfeld, London, 1989).

Hatch, Alden, *The Mountbattens* (W.H. Allen, London, 1966).

Heald, Tim, *The Duke: A Portrait of Prince Philip* (Hodder, London, 1991).

Heald, Tim, *Barbara Cartland* (Sinclair-Stevenson, London, 1994).

Healey, Denis, *The Time of My Life* (Michael Joseph, London, 1989).

Hemming, Henry, *Churchill's Iceman* (Preface, London, 2014).

Hennessy, Peter, *Having It So Good* (Allen Lane, London, 2006).

Henriques, Robert, *From a Biography of Myself* (Secker & Warburg, London, 1969).

Heward, Edmund, *The Great and the Good: A Life of Lord Radcliffe* (Barry Rose, London, 1994).

Hicks, Ashley, *David Hicks: Designer* (Scriptum Editions, London, 2002).

Hicks, Pamela, *India Remembered: A Personal Account of the Mountbattens During the Transfer of Power* (Pavilion, London, 2007).

Hicks, Pamela, *Daughter of Empire: Life as a Mountbatten* (Weidenfeld & Nicolson, London, 2012).

Higham, Charles, *Elizabeth and Philip: The Untold Story* (Sidgwick & Jackson, London, 1991).

Higham, Charles, *Mrs Simpson: Secret Lives of the Duchess of Windsor* (Sidgwick & Jackson, London, 2004).

Higham, Charles and Moseley, Roy, *Merle: A Biography of Merle Oberon* (New English Library, London, 1983).

Hitchcock, Eric, *Making Waves: Admiral Mountbatten's Radio SEAC 1945–49* (Helion, Warwick, 2014).

Hoare, Philip, *Noel Coward* (Sinclair-Stevenson, London, 1995).

Hodson, H.V., *The Great Divide: Britain–Pakistan* (Hutchinson, London, 1969).

Hoey, Brian, *Mountbatten: The Private Story* (Sidgwick & Jackson, London, 1994).

Holman, Dennis, *Lady Louis: Life of the Countess Mountbatten of Burma* (Odhams, London, 1952).

Horrie, Chris, *Tabloid Nation* (André Deutsch, London, 2003).

Selected Bibliography

Horsfield, John, *Mountbatten, Somerville and the South East Asia Command: The War Against Japan 1943–1944* (California State University, Los Angeles, 2017).

Hough, Richard, *Louis and Victoria* (Hutchinson, London, 1974).

Hough, Richard, *Mountbatten: Hero of our Time* (Weidenfeld & Nicolson, London, 1981).

Hough, Richard, *Edwina: Countess Mountbatten of Burma* (Weidenfeld & Nicolson, London, 1983).

Hough, Richard, *Bless Our Ship: Mountbatten and the Kelly* (Hodder, London, 1991).

Hough, Richard, *Other Days Around Me* (Hodder, London, 1992).

Hughes-Wilson, John, *Military Intelligence Blunders* (Constable, London, 2004).

Hutchins, Chris and Thompson, Peter, *Diana Nightmare: The Family* (Christopher Hutchins, London, 2011).

Ingall, Francis, *The Last of the Bengal Lancers* (Pen & Sword, Barnsley, 1989).

Ismay, Hastings, *The Memoirs of Lord Hastings* (William Heinemann, London, 1960).

Joshi, Shashi, *The Last Durbar* (Oxford University Press, Oxford, 2006).

Joubert de la Ferte, Philip, *The Fated Sky: An Autobiography* (Hutchinson, London, 1952).

Judd, Denis (ed.), *A British Tale of Indian and Foreign Service: The Memoirs of Sir Ian Scott* (The Radcliffe Press, London, 1999).

Kahn Jr, E.J., *Jock: The Life and Times of John Hay Whitney* (Doubleday, New York, 1981).

Keay, John, *Midnight's Descendants South Asia from Partition to the Present Day* (Collins, London, 2014).

Keegan, John (ed.), *Churchill's Generals* (Weidenfeld and Nicolson, London, 1991).

Kelley, Kitty, *The Royals* (Grand Central, New York, 1997).

Kennedy, Ludovic, *On My Way to the Club* (Collins, London, 1990).

Kent, Barrie, *Signal!: A History of Signalling in the Royal Navy* (Hyden House, Clanfield, 1993).

Kerr, Mark, *The Life of Prince Louis of Battenberg* (Longmans, Harlow, 1934).

Khan, Yasmin, *The Great Partition: The Making of India and Pakistan* (Yale, New Haven, 2007).

King, Cecil, *The Cecil King Diary 1965–70* (Cape, London, 1972).

King, Greg, *The Duchess of Windsor: The Uncommon Life of Wallis Simpson* (Aurum, London, 1999).

Kirkpatrick, Lyman, *Captains Without Eyes: Intelligence Failures in World War II* (Macmillan, London, 1969).

Knatchbull, Timothy, *From a Clear Blue Sky* (Hutchinson, London, 2009).

Knight, John, *The Kelly: Mountbatten's Ship* (John Knight, London, 1997).

Knowles, Sydney, *A Diver in the Dark* (Weidenfeld & Nicolson, London, 2009).

Lacey, Robert, *Majesty: Elizabeth II and the House of Windsor* (Hutchinson, London, 1977).

Laffaye, Horace, *Polo in Britain* (McFarland, Jefferson, 2012).

Lamb, Alastair, *Birth of Tragedy: Kashmir 1947* (Roxford, Hertingfordbury, 1994).

Lambton, Anthony, *The Mountbattens: The Battenbergs and Young Mountbatten* (Constable, London, 1989).

Lampe, David, *Pyke: The Unknown Genius* (Evans, London, 1959).

Leigh, David, *The Wilson Plot* (William Heinemann, London, 1988).

Liversidge, Douglas, *The Mountbattens: From Battenberg to Windsor* (Arthur Barker, London, 1978).

Louis, W. Roger, *More Adventures with Britannia: Personalities, Politics and Culture in Britain* (Tauris, London, 1998).

Louis, W. Roger, *Ends of British Imperialism* (Tauris, London, 2006).

Lovat, Lord, *March Past* (Weidenfeld & Nicolson, London, 1978).

Lovell, Mary, *The Riviera Set* (Little, Brown, London, 2016).

Lyman, Robert, *The Generals: From Defeat to Victory, Leadership in Asia 1941–45* (Constable, London, 2008).

McBeth, George, *The Katana: A Novel Based on the Wartime Diaries of John Beeby* (Simon & Schuster, New York, 1981).

McGeoch, Ian, *Mountbatten of Burma: Captain of War – Guardian of Peace* (Haynes, Sparkford, 2009).

Mansergh, Nicholas and Moon, Peverell, *Transfer of Power: The Mountbatten Viceroyalty*, vol. 10, 'Formation of a Plan, 22 March–30 May 1947' (HMSO, London, 1983).

Mansergh, Nicholas and Moon, Peverell, *Transfer of Power: The Mountbatten Viceroyalty*, vol. 11, 'Announcement and Reception of the 3 June plan, 31 May–7 July 1947 (HMSO, London, 1983).

Mansergh, Nicholas and Moon, Peverell Moon, *Transfer of Power: The Mountbatten Viceroyalty*, vol. 12, 'Princes, Partition and Independence, 8 July–15 August 1947' (HMSO, London, 1983).

Marshall, Arthur, *Life's Rich Pageant* (Hamish Hamilton, London, 1984).

Marston, Daniel, *The Indian Army and the End of the Raj* (Cambridge University Press, Cambridge, 2014).

Massingberd, Hugh, *Daydream Believer: Confessions of a Hero-Worshipper* (Macmillan, London, 2001).

Masson, Madeleine, *Edwina: The Biography of the Countess Mountbatten of Burma* (Robert Hale, London, 1958).

Mathai, M.O., *Reminiscences of the Nehru Age* (Vikas, New Delhi, 1978).

Mathai, M.O., *My Days with Nehru* (Vikas, New Delhi, 1979).

Mead, Richard, *General Boy: The Life of Lieutenant General Sir Frederick Browning* (Pen & Sword, Barnsley, 2010).

Meyer-Stabley, Bertrand, *Edwina Mountbatten* (Bartillat, Paris, 2005).

Meyrick, Kate, *Secrets of the 43: Reminiscences by Mrs Meyrick* (John Long, London, 1933).

Milton, Giles, *The Ministry of Ungentlemanly Warfare: Churchill's Mavericks: Plotting Hitler's Defeat* (John Murray, London, 2016).

Mitchell, L.M., et al. (eds.), *A Summary Catalogue of the Papers of Earl Mountbatten of Burma. Occasional Papers #9* (Southampton University Library, Southampton, 1991).

Mitchell, Norval, *Sir George Cunningham* (Blackwood, Edinburgh, 1968).

Montgomery, Bernard, *The Memoirs of Field Marshal the Viscount Montgomery of Alamein* (Collins, London, 1958).

Moon, Penderel, *Divide and Quit* (Chatto, London, 1961).

Moon, Penderel (ed.), *Wavell: The Viceroy's Journal* (Oxford University Press, Oxford, 1973).

Moore, R.J., *Escape from Empire: The Attlee Government and the Indian Problem* (Clarendon Press, Oxford, 1983).

Morgan, Janet, *Edwina Mountbatten: A Life of Her Own* (Collins, London, 1991).

Morley, Peter, *A Life Rewound: Memoirs of a Freelance Producer* (Bank House Books, New Romney, 2010).

Morton, John, *Family of the Raj* (The Memoir Club, Durham, 2017).

Selected Bibliography

Mosley, Leonard, *The Last Days of the British Raj* (Weidenfeld & Nicolson, London, 1961).

Mountbatten, Earl, *Time Only to Look Forward* (Nicholas Kaye, London, 1949).

Mountbatten, Earl, *Reflections on the Transfer of Power and Jawaharlal Nehru* (Cambridge University Press, Cambridge, 1968).

Mountbatten, Earl, 'A Viceroy Remembers' in Kalid Hasan (ed.), *Quaid-I-Azam: Mohamed Ali Jinnah: A Centenary Tribute 1876–1976* (Embassy of Pakistan, Karachi, 1976).

Mountbatten, Earl, *Eighty Years in Pictures* (Macmillan, London, 1979).

Mountbatten, Earl, *Apocalypse Now?* (Spokesman, Nottingham, 1980).

Murfett, Malcolm (ed.), *The First Sea Lords from Fisher to Mountbatten* (Praeger, Westport, 1995).

Murphy, Ray, *The Last Viceroy* (Jarrolds, London, 1948).

Murphy, Robert, *British Cinema and the Second World War* (Continuum, London, 2000).

Neillands, Robin, *A Fighting Retreat: British Empire 1947–1997* (Hodder, London, 1996).

Neillands, Robin, *The Dieppe Raid* (Aurum, London, 2005).

Nicol, Allan, *The Monster Butler* (Black & White, Edinburgh, 2011).

Nicolson, Nigel (ed.), *Harold Nicolson Diaries and Letters 1939–1945* (Collins, London, 1967).

Obolensky, Serge, *One Man in His Time* (Hutchinson, London, 1960).

O'Keefe, David, *One Day in August: The Untold Story Behind Canada's Tragedy at Dieppe* (Knopf, New York, 2013).

Oppenheimer, A.R., *IRA, The Bombs and the Bullets: A History of Deadly Ingenuity* (Irish Academic Press, Newbridge, 2008).

Page, Elizabeth, *A Taste of Life* (Librario, Kinloss, 2004).

Parker, John, *Prince Philip: A Critical Biography* (St Martin's Press, New York, 1990).

Pattinson, William, *Mountbatten and the Men of the Kelly* (Patrick Stephens, Sparkford, 1986).

Payn, Graham and Morley, Sheridan (eds.), *The Noel Coward Diaries* (Weidenfeld & Nicolson, London, 1982).

Payn, Graham with Day, Barry, *My Life with Noel Coward* (Applause, London, 1994).

Pender, Paul, *The Butler Did It* (Mainstream, Edinburgh, 2012).

Penrose, Barry, *The Pencourt File* (Secker & Warburg, London, 1978).

Petropoulos, Jonathan, *Royals and the Reich* (Oxford University Press, Oxford, 2006).

Peyton, John, *Solly Zuckerman* (John Murray, London, 2001).

Philips, C.H. and Wainwright, Mary D. (eds.), *The Partition of India: Policies and Perspectives, 1935–1947* (Allen & Unwin, London, 1970).

Picknett, Lynn and Prince, Clive, *War of the Windsors* (Mainstream, Edinburgh, 2003).

Pimlott, Ben (ed.), *The Second World War Diary of Hugh Dalton 1940–45* (Jonathan Cape, London, 1986).

Pimlott, Ben, *The Queen: A Biography of Elizabeth II* (Collins, London, 1996).

Plummer, Christopher, *In Spite of Myself* (Knopf, New York, 2008).

Pollack, Howard, *George Gershwin: His Life and Work* (University of California Press, Berkeley, 2006).

Poolman, Kenneth, *Kelly* (William Kimber, London, 1954).

Powell, Ted, *King Edward VIII* (Oxford University Press, Oxford, 2018).

Pugsley, Alan, *Destroyer Man* (Weidenfeld & Nicolson, London, 1957).

Rankin, Nicholas, *Ian Fleming's Commandos: The Story of 30 Assault Unit in WWII* (Faber, London, 2011).

Rasor, Eugene, *Earl Mountbatten of Burma 1900–1979* (Greenwood Press, Westport, 1998).

Read, Anthony and Fisher, David, *The Proudest Day: India's Long Road to Independence* (Norton, New York, 1998).

Reddy, Sheela, *Mr and Mrs Jinnah: The Marriage That Shook India* (Penguin, London, 2017).

Reid, Charles, *Malcolm Sargent: A Biography* (Hamish Hamilton, London, 1968).

Reid, Walter, *Keeping the Jewel in the Crown: The British Betrayal of India* (Birlinn, Edinburgh, 2016).

Reynolds, David, *In Command of History* (Allen Lane, London, 2004).

Rhodes James, Robert (ed.), *Chips: The Diaries of Sir Henry Channon* (Weidenfeld, London, 1967).

Ritchie, Charles, *Diplomatic Diaries 1946–1962* (Macmillan, London, 1981).

Ritter, Jonathan Templin, *Stilwell and Mountbatten in Burma: Allies at War, 1943–1944* (University of North Texas Press, Denton, 2017).

Roberts, Andrew, *Eminent Churchillians* (Weidenfeld & Nicolson, London, 1994).

Roose-Evans, James (ed.), *The Time of My Life: Entertaining the Troops* (Hodder, London, 1989).

Roskill, Stephen, *Churchill and the Admirals* (Collins, London, 1977).

Ryder, Rowland, *Oliver Leese* (Hamish Hamilton, London, 1987).

Sain, Kanwar, *Reminiscences of an Engineer* (Young Asia Publications, New Delhi, 1978).

Sarila, Narendra Singh, *The Shadow of the Great Game: The Untold Story of India's Partition* (Constable, London, 2005).

Sarila, Narendra Singh, *Once a Prince of Sarila: Of Palaces and Elephant Rides, Of Nehrus and Mountbattens* (Tauris, London, 2008).

Schofield, Victoria, *Kashmir in Conflict: India, Pakistan and the Unending War* (Tauris, London, 2000).

Segrave, Elisa, *The Girl from Station X* (Union Books, London, 2013).

Seton, Marie, *Panditji: A Portrait of Jawaharlal Nehru* (Dobson, London, 1967).

Singh, Karan, *Heir Apparent* (Oxford University Press, Oxford, 1982).

Singh, Khushwant, *Truth, Love and a Little Malice: An Autobiography* (Viking, London, 2002).

Singh, Khushwant, *The Vintage Sardar* (Penguin, India, 2002).

Singh, Natwar, *Profiles and Letters* (Sangam Books, Hyderabad, 1998).

Singh, Natwar, *One Life Is Not Enough* (Rupa, New Delhi, 2014).

Slim, William, *Defeat into Victory* (Cassell, London, 1956).

Smith, Adrian, *Mountbatten: Apprentice War Lord* (Tauris, London, 2000).

Smith, Charles, *Fifty Years with Mountbatten* (Sidgwick & Jackson, London, 1980).

Spence, Lyndsy, *The Mistress of Mayfair* (The History Press, Stroud, 2016).

Spencer, Herbert (ed.), *Chakkar: Polo Around the World* (World Polo Associates, 1994).

Stadiem, William, *Madame Claude* (St Martin's Press, New York, 2018).

Stephens, Ian, *Horned Moon; An Account of a Journey Through Pakistan, Kashmir and Afghanistan, 1953 and 1966* (Benn, London, 1966).

Stephen, Martin, *The Fighting Admirals: British Admirals of the Second World War* (Leo Cooper, London, 1991).

Stout, Mark, 'The Alternate Central Intelligence Agency: John Grombach and the Pond' in Christopher Moran (ed.), *Spy Chiefs*, vol. 1 (Georgetown University Press, Washington, 2018).

Summers, Anthony and Dorril, Stephen, *Honeytrap* (Weidenfeld & Nicolson, London, 1987).

Swinson, Arthur, *Mountbatten* (Pan, London, 1971).

Talbot, Ian and Singh, Gurharpal, *The Partition of India* (Cambridge University Press, Cambridge, 2009).

Taylor, A.J.P., *Beaverbrook* (Hamish Hamilton, London, 1972).

Terraine, John, *The Life and Times of Lord Mountbatten* (Hutchinson, London, 1968).

Tharoor, Shashi, *Inglorious Empire: What the British Did to India* (Hurst, London, 2017).

Thomas, Howard, *With an Independent Air* (Weidenfeld & Nicolson, London, 1977).

Thorne, Christopher, *Allies of a Kind: United States, Britain and the War Against Japan 1941–45* (Hamish Hamilton, London, 1978).

Thorpe, D.R., *Eden: The Life and Times of Anthony Eden 1897–1977* (Chatto, London, 2003).

Thorpe, D.R. (ed.), *Who's In, Who's Out: The Journals of Kenneth Rose* (Weidenfeld & Nicolson, London, 2018).

Trevelyan, Raleigh, *Grand Dukes and Diamonds: The Wernhers of Luton Hoo* (Secker & Warburg, London, 1991).

Tsang, Rhiannon Jenkins, *The Last Vicereine* (Penguin, New Delhi, 2017).

Tuchman, Barbara, *Sand Against the Wind: Stilwell and the American Experience in China 1911–1945* (Macmillan, London, 1971).

Tucker, Sophie, *Some of These Days* (Doubleday, New York, 1945).

Turner, Jon Lys, *The Visitors Book* (Constable, London, 2016).

Vickers, Hugo, *Alice: Princess Andrew of Greece* (St Martins, New York, 2000).

Vickers, Hugo, *Elizabeth: The Queen Mother* (Hutchinson, London, 2005).

Vickers, Hugo, *Behind Closed Doors: The Tragic, Untold Story of the Duchess of Windsor* (Hutchinson, London, 2011).

Villa, Brian Loring, *Mountbatten and the Dieppe Raid 1942* (Oxford University Press, Oxford, 1989).

Von Tunzelmann, Alex, *Indian Summer: The Secret History of the End of an Empire* (Simon & Schuster, London, 2007).

Wainwright, Robert, *Sheila: The Australian Ingenue Who Bewitched British Society* (Allen & Unwin, London, 2014).

Walker, David, *Lean, Wind, Lean* (Collins, London, 1984).

Walton, Calder, *Empire of Secrets: British Intelligence, the Cold War and the Twilight of Empire* (Collins, London, 2013).

Warner, Oliver, *Admiral of the Fleet: The Life of Sir Charles Lambe* (Sidgwick & Jackson, London, 1969).

Warner, Philip, *Auchinleck: The Lonely Soldier* (Buchan & Enwright, London, 1981).

Warren, Allan, *The Confessions of a Society Photographer* (Jupiter Books, London, 1976).

Wedemeyer, Albert, *Wedemeyer Reports* (Henry Holt, New York, 1958).

West, Nigel, *A Matter of Trust* (Weidenfeld & Nicolson, London, 1982).

Selected Bibliography

Wheen, Francis, *Tom Driberg: His Life and Indiscretions* (Chatto & Windus, London, 1990).

White, T.H. (ed.), *The Stilwell Papers* (Macdonald, London, 1949).

Williams, Francis (ed.), *A Prime Minister Remembers* (William Heinemann, London, 1961).

Williams, Masha, *In the Bey's Palace* (Book Guild, Kibworth, 1990).

Wilson, A.N., *After the Victorians* (Hutchinson, London, 2005).

Wilson, A.N., *Our Times: The Age of Elizabeth II* (Hutchinson, London, 2008).

Wilson, Jon, *India Conquered: Britain's Raj and the Chaos of Empire* (Simon & Schuster, London, 2017).

Windsor, Duchess of, *The Heart Has Its Reasons* (Michael Joseph, London, 1956).

Wingate, Ronald, *Lord Ismay* (Hutchinson, London, 1970).

Winn, Godfrey, *The Positive Hour* (Michael Joseph, London, 1970).

Winton, John, *Cunningham: The Greatest Admiral Since Nelson* (John Murray, London, 1998).

Wolpert, Stanley, *Nehru: A Tryst with Destiny* (Oxford University Press, Oxford, 1996).

Wolpert, Stanley, *Shameful Flight: The Last Years of the British Empire in India* (Oxford University Press, Oxford, 2006).

Woolgar, Christopher and Robson, Karen (eds.), *A Guide to the Archive and Manuscript Collections of the Hartley Library, Occasional Paper #11* (Southampton University Library, 1992).

Woolgar, Christopher, *Mountbatten on the Record* (University of Southampton, 1997).

Wyatt, Woodrow, *Confessions of an Optimist* (Collins, London, 1985).

Young, Kenneth (ed.), *The Diaries of Sir Robert Bruce Lockhart, vol. 1, 1915–1938* (Macmillan, London, 1973).

Young, Kenneth (ed.), *The Diaries of Sir Robert Bruce Lockhart, vol. 2, 1939–1965* (Macmillan, London, 1980).

Zec, Donald, *The Queen Mother: with unique recollections by the late Earl Mountbatten of Burma* (Sidgwick & Jackson, London, 1990).

Ziegler, Philip, *Mountbatten: The Official Biography* (Collins, London, 1985).

Ziegler, Philip (ed.), *The Diaries of Lord Louis Mountbatten 1920–1922* (Collins, London, 1987).

Ziegler, Philip (ed.), *Personal Diary of Admiral the Lord Louis Mountbatten 1943–1946* (Collins, London, 1988).

Ziegler, Philip (ed.), *From Shore to Shore: The Final Years, The Diaries of Earl Mountbatten of Burma 1953–1979* (Collins, London, 1989).

Ziegler, Philip, 'Mountbatten Revisited' in Wm Roger Louis, *More Adventures with Britannia* (University of Texas Press, Austin, 1998).

Ziegler, Philip, *King Edward VIII: The Official Biography* (Collins, London, 1999).

Zuckerman, Solly, *From Apes to Warlords: An Autobiography 1904–45* (Hamish Hamilton, London, 1978).

Zuckerman, Solly, *Monkeys, Men and Missiles: An Autobiography 1946–88* (Collins, London, 1988).

Zuckerman, Solly, *Six Men Out of the Ordinary*, (Peter Owen, London, 1992).

Selected Bibliography

ARTICLES

Abid, Massarrat, 'Quaid-I-Azam and Mountbatten: Nature of Relationship', *Journal of the Research Society of Pakistan*, vol. 36, issue 2, 1999, pp. 1–19.

Adamthwaite, Anthony, 'Suez Revisited', *International Affairs* 64 (Summer 1988), pp. 449–64.

Akbar, Ahmed, 'The Hero in History: Myth, Media and Realities', *HISTOD*, March 1996, pp. 7–10.

Akbar, Ahmed, 'Edwina & Nehru', *History Today*, March 1996.

Ali, Rabia Umar, 'Mountbatten and the Partition of British India: A Role Analysis', *Pakistan Journal of History and Culture*, vol. 21, issue 2, June 2000, pp. 89–98.

Ankit, Rakesh, 'Mountbatten and India, 1948–64', *The International History Review*, vol. 37, no. 2, 2015.

Ashton, S.R., 'Mountbatten, the Royal Family, and British influence in Post-Independence India and Burma, *The Journal of Imperial and Commonwealth History*, vol. 33, no. 1, 2007, pp. 73–92.

Aster, Sydney, 'Mountbatten', *American Historical Review*, vol. 91, February 1986, p. 115.

Brown, David, 'Mountbatten as First Sea Lord', *Journal of the Royal United Services Institute for Defence Studies*, vol. 131, issue 2, 1986, pp. 63–8.

Chawla, Muhammad Iqbal, 'Mountbatten and Balochistan: An Appraisal', *Proceedings of the Indian History Congress*, no. 75, 2014, pp. 928–57.

Chawla, Muhammad Iqbal, 'Mountbatten's Response to the Communal Riots in the Punjab, 20 March to 15 August 1947: An Overview', *Journal of the Royal Asiatic Society*, vol. 26, issue 4, October 2016, pp. 683–706.

Chester, Lucy, 'Drawing the Indo-Pakistani Boundary', *American Diplomacy*, 15 February 2002.

Coll, Rebecca, 'Autobiography and Screen: The Life and Times of Lord Mountbatten', *Historical Journal of Film, Radio and Television*, vol. 37, issue 4, December 2017, pp. 665–82.

Copland, Ian, 'Lord Mountbatten and the Integration of the Indian States: A Reappraisal', *Journal of Imperial and Commonwealth History*, vol. 21, no. 2, pp 385–408.

Crawley, William and Hitchcock, Eric, 'Making Waves: Admiral Mountbatten's SEAC 1945–49', *Asian Affairs*, vol. 46, issue 3, November 2015, pp. 534–5.

Cuneo, Ernest, 'Mountbatten: A Life Struggle for Vindication', *The American Legion*, vol. 107, December 1979, pp. 8–9.

Dar, Farooq Ahmad, 'British Policy and the Transfer of Power', *Journal of Political Studies*, vol. 21, issue 1, 2014, pp. 199–213.

Davies, Philip, 'Defence Intelligence in the UK after the Mountbatten Reforms: Organisational and Inter-Organisational Dilemmas of Joint Military Intelligence', *Public Policy and Administration*, vol. 28, issue 2, April 2013, pp. 196–213.

Doherty, Frank and Byrne, John, 'Mountbatten was Part of Gay Ring which was Linked with Kincora', *NOW*, April 1990, pp. 13–17.

Forbes, Alastair, 'Edwina Mountbatten: A Life of Her', *Times Literary Supplement*, issue 4605, 5 July 1991, p. 28.

Grigg, John, 'Myths About the Approach to Indian Independence', University of Texas at Austin, 1995.

Grove, Eric and Rohan, Sally, 'The Limits of Opposition: Admiral Earl Mountbatten of Burma, First Sea Lord and Chief of Naval Staff', *Contemporary British History*, vol.13, issue 2, June 1999, pp. 98–116.

Gupta, Shyamratna, 'The Mountbatten Saga: Myths, Images, and

Facts of Current History', *International Studies*, vol. 23, no. 3, 1986.

Hassan, Syed Minhajul, 'The Impact of Mountbatten–Nehru Relationship on the Partition of India', *Journal of the Pakistan Historical Society*, vol. 44, issue 3, July 1996, pp. 229–42.

Henshaw, Peter, 'The British Chiefs of Staff and the Preparation of the Dieppe Raid', March–August 1942: Did Mountbatten Really Evade the Committee's Authority?', *War and History*, vol. 1, no. 2, 1994, pp. 197–214.

Henshaw, Peter, 'The Dieppe Raid: A Product of Misplaced Canadian Nationalism?: Notes and Comments', *CANHISREV*, vol. 77, June 1996, pp. 250–66.

Ilahi, Shereen, 'The Radcliffe Boundary Commission and the Fate of Kashmir', *India Review*, vol. 2, issue 1, January 2003, pp. 77–102.

Jeffrey, Robin, 'The Punjab Boundary Force and the Problem of Order, August 1947', *Modern Asian Studies*, vol. 8, no. 4, 1974, pp. 491–520.

Johnson, Paul, 'Mountbatten', *The Wall Street Journal*, vol. 205, 10 May 1985, p. 22.

Kaul, Chandrika, 'At the Stroke of the Midnight Hour: Lord Mountbatten and the British Media at Indian Independence', *The Round Table*, 2008.

Kedourie, Elie, 'Scuttling an Empire', *Quadrant*, vol. 30, no. 3, March 1986, pp. 60–6.

Kennedy, Thomas C., 'Mountbatten: A Biography', *The Historian*, vol. 49, no. 3, 1987, pp. 401–3.

Khan, Mahboobul Rahman, 'Mountbatten and the Hurried Scuttle', *Pakistan Journal of History and Culture*, vol. 19, issue 1, January 1998, pp. 17–25.

King, Cecil, 'The So-Called Military Coup of 1968: What Really Happened', *Encounter*, August 1981.

Klare, Hugh J., 'The Mountbatten Report', *The British Journal of Criminology*, vol. 8, no. 1, 1968, pp. 80–2.

Krishan, Y., 'Mountbatten and the Partition of India', *History*, vol. 68, February 1983, pp. 22–37.

Kumarasingham, Harshan, 'The "Tropical Dominions": The Appeal of Dominion Status in the Decolonisation of India, Pakistan and Ceylon', *Transactions of the Royal Historical Society*, vol. 23, December 2013, pp. 223–45.

Lodhi, M. Zahid Khan, 'Mountbatten Changed the Original Boundary Award', *Journal of the Research Society of Pakistan*, vol. 32, issue 1, 1995, pp. 55–61.

McClung, Stuart, 'Stilwell and Mountbatten in Burma: Allies at War, 1943–1944', *Journal of America's Military Past*, vol. 42, issue 2, Spring/Summer 2017, pp. 102–4.

McDonald, Henry, 'Royal blown up by IRA "backed united Ireland"', *Guardian*, 29 December 2007.

Moore, R.J., 'Mountbatten, India, and the Commonwealth', *Journal of Commonwealth and Comparative Politics,* vol. 19, no. 1, 1981, pp. 5–43.

Moore, R.J., 'The Mountbatten Viceroyalty: A Review Article', *Journal of Commonwealth and Comparative Politics*, vol. 22, issue 2, 1984, pp. 204–15.

Morris-Jones, W.H., 'The Transfer of Power, 1947: A View from the Sidelines', *Modern Asian Studies,* vol. 16, 1982.

Morris-Jones, W.H., 'Thirty-Six Years Later: The Mixed Legacies of Mountbatten's Transfer of Power', *International Affairs*, vol. 59, no. 4, 1983, pp. 621–8.

Mountbatten, Louis, 'Reflections on the Transfer of Power and Jawaharlal Nehru', The Second Jawaharlal Nehru Memorial Lecture, London, 1968.

Murphy, Philip, 'By invitation only: Lord Mountbatten, Prince Philip and the attempt to create a Commonwealth Bilderberg Group, 1964–1966', *The Journal of Imperial and Commonwealth History*, vol. 33, no. 2, May 2005, pp. 245–65.

Ninian, Alex, 'India and Mountbatten's Legacy', *Contemporary Review*, vol. 289, issue 1686, Autumn 2007, p. 382.

Pachauri, S.K., 'Mountbatten in India and 15th August 1947', *Proceedings of the Indian History Congress*, vol. 68, 1 January 2007, pp. 889–94.

Philip, Duke of Edinburgh, 'Lord Louis', *NIPROC*, vol. 106, February 1980, pp. 26–35.

Roberts, Andrew, 'Why Mountbatten should have been Impeached', *Sunday Times*, 24 July 1994.

Romanes, Aline, 'The Dear Romance', *Vanity Fair*, June 1986, p. 68.

Roskill, Stephen, 'The Dieppe raid and the question of German foreknowledge', *RUSI Journal*, vol. CIX, no. 633, 1964, pp. 27–31.

Sbrega, John J., 'Anglo-American Relations and the Selection of Mountbatten as Supreme Allied Commander, South East Asia', *Military Affairs*, vol. 46, issue 3, October 1982, pp. 139–45.

Scott Plummer, Simon, 'How Mountbatten Bent the Rules and the Indian Border', *Daily Telegraph*, 24 February 1992, p. 10.

Singh, Khushwant, 'The Edwina–Nehru Affair', *The Hindustan Times*, 20 April 1996.

Sinha, S.K., 'Mountbatten as I Saw Him', *USI Journal*, vol. 140, issue 579, January–March 2010, pp. 110–18.

Skow, John, 'Great Britain's Uncle Dickie', *Time*, vol. 125, issue 19, 13 May 1985, p. 73.

Smith, Adrian, 'Rewriting History? Admiral Lord Mountbatten's Efforts to Distance Himself from the Suez Crisis', *Contemporary British History*, vol. 26, issue 4, December 2012, pp. 489–508.

Smith, Adrian, 'Resignation of a First Sea Lord: Mountbatten and the 1956 Suez Crisis', *History*, vol. 98, no. 329, January 2013, pp. 105–34.

Smith, Adrian, 'Admiral Lord Mountbatten: Man of Science and Royal Role Model', *The Historian*, issue 131, Autumn 2016, pp. 20–23.

Smith, Adrian, 'Mountbatten goes to the movies: the cinema as a vehicle for promoting the heroic myth', *Historical Journal of Film, Radio and Television*, vol. 26, no. 3, August 2006, pp. 395–416.

Springhall, John, 'Mountbatten versus the Generals: British Military Rule of Singapore 1945–46, *Journal of Contemporary History*, vol. 36, no. 4, 2001, pp. 635–52.

Stout, Mark and Kadar Lynn, Katalin, 'Every Hungarian of any Value to Intelligence: Tibor Eckhardt, John Grombach and the Pond', *Intelligence and National Security*, vol. 31, issue 5, August 2016, pp. 699–714.

Talbot, Ian, 'Mountbatten and the Partition of India: A Rejoinder', *History*, vol. 69, no. 225, 1984, pp. 29–34.

Tarling, Nicholas, 'Lord Mountbatten and the Return of Civil Government to Burma', *Journal of Imperial and Commonwealth History*, vol. 11, issue 2, January 1983, pp. 197–226.

Tinker, Hugh, 'Jawaharlal Nehru at Simla, May 1947: A Moment of Truth?', *Modern Asian Studies,* vol. 4, no. 4, 1970, pp. 349–58.

Selected Bibliography

Tinker, Hugh, 'Incident at Simla, May 1947 – what the documents reveal: A moment of truth for the historians?' *Journal of Commonwealth and Comparative Politics*, July 1982.

Villa, Brian Loring, 'Mountbatten, the British Chiefs of Staff and Approval of the Dieppe Raid', *The Journal of Military History*, vol. 54, no. 2, 1990, pp. 201–26.

Villa, Brian Loring and Henshaw, Peter J., 'The Dieppe Raid Debate', *Canadian Historical Review*, vol. 79, 1998, pp. 304–15.

Willey, Scott A., 'Stilwell and Mountbatten in Burma: Allies at War 1943–1944', *Air Power History*, vol. 64, issue 2, Summer 2017, p. 62.

Ziegler, Philip, 'Unauthorised Action Mountbatten and the Dieppe Raid 1942', *Spectator*, 10 March 1990.

Source Notes

Preface

1 Mountbatten to Richard Hough, 14 January 1974, Hough Papers.
2 'The Man and his Murders', *Spectator*, 1 September 1979, p. 7.
3 Interview with Sir Robert Scott, Ziegler. p. 53.
4 Pat MacLellan to Brian Kimmons, 3 March 1980, by kind permission of Pat MacLellan.

Prologue

5 Mountbatten lent Prince Philip the sword for his wedding in 1947.
6 Numbers vary according to newspaper accounts. Philip Ziegler, *Mountbatten: The Official Biography* (Collins, 1985), p. 70, says 1,400 guests.
7 It can be found at https://www.britishpathe.com/video/lord-louis-mountbatten-and-edwina-cynthia-annette.

Chapter 1: Beginnings

8 Belt 4, p. 4 MB1/K319, Hartley Library.
9 Prince Alexander was actually the son of the court chamberlain,

Baron von Senarclens de Grancy, rather than Grand Duke Louis II of Hesse, a further embarrassment to Mountbatten, who prided himself on his noble heritage.

10 Mountbatten acknowledged his half-sister at a charity event in October 1978 whilst a TV series on Langtry was being shown, but there is some evidence the child's father was actually Arthur Jones. Jeanne Marie married Sir Ian Malcom and their daughter, Mary Malcolm, became a well-known BBC television announcer. It has been alleged Prince Louis also fathered a daughter, Mary, in November 1911 with Katherine Burton, the daughter of a Lincolnshire solicitor. Interview with Mary's daughter, Jade Neergaard, 11 September 2017.

11 Mountbatten's interview on his father can be found at MB1/K319, Hartley Library.

12 Richard Hough, *Mountbatten: Hero of Our Time* (Weidenfeld & Nicolson, 1980), p. 10.

13 The Grand Duke was assassinated shortly afterwards.

14 Mountbatten claimed he later became friendly with the other conspirator, Prince Felix Youssoupoff. Louis Mountbatten, *Eighty Years in Pictures* (Macmillan, 1979), p. 27.

15 At five Dickie lived in Gibraltar and at seven in Malta, when his father became Second-in-Command of the Mediterranean Fleet.

16 Maurice Battenberg was killed in October 1914 on the Ypres Salient just after his twenty-third birthday.

17 Mountbatten to his mother, 8 May 1910, MB6/M/164, Hartley Library.

18 MB1/A4, Hartley Library.

19 MB1/A4 folder 3, Hartley Library.

20 MB1/A4, Hartley Library.

21 Scott, the son of Admiral Sir Percy Scott, often described as the 'father of modern gunnery', was killed in action three years later.

22 MB1/A5, Hartley Library.

23 Ibid.

[24] Hough, *Mountbatten*, p. 23.

[25] Mountbatten, *80 Years*, p. 42.

[26] MB6/M/57, Hartley Library.

[27] Mountbatten confirmed the story was true to Richard Hough. Hough, *Mountbatten*, p. 31.

[28] Janet Morgan, *Edwina Mountbatten: A Life of Her Own* (Collins, 1991), p. 48.

[29] Richard Hough, *Edwina: Countess Mountbatten of Burma* (Weidenfeld, 1983), p. 41.

Chapter 2: Students

[30] Mountbatten to his mother, 15 June 1915, MB6/M/58 and Mountbatten to his mother, 13 June 1915, MB6/M/164, Hartley Library.

[31] Ziegler, p. 39.

[32] Mountbatten to his mother, 12 March 1916, MB6/M/59, Hartley Library.

[33] Mountbatten to his mother, 27 June 1916, MB6/M/164, Hartley Library.

[34] Mountbatten to his mother, 28 July 1916, MB6/M/59, Hartley Library.

[35] Conditions only improved after one 'snottie' broke his back and was permanently crippled when the ropes of his hammock were cut and he crashed onto the steel deck.

[36] Morgan, p. 65.

[37] Richard Hough, *Edwina*, p. 46, says January 1919.

[38] His friend from Osborne, Kit Bradford, was art director. Copies at MB6/M3, Hartley Library.

[39] Mountbatten to his mother, MB6/M/164, Hartley Library.

[40] Further stories appeared in *Royal Magazine*, September 1919 and January 1920.

41 Peter Murphy reminiscences, pp. 36–7, Hartley Library.

42 Its Commander, Geoffrey Layton, later served under Dickie as Commander-in-Chief Ceylon during the Second World War.

43 Mountbatten to his mother, 30 November 1917, MB6/M/60, Hartley Library.

44 Ibid., 22 January 1918.

45 Ibid. Hilda Blackburne, two years younger than Dickie, was like the Queen Mother, the granddaughter of the 13th Earl of Strathmore.

46 MB1/A11, Hartley Library. The girls were: Peggy Peyton, daughter of a retired colonel in the Indian Army, whom he thought he would marry; Poppy Baring, who was to become a close friend; the actress Phyllis Clare.

47 The sister of Nada married to Dickie's brother George.

48 Morgan, p. 77.

49 Mountbatten to his mother, 16 December 1916, MB6/M/151, Hartley Library.

50 B.B. Cubett to Under Secretary of State at Foreign Office, 22 March 1918, WO 339/55276, TNA.

51 Peter Murphy, 'Reminiscences and Comments concerning Lord Mountbatten', BA S319, quoted Ziegler, p. 51.

52 Anon, *Demosthenes Demobilised* (W. Heffer, 1920), p. 49.

53 *Demosthenes*, p. 76.

54 Mountbatten to his mother, 20 December 1919, MB6/M/60, Hartley Library.

55 She later became less favourably disposed. 'Lady Cunard, who is always original, said that Lord Louis Mountbatten was one of the most tedious men she knew; he thought a mask of superficial charm could compensate for never having read a book', 19 December 1947, John Colville, *The Fringes of Power: Downing Street Diaries 1939–1955* (Hodder, 1985).

56 Mountbatten to his mother, 28 December 1919, MB6/M/60, Hartley Library.

57 Mountbatten to his father, 16 December 1919, MB6/M151, Hartley Library. Her other suitors included the son of the Duke of Marlborough and Peregrine Cust, later 6th Baron Brownlow, a Lockers Park contemporary of Mountbatten, who became a great friend of both him and the future Edward VII. Audrey later also had an affair with Edward.

58 Mountbatten to his mother, 28 December 1919, MB6/M/60, Hartley Library.

59 Ibid., 12 October 1919.

Chapter 3: First Loves

60 Rupert Godfrey (ed.), *Letters from a Prince* (Little, Brown, 1998), p. 256.

61 Mountbatten to his mother, 21 March 1920, MB6/M/61, Hartley Library.

62 Ibid.

63 Interview Mike Hutchinson, 2 May 2017.

64 Briefing note 'Edwina', A3002/2/1/9, p. 1, Hartley Library.

65 Unofficial diary 8 July 1920 and 5 July 1920, quoted Ziegler, p. 58.

66 Mountbatten to his father, 29 June 1920, MB6/M/151, Hartley Library.

67 Godfrey, *Letters*, p. 280.

68 For years afterwards Mountbatten was giving Brooks money and telling him to stop pestering him, suggesting some form of blackmail. MB1/ C37, Hartley Library.

69 Mountbatten to his mother, 15 July 1920, MB6/M/61, Hartley Library.

70 MB1/A10, Hartley Library. Mountbatten's inventions of the period can be found at MB1/N11, Hartley Library.

71 He made a point of keeping George V abreast of the tour, for example, writing him a 12-page letter with illustrations after the

Royal Train was in an accident in Australia in July, Royal Archives (hereafter RA) PS/PSO/GV/C/O/1548A/48.

[72] Hough, *Edwina*, p. 51.

[73] He was later a Conservative MP and 8th Baron Dynevor.

[74] Morgan, p. 85.

[75] Mountbatten to his mother, 3 January 1921, MB6/M/61, Hartley Library.

[76] Ibid., 30 January 1921.

[77] Ibid., 31 January 1921.

[78] Ibid., 30 June 1921. In March 1922 she married Dudley Coats, heir to a textile fortune, or as the wags put it, swopping coats of arms for the arms of Coats.

[79] They were married in April 1923.

[80] Their children, Charles and Poppy, were friendly with Edwina and Poppy was an ex-girlfriend of Dickie and the Prince of Wales.

[81] Mountbatten to his mother, 8 August 1921, MB6/M/61, Hartley Library.

[82] 'Edwina', MS350 A3002/2/1/9, Hartley Library.

[83] Morgan, p. 90.

[84] 'Edwina', p. 3, MS350 A3002/2/1/9, Hartley Library.

[85] Ibid., p. 4.

[86] Hough, *Edwina*, p. 65.

[87] 'Edwina', MS350 A3002/2/1/9, Hartley Library.

[88] Mountbatten later claimed he had not proposed, one of many examples of his rewriting the truth. 'Edwina', p. 6, MS 350 A3002/2/1/9, Hartley Library.

Chapter 4: Duty

[89] Mountbatten to Edwina, 26 October 1921, BA S131, quoted Ziegler, p. 68.

[90] Michael Torby to Zia Werner, 11 November 1921, quoted Raleigh

Trevelyan, *Grand Dukes and Diamonds: The Wernhers of Luton Hoo* (Secker & Warburg, 1991), p. 293.

91 She was the great-grandmother of TV presenter and historian Dan Snow.

92 Olwen Carey Evans, *Lloyd George Was My Father* (Gomer Press, 1985), p. 121.

93 Carey Evans, *Lloyd George*, p. 122. Evans was cross Edwina never thanked for the silver trinket box given as a wedding present.

94 Mountbatten unofficial diary, 13 January 1922.

95 Morgan, p. 108.

96 Lady Reading to Wilfrid Ashley, 20 February 1921, Reading Papers, quoted Philip Ziegler (ed.), *The Diaries of Lord Louis Mountbatten 1920–1922* (Collins, 1987), p. 254.

97 Mountbatten to his mother, 14 February 1921, MB6/M/63, Hartley Library.

98 Dickie's school and naval friend Kip Bradford had thought he would be best man. Ziegler says 14th, p. 69 and Smith the 13th, p. 41 and Morgan, 10 February, p. 112.

99 Richard Thorpe, *Eden: The Life and Times of Anthony Eden 1897– 1977* (Chatto, 2003), p. 52.

100 Ziegler, *1920–1922*, p. 255.

101 Margaret Greville to Lord Reading, 20 February 21922, Reading MSS Eur E 238, F 118, British Library.

102 Ziegler, *1920–1922*, p. 257 and Ziegler, p. 69.

103 Ibid., pp. 257–8.

104 Mountbatten to his mother, 21 February 1921, MB6/M/63, Hartley Library.

105 Ibid.

106 Morgan, p. 124.

107 His report to Admiral Halsey is at MB1/A16, Hartley Library.

108 Hough, *Edwina*, p. 78 incorrectly claims Edwina met him at Plymouth.

109 It included 700 hand-painted dinner place cards.

Chapter 5: Honeymoon

[110] Thorogood the valet had gone ahead by rail with most of the luggage.

[111] Mountbatten to his mother, 30 July 1922, MB6/M/63, Hartley Library.

[112] Mountbatten to his mother, MB1/A107 folder 2, Hartley Library. According to Hough, *Edwina*, p. 91, Edwina made a pass at Chaplin.

[113] https://www.charliechaplin.com/en/films/1-The-Kid/articles/300-Nice-and-Friendly. Together with the film of his wedding, it remained amongst Dickie's favourite viewing pleasures.

[114] *The World*, 5 October 1922.

[115] *Meriden Daily Journal*, 16 October 1922.

[116] Edward certainly took credit. He wrote 'it was my intervention with my papa that saved your neck from the Navy axe in 1922!' Windsor to Mountbatten, 7 October 1966, RA EDW/PRIV/MAIN/A/11349. He had invested in a business producing gramophones with the Prince of Wales and Duke of York.

[117] Richard Baker, *The Terror of Tobermory* (W.H. Allen, 1972), p. 85.

[118] Len Wincott, MB1/N100, Hartley Library.

[119] Morgan, p. 154.

[120] He celebrated by racing down from the island's summit in basket toboggans and then gambling in the casino, buying a tiny rocking chair with his winnings.

[121] Mountbatten to Edwina, 14 February 1924, BA S138, quoted Ziegler, pp. 106–17.

[122] She later married P.G. Wodehouse's co-librettist Guy Bolton, most famous for *Three Blind Mice*.

Chapter 6: A Marriage Under Threat

[123] The notes of his lectures can be found at MB5/8.

[124] Joan Alexander, *Mabel Strickland* (Progress Press, 1996), p. 86.

[125] Davis later married the actress Louise Brooks.

[126] It may have lasted longer. Kate Meyrick, whose Regent Street club the 'Silver Slipper' opened in 1927, writes in her memoirs of Sefton and 'Lady Louis Mountbatten with her priceless jewellery, her arms covered with diamond bracelets' sharing a table. Kate Meyrick, *Secrets of the 43* (John Long, 1933), p. 160.

[127] She was also the lover of Randolph Churchill and allegedly, his father, Winston. She married Lord Castlerosse in 1928 but divorced him in 1938 – the co-respondent was the homosexual Robert Heber-Percy, whom she was claiming to 'cure'. See Lyndsy Spence, *The Mistress of Mayfair* (The History Press, 2016).

[128] Mountbatten diary, 3 December 1925, quoted Morgan, p. 191 and Ziegler, p. 111.

[129] *San Francisco Chronicle*, 3 October 1926.

[130] Mountbatten to Edwina, 12 January 1927, BA S139, quoted Ziegler, pp. 112–13.

[131] Mountbatten to Andrew Yates, 13 October 1926, quoted Ziegler, p. 80.

[132] Hough, *Mountbatten*, p. 77.

[133] Hugh Molyneux and Laddie Sandford were amongst the guests. For footage, see https://www.youtube.com/watch?v=KjIsneWNXoo.

[134] Morgan, p. 204.

[135] Beaverbrook to Paul Cravath, 20 January 1928, BBK/C/255, House of Lords Record Office.

[136] Edwina to Mountbatten, 3 September 1928, BA S52, quoted Ziegler, p. 113.

[137] Mountbatten to his mother, 18 August 1928, MB6/M/65, Hartley Library.

[138] Ibid., 15 September 1928.

139 *New York Mirror*, 15 September 1928.

140 *New York News*, 15 September 1928.

141 *Troy Budget*, 16 September 1928.

Chapter 7: Divergent Paths

142 Mountbatten to his mother, 25 April 1929, MB6/M/65, Hartley Library. However, Hough claims the lack of a male heir 'became a subject of much bitterness between them.' *Edwina*, p. 119.

143 Edwina to Mountbatten, 29 April 1929, BA S55, quoted Ziegler, p. 114.

144 Mountbatten to his mother, 30 June 1929, MB6/M/65, Hartley Library.

145 J77/2681/3249, TNA.

146 His record can be found at ADM 196/145/516 and service in SOE at HS 9/1364/4, TNA. Details of the case are at MB1/A89, Hartley Library.

147 An assessment of Mountbatten as a signal officer can be found in 'Mountbatten – Signal Officer Supreme' by Captain Gordon Wilson, a paper given at the September 1990 conference 'Aspects of British Defence and Naval Policy in the Mountbatten Era' kindly supplied by Captain Wilson.

148 Vice Admiral Sir Peter Dawnay, MB1/N99, Hartley Library.

149 1 January 1930, MB1/O5, Hartley Library.

150 Stefan Buczacki, *My Darling Mr Asquith* (Cato Clark), p. 293 and John Carswell, *The Exile: A Life of Ivy Litvinov* (Faber, 1983), p. 124.

151 John Foster Dulles was another passenger.

152 Morgan, p. 212.

153 Ibid., p. 214.

154 Ibid., p. 216.

155 Mountbatten diary, March 1931, quoted Morgan, p. 217.

156 Morgan, p. 218.

[157] Ibid., p. 219.

[158] May 1931, BA S 139, quoted Ziegler, p. 112.

[159] Morgan, p. 220.

[160] Ibid.

[161] Ibid.

Chapter 8: A Terrible Scandal

[162] His later girlfriends included Barbara Hutton and Beaverbrook's daughter Janet.

[163] Morgan, p. 221.

[164] The Cassell will settlement can be found at J84/161, TNA.

[165] Morgan, p. 223.

[166] Ibid., p. 224.

[167] Mountbatten to his mother, 22 September 1931, MB6/M/65, Hartley Library.

[168] Charlotte Breese, *Hutch* (Bloomsbury, 1999), pp. 105–6. Ziegler says 20 May.

[169] Mountbatten to his mother, 27 June 1932, MB6/M/65, Hartley Library.

[170] Ibid.

[171] The deposition for the case J54/2101 is one of the few cases of the period missing from the National Archives, nor is there any material lodged in the Mountbatten papers at Southampton.

[172] Edwina's diary, 3 July 1932, quoted Ziegler, p. 114.

[173] Ziegler, p. 114.

[174] Morgan, p. 225.

[175] Ibid., p. 227.

[176] Ibid., p. 238.

[177] Duberman, pp. 160–1. Certainly, according to the producer, John Krimsky, Edwina knew Robeson in 1933 because he met her and Dickie then in Robeson's suite at The Dorchester. Duberman, p. 618.

[178] Breese, p. 109.

[179] Ibid., p. 108.

[180] Hough, *Edwina*, p. 128.

[181] Pamela Hicks interview, 28 April 2017.

[182] Breese, pp. 111–12, lists various occurrences of them being seen together intimately.

[183] Lesley Blanch, *On the Wilder Shores of Love: A Bohemian Life* (Virago, 2015), p. 152.

[184] Charlotte Breese to the author, 28 December 2016.

[185] Breese, p. 56.

[186] Ibid., p. 106. 'Rosemary d'Avigdor Goldsmid was the original source of this story, and in the author's hearing she rang three contemporaries who confirmed that "everyone knew it was true".' Breese, p. 314.

[187] Ibid., p. 111.

[188] Ibid., p. 113.

[189] In 1969, on Hutch's death, Mountbatten offered to pay for the costs of his grave.

[190] *Time*, 7 January 1929.

[191] Ziegler, who mentions her only once, says 1926, p. 113.

[192] Morgan, p. 228.

[193] Ibid.

Chapter 9: Playing to Win

[194] Mountbatten diary, 17 December 1932, quoted Ziegler, p. 111.

[195] Imprisoned during the Second World War in Mauthausen Concentration Camp, Szapary was saved by the intervention of the future King Gustav VI of Sweden and Dickie's brother-in-law. Szapary emigrated to America and married Gladys Vanderbilt's daughter in 1949.

[196] Morgan, p. 229.

197 *Daily News,* 4 July 1933.

198 His notes can be found at MB1/I4, Hartley Library.

199 Morgan, p. 232.

200 Ibid.

201 Pamela Hicks, *Daughter of Empire: Life as a Mountbatten* (Weidenfeld, 2012), pp. 25–6.

202 'South American Trip', Marjorie Brecknock diary, p. 37, by kind permission of 6th Marquess Camden.

203 Brecknock, p. 50.

204 Ibid., p. 52.

205 Captain E.G. Roper, MB1/N100A, Hartley Library.

206 MB1/A48, Hartley Library.

207 The press sometimes reported that her secretary Major Phillips accompanied her.

208 Quoted https://www.townandcountrymag.com/society/tradition/a8013/gloria-vanderbilt-custody-trial/.

209 She quickly lost interest in her young charge, who went on to marry four times, including the conductor Leopold Stokowski and film director Sidney Lumet.

210 The Milford Haven visitors book shows her staying almost continuously between mid-August to the end of October 1929, ten weeks during the last six months of 1930 and from April to June 1931. MB2/J5, Hartley Library.

211 Mountbatten, *Eighty Years*, p. 117.

212 Brian Hoey, *Mountbatten: The Private Story* (Sidgwick, 1994), p. 171.

213 Morgan, p. 243.

214 Ibid., p. 245.

215 Ibid., p. 245.

216 Ibid., p. 246.

217 Ibid., p. 248.

218 Edwina to Mountbatten, 1 January 1936, BA S62, quoted Ziegler, p. 117.

219 Hicks, *Daughter of Empire,* p. 40.

220 Ibid., p. 29.

221 MB1/A38, Hartley Library, for further details.

Chapter 10: Problems in the Family

222 Mountbatten diary, 25 January 1936, quoted Ziegler, p. 93.

223 Claud Cockburn, *In Time of Trouble* (Rupert Hart-Davis, 1956), pp. 250, 252.

224 Charles Higham, *Mrs Simpson: Secret Lives of the Duchess of Windsor* (Sidgwick, 1988), pp. 195–6.

225 7 December 1937, RA EDW/PRIV/MAIN/A/3050.

226 Edwina diary, 10 December 1936.

227 Edwina diary, 9 February 1937, quoted Morgan, p. 256.

228 Morgan, p. 256.

229 Mountbatten diary, 12 March 1937, quoted Anne de Courcy, *The Viceroy's Daughters* (Weidenfeld, 2000), p. 252.

230 Morgan, p. 256.

231 Mountbatten to Edward, 15 March 1937, RA EDW/PRIV/ MAIN/A/3172.

232 Mountbatten to Edward, 5 May 1937, RA EDW/PRIV/ MAIN/A/3206.

233 Ibid.

234 Hicks, *Daughter of Empire*, p. 44.

235 Mountbatten to his mother, 12 February 1938, MB6/M/66, Hartley Library.

236 Mountbatten, *Eighty Years,* p. 127.

237 Part of the collection is at the British Library and part at the Harry Ransom Center, University of Texas at Austin. For example, the Paris Catalogue 1901–2, has 'of the latest Photographic Novelties' the Square Game 'a splendid ensemble of rakes in rut enlightened by the charming novelty and the sketched forms of a virgin of eleven', CUP 364 G 48 Album 7, British Library.

[238] Hough, *Mountbatten,* p. 85.

[239] Mountbatten to Edwina, 16 March 1938, Lady Mountbatten papers, quoted Ziegler, p. 102.

[240] Mountbatten to Duff Cooper, 1 October 1938, DUFC 2/14, Churchill College, Cambridge.

[241] Morgan, p. 266.

[242] Ibid., p. 268.

[243] Ibid., p. 269.

[244] Ibid., p. 271.

[245] Michael Cunningham-Reid (1928–2014), a hotelier in Kenya and the first non-national to be granted a Republic of Kenya passport, and Noel Cunningham-Reid (1930–2017), later a racing driver.

[246] The films can be seen at https://www.pbsamerica.co.uk/series/real-country-house/.

[247] According to a family story, 'Bobby hired the actor, Henri Garat, to have an affair with Mary . . .', Fiona Cunningham-Reid, his granddaughter, email to the author, 30 March 2018.

Chapter 11: At War

[248] Michael Wardell, 'With Mountbatten in the Kelly' in *The Atlantic Advocate,* November 1957, vol. 48, no. 3.

[249] It was repainted in the more orthodox Admiralty Dark Grey almost immediately afterwards.

[250] Morgan, p. 274.

[251] Richard Hough, *Bless Our Ship: Mountbatten and the Kelly* (Hodder & Stoughton, 1991), p. 68.

[252] Ray Murphy, *The Last Viceroy* (Jarrolds, 1948), p. 93.

[253] *Daily Mirror,* 7 December 1940.

[254] Morgan, p. 275.

[255] Ibid.

256 Mountbatten to his mother, 13 September 1940, MB6/M/66, Hartley Library.

257 Breese, p. 161.

258 Sonia Purnell claims that the company of *Javelin* mutinied and the leaders were removed from the ship never to be heard of again, but this episode took place later in the war. *Daily Mail,* 7 April 1999.

259 It is confirmed in MB1/K129, Hartley Library. George VI discusses the offer with Mountbatten, RA GVI/PRIV/DIARY/1940: 9 December.

260 Mountbatten later claimed, contrary to the testimony of other officers, that the Germans had machine-gunned the survivors in water. Andrew Roberts, *Eminent Churchillians* (Weidenfeld & Nicolson, 1994), p. 63.

261 Ziegler, p. 145.

262 Coote to Hough, 26 September 1990, Hough papers and *Bless This Ship,* p. 172.

263 Morgan, p. 309.

264 Ibid., p. 307.

265 Stark to Pound, 15 October 1941, MB1/B14, Hartley Library and PREM 3/330/2, TNA. Pound sent the letter to Churchill, who sent it to King George VI.

Chapter 12: Combined Operations

266 Throughout his career, Mountbatten would be criticised for empire-building and extravagance.

267 Robert Henriques, *From a Biography of Myself* (Secker & Warburg, 1969), p. 54. Waugh's 'Marchmain House' in *Officers and Gentlemen* is based on Combined Operations.

268 12 November 1942, Ben Pimlott (ed.), *The Second World War Diary of Hugh Dalton 1940–45* (Jonathan Cape, 1986), p. 518.

269 Murphy, p. 137.

270 31 May 1943, Michael Davie (ed.), *The Diaries of Evelyn Waugh* (Weidenfeld, 1976), p. 538.

271 Murphy, p. 128.

272 Alex Danchev and Daniel Todman (eds.), *Field Marshall Lord Alanbrooke War Diaries 1939–1945* (Weidenfeld, 2001), p. 236.

273 Graham Payne and Sheridan Morley (eds.), *The Noel Coward Diaries* (Weidenfeld, 1982), p. 7.

274 12 December 1941, *Noel Coward Diaries*, p. 13. Four days later the Mountbattens were at Coward's forty-second birthday with John Gielgud, Celia Johnson and David Niven.

275 Noël Coward, *Future Indefinitive* (William Heinemann, 1954), p. 210.

276 Barry Day (ed.), *The Letters of Noel Coward* (Methuen, 2007), p. 467.

277 The filming is recounted in Coward's *Future Indefinite*, pp. 210–31.

278 Coward to Mountbatten, 17 September 1941, MB1/A48, Hartley Library.

279 Churchill had considered making Mountbatten First Sea Lord in 1942, replacing Dudley Pound. In the end Pound stayed and Andrew Cunningham succeeded him in 1943.

280 Neither Alan Brooke's diary nor the records of the Chiefs of Staff sustain Mountbatten's interpretation, but he later claimed, 'the minutes rather blurred over the clash', cf. correspondence with Stephen Roskill, MB1/K20b, Hartley Library.

Chapter 13: The Dieppe Raid

281 In a handwritten note on the minutes of 1 June 1942 – the first meeting of Combined Force Commanders that Mountbatten attended – Baillie-Grohman had added that 'a battleship was refused "by the highest authorities", the reason being that, should

the battleship be sunk, we could never claim Dieppe as a victory; and it was highly important at this period to be able to report a victory.' GRO 22 NMM, National Maritime Museum.

[282] Unpublished manuscript, *Before I Forget*, John Hughes-Hallett, p. 168, MB1/B47.

[283] RA, 12 July 1941, George VI diary.

[284] F.R. Hinsley, et al., *Intelligence in the Second World War: Its Influence on Strategy and Operations, vol. 2* (HMSO, 1981), p. 695.

[285] Martin Gilbert, *Road to Victory: Winston S Churchill 1941–1945* (Heinemann, 1986), p. 198.

[286] Churchill to Ismay, 15 August 1942, CAB 120/66, TNA.

[287] Ismay to Churchill, 16 August 1942, CAB 120/69, TNA.

[288] Peter Murphy interview, FO 898/375, TNA.

[289] The report is at MB1/B33, Hartley Library.

[290] 25 October 1942, GRO/26, National Maritime Museum and 'Lessons to be drawn from the Assault on Dieppe', November 1942, GRO/28, NMA.

[291] Lyman Kirkpatrick, *Captains Without Eyes* (Westview Press, 1987), p. 192.

[292] Montgomery in his memoirs claimed he would not 'have agreed to either of these changes'. *The Memoirs of Field-Marshal the Viscount Montgomery* (Collins, 1958), p. 76.

[293] After Dieppe was captured in 1944, it was revealed that the gun emplacements were hidden during daylight hours and therefore could not have been picked up by photographic reconnaissance.

[294] Montgomery memoirs, p. 77.

[295] 'You may be surprised to hear that my responsibility was confined to the initial conception and plan. The plan was subsequently changed and the raid did not take place under my command.' Mountbatten to Raymond de Boer, 19 June 1962, DEFE 2/1795, TNA.

[296] David O'Keefe, *One Day in August* (Knopf, 2013). If so, it was a costly exercise given an Enigma machine was recovered from a captured U-boat within two months of Dieppe.

[297] 23 December 1942, COIS (42) 355 meeting, Ismay 2/3/245, King's College London.

[298] See Adrian Smith, *Mountbatten: Apprentice War Lord* (Tauris, 2000), pp. 233–4 for examples of the favourable press coverage, not least on Mountbatten.

[299] 15 June 1942, Kenneth Young (ed.), *The Diaries of Sir Robert Bruce Lockhart: 1939–1965* (Macmillan, 1980), p. 174.

[300] Mountbatten to Alan Brooke, 31 August 1942, MB1/B18, Hartley Library.

[301] Roberts' fate was to be relieved of his command and sent to run a recruiting depot.

[302] *Alanbrooke War Diaries 1939–1945*, p. 350.

[303] 'My Time with Mountbatten and Other Political Topics', Head of Secretariat, p. 7, MB1/B53, Hartley Library.

[304] Arthur Marshall, *Life's Rich Pageant* (Hamish Hamilton, 1984), p. 156.

[305] Haydon to Mountbatten, 8 October 1942, MB1/B28, Hartley Library.

[306] Interview Dr Brooks, Ziegler, p. 212.

[307] Morgan, p. 320.

[308] Hough, *Edwina*, p. 161.

[309] 'Habbakuk' was abandoned in favour of the cheaper option of conventional aircraft carriers and after Allies gained access to airfields on the Azores and the development of long-range aircraft, which allowed convoys to be protected in the Atlantic.

Chapter 14: Supremo

[310] 31 May 1943, John Barnes (ed.), *The Empire at Bay: The Leo Amery Diaries 1929–1945* (Hutchinson, 1988), pp. 890, 893.

[311] 6 August 1943, Alan Brooke diary, p. 437.

[312] Pownall private diary, Ms 350 A 3002 4/2/13, Hartley Library.

313 28 August 1943, MB1/N41, Hartley Library.

314 Mountbatten to Edwina, 21 August 1943, BA S144, quoted Ziegler, pp. 224–5.

315 28 October 1943, Brian Bond (ed.), *Chief of Staff: The Diaries of Lieutenant-General Sir Henry Pownall*, vol. 2 (Leo Cooper, 1974), p. 117.

316 9 December 1943, IV/Som 3a, Ismay papers, King's College London.

317 3 December 1943, Somerville to Ismay, Ismay 4/30/2, Ismay Papers, King's College London.

318 Mountbatten, *Eighty Years*, p. 146 and John Terraine, *The Life and Times of Lord Mountbatten* (Hutchinson, 1968), p. 103.

319 Mountbatten to Eden, 23 September 1943, MB1/C96, Hartley Library.

320 Adam to Mountbatten, 21 October 1944, MB1/C2, Hartley Library.

321 Ralph Arnold, *A Very Quiet War* (Hart-Davis, 1962), p. 153.

322 22 November 1943, Pownall diary, p. 118.

323 Another version was Supreme Example of Allied Confusion.

324 12 January 1944, T.H. White (ed.), *The Stilwell Papers* (Macdonald, 1949), pp. 258–9.

325 Morgan, p. 330.

326 Ibid.

327 2 February 1944, Ismay to Auchinleck, Ismay 4/9/6a, King's College London.

328 Rowland Ryder, *Oliver Leese* (Hamish Hamilton, 1987), p. 201. A picture of SEAC can be found in Elizabeth Page, *A Taste of Life* (Librario, 2004), pp. 51–7.

329 Mountbatten to General Wheeler, 26 September 1962, MB1/J679, Hartley Library. John Barratt describes her – and Janey Lindsay – as a girlfriend, Barratt, p. 62, but Dean's family deny this.

330 Mountbatten diary, quoted Ziegler, p. 307.

331 Philip Ziegler, *Personal Diary of Admiral the Lord Louis Mountbatten 1943–1946* (Collins, 1988), p. 70.

332 RA GVI/PRIV/RF/24/195: Diary, p. 102.

333 Mountbatten to Edwina, 5 May 1944, BA s145, quoted Ziegler, p. 307.

334 *Diary 1943–1946*, p. 163 and Ziegler, p. 307.

335 Pamela's wartime lovers included Charles Portal, Chief of the Air Staff, and Jock Whitney, a future ambassador to London and the ex-husband of the Mountbattens' friend Liz Altemus.

336 Duff Cooper claimed the affair was over by mid-April. The 'walkout with Edwina is over, which on the whole is just as well as it was really over-publicised and generally badly handled'. DUFC 12/39, Churchill College Archives.

337 Sally Bedell Smith, *In All His Glory: The Life and Times of William S. Paley* (S&S, 1990), pp. 218–19.

338 Daphne Straight to Duff Cooper, 22 March 1944, DFC 12/39, Churchill College Archives.

339 Interview Lady Pamela Hicks, 26 April 2017.

340 Trevelyan, p. 394.

341 *Daughter of Empire*, p. 93.

342 Mountbatten to Edwina, 22 August 1944, BA S145, Ziegler, p. 305.

343 Edwina to Mountbatten, 30 August 1944, BA S67, Ziegler, p. 306.

344 Morgan, p. 336. It took Edwina two years to recover from the news of Bunny's wedding.

345 Ibid., p. 337.

346 Ibid.

347 *Daughter of Empire*, p. 93. Dickie had asked Edwina to choose a wedding present, which likewise wasn't the most tactful of requests. MB1/C210, Hartley Library.

348 Morgan, p. 339.

349 Brian Connell, *Manifest Destiny: A Study in Five Profiles of the Rise and Influence of the Mountbatten Family* (Cassell, 1953), p. 110.

350 Morgan, p. 342.

Chapter 15: Relief Work

[351] 9 February 1945, James Roose-Evans (ed.), *The Time of My Life: Entertaining the Troops* (Hodder & Stoughton, 1989), p. 254.

[352] Morgan, pp. 343–4.

[353] Ibid., p. 348.

[354] Dennis Holman, *Lady Louis: Life of the Countess Mountbatten of Burma* (Odhams, 1952), p. 82.

[355] Philip Christison unpublished autobiography, p. 176, Imperial War Museum.

[356] Ziegler, p. 306, quoting BA S146.

[357] Private information.

[358] Morgan, p. 356.

[359] Mountbatten diary, 12 September 1945, Ziegler, p. 304.

[360] In May 1945, the Commander-in-Chief, Land Forces, General Leese told Mountbatten he wanted to replace William Slim, whom he felt was exhausted, as commander of the 14th Army with General Philip Christison. Slim would be offered command of a newly formed 12th Army charged with garrisoning Burma. Mountbatten said that he retained confidence in Slim, but that he could be 'sounded out' on the suggestion. Leese, either deliberately or mistakenly, interpreted this as support, and informed Slim of his demotion, whereupon the victorious general of the 14th Army offered his resignation. When Alan Brooke learnt of Leese's behaviour, he immediately ordered that he should be replaced by Slim as C-in-C.

[361] Pownall, pp. 202–3.

[362] Brian Kibbins, 'Reminiscences', MB1/N99, Hartley Library.

[363] Ward had previously served with Special Operations Executive, worked at a secret radio station in Italy, and been a PA to the Australian Military Mission in Berlin before being attached to SEAC.

[364] Tom Driberg, *Ruling Passions* (Cape, 1977), p. 223.

[365] 28 November 1945, Morgan, p. 369.

366 Mountbatten to George VI, 14 December 1945, RA GVI/PRIV/ RF/24/129.

367 Mountbatten to George VI, 12 December 1945, RA GVI/PRIV/ RF/24/131.

368 17 December 1945, Duff Hart-Davis (ed.), *King's Counsellor: Abdication and War: The Diaries of Sir Alan Lascelles* (Weidenfeld, 2006), pp. 374–5.

369 Peter Murphy to Edwina, 3 January 1946, MB1/C301, Hartley Library.

370 Morgan, p. 371.

371 cf. 'Visit of Pandit Jawaharlal Nehru to Malaya', CO 717/149/8, TNA.

372 Interview Joyan Chaudhuri, 23 March 1973, Nehru Memorial Museum.

373 Ziegler, *1943–1946*, p. 304 and diary, 18 March 1946, Ziegler, p. 327.

374 Mountbatten interview recorded 26 July 1967, transcript 351, Nehru Memorial Museum.

375 Diary, 26 May 1946, quoted Ziegler, p. 338.

376 Mountbatten to Edwina, 16 April 1945, BA S146, quoted Ziegler, p. 346 and Morgan, p. 377.

Chapter 16: Love and Marriage

377 Hoey, p. 239.

378 John Barratt, *With the Greatest Respect: Private Lives of Earl Mountbatten and Prince and Princess Michael of Kent* (Sidgwick, 1991), p. 94.

379 Mountbatten to Patricia, 31 December 1953, Lady Mountbatten Papers, quoted Ziegler, pp. 573–4.

380 The wedding can be seen at https://www.youtube.com/ watch?v=WhneY8v1iaU.

381 Benning (1921–74) married John Henniker-Major, later 8th Baron Henniker in 1946.

382 21 January 1941, Robert Rhodes James (ed.), *Chips: The Diaries of Sir Henry Channon* (Weidenfeld & Nicolson, 1967), p. 287.

383 Mountbatten to King George VI, 20 February 1944, RA GVI/PRIV/RF/24/084.

384 Mountbatten to King George VI, 10 May 1944, RA GVI/PRIV/RF/24/088.

385 Ziegler, p. 308.

386 BA, S96, quoted Ziegler, p. 308.

387 Mountbatten to King George VI, 23 August 1944, RA GVI/PRIV/RF/24/94.

388 Ibid.

389 Mountbatten to his mother, 28 August 1944, BA vol. XIII, quoted Ziegler, p. 308.

390 Mountbatten to his mother, 9 February 1945, MB6/M/67, Hartley Library.

391 Sargent divorced in 1946.

Chapter 17: A Poisoned Chalice

392 RA GVI/PRIV/DIARY/1946: 17 December 1946.

393 Ronald Lewin, *The Chief: Field Marshall Lord Wavell* (Hutchinson, 1980), p. 238.

394 John Christie, *Morning Drum* (BACSA, 1983), p. 95.

395 Julian Amery to Mountbatten, 30 January 1968, AME J 2/1/53, Churchill College Archives: cf. Julian Amery to Mountbatten, 5 February 1968, MB1/K293, Hartley Library. Mountbatten went to SEAC.

396 Clement Attlee, *As It Happened* (Heinemann, 1954), p. 184.

397 Mountbatten to Attlee, 3 January 1947, Nicholas Mansergh and Peveral Moon (eds.), *The Transfer of Power, vol. IX* (HMSO, 1983), pp. 451–2.

398 *The Letters of Noel Coward*, p. 83.

399 Ziegler, p. 359.

400 Attlee to Mountbatten, 18 March 1947, MB1/D254, Hartley Library.

401 Mountbatten to his mother, 23 March 1947, MB6/M/68, Hartley Library.

402 Pamela Mountbatten, *India Remembered: A Personal Account of the Mountbattens During the Transfer of Power* (Pavilion, 2007), p. 50.

403 Narendra Singh Sarila, *Once a Prince of Sarila: Of Palaces and Elephant Rides, Of Nehrus and Mountbattens* (IB Tauris, 2008), pp. 239–40.

404 *TTOP, vol. X*, p. 9.

405 Morgan, p. 389.

406 *TTOP, vol. IX*, p. 303.

407 Hoey, p. 204.

408 Morgan, p. 391.

409 Ibid.

410 23 March 1947, Shahid Hamid, *Disastrous Twilight: A Personal Record of the Partition of India* (Pen & Sword Books, 1993), p. 150. Hamid (1910–93), the uncle of the novelist Salman Rushdie, founded Inter-Services Intelligence.

411 There were 133 of these meetings from 24 March to 6 May. One problem about such record taking was it only reflected Mountbattens' version of events.

412 31 March 1947, Hamid, p. 153.

413 In March 1957, Edwina wrote to Nehru, 'Ten years . . . monumental in their history and so powerful in the effects on our personal lives', suggesting a close relationship from the Mountbatten's arrival. Morgan, p. 474.

414 Maulana Abul Kalam Azad, *India Wins Freedom: An Autobiographical Narrative* (Longman, 1959), p. 184.

415 *Daughter of Empire*, p. 119. See Ziegler, p. 367 for Mountbatten's relationship with Nehru.

[416] 1 July 1947, Hamid, p. 201.

[417] 23 April 1947, *TTOP, vol. X*, p. 388.

[418] Ismay to Lady Ismay, 25 March 1947, Ismay papers III/8/1, King's College London.

[419] Hastings Ismay, *The Memoirs of Lord Hastings* (Heinemann, 1960), p. 417.

[420] Ibid.

[421] Ibid.

[422] Ismay, p. 419.

[423] 2 April 1947, *TTOP, vol. X*, p. 59.

[424] Mountbatten to King George VI, 2 April 1947, RA PS/PSO/GV1/GOV/IND 1947 Viceroy Reports.

Chapter 18: A Tryst with Destiny

[425] *TTOP, vol. X*, p. 193.

[426] *TTOP, vol. X*, p. 232.

[427] Estimated numbers vary from 60,000, later changed to 150,000 in the official 'Notes on her Excellency's Tour of the N.W.F.P. and Punjab', MB1/Q79, Hartley Library, to 100,000 in Mountbatten's own estimation MB2/N14, Hartley Library.

[428] 1 May 1947, Report no. 5, *TTOP, vol. X*, p. 534.

[429] Hamid, p. 168, claims this is myth-making, that there was never a risk and it was a friendly crowd.

[430] Mountbatten to Attlee, 1 May 1947, *TTOP, vol. X*, p. 537.

[431] Ibid., p. 540.

[432] *India Remembered*, p. 88.

[433] Christie, 10 Mss Eur D 718/3 Part 2, India Office Library.

[434] Hamid, pp. 166–7.

[435] 15 May 1947, Personal Report no. 7, *TTOP, vol. X*, p. 836.

[436] Contrary to Mountbatten's claim that it was a spur-of-the-moment decision, the date had already been agreed with the India Office.

PREM 8/541/10. However, it proved to be an inauspicious date for the astrologers, so it was officially changed to midnight on 14 August.

[437] Francis Ingall, *The Last of the Bengal Lancers* (Pen & Sword, 1989), p. 154. Ingall was the founder-commandant of the Pakistan Military Academy.

[438] 4 June 1947, Hamid, p. 179.

[439] Alex von Tunzelmann, *Indian Summer: The Secret History of the End of an Empire* (Simon & Schuster, 2007), p. 202.

[440] Ismay, pp. 427–8.

[441] Mountbatten to Nye, 19 June 1947, MB1/D1, Hartley Library. Some of the correspondence is missing such as a 'strictly personal' letter from Nye, 1 July 1947.

[442] According to John Christie, he threatened 'sanctions – such as withholding arms, ammunition, and other supplies – against States not agreeing to accede'. Christie Papers, MSS Eur D718/3, India Office Library.

[443] Charles Chenevix Trench, *Viceroy's Agent* (Cape, 1987), p. 347.

[444] Anthony Read and David Fisher, *The Proudest Day: India's Long Road to Independence* (Norton, 1998), p. 465.

[445] Chaudry Muhammad Ali, *The Emergence of Pakistan* (Columbia University Press, 1967), p. 178.

[446] Mountbatten to Patricia, 5 July 1947, Lady Mountbatten papers, quoted Ziegler, pp. 398–9.

[447] Morgan, p. 409.

[448] Sir Patrick Spens, the resigning Chief Justice of India, had been a unanimous choice by all parties, but for some reason he was never called upon.

[449] He had arrived expecting to be given several months.

[450] Leonard Mosley, *The Last Days of the British Raj* (Weidenfeld & Nicolson, 1961), p. 199.

[451] 9 August 1947, Hamid, p. 222. See also Ziegler, p. 417, for why the awards were not announced before Independence.

[452] Ismay to his wife, 5 August 1947, Ismay papers 111/8/13A, quoted Ziegler, p. 365.

[453] 13 August 1947, Hamid, p. 228.

[454] Hamid claims that Mountbatten had actually wanted the drive cancelled or a closed car used. 14 August 1947, Hamid, p. 229.

[455] *TTOP, vol. XII*, p. 773.

[456] Ibid., p. 771.

[457] Attlee to Mountbatten, 16 August 1947, S 147, quoted Ziegler, p. 427.

[458] Supposedly the title was suggested by George VI, Mountbatten to King George VI, 19 August 1947, RA GVI/PRIV/RF/24/160.

[459] Mountbatten to Edwina, 18 August 1947, S 147, quoted Ziegler, p. 427 and Morgan, p. 412.

[460] Radcliffe destroyed all his notes and drafts in connection with the Boundary Commissions before he left India.

Chapter 19: Governor-General

[461] It consisted of three separate reports and maps – the Punjab, Bengal and Sylhet/Assam.

[462] Chittagong was completely cut off from India by East Pakistan, so though the population was predominantly Buddhist and Hindu, it made logical sense.

[463] Kanwar Singh, *Reminiscences of an Engineer* (Young Asia Publications,1978), p. 90 and Hamid, p. 234. Radcliffe, aware of the complexities of the irrigation system, had hoped the two states might exercise joint control in certain areas, but this never happened.

[464] This role should have been taken by someone independent, probably from Britain.

[465] Hamid, p. 222.

[466] P28 Stephens box 45/59, South East Asia Studies Centre and India Office Library, Mss Eur F 180/79, British Library.

⁴⁶⁷ 2 April 1948, Ismay Mss, 111/7/24a, Mountbatten told Ismay to burn the letter. Von Tunzelmann argues that Chittagong was already a compensation for the loss of Calcutta, p. 234.

⁴⁶⁸ The full story is in Christopher Beaumont, 'The Truth of the Partition of the Punjab in August 1947' (privately distributed, 1992). By kind permission of Robert Beaumont.

⁴⁶⁹ Christie, 10 Mss Eur D 718/3 Part 2, India Office Library.

⁴⁷⁰ Noel Baker to Attlee, 26 February 1948, PREM 8/821, TNA.

⁴⁷¹ *TTOP, vol. XII*, pp. 131–7.

⁴⁷² Ibid., p. 267.

⁴⁷³ Robin Neillands, *A Fighting Retreat* (Hodder & Stoughton, 1996), p. 77.

⁴⁷⁴ Philip Ziegler, 'Mountbatten Revisited' (Harry Ransom Humanities Research Centre, 1995), p. 22.

⁴⁷⁵ Philip Ziegler, 'Mountbatten Revisited' in Wm Roger Louis (ed.), *More Adventures with Britannia* (University of Texas Press, 1998), p. 199.

⁴⁷⁶ For more background see Robin Jeffrey, 'The Punjab Boundary Force and the Problem of Order, August 1947', *Modern Asian Studies*, 8.4 (1974), pp. 491–520.

⁴⁷⁷ Mountbatten to King George VI, 2 September 1947, RA PS/PSO/GVI/C/052/098B.

⁴⁷⁸ Lawrence James, *The Raj* (Abacus, 1997), p. 636.

⁴⁷⁹ Khalid Sayeed, *Pakistan: The Formative Phase* (1968), pp. 168–9.

⁴⁸⁰ Mountbatten to George VI, 11 September 1947, BA D86.

⁴⁸¹ Stephens, pp. 109–10 and Stephens box 41/47, South East Asia Centre, Cambridge University.

Chapter 20: A Deeper Attachment

⁴⁸² Ismay papers, 111/8/20 H, King's College London.

⁴⁸³ RA GVI/PRIV/DIARY/1945: 14 October.

484 The forms and Mountbatten's instructions can be found at RA PS/ PSO/GVI/C/270/25 and 26.

485 M to Chuter Ede, 27 January 1947, RA PS/PSO/GVI/C/270/30.

486 Philip to Mountbatten, 29 February 1947, BA S 176, cited Ziegler, p. 457.

487 In fact, under the 1705 Act of Parliament, all descendants of the Electress Sophie of Hanover were British subjects, which Philip was through Queen Victoria, as Dilhorne, a former Lord Chancellor, subsequently pointed out to Mountbatten. Dilhorne to Mountbatten, 22 November 1972, MB1/K200, Hartley Library.

488 Mountbatten to Driberg, 3 August 1947, MB1/ E49, Hartley Library.

489 Morgan, p. 419.

490 Ibid., pp. 423–4.

491 Edwina to Sargent, 23 January 1948, MS Mus 1784/1/12, British Library.

492 *Eighty Years*, p. 184

493 Fortunately, it turned out to be a member of the extremist group Hindu Mahasabha.

494 Edwina to Nehru, 28 September 1947, Nehru papers by kind permission of Susan Williams.

495 Edwina to Nehru, 3 October 1947, Nehru papers, Susan Williams papers.

496 Nehru to Edwina, 14 April 1948, quoted Ziegler, p. 473 and Morgan, p. 428.

497 Mountbatten to King George VI, 14 May 1948, RA C 052/1148.

498 Morgan, p. 428.

499 *Daughter of Empire*, p. 173.

500 Morgan, p. 428.

501 Ibid., p. 429.

502 Nehru to Edwina, 12 March 1957, Broadlands un-catalogued Archives, quoted Ziegler, p. 473.

503 *Daughter of Empire*, pp. 174–5.

504 Morgan, p. 430.

505 Ibid.

506 Ibid.

507 Ziegler, p. 479.

508 Alan Campbell-Johnson, *Mission with Mountbatten* (Robert Hale, 1951), p. 351.

509 Stanley Wolpert, *Nehru: A Tryst with Destiny* (OUP, 1996), p. 436.

510 *India Remembered*, p. 228.

511 *Daughter of Empire*, p. 177. Nehru recovered fast. Within a few days he was seeing a former lover, the diplomat Clare Boothe Luce. Wolpert, *Nehru*, p. 436.

Chapter 21: Malta Again

512 *Daughter of Empire*, p. 178.

513 Morgan, p. 433.

514 Ibid., p. 434.

515 Ibid.

516 Mountbatten to Duke of Windsor, 14 September 1948, RA EDW/ PRIV/MAIN/A/7302.

517 Morgan, p. 434.

518 MB1/J51, Hartley Library.

519 The options to the Prime Minister are given in ADM 1/22697, TNA.

520 Mountbatten interviewed May 1972, MB6/M/151, Hartley Library.

521 Morgan, p. 437.

522 *Daughter of Empire*, p. 185.

523 Manley Power, unpublished memoir, MANP 1, Churchill College Archives, pp. 93–6.

524 Interview Ron Perks, 19 May 2018.

525 Ibid.

[526] Ibid.

[527] Morgan, p. 439.

[528] Mountbatten to his mother, 30 November 1948, MB6/M/68, Hartley Library.

[529] Morgan, p. 440.

[530] The guest in between was Malcolm Sargent.

[531] Morgan, p. 450.

[532] Mountbatten to Edwina, 17 June 1949, BA S147, quoted Ziegler, pp. 483–4 and Morgan, p. 442.

[533] Morgan, p. 443.

[534] Mountbatten to Edwina, 17 June 1949, BA S147, quoted Ziegler, p. 484 and Morgan, p. 443.

[535] Mountbatten to his mother, 12 July 1949, MB6/M/68, Hartley Library.

[536] Morgan, p. 448.

[537] Ibid.

[538] *Daughter of Empire*, pp. 187–8.

[539] Mountbatten to Edwina, 11 July 1949, BA S147, quoted Ziegler, p. 489 and Morgan, p. 445.

[540] Beaverbrook to Driberg, 1 August 1952, Beaverbrook papers c/122, quoted Ziegler, p. 489.

[541] *Ruling Passions*, p. 225.

[542] Martin Dillon to the author, 4 April 2018.

[543] MB1/H39, Hartley Library. cf. MB1/C20/1 on Mountbatten's account of the feud.

[544] Wardell to Mountbatten, 7 June 1972, MB1/K25, Hartley Library.

[545] Driberg, *Ruling Passions,* p. 225.

[546] Anne Chisholm and Michael Davie, *Lord Beaverbrook: A Life* (Hutchinson, 1992), pp. 493–4. Mountbatten told Richard Hough that the vendetta was because of his suspected affair with Jean Norton but denied it. Hough, *Mountbatten*, pp. 141–2.

[547] Philip Eade, *Young Philip* (Collins, 2011), p. 186 and Janet Aitken, *The Beaverbrook Girl: An Autobiography* (Collins, 1987), p. 133.

[548] Morgan, p. 444.

[549] Ziegler, p. 513.

[550] Sarah Bradford, *Elizabeth: A Biography of Her Majesty the Queen* (Heinemann, 1996), p. 158.

[551] Mountbatten to his mother, 20 December 1949, MB6/M/68, Hartley Library.

[552] Ziegler, p. 495.

[553] Ibid.

[554] MB1/ O5, Hartley Library.

[555] Mountbatten to Patricia, 12 August 1949, Ziegler, p. 497.

[556] Morgan, p. 457.

[557] After Queen Mary's death, it was agreed just before the birth of Prince Andrew in 1960 that all descendants not entitled to be called Royal Highness would take the name Mountbatten-Windsor. Mountbatten in his lineage tables stated the House of Mountbatten reigned from 8 February to 9 April 1952.

[558] John Gordon to Beaverbrook, May 1952, BBK H/121, House of Lords.

[559] Michael Bloch, *The Secret File of the Duke of Windsor* (Bantam Press, 1988), pp. 257, 265.

[560] Mountbatten to Edwina, 28 February 1952, BA S149, Ziegler, p. 501 and Morgan, p. 466.

[561] 28 February and 5 March 1952, Guy Liddell Diary, KV 4/474 TNA. I am grateful to Nigel West for the reference.

[562] James Thomas to Mountbatten, 4 September 1952, MB1/H260, Hartley Library.

[563] 19 September 1944, *Chips Channon*, p. 394.

[564] Interview Lady Pamela Hicks, 26 April 2017.

[565] The correspondence can be found at CHAN 4/8-4/9 Churchill College Archive, Cambridge. In 1954 the FBI opened a file on her, concerned about her relationship with Krishna Menon, who was suspected of being anti-American.

Chapter 22: Separate Lives

566 *Daughter of Empire*, p. 207.

567 Lt Commander Brian Smith, email to author, 21 May 2019.

568 Ibid.

569 An account of the cruise and Sargent's chasing of teenage girls can be found in Masha Williams' *In the Bey's Palace* (Book Guild, 1990), pp. 139–57.

570 Barratt, p. 62. This may be the relationship with the wife of a junior officer where Mountbatten was required to pay off the press. Private information.

571 Philip to Mountbatten, 10 February 1953, BA S180, Ziegler, p. 514. Asked who saluted whom when they met, Philip replied, 'We both salute, but only one of us means it.'

572 Morgan, p. 475. John Barratt claims they had also discussed divorce so Edwina could marry Bunny Phillips, Barratt, p. 61, and that they had contemplated divorce in 1946. Private information.

573 She had initially thought of giving them to Paula Long. Morgan, p. 475.

574 Edwina to Mountbatten, 8 February 1952, BA S72 quoted Ziegler, p. 474 & Morgan, p. 476.

575 BA S149, quoted Ziegler, p. 474 & Morgan, p. 476.

576 Morgan, p. 438.

577 Ibid., p. 447.

578 A.N. Wilson, *After the Victorians* (Hutchinson, 2005), p. 494.

579 Interview Karan Tharpar, *Outlook*, 7 October 2009.

580 Ziegler, p. 473.

581 Ashley Hicks, 1 February 2017, *Daily Telegraph*. Pandit is also supposed to have said, when asked if her brother had an affair with Edwina, 'If the relationship did become intimate . . . I'm glad.' *Los Angeles Times,* 2 January 1988.

582 Edwina to Mountbatten, 8 February 1952, BA S72, quoted Ziegler, p. 474 & Morgan, p. 476.

583 Hough, *Edwina*, p. 185.

584 Ibid.

585 Hamid, p. 172.

586 https://www.outlookindia.com/magazine/story/if-i-werent-a-sanyasin-he-would-have-married-me/223036.

587 Dr Zareer Masani to the author, 12 February 2017.

588 Ahmed, p. 147 and M.J. Akbar, *Nehru: The Making of India* (Viking, 1988), p. 391.

589 Ahmed, pp. 146–147.

590 Wolpert, *Nehru*, p. viii.

591 Breese, pp. 307–8.

592 Hamid, p. 153.

593 Ahmed, pp. 132–3.

594 Morgan, pp. 477–8.

Chapter 23: Sea Lord

595 Edwina to Ismay, 5 August 1954, Ismay papers IV/Mou/43b, King's College London.

596 McGrigor to Mountbatten, 15 September 1954, MB1/H266, Hartley Library.

597 Manley Power unpublished memoir, p. 106, Churchill College Archive, Cambridge.

598 Ziegler, p. 528.

599 Morgan, p. 459.

600 Barratt, p. 36.

601 Ibid., p. 37, for the rest of the story.

602 Ibid., pp. 37–8.

603 See Mike and Jacqui Welham, *The Crabb Enigma* (Matador, 2010) and Don Hale, *The Final Dive* (Sutton, 2007).

604 Vice Admiral Sir Norman Denning, 11 April 1972. The document is retained under section 3(4) but was supplied to the author on 16 June 2018.

[605] Sydney Knowles, *A Diver in the Dark* (Weidenfeld & Nicolson, 2009), pp. 92, 132.

[606] Dick White to Mountbatten, 20 July 1965, MB1/J327a, Hartley Library.

[607] Personal and Confidential Note, 7 or 8 September 1956, MB1/N106, Hartley Library.

[608] Draft, 20 August 1956, MB1/N106, Hartley Library.

[609] Mountbatten to Eden, 2 November 1956, MB1/N106, Hartley Library, cf. PREM 11/1090, TNA.

[610] Mountbatten interviewed May 1972, MB6/M/151, Hartley Library.

[611] The couple had been introduced by Chips Channon. Hicks 'unwisely boasted his "grand" engagement to Tony Armstrong-Jones. "Oh, I don't call *that* grand," was Tony's testy reply. A few days later Tony announced his own engagement to Princess Margaret.' Nicky Haslam, *Redeeming Features* (Knopf, 2009), pp. 98–9. Film of the wedding can be seen at https://www.youtube.com/watch?v=ohtsWIXdZZA.

[612] William Evans, *My Mountbatten Years* (Headline, 1989), p. 48.

[613] Edwina to Mountbatten, 7 January 1960, BA S75, quoted Ziegler, p. 569.

[614] Robert Turner, 'From the Depths of my Memory', pp. 89–90, GB 0162 Mss Brit Emp. S 454, Bodleian Library. There are also copies at MB1/J332 and MB1/R674, Hartley Library.

[615] Turner, p. 89.

[616] Ibid., p. 90.

[617] Robin Bryans claimed she committed suicide 'rather than face further violent quarrels with her husband', Robin Bryans, *Blackmail and Whitewash* (Honeyford Press, 1996), p. 397 and argued she was buried at sea because suicides cannot be buried in consecrated ground, Robin Bryans, *Checkmate* (Honeyford Press, 1994), p. 437. Another rumour circulated that she had been murdered by her lover's family after being caught in bed with a servant. Private information.

[618] Hough, *Edwina*, p. 219.

[619] Interview Lady Pamela Hicks, 26 April 2017.

[620] Ziegler, p. 570.

[621] Barratt, p. 47.

[622] The condolence letters can be found at MB1/R598-MB1/R641, Hartley Library.

[623] Charles Smith, *Fifty Years with Mountbatten* (Sidgwick, 1980), p. 125.

[624] Ronald Brooke to Mountbatten, 22 February 1960, MB1/R601, Hartley Library.

[625] Smith, p. 129.

[626] Terry Cattermole, 'The Last Salute', email to author, 9 May 2017.

Chapter 24: After Edwina

[627] E.H. Cookridge, *From Battenberg to Mountbatten* (Arthur Barker, 1965), pp. 226–7.

[628] Nehru to Mountbatten, 18 March 1960, MB1/J303, Hartley Library.

[629] Sargent to Mountbatten, 22 November 1960, MB1/J391, Hartley Library.

[630] Fairbanks to Mountbatten, 20 March 1960, MB1/J161, Hartley Library.

[631] Mountbatten to Fairbanks, 31 March 1960, MB1/J161, Hartley Library.

[632] Interview William Evans, 2 February 2017.

[633] Ibid.

[634] Ibid.

[635] Mountbatten to Patricia, Lady Mountbatten papers, quoted Ziegler, p. 572.

[636] Mountbatten to Grace Stevens, 29 September 1961, MB1/J428, Hartley Library.

[637] MB1/J95, Hartley Library.

638 *The Mariner's Mirror*, vol. 73, issue 1, 1987, p. 78.

639 Philip Ziegler (ed.), *From Shore to Shore: The Final Years, The Diaries of Earl Mountbatten of Burma 1953–1979* (Collins, 1989), p. 572. According to John Barratt, his employer although 'he had quite a number of sexual liaisons, he seemed to be quite happy, even during the years he was married, with long periods of celibacy', Barratt, p. 56.

640 Mountbatten to Sibilla O'Donnell, 24 November 1962, by kind permission of Sibilla Tomacelli.

641 *Tour Diary 1953–1979*, p. 6 and MB8/10, Hartley Library.

642 Mountbatten to Sibilla O'Donnell, 5 March 1963, by kind permission of Sibilla Tomacelli.

643 Ibid., 28 March 1963.

644 Sibilla O'Donnell to Mountbatten, 17 January 1964, by kind permission of Sibilla Tomacelli.

645 Barratt, p. 68.

646 Hoey, pp. 83, 86.

647 Ibid., p. 87.

648 Ibid., p. 88.

649 Ibid., p. 88.

650 Ibid., p. 89.

651 Ibid., p. 90.

652 Ibid., p. 89.

653 Ibid., p. 83.

654 Barratt, p. 66.

655 Interview William Evans, 2 February 2017.

656 Barratt, pp. 56, 63. Writing to a friend in 1949, Mountbatten had requested pictures of women riding in a rodeo 'from the side and back'. Mountbatten to Jock Lawrence, 24 July 1949, Academy of Motion Picture Arts and Sciences Archives.

657 William Evans, quoted Hoey, p. 96.

658 Barratt, p. 64.

659 Interview Mary Lou Emery, 13 June 2017.

660 Barratt, pp. 64–5.

661 Philippa de Pass to the author, 4 May 2019.

662 Private information.

663 William Stadiem, *Madame Claude* (St Martin's Press, 2018), p. 269. Mountbatten knew de Rothschild on the polo circuit.

664 *Mountbatten Diaries 1953–1979*, p. 117.

665 Christopher Plummer, *In Spite of Myself* (Knopf, 2008), p. 415. The film was released in 1963.

666 *Mountbatten Diaries 1953–1979*, 20 March 1965, quoted Ziegler, p. 606.

667 Interview William Evans, 27 March 2018, and phone call William Evans to author, 7 February 2017. Sibilla Tomacelli also thought they had an affair. Interview Sibilla Tomacelli, 21 April 2017.

668 According to John Barratt, she had an affair with Prince Philip, quoted Davies, p. 181. When she divorced Ford in 1976, he accused her of being the lover of Imelda Marcos.

669 Mountbatten to Sibilla Tomacelli, 13 January 1969, by kind permission of Sibilla Tomacelli.

670 Richard Hough, *Other Days Around Me* (Hodder, 1992), p. 198.

671 Evans, p. 76.

672 Mountbatten to Barbara Cartland, 7 December 1961, MB1/J277, Hartley Library.

673 Ibid., 13 December 1962.

674 Tim Heald, *Barbara Cartland* (Sinclair-Stevenson, 1994), p. 181. A 2006 BBC4 drama *In Love with Barbara* suggested they had an affair. According to her son, 'she destroyed her letters from him before she died', Ian McCorquodale email to the author, 24 October 2016. According to the *Daily Mail*, 18 March 2017, she claimed Mountbatten had told her that Prince Philip had an illegitimate daughter in Australia.

675 She called him 'Dearest Dickie, Dearest One and Dearest Supremo'. Her file is MB1/J380 and MB1K248, Hartley Library.

676 More details, Barratt, p. 175. Telling Sibilla about the swimming

pool, in which Mountbatten would swim nude each day, he asked Sibilla when 'next you come over you can put on one of your brief bikinis and lie by the pool, looking more entrancing than ever.' Mountbatten to Sibilla Tomacelli, 11 March 1970, by kind permission of Sibilla Tomacelli.

677 'All his girlfriends are listed in the archives, with their letters to him carefully filed under their names.' Barratt, p. 62.

678 Sally Dean to Mountbatten, 22 September 1966, MB1/K304, Hartley Library.

679 Robin's father, Eddy, had many years earlier proposed unsuccessfully to her mother, Mary.

680 Mountbatten to Janey Lindsay, 13 January 1969, private collection.

Chapter 25: Retirement

681 Post-war reorganisation of services, MB1/C203, Hartley Library.

682 Disarmament 1957–8, MB1/I120, Hartley Library.

683 Lord Bramall, Reel 10, 12502, Imperial War Museum.

684 Edward Ashmore, *The Battle and the Breeze* (Sutton, 1997), p. 125.

685 Ashmore, pp. 153–4.

686 Solly Zuckerman, *Six Men Out of the Ordinary* (Peter Owen, 1992), p. 147.

687 Interview Pat MacLellan, 28 February 2017.

688 Denis Healey, *The Time of My Life* (Michael Joseph, 1989), p. 258.

689 Healey, p. 258.

690 Ziegler, p. 617. Denis Healey claimed only one out of the top 40 people in the Ministry was in favour of his reappointment. Healey, p. 258.

691 He was pleased to also be given the Ethiopian Order of the Seal of Solomon, especially as Prince Philip only had the Order of Sheba.

692 *Sunday Telegraph*, 11 July 1965.

693 Private information from someone who used to shoot with him.

694 Draft letter Mountbatten to Wilson, 17 October 1965, SZ/
GEN/72/Mountbatten, University of East Anglia.

695 PREM 13/553, TNA.

696 Though part of their correspondence – 17 pages were closed in
2017 until 2053 – is in the National Archives at MEPO 10/30,
none of their correspondence has been released at Southampton
University. One has to ask why.

697 Mountbatten to Robert Laycock, 1 February 1965, MB1/J266,
Hartley Library.

698 Mountbatten to Sibilla Tomacelli, 7 February 1965, by kind
permission of Sibilla Tomacelli.

699 United World Colleges consists of 17 schools and colleges on four
continents and presidents have included Nelson Mandela and
Queen Noor of Jordan.

700 The recordings were carried out between January 1961 and
November 1966, MB1/K39. They remain closed.

701 Robin Bousfield to Mollie Travis, 11 November 1966, MB1/K38,
Hartley Library. Some 30 pages were transcribed but remain
unavailable. There is some correspondence in the Royal Archives.
Many papers were destroyed at this stage, MB1/H17, Hartley
Library.

702 Robin Bousfield to Mollie Travis, 23 January 1967 and 13 April
1967, MB1/K38, Hartley Library. Some of the transcribed letters
are available but not the originals. John Barratt later claimed
that whilst sorting out Murphy's papers, he found 'a sheaf of
indiscriminate and intimate letters from the old Duke of Kent . . .
after consulting Lord Mountbatten, I burned them', Barratt, p. 54.

703 CAB 21/5987, CAB103/640, TNA. cf. also LCO 67/88, TNA.

704 Mountbatten to C.S. Forester, 5 June 1944, MB1/ C101, Hartley
Library. The central character of Forester's *The Ship* is based on
Mountbatten. Mountbatten falsely claimed the writer to be 'a
boyhood friend of mine', Adrian Smith, *Mountbatten: Apprentice
War Lord* (Tauris, 2000), p. 9.

705 MB1/K26a, Hartley Library. When books did come out, even if unauthorised, Mountbatten bought scores of copies to be sent to friends and family. MB1/K31 & MB1/G14, Hartley Library.

706 Ray Murphy, American author, 1946–8, MB1/E110, Hartley Library.

707 The various reminiscences can be found at MS350, Hartley Library.

708 MB1/G14, Hartley Library.

709 Sir N. Flower to L. Pollinger, 13 October 1944 and A. Campbell Johnson to L. Pollinger, 27 March 1945, MB1/C40, Hartley Library.

710 CAB 21/4302, TNA.

711 Details of the various interactions with authors can be found at MB1/I15, Hartley Library.

712 Brian Connell and Ronald Seth later offered themselves.

713 Edwina to Elizabeth Collins, undated, MB1/R144, Hartley Library.

714 Stephen Prior interview with Madeleine Masson, Clive Prince et al., *War of the Windsors: A Century of Unconstitutional Monarchy* (Mainstream, 2002), p. 255. I'm grateful to Clive Prince for trying to locate the original interview.

715 Ismay to M, 6 March 1962, Ismay 4/24/51, King's College London and Mss Eur, Jenkins D 807,166–7, India Office Library. Mountbatten had discouraged Evan Jenkins from talking to Mosley.

716 Ismay to M, 6 March 1962, Ismay 4/24/51, King's College London.

717 Ismay to M, 21 March 1962, Ismay 4/24/52c, King's College London.

718 The correspondence can be found at MB1/K15, Hartley Library.

719 Ziegler, pp. 666–7.

720 'Publication of official documents: Broadlands Archive Trust (Earl Mountbatten), 1965 Jun–Dec', CAB 21/5987, TNA.

721 'Lord Mountbatten private collection of official documents' (The

Broadlands Archive Trust), 1966 Jan 21–1969 Jun 17, CAB
103/640, TNA.

[722] 'Lord Mountbatten private collection of official documents (The
Broadlands Archive Trust), 1966 Jan 21–1969 Jun 17, CAB
203/640, TNA.

[723] Papers related to his time as Viceroy were cleared by the Royal
Archives and Foreign Office in 1970. FCO 37/643, TNA. However
there were culls in the 1980s and then in 2010.

[724] Ludovic Kennedy was offered but turned down the job.

[725] See Rebecca Coll, 'Autobiography and History on Screen: The Life
and Times of Lord Mountbatten', *Historical Journal of Film, Radio
and Television*, December 2017, vol. 27, Issue 4, pp. 665–82.

[726] The success of the series persuaded the Royal Family to agree to a
BBC programme on them in 1969.

Chapter 26: Fixer

[727] 12 August 1967, Cecil King, *The Cecil King Diary: 1965–70*
(Cape, 1972), pp. 138–9.

[728] Hugh Cudlipp to Cecil King, 29 April 1968, 432/2/4 Cudlipp
Archive, Cardiff University.

[729] Ibid.

[730] Ibid.

[731] Ibid.

[732] Cudlipp, pp. 325–7. cf. Solly Zuckerman, *Monkeys, Men and
Missiles: An Autobiography 1946–88* (Collins, 1988), pp. 463–6.

[733] 6 November 1975, Mountbatten to Brabourne, SZ/GEN92/
Mountbatten, University of East Anglia.

[734] King expected a hereditary peerage from Wilson in return for the
paper's support for Labour and was upset to be offered only a life
peerage. In the end he got nothing.

[735] Cecil King to Mountbatten, 13 July 1970, SZ/GEN92/ Mountbatten 1970–1, University of East Anglia, UEA.

[736] Mountbatten to Cecil King, 15 July 1970, SZ/GEN92/ Mountbatten 1970–1, UEA.

[737] Mountbatten to Zuckerman, 15 July 1970, SZ/GEN92/ Mountbatten 1970–1, UEA.

[738] Hugh Cudlipp to Mountbatten, 4 November 1975, King–Cudlipp file 1975–8, SZ/GEN and Cardiff 462/2/6, UEA.

[739] Mountbatten to Hugh Cudlipp, 6 November 1975, King–Cudlipp file, 1975–8, SZ/GEN & Cardiff 462/2/6, UEA.

[740] Cecil King to Hugh Cudlipp, 13 October 1976, King–Cudlipp file, 1975–8, SZ/GEN, UEA.

[741] Ruth Dudley Edwards, *Newspaperman Hugh Cudlipp, Cecil Harmsworth King and the Glory Days of Fleet Street* (Secker & Warburg, 2003), pp. 370–1, quoting 'The So-Called "Military Coup" of 1968' by Hugh Cudlipp, *Encounter,* September 1981.

[742] *The Times*, 3 April 1981. In September, Cudlipp returned to the fray with an article in *Encounter.*

[743] 14 November 1975, SZ/GEN, Cecil King–Cudlipp file, UEA.

[744] The list can be found in Hugh Cudlipp to Cecil King, 30 April 1968, 432/2/4 Cudlipp Archive, Cardiff University. Troughton later became chairman of the British Council and a trustee of the Broadlands Archive Trust.

[745] Ibid.

[746] Ibid.

[747] *Six Men*, p. 142.

[748] 7 December 1947, Robert Bruce Lockhart diary, Loc 60, Beaverbrook Papers, House of Lords.

[749] *Six Men*, p. 143.

[750] Peter Wright in *Spycatcher* claims Cecil King was a long-term MI5 agent. He certainly had been used on specific occasions by the intelligence services, as had his son Michael, the foreign editor of the *Daily Mirror.*

751 3 August 1977, Zuckerman memo, SZ/GEN Cudlipp–King film, University of East Anglia.

752 3 August 1977, SZ/GEN Cudlipp–King film, University of East Anglia.

753 He describes it in a 1974 interview, part of which is featured in Adam Curtis' documentary, *The Mayfair Set*.

754 Charles Higham, *Elizabeth and Philip: The Untold Story* (Sidgwick & Jackson, 1991), p. 86.

755 Mountbatten's otherwise voluminous correspondence with Zuckerman in the Southampton and UEA archives is missing between 29 January and 18 October 1968.

756 *Private Eye*, no. 362, 31 October 1975, p. 5, copy at MB1/K162a, Hartley Library.

757 Von Tunzelmann, p. 362.

758 Ben Pimlott, *The Queen: A Biography of Elizabeth II* (Collins, 1996), pp. 470–1.

759 22 February 1970, *From Shore to Shore*, p. 190.

760 A reminder was that the Royal Archives and Government had insisted in 1970 on reviewing his archives to ensure there was nothing embarrassing in them on his time in India. FCO 37/643, TNA.

761 Mountbatten diary, 2 June 1972, quoted Ziegler, p. 680.

762 3 June 1972, MB1/K45, Hartley Library.

763 Charles Higham, *Mrs Simpson: Secret Lives of the Duchess of Windsor* (Sidgwick & Jackson, 2004), pp. 484–5.

764 Linda Mortimer interview, quoted Greg King, *The Duchess of Windsor: The Uncommon Life of Wallis Simpson* (Aurum, 1999), p. 48.

765 More details can be found in Hugo Vickers, *Behind Closed Doors: The Tragic, Untold Story of the Duchess of Windsor* (Hutchinson, 2011), p. 130.

766 8 August 1978, Richard Thorpe (ed.), *Who's In, Who's Out: The Journals of Kenneth Rose, vol. 1* (Weidenfeld & Nicolson, 2018), p. 563.

767 When no member of the family planned to attend Charles' Dartmouth graduation, Mountbatten went himself. Hoey, p. 255.

768 Mountbatten Diary, 31 January 1972, quoted Ziegler, p. 685.

769 Mountbatten to Prince Charles, 13 November 1972, quoted Jonathan Dimbleby, *The Prince of Wales* (Little Brown, 1994), p. 176.

770 Prince Charles to Mountbatten, 19 March 1973, BA S 33, quoted Ziegler, p. 685.

771 Mountbatten to Prince Charles, 28 February 1973, BA S33, quoted Ziegler, p. 685.

772 Barratt, p. 70.

773 Sarah Bradford, *Elizabeth: A Biography of Her Majesty the Queen* (Heinemann, 1996), p. 397.

774 MB1/K303, Hartley Library. Though widely tipped as a future bride, in spite of relationships with Melvyn Bragg and Lloyd Grossman, she has never married.

775 Nigel Dempster and Peter Evans, *Behind Palace Doors* (Orion, 1993), p. 80.

776 Mountbatten to Prince Charles, 14 February 1972, BA S33, Ziegler, p. 687.

777 Bradford, p. 426.

778 Sally Bedell Smith, *Princes Charles* (Random House, 2017), p. 115.

779 Dimbleby, p. 263.

780 Bedell Smith, p. 116. She subsequently married the novelist and property developer Charles Ellingworth in 1987.

781 Prince Charles to Mountbatten, 15 December 1977, BA S35, quoted Ziegler, p. 694.

782 M to Charles, 21 April 1979, BA S35, quoted Ziegler, p. 687.

Chapter 27: Ireland

783 TAOIS/2005/151/508, National Archives, Dublin.

784 Declan Foley email to the author, 17 January 2017.

785 Interview India Hicks, 28 April 2017.

786 Hoey, p. 247.

787 Ibid., p. 248.

788 Interview girlfriend, 7 June 2017.

789 Hoey, p. 251.

790 Timothy Knatchbull, *From a Clear Blue Sky* (Hutchinson, 2009), p. 19.

791 Ibid., p. 20.

792 Interview Emma Temple, 15 March 2019.

793 6 September 1960, 'Residence in Ireland', DFA/90/2/360, National Archives, Dublin.

794 *Belfast Telegraph*, 17 August 2009, and RTE 'Return to Mullaghmore', broadcast 17 August 2009.

795 12 September 1960, 'Residence in Ireland', DFA/90/2/360, Dublin Archives.

796 1 September 1971, *From Shore to Shore*, p. 221 and BA S19, Ziegler, p. 697.

797 17 July 1972, Brabourne Papers, quoted Ziegler, p. 697.

798 'Holiday visit by Lord Mountbatten and Lord and Lady Brabourne to Republic of Ireland', August 1974, FCO 87/331, TNA.

799 Interview, 16 August 2018.

800 12 June 1974, Brabourne papers, quoted Ziegler, p. 698.

801 Graham Yuill to author, 28 October 2018.

802 Ludovic Kennedy, *On My Way to the Club* (Collins pb edition, 1990), p. 371.

803 Kennedy, p. 37.

804 David Roberts email to the author, 2 January 2019.

805 David Bicknell email to the author, 10 September 2018.

806 Amongst the protective measures was a transmitter in the house linked to the police. Interview Graham Yuill, 15 March 2019.

807 *Sunday Express*, 22 October 2017 and interviews Graham Yuill, 23 October 2017 and 30 November 2018.

808 Graham Yuill to the author, 28 October 2018.

809 'Sections of the Garda . . . were dubbed by military intelligence as "nests of vipers".' Graham Yuill to the author, 30 October 2018.

810 Robin Haydon to Lord Carrington, 26 September 1979, FCO 87/841, TNA.

811 Those who also died immediately or as a result of their wounds were Doreen Knatchbull, Nicholas Knatchbull and Paul Maxwell. A second attack at Warren Point that afternoon killed 18 soldiers and a civilian.

812 Details can be found at MB1/K381, including his 'Philosophy of Life' with his views on his career, family, the monarchy and religion, CAB 130/718 and DEFE 68/350, TNA.

813 DEFE 49/22, TNA.

814 There were more volunteers than slots and a number of petty officers asked to take part as ordinary sailors.

815 ROSK 10/47, Churchill College Archives, Cambridge.

816 It can be found at MB1/K381(7), Hartley Library.

817 One of them had given a false name, which turned out by chance to be the name of a known IRA member. There were rumours that Russian intelligence or, according to Enoch Powell, the CIA were involved – https://wais.stanford.edu/Russia/KGBDeathMountbatten.htm, POLL 3/2/1/89, Churchill College Archives and *Sunday Telegraph*, 19 August 1984.

818 Graham Yuill to author, 25 October 2018, based on information from Major General David Miller, commander of the UDR, interview with Garda Special Branch officer, 22 May 2018 and Liam Clarke and Kathryn Johnston, *Martin McGuinness* (Mainstream, 2001), p. 116.

819 McMahon served 19 years before being let out under the Good

Friday Agreement. McGirl died in 1995 in a mysterious accident when his tractor overturned. There were rumours the SAS had been involved. 'Of the 400 odd IRA Maze prisoners released under the Good Friday Agreement, something like 90 returned to the town or its environs, which says something (each was given a grant towards setting himself up as a taxi driver).' Private information.

820 Courtney later published his autobiography, *It Was Murder. Murders and Kidnappings in Ireland: The Inside Story* (Blackwater Press, 1996), which remains unavailable on Amazon or even at the British Library.

821 An Irish career criminal Patrick Holland stated Mountbatten had been killed by the British Security Services 'because of a deep-rooted secret Mountbatten knew that if revealed would have been so damaging to the Royal Family that it may have damaged their reputation for ever'. 'Secrets from the Grave Reveal Provisional IRA did not Murder Lord Mountbatten', *OPC Global News and Media*, 21 June 2012.

822 Martin Dillon to the author, 4 April 2018.

823 29 August 1979, 'Murder of Lord Mountbatten and others', PREM 19/13, TNA. Some parts of the file remain closed.

824 Ibid.

825 Interview Garda intelligence officer, 22 May 2018 and conversation Donal O'Sullivan, Irish Ambassador in London, 11 April 1972. 'Return to Mullaghmore'.

Chapter 28: Rumours

826 Driberg and Mountbatten certainly talked openly about sex. 'Have you seen Dr Kinsey's fascinating book on the sex-life of the American male?' Driberg to Mountbatten, 11 May 1948, MB1/E49, Hartley Library. Attempts in 1968 to prosecute Driberg, an associate of the Kray Brothers who had already been arrested several times for importuning, for offences against young men were

dropped by the Director of Public Prosecutions. It emerged in 1990 that Driberg had been a Soviet agent codenamed Lepage.

827 Ziegler, pp. 52–3.

828 Barratt, p. 53. Barratt also told Hoey the same thing, Hoey, p. 91. A source close to Barratt told the author that it was assumed that Barratt and Mountbatten had been lovers though Barratt denied this. Hoey, p. 92.

829 Hoey, p. 96.

830 Ibid., p. 95.

831 *Private Eye*, 12 October 1979, issue 465, p. 6.

832 Michael Thornton to the author, 19 December 2018.

833 Jeremy Norman to the author, 3 June 2017.

834 Interview Derrick Meakins, 3 May 2017.

835 Hugh Massingberd, *Daydream Believer: Confessions of a Hero-Worshipper* (Macmillan, 2001), p. 147.

836 Interview Jackie Crier, 23 June 2018.

837 Nicholas Davies, *Queen Elizabeth II* (Carol Publishing Group, 1996), p. 202. According to one of the journalists on the story, three MPs were also discovered to be involved in the vice ring. Edward Laxton to the author, 11 December 2018.

838 Francis Wheen to the author, 17 January 2017.

839 Ibid., 24 April 2018.

840 Breese, p. 306.

841 Philip Hindin interview 1990, by kind permission of Charlotte Breese.

842 Elisa Segrave, *The Girl from Station X* (Aurum, 2014), p. 188.

843 Interview private source, 18 April 2017.

844 Private information, 8 January 2019.

845 Interview Special Branch Garda officer, 22 May 2018.

846 Michael Bloch (ed.), *James Lees-Milne Diaries 1942–1954* (John Murray, 2006), pp. 58–9. The editor Michael Bloch speculates MB was Mountbatten though Mountbatten never lived in Eaton Square.

847 Roy Archibald Hall, *To Kill and Kill Again* (John Blake, 2002), p. 23.

848 Paul Pender, *The Butler Did It*, (Mainstream, 2012), pp. 84–5.

849 A.M. Nicol, *The Monster Butler* (Black & White Publishing, 2011), p. 68.

850 Harris had achieved notoriety in a sex scandal ten years earlier with the Vicar of Stiffkey, who was unfrocked for associating with a prostitute. He was later eaten by a lion.

851 Mountbatten was off duties in May 1943 from exhaustion.

852 The article can be found at https://forums.richieallen.co.uk/archive/index.php?thread-1206.html. Twig was Nield's boss, Chief Petty Officer Birch.

853 Peter Thompson, *Diana's Nightmare* (Simon & Schuster, 1991), p. 121.

854 Ibid., p. 241. Richard Benjamin Douglas Wright (7/1/1907–22/9/1977).

855 Anthony Daly to the author, 24 February 2019.

856 Ibid., 22 February 2019.

857 Ibid. According to *The Abuse of Power*, the founder of the National Association of Freedom, Viscount de L'Isle, was a client of the Playland homosexual syndicate. Other clients included Tom Driberg, Sir Michael Havers, James Molyneux and the former Governor of the Bank of England, Gordon Richardson.

858 Ibid.

859 *International Times*, 1 January 1980.

860 'Mountbatten was part of a gay ring which was linked with Kincora', *Now Magazine*, April 1990, pp. 13–14.

861 Ibid., p. 16.

862 *Now Magazine*, September 1989. Bryans' file with the Metropolitan Police was destroyed at an unknown date.

863 Robin Bryans to A.K. Seedhar, 3 November 1989, letter kindly supplied by David Burke/Joseph de Burca.

864 Ibid.

865 Interview 'Sean', 19 November 2018.

866 The two hotels in Mullaghmore by the harbour are the Pier Head hotel and Beach hotel.

867 Interview 'Amal', 25 May 2019.

868 Interview Ron Perks, 19 May 2018.

869 Private information from a university friend of the author, 3 March 2018.

870 Private information from a university friend of the author. 3 March 2018.

871 Nick Best to the author, 21 March 2018. According to a former Life Guards officer, Mountbatten set up a young Life Guards officer in a flat in the mid-1960s close to Kinnerton Street. Interview 24 June 2019.

872 Nigel West to the author, 19 February 2016.

873 Interview with Nigel West's friend, 27 April 2018. He said his mother-in-law, a Wren, had been one of Mountbatten's lovers at SEAC. West is General Sir Michael West.

874 Interview Mr 'A', 28 March 2019.

875 E.A. Conroy to Director, FBI, 23 February 1944, FBI file 75045. Half the file, declassified for the author in 2016, remains closed.

876 1 November 1956, FBI file 58216.

877 Mark Stout, 'The Alternate Central Intelligence Agency: John Grombach and the Pond', p. 41 in Christopher Moran (ed.), *Spy Chiefs*, vol. 1 (Georgetown University Press, 2018). cf. 'John Grombach and the Pond', *Intelligence and National Security*. Aug 2016, vol. 31, issue 5, pp. 699–714.

878 Stout, p. 41.

879 Memo 29 May 1968, FBI file 62-75045.

880 One of the other allegations was that 'Lord Norwich had caught Eden sleeping with his (Norwich's) wife; that Norwich had complained to Churchill, who had quieted Norwich down'. 'Allegations of Homosexuality: Anthony Eden and Admiral Mountbatten 1956', FBI file 202315.

881 Frederic Long to M, 26 February 1916, MB1/A7. Prince John Bryant Digby de Mahe was the son of Prince Charles Digby Mahe de Chenal de la Bourbonnais and two years younger than Mountbatten.

882 Frederic Long to Mountbatten, 1 May 1918, MB1/A7, Hartley Library.

883 Frederic Long to Mountbatten, 29 May 1918, MB1/A7, Hartley Library. Long died unmarried, aged seventy-five, in December 1960.

Chapter 29: Legacy

884 Andrew Hardman to Christine Stewart, 5 November 1979, FCO 87/842, TNA.

885 Quoted William Pattinson, *Mountbatten and the Men of the Kelly* (Patrick Stephens, 1986), pp. 11–12. Allan Warren, a close friend of Mountbatten, successfully lobbied for an inscription on the outside of the green. In 1985 a brass plaque to Mountbatten was also unveiled by Prince Philip in Westminster Abbey.

886 Rubinstein Callingham to Hough, 14 August 1981, Hough papers. It was also claimed that Brabourne 'wanted a rake-off from the Hough book for the Mountbatten Memorial Trust and he wanted Hough to remove some references to the Royal Family, in particular some quotes given by the Queen.' *Private Eye*, 13 February 1981, p. 6. The family also warned off Barbara Cartland, who was collecting a volume of tributes to Mountbatten.

887 Kennedy, p. 373.

888 Ibid., p. 374.

889 ROSK 7/224-226, Churchill College Archives, Cambridge.

890 5 November 1980, PREM 19/294, TNA.

891 Kennedy, p. 374.

892 *The Times*, 5 November 1980. Admiral Sir William Davis wrote to

Hailsham the same day: 'Dickie's memory at times was a bit faulty as I had more than once to point out to him. The trouble was he tried to tackle three whole men's jobs simultaneously. He was not as clever a man as his brother, nor for that matter as his wife, for whom I had a great regard.' HLSM 1/1/16, Churchill College Archives, Cambridge.

893 Somerville to Howard, 23 November 1982, R78/3190/1, BBC Written Archives.

894 ROSK 7/224-226, Churchill College Archives.

895 Ziegler had first suggested Ludovic Kennedy and Charles Douglas-Home, before it was suggested he might be the best candidate. Interview Philip Ziegler, 3 May 2017.

896 Yola Letellier has one reference. The book was read by the Cabinet Secretary Robert Armstrong before publication.

897 Marjorie Brecknock's list of the inaccuracies in the book. MB1/K41a, Hartley Library.

898 After Mountbatten's death, he had worked briefly for a multi-millionaire in Los Angeles, where he had come out as gay and caught Aids. When that job ended, he returned to Britain where he had worked as a road sweeper and died destitute in 1993. Allan Warren, *Nein Camp* (Bunnywar Books, 2012), p. 366. On the evening of Mountbatten's death, a suicidal Barratt brought several bottles of 1947 claret to Allan Warren and they drowned their sorrows, Barratt subsequently retiring to bed with another male house guest, 'Sooty'. Interview Allan Warren, 5 March 2019.

899 Andrew Roberts, *Eminent Churchillians* (Weidenfeld & Nicolson, 1994), p. 55.

900 Mountbatten has continued to be the subject or a main character in various films, including a drama, *The Last Viceroy* with Nicol Williamson in 1985; a 1998 film on Jinnah where James Fox played Mountbatten; a drama documentary, *The Last Days of the Raj* in 2007 with James Wilby as Mountbatten; and a 2017 film, *The Viceroy's House*, starring Hugh Bonneville and Gillian

Anderson. A drama based on Alex von Tunzelmann's *Indian Summer*, starring Hugh Grant and Cate Blanchett, was cancelled after the Indian government took exception to the suggestion Nehru and Edwina had had a physical relationship. Mountbatten has also figured in numerous works of fiction, notably George McBeth's *The Katana* and Christopher Creighton's *The Khrushchev Objective*, which suggests he was murdered 'for his role in preventing the assassination of Khruschev during a summit meeting in England in 1956'. The story of Edwina's love affair with Nehru has inspired Catherine Clement's *Edwina and Nehru* and Rhiannon Jenkins Tsang's *The Last Vicereine*. Jeremy Kingston's comedy, *Making Dickie Happy*, featuring Dickie, Noël Coward and Agatha Christie, was first performed in 2004.

901 The collection also included material from the former Prime Minister Lord Palmerston and the nineteenth-century social reformer, the 7th Earl of Shaftesbury.

902 Pat MacLellan to Malcolm Kimmins, 3 March 1980, by kind permission of General Pat MacLellan.

903 Breese, p. 306.

904 *Daily Telegraph*, 16 December 2012. Known lovers include Hugh Sefton, Tony Simpson, Leslie Hutchinson, Laddie Sandford, Antonio Portago, Mike Wardell, Larry Gray, Ted Phillips, Sergei Obolensky, Antony Szapary, Bobby Sweeney, Winston Guest, 'Bunny' Phillips, Bill Paley, Malcolm Sargent and Nehru and possibly Sophie Tucker and Edwina's sister-in-law Nada.

905 Ziegler, p. 53.

906 Barratt, p. 56.

907 Lambton, p. 10.

908 David Cannadine, *New York Review of Books*, 5 September 1985.

909 Rear Admiral Royer Dick, 'Earl Mountbatten as a Younger Officer: Some Comments of a Contemporary', p. 2, MB1/N100, Hartley Library.

910 'The Viceroy's Verdict', *The Spectator*, 4 September 2004.

911 Robin Neillands, *A Fighting Retreat: British Empire 1947–1997* (Hodder & Stoughton, 1996), p. 80.

912 Barratt, p. 133.

913 Kennedy, p. 370.

914 Interview John Festing, 17 April 2019.

915 Interview Pat MacLellan, 28 February 2017.

916 Philip Christison autobiography, p. 176. Churchill College Archives, Cambridge.

917 Hoey, p. 208.

918 Belt 3, *Life & Times*, p. 4, MB1/K319, Hartley Library.

919 Woodrow Wyatt, *Confessions of an Optimist* (Collins, 1985), p. 162.

Index

Index

Index

Index

Index

Index